The Gilded Age

ESSAYS ON THE ORIGINS OF MODERN AMERICA

EDITED BY

Charles W. Calhoun

A Scholarly Resources Inc. Imprint
Wilmington, Delaware

© 1996 by Scholarly Resources
All rights reserved
First published 1996
Printed and bound in the United States of America

Scholarly Resources Inc.
104 Greenhill Avenue
Wilmington, DE 19805-1897

Library of Congress Cataloging-in-Publication Data

The gilded age : essays on the origins of Modern America /
  edited by Charles W. Calhoun.
      p.   cm.
  Includes bibliographical references and index.
    ISBN 0-8420-2499-9 (cloth : alk. paper). — ISBN 0-8420-
2500-6 (pbk. : alk. paper)
    1. United States—History—1865–1898. I. Calhoun,
Charles W. (Charles William), 1948–
E661.G46   1995
973.8—dc20   95-17891
                                                  CIP

For

Judy, Mary, and A. B.

About the Editor

Charles W. Calhoun received his B.A. from Yale University and his Ph.D. in history from Columbia University, where he did his doctoral work with John A. Garraty. He is a professor of history at East Carolina University, Greenville, North Carolina, where he has served as department chair. He is a past president of the Society for Historians of the Gilded Age and Progressive Era. The recipient of several research grants, including a National Endowment for the Humanities fellowship, he is a specialist in the politics and diplomacy of the Gilded Age. His publications include *Gilded Age Cato: The Life of Walter Q. Gresham* (1988), *A Biographical Directory of the Indiana General Assembly, 1816–1899* (1980, coeditor), and several articles, book chapters, and reviews. He is currently working on a study of Republican party thought in the late nineteenth century.

Contents

Preface

The idea for this book grew out of conversations I have had over the years with several colleagues who pointed to the need for a reconsideration of the various aspects of American life in the Gilded Age. This need seemed particularly acute to college and university instructors, who lamented that no such up-to-date comprehensive overview was available in print for student use. In agreeing to prepare this volume, I concluded that the most useful result could come from soliciting the aid of experts in the various fields of American history in the late nineteenth century. I invited the authors to discuss the major trends, events, and personalities associated with their subjects and also to cast their essays within the framework of their own interpretations. The happy result is that these writings are not mere dry recitations of facts but instead lively syntheses of modern scholarship, each of which makes its own interpretive argument. The hope is that readers will find them not only informative but provocative as well.

Needless to say, the greatest debt I have incurred in preparing this work is to the contributors. All of them were deeply involved in research projects of their own, but each saw the great value that a collection such as this could have, and each was willing to take the time and effort to produce a significant essay. They were prompt in submitting material and remarkably patient and obliging in accepting editorial suggestions. In addition, we all appreciate the excellent work done by the fine editorial staff at Scholarly Resources. I thank the chair of my department, Roger Biles, for a teaching schedule conducive to work on this book and for his encouragement. I am also grateful to Ms. Mary Lou Harrold for her assistance in running three of the chapters through unfamiliar word-processing programs. I wish to express my deepest thanks to my wife, Bonnie, and daughter, Elizabeth, for their great tolerance when I too often excused myself from a designated family time to "go over" this or that essay "just one more time."

C.W.C.

Introduction

Charles W. Calhoun

Every period of history is characterized by change. This is true because of the nature of human existence and also because of the way historians define periods in the past. But some eras exhibit greater change than others, and that certainly was true of the nineteenth century in the United States. During that time the central fact of American life was the evolution of the nation from a largely agricultural, rural, isolated, localized, and traditional society to one that was becoming industrialized, urban, integrated, national, and modern. The process began before the 1870s and continued after 1900, but the last third of the century—roughly the period known as the Gilded Age—saw a rapid acceleration in the country's transformation.

The term "Gilded Age" derives from the title of a novel published in 1873 by Mark Twain and Charles Dudley Warner. Responding to a dare from their wives, Twain and Warner whipped the book out in four months, with the aim, as Twain put it, of satirizing "speculativeness" in business and "shameful corruption" in politics. Alas for historical truth, scholars for decades tended to view Twain and Warner's gross caricature as an accurate, if somewhat overdrawn, portrait of late nineteenth-century American life.[1] In the last generation, however, many historians have undertaken a reevaluation of the Gilded Age with a view not to deny the era's problems but rather to assess their true nature. While these scholars recognize that the benefits of industrialization and other new ways of doing things were not evenly distributed among the American people, the picture that emerges from their research nonetheless shows the period to be one of substantial accomplishment.

Whatever measure one might apply, the nation that entered the twentieth century was vastly different from the one that had emerged from the Civil War. Between 1870 and 1900 the nation's population nearly doubled, reaching just under 76 million people in the latter year. Much of that growth was due to the influx of immigrants; in the same thirty-year span the number of foreign-born persons in the population rose 86 percent. The number of all Americans engaged in gainful employment increased by 132 percent, while the number of women who held paying jobs jumped 190 percent. Workers in agriculture outnumbered all others by 52 to 48 percent in 1870, but by 1900 nonfarm labor constituted 60 percent of the work force. In 1870 the nation had only twenty-five cities with over fifty thousand in population; thirty years later there were seventy-eight, and three had passed the million mark by 1890. Railroad mileage—53,000 miles in 1870—had nearly quadrupled by 1890; the telephone, invented in 1876, grew steadily in service to include more than 1.3 million units by 1900; and between 1870 and 1900 wheat production grew from 254 million bushels to 599 million bushels, while steel production rose from 77,000 tons to 11.2 million tons. This last statistic is perhaps the most telling of all, for it symbolizes the extraordinary changes wrought by industrialization with its concomitant influences on how Americans lived and worked.[2]

Historians and others might argue about the meaning of the term "modern," but few would dispute that the alterations in American society in the late nineteenth century had a lasting impact in the next century or that modern America, in a variety of ways, could trace its roots to the transformations in the Gilded Age. The essays that follow examine several important facets of American life in this formative and momentous period in the nation's history.

Glenn Porter traces the twin developments of industrialization and the rise of big business. Industrialization, he argues, appeared as a confluence of scientific, technical, and organizational improvements that built on the nation's abundant natural resources, plentiful labor, availability of capital, political stability, and transportation and communications systems permitting an integrated national market. Referring to the rise of big business as "the harsher face of industrialization," he notes the pioneering efforts of the large integrated rail systems followed by the emergence of giant manufacturing enterprises utilizing both vertical integration and horizontal combination. While not denying the greed and self-indulgence of many of the so-called robber barons of business, Porter emphasizes instead their achievements in crisscrossing the nation with railroads, building efficient factories, and feeding Americans' growing desire for material goods.

Between 1870 and 1900 the U.S. government issued over five hundred thousand patents for new inventions. Advances in science and technology formed indispensable elements in the nation's industrial transformation. As James Rodger Fleming observes, American scientists in the late nineteenth century were at last moving out of the shadow of their more accomplished counterparts in Europe. They pursued basic research with more confidence and with greater support, especially from the emerging research universities and the federal government. Moreover, mechanical wizards (such as Thomas Edison) and entrepreneurs (such as Gustavus Swift) produced a cornucopia of machines, processes, and products, ranging from electric lights to refrigerated railroad cars, that took Americans giant strides forward into modern ways of living.

Yet the nation's industrial transformation did not occur without severe strains, and, as Eric Arnesen demonstrates, none experienced those strains more than working people. Small shops employing artisans or skilled workers increasingly gave way to larger mechanized factories using more unskilled labor. American workers found their economic lives reduced from independence to dependence as the wage system of labor came to dominate the workplace. Most were convinced that they were not receiving their fair share of the nation's new abundance, and some of them sought to regain lost power through organization. At first "reformist" organizations, such as the Knights of Labor, advocated political solutions through government-instituted economic reform. In the 1880s this approach gave way to the "bread-and-butter" unionism exemplified by Samuel Gompers's American Federation of Labor, which essentially accepted the wage system and espoused collective bargaining, the strike, and other methods to gain better treatment from employers. Organized capital, clinging to notions of the primacy of the owner's right to manage his property, resisted both forms of activism. Labor scored few successes before the turn of the century, but the acceptance of Gompers's philosophy of unionism positioned workers for more effective contention with management in the atmosphere more congenial to labor that developed in the twentieth century.

Among those who swelled the ranks of labor in the new industrializing economy were millions of newly arrived immigrants. In 1870 one third of industrial workers were foreign born; by 1900 more than half were. Roger Daniels chronicles the story of these new Americans, including who they were, where they came from, their motives for migration, how they came to the United States, where they took up residence, and how they lived once they had settled. He analyzes the communities of several ethnic groups, with special attention paid to the work they performed in the evolving industrial economy. Daniels also explores the nativist reaction to newcomers and the drive for legislation to restrict immigration that presaged the exclusion laws of the twentieth century.

Immigrants tended to concentrate in cities that offered them employment in the new industrial factories. Their numbers contributed significantly to the enormous growth in urban places, as described by Robert G. Barrows. No matter how one wishes to state the case, the nation's "urbanization" showed prodigious advances in the last third of the nineteenth century: the total number of Americans living in cities grew substantially; the proportion of those living in cities rose; and the number of cities, including big cities, showed dramatic increases. In addition to these population trends, Barrows examines the physical transformation of the cities, including the creation of transportation systems that permitted spatial growth and differentiation of function, architectural innovations in both residences and business structures, and the institution of services such as waterworks, sanitation systems, gas, and electricity. He also explores the nature of urban government while taking note of the evolution in historians' views of the impact of bosses and reformers.

Of great importance to urban reform movements were the activities of women, mostly from the middle class, whose wide-ranging efforts on behalf of improvement have been described as "municipal housekeeping." That women were enabled to pursue such efforts was one of the many ways that industrialization affected their lives. As Stacy A. Cordery shows, middle-class men believed that a symbol of their economic success in the new industrializing America was the ensconcing of their wives in a leisured domestic life. But, she notes, the very fact of that leisure (in part born of the time-saving appliances wrought by industrialization) allowed women to strike out on their own in a variety of ways. Many chose reform, including participation in such groups as the Women's Christian Temperance Union, work in the urban settlement houses, or endeavors to improve women's lot through agitation for the suffrage. Others engaged in remunerative labor; and for most working-class women, especially those in the new industrial sector, this was by necessity rather than by choice. Increasing numbers of women pursued higher education, and some began to enter law, medicine, and other learned professions. The ways in which Gilded Age women broke out of their "proper sphere" set the stage for the emergence of the "new woman" of the Progressive Era in the next century.

While women strove to improve their lot, African Americans struggled against enormous obstacles blocking their advancement. As Leslie H. Fishel, Jr., shows, some African Americans moved out of the agricultural South, but the vast majority remained there, more or less tied to a tenant farming system that offered little hope of economic independence or improvement. Despite the Fourteenth and Fifteenth Amendments to the Constitution and other progress achieved during Reconstruction, by the end of the century blacks found themselves relegated to a position of legal inferiority, with segregation firmly entrenched and sanctioned by the Supreme Court, the right to vote effectively nullified throughout the South, and lynching becoming an increasing menace. Outside the agricultural South, African Americans usually found employment only at the lowest economic rungs. Still, blacks strove to build their communities, focusing on schools, churches, and social associations. Reform organizations took form, and, despite quarrels over strategy among black leaders, they began to lay the groundwork for the decades-long battle for equality that began to achieve success in the midtwentieth century.

As industrialization fueled the nation's modernization, black Americans often found themselves excluded from its benefits. Another group, Native Americans, or Indians as they were usually called, doubted the value of such "benefits," and many clung tenaciously to a premodern existence. During the Indian wars of the period, Edmund J. Danziger, Jr., writes, they suffered from a distinct disadvantage, both in sheer numbers and in technology. Superior weaponry not only overpowered the aboriginal peoples of the Plains, but it also led to the near extinction of their principal resource, the buffalo. Some resigned themselves to a loss of traditional ways on reservations and began to farm or do other work, send their children to school, and attend church. Yet, there was also much resistance to the U.S. government's Americanization programs as many Indians sought to keep tribal customs alive. Danziger examines the efforts of the government and the so-called Friends of the Indian to deal with these anomalous "nations within the nation," including the establishment of Indian schools and the passage of the Dawes Severalty Act, which stressed individual ownership and working of land. By the end of the century the Indians' nomadic life had ended and armed resistance had subsided, and they were more or less settled in island communities. Still, contrary to policymakers' expectations, they did not meld into the dominant society but remained a significant cultural minority that displayed increasing assertiveness and power in the century that followed.

Among the most neglected and least understood aspects of the late nineteenth century is its political life. Charles W. Calhoun offers an explanation for traditional historians' misperceptions of the period and then examines the nature of political culture in the Gilded Age. Most politicians who held office at the national level were not simply self-interested spoilsmen; rather, they were sincere, dedicated, hardworking public servants if not inspiring, charismatic crusaders. Although an evenly divided electorate and a politically divided national government diminished the prospect for action, politicians did achieve some important successes, not the least of which was the growing acceptance of the primacy of economic policymaking among the federal government's responsibilities. As the nation's industrialization progressed, Republicans in particular pushed for stimulus policies such as the protective tariff, which most Democrats attacked as legislation favoring special interests. Thus, national politics was not a venal battle for office between two parties that offered little choice to voters. Instead, Republicans and Democrats argued vehemently over the nature of government and its role in society—and voters listened.

The effort to break the equilibrium between the two major parties was a defining characteristic of the period's political life. Lewis L. Gould examines the struggle for supremacy between the Republicans and the Democrats in the post-Reconstruction decades. He discusses the image each party projected to the electorate and notes where the voting strength of each lay. Election by election he traces the prospects and campaign strategies of the parties, and he explores how events during the succeeding presidential administrations affected the parties' fortunes. By the 1890s the electorate seemed ready for a major realignment, and the Panic of 1893 and the subsequent depression provided the spark. Voters rejected the Democrats then in power, who seemed incapable of dealing with the economic crisis, and swung to the Republicans, who promised tariff protection, a stable currency, and prosperity. When economic recovery did arrive, Republicans took the credit, and a majority of voters remained attached to their party well into the succeeding century.

Although the vast majority of voters allied themselves with one of the two major parties, occasional third parties appeared. As Worth Robert Miller shows, these third parties found their greatest support in the agricultural areas of the nation. As industrialization and other developments were transforming American life, many farmers remained skeptical, certain that few of the profits of progress were coming their way. Americans achieved unheard-of rates of agricultural production, and yet it was the farmers' very success (due in part to industrialization) that led to their economic distress and political unrest. Because of a general downward price trend, the more farmers produced, the less they seemed to get paid; and they increasingly turned to government for solutions. Believing that the two major parties were unsympathetic, many farmers backed the Greenback party in the 1870s and 1880s. In the 1890s the farmer-supported Populists came as near as any third party to moving into major party status. But the farmers' preferred solution to their difficulties, inflation of the currency, found little support outside their own ranks. By the end of the century, with the return of general prosperity, their breakaway political effort had collapsed. Even so, they had exhibited an organizational solidarity that served as a model for farmers and other economic groups that sought to influence government policy in the twentieth century.

While the United States experienced numerous changes in its internal economic and social arrangements in the late nineteenth century, the period also gave rise to important transformations in the nation's international relations, as Joseph A. Fry writes in his essay on foreign affairs. As in domestic policy, Republican administrations were more activist in pursuing an energetic foreign policy than were Democratic ones, and under President William McKinley the nation acquired an overseas island empire at the end of the century. Historians debate the degree to which this new role for the United States was actually "new," and Fry sees important antecedents for the country's imperial behavior. While denying that there existed a master plan or completely consistent pattern of actions culminating in empire, he posits an emerging imperial mindset born of past domineering treatment of nonwhites (such as Native Americans), a prevailing sense of American mission, and a tendency to link commercial expansion with prosperity. That mindset prepared

Americans to accept distant island possessions as a result of the Spanish-American War. That step, along with its myriad consequences, moved the nation a long way toward the world power status it achieved in the next century.

In the face of tremendous economic and other transformations in the Gilded Age, the institution most resistant to change was the American legal system, which, in the words of Michael Les Benedict, tended to "reinforce conservatism in matters of public policy." Benedict focuses on developments in judicial thought, especially the emergence of "laissez-faire constitutionalism," which he argues was not simply a probusiness bias on the part of judges who were more willing to uphold property rights than human rights. Rather, he sees this judicial philosophy as an amalgam of "classical" laissez-faire economic thought, a concern for fairness that opposed government policies favoring one economic interest over another, and a Victorian moralism hostile to "class legislation" that bestowed benefits on lazy, dissipated, or otherwise undeserving members of society at the expense of hardworking and moral citizens. Adopting the principle of "substantive due process," the Supreme Court began to invalidate regulatory legislation that allegedly denied businessmen their property rights without due process of law. This conservative doctrine, which tended to confound government efforts at business regulation, set the trend for the early twentieth century and was not finally abandoned until the 1930s. Ironically, the restraints thus imposed represented an unprecedented activism by judges that characterized much of constitutional jurisprudence in the twentieth century.

While the courts may have momentarily limited the effective regulation of business, at the state level positive legislative action in a wide range of areas abounded in the period. According to Ballard C. Campbell, "the vast majority of legal complaints about state action were rejected," and "the states were beehives of political activity in the Gilded Age." The nation's tradition of "dual federalism" assigned vast areas of government responsibility to the states, which produced numerous legislative enactments based on their broadly defined "police powers" to promote the public good or on their authority to exercise control over local governments. State legislatures passed laws supporting education, instituting care for orphans, the insane, and other unfortunates, upholding morals through regulation of prostitution and alcohol consumption, furthering the assimilation of immigrants by mandating use of the

English language in their schools, reforming the political process, regulating the conditions of labor, licensing certain professional practitioners, such as physicians, dentists, and lawyers, and protecting public health through the imposition of a variety of controls on activity by businesses and other entities. As Campbell notes, the principal impetus for this quickened pace of state government activity was industrialization and all the associated transformations it wrought in American society. Decades before the Progressive Era of the early twentieth century, these "laboratories of democracy," as some observers called the states, began to respond to the problems and challenges that confronted Americans in the new industrial age.

Notes

1. Mark Twain and Charles Dudley Warner, *The Gilded Age: A Tale of Today* (Hartford, CT, 1874); John A. Garraty, *The New Commonwealth, 1877–1890* (New York, 1968), 1–4.

2. *The Statistical History of the United States: From Colonial Times to the Present* (New York, 1976), 11, 14–15, 127, 129, 512, 693–94, 731, 783–84.

1

Industrialization and the Rise of Big Business

Glenn Porter

Every historical period is marked by stresses as change undermines seemingly settled arrangements and brings new challenges. Every age can say, with Thomas Paine's Revolutionary War generation, that "these are the times that try men's souls." The Civil War brought through fire and pain the resolution of some fundamental and long-standing questions about the nature of the American political union and the meaning of American democracy. At its end an exhausted nation surely hoped for rest. The succeeding decades saw nothing like the fiery conflict concluded at Appomattox, but neither did they bring peace.

What these years did yield was the origins of the modern American economy and society. This period was the great watershed between two eras in American history. From the Revolution to the Civil War the economy had seemed to offer, at least to most white males, not only a means of earning a living for themselves and their families but also a landscape of opportunities where they might hope to improve their lot in life. The economy and the business system had appeared to most to be an environment that, on the whole, fit in comfortably with the republican virtues and democratic aspirations of the young United States. The antebellum "republican" economic world of small units, mostly operating locally, was a very different one from the twentieth-century environment ruled by giant multinational corporations. Today, the institutions of the modern economy suggest little of republican virtues and democratic possibilities. It was during the passage from the end of

the Civil War to the first years of the twentieth century that the
main outlines of that transition emerged.

In that time there appeared the most powerful and influential
institution of the twentieth century—the modern corporation. During those decades the new giants of business embraced and began
to shape technology and science to nourish and to serve the culture
of consumption that defines modern America. The corporation's
thoroughgoing use of system, of bureaucratic organization, and of
what it saw as rational, conscious, and measurable ways of setting
and reaching objectives would come in time to influence the way
other institutions behaved—those in government, unions, agriculture, voluntary associations, the military, and the schools and universities. From Appomattox to the years just before World War I,
the business executive, the engineer, and the wizards of marketing
would assume their roles as the most powerful shapers of American civilization. The first major meaning of the era of industrialization and the rise of big business, then, was that it formed the
bridge that led from the America of Thomas Jefferson and Abraham
Lincoln to that of Henry Ford, Franklin Roosevelt, and Walt Disney.

It is also important to note that the transition did not occur
mostly or merely as the result of conspiracies or unbridled greed.
Then, and for a long time afterward, Americans and their historians attributed the decline of the old order to the extraordinary evil
genius and avarice of the swashbuckling "robber barons," who stole
from the people and paid the politicians to look the other way.[1]
That explanation, though, is too simple and too convenient. In some
ways, the late nineteenth century was a time of spectacular excess,
of brass-knuckled business and shady politics on a grand scale, a
long national carnival of fraud and bribery. Those qualities appalled
middle-class reformers and some later historians, who gave the times
such labels as the Gilded Age, the Era of Excess, and the Great
Barbecue. Failings of character may have been especially prominent in that age, but they are part of life in every age. In any case,
they could hardly account for the era's deep-seated, widespread
changes in the economy and business system. Instead, new technical and economic factors made a different industrial and corporate
order possible, one with many large-scale enterprises operating all
over the country.

In the end, Americans accepted it because the results satisfied
the emerging central purpose in modern life—that is, getting and
enjoying new and abundant material goods. Human beings always

want to do and to be and to have a wide variety of things in their lives. Some of those desires contradict others. Industrialization and the coming of big business brought a variety of disturbing and painful developments to life in the United States, but, over and above all, they were the means through which Americans could have an economy that yielded novel and alluring goods and services on a scale never seen before. The new order thus met the central needs of an increasingly materialistic society. Though many felt uneasy, uncomfortable, and even fearful about important aspects of their industrial and corporate society, in the end most simply accepted the costs because the benefits were so appealing. The decades after the Civil War were the crucible in which the modern United States came to be.

Industrialization

To many Americans, the war had symbolized the triumph of the industrial North over the agrarian South, and there can be no doubt that the superior industrial base of the northern states was one of the decisive factors in that struggle. For many years following the armed conflict, leaders in the South worked toward the goal of transforming their region into a so-called New South, one with more manufacturing, better transportation and communications, and a strengthened financial sector. Moreover, in the rest of the country, the late nineteenth century saw an explosive growth of industry as the nation built vigorously on the advanced economic base that had done so much to doom the Confederacy.

The bundle of economic changes that historians crudely summarize with the term industrialization was a multifaceted and complex phenomenon with many different meanings. As the process of change went forward at an accelerated pace in the late nineteenth century, it was intimately tied to many of the topics discussed in this volume—to science and technology, urbanization, labor, immigration, the changes in rural America, and politics and issues of public policy. Although its force was increasingly strong, it was not, however, something new in American life. Industrial development had been the centerpiece of much of Alexander Hamilton's late eighteenth-century vision of the future, in contrast to the competing Jeffersonian vision; and the United States had followed closely on Britain's heels as that island nation led the Western world into the Industrial Revolution in the latter half of the eighteenth century and the first half of the nineteenth. The factory had spread across much of New England and the Middle Atlantic states, American technical and business prowess had achieved a position of leadership by the time of the first great world's fair at London's Crystal Palace in 1851, and by 1860 the United States had in operation more than half the railroad track on the globe.

To many citizens, this was progress. It made national independence secure, and it brought faster and more reliable transportation, new and improved goods for consumers, and rising incomes for most families. However, its blessings were by no means universally appreciated or equally shared by all. The benefits of economic and technical changes were highly unevenly distributed across society, as they had been previously and have remained since. Major segments of the population—especially African Americans, Native Americans, and women—stood at the margins of the emerging industrial United States. Even to some among the privileged elites, such as Henry David Thoreau, the introduction of steam engines and factories had seemed only a hollow and false sort of improvement. Yet, for those who believed that economic growth was a good thing and who saw tangible progress in technical innovations such as the railroad and the telegraph, industrialization seemed on the whole to be clearly a positive development in the nation's life.

As the pace of change quickened after the Civil War, however, the costs and the benefits were more heatedly debated. The Midwest emerged as a major part of the industrial, as well as the agrarian, heartland. Even the South moved toward industrialization, welcoming in particular the textile factories that had expanded out of New England after the war. Industry always had been associated with such problems as crowding in the cities, conflicts involving new immigrants, and social and economic inequalities. For many, what seemed especially worrisome about these events was that they meant the gradual and seemingly relentless decline of agriculture's place in American life.

That decline was in fact a relative, not an absolute, one. In many respects agriculture flourished. The volume and value of foodstuffs increased, exports grew, more acreage came under cultivation from 1870 to 1900 than in the whole of prior American history, and farming continued to become ever more productive in the latter part of the century as advanced mechanization came to the farm in the shape of improved reapers and other agricultural implements. Despite these positive elements, the influence of things agrarian carried less and less weight as the nation moved toward the twentieth century. The percentage of the work force engaged in agriculture declined almost continuously from the late eighteenth century onward, as dramatic increases in productivity on the farm meant that more and more output could be brought forth by fewer and fewer hands. In 1800 almost three-quarters of the work force was in agriculture, but that proportion had dropped by 1860 to barely more than half. By 1900 only four in ten were working in agriculture. Cities swelled with millions of people depending for a living not on agriculture but on industry, commerce, transportation, and the service industries. To many in the countryside, cities were simply sinkholes of sin overrun with unwelcome foreigners, Jews, and Catholics. Although the heartland's values retained remarkable and disproportionate force despite the shifting economic realities, America's cultural tune was in fact gradually coming to be called more by the urban and industrial sectors and less by the rural and agrarian ones. Industrial and financial elites became, in the eyes of many farmers and their families, evil conspirators winning a growing place in American life through underhanded and secretive means. Such concerns fed the growth of farmers' organizations, including the Grange and the Populist party, as well as a wide variety of confused and fervent monetary reformers, from the Greenbackers (who advocated an expanded paper currency) to the proponents of "free silver."

Despite the critics in the rural reaches and among concerned but largely ineffectual intellectuals, the big train of industrialization rolled on. The period covered by this essay, in fact, witnessed what Peter Temin called "the greatest industrial growth the country has seen. Industry as a whole grew rapidly, firms expanded, and the size of individual plants shot up. Americans became conscious of living in an *industrial* economy, a conciousness that was not altogether welcome."[2]

It is never easy to explain briefly such a large and complex development as industrialization. Nevertheless, some factors seem clear. At a time when technical, scientific, and organizational improvements were particularly numerous and fertile, the U.S. economy benefited from its large and rich internal market, abundant natural and human resources, excellent transportation and communications systems, a sophisticated financial system, the relatively easy movement of people and capital within its boundaries, and a high degree of political stability. The unease about industrialization and the opposition to it never raised truly fundamental doubts about the legitimacy and the desirability of the nation's economic expansion, at least in those segments of society that had decisive power in America. In such a context, the stream of technical and organizational innovations that spurred growth throughout the industrial world had a particularly powerful effect in the United States. Mechanization and the factory system, well under way before the Civil War, experienced heightened growth. Production in volume through the use of special-purpose and ever more precise and durable machinery, a hallmark of what came to be known as the "American System" of manufactures, spread steadily. From the industries that had dazzled observers in the 1850s (such as guns, clocks, axes, and woodworking machines), the American System moved to others (such as reapers, sewing machines, bicycles, and early automobile production).[3] The diffusion of a range of new manufacturing techniques was the work of a talented network of mechanics and inventors who carried their knowledge throughout important sectors of the economy. Innovations in marketing (such as installment sales and the heavy use of advertising to establish brand names) and advances in the production, cutting, and shaping of metals were important factors in the success of many firms at the forefront of change. New sources of lighting and of power, especially electricity, further confirmed the nineteenth century's belief in progress. Within the factory itself, engineers reorganized work processes through what was known first as systematic and then as scientific management, or Taylorism (for its messianic leader, Frederick W. Taylor). The result was the strongest expansion of industry in American history up to that time.

Most of that expansion, it should be emphasized, was not carried out by giant organizations. Big business was not the same as industrialization. Large-scale corporations appeared almost entirely in industries dominated by a few enterprises, which were organized and functioned in ways quite different from the much more numerous and, generally, smaller concerns elsewhere in the industrial economy. Those giant firms received most of the attention from late nineteenth-century contemporaries, and they have been the focus of most of the historical analysis about business since the late nineteenth century. The vast majority of industrial firms, however, were not big businesses. Before turning to the topic of the modern corporation, it is important to understand a bit more about the varieties of America's industrial enterprises. Industrialization

The New Industrial Landscape. General view of the blast furnaces at the giant Homestead Works of U.S. Steel, from a stereo view by H. C. White Company, 1907. *Courtesy Hagley Museum and Library*

began and flourished well before the rise of big business, and it took many forms.

Custom and Batch Production

Philip Scranton, the leading historian of the numerous manufacturing firms that largely fell *outside* the arena of big business, noted that the key characteristic of these companies was that they were custom or batch producers. Unlike most of the giant firms in the manufacturing sector, they dealt in products and markets that did not lend themselves to truly large-scale bulk or mass production. Instead, they manufactured either specialty goods in small lots or batches of products that had fairly short lives in the marketplace and then had to be replaced by a new and different run of goods. In an essay published in 1900, woodworking machinery maker John

Richards noted that "industry can be divided into two classes." The first was firms "producing articles of uniform character." The other was companies manufacturing goods "involving special and progressive skill" and "constant change."[4]

Although Scranton emphasized nothing so much as the diversity of such firms, he did offer a number of generalizations about them, beyond their shared reliance on custom or batch production processes. Often their customers had special requirements that made it difficult or simply uneconomical to set up the long production runs characteristic of the large bulk/mass producers. For firms supplying such special goods, frequent and close contact with the market was usually necessary. Almost all firms using batch production methods were relatively small concerns. A few of the custom production businesses, such as some of the locomotive and specialty machine builders, did in fact grow to be large,[5] but most did not. Customarily, the batch production companies operated in lines where demand ebbed and flowed quickly and unpredictably because the goods were subject to the shifting winds of fashion. This was particularly the case in consumers' goods industries such as hardware, jewelry, clothing, styled fabrics, furniture, publishing, and many household items. In such businesses, manufacturers seldom ventured into doing their own marketing, because it made better economic sense to leave that to the traditional networks of numerous wholesalers distributing the goods to even more numerous and smaller retailers.

For all those involved in making and selling custom or batch goods, flexibility was a key requirement. These companies had to be supple, and they had to be quick. Time pressures were severe. Whether the customer was a single firm needing a new power plant to get a factory back on line, or a diffuse network of customers selling jewelry or clothing held hostage to the sudden turns of fashion, time was of the essence. For almost every business in this sector of the industrial economy, success required the ability to design and manufacture a frequently changing menu of goods to satisfy a demanding and unforgiving market. These concerns could seldom produce ahead of demand, they could not stock large inventories, and they had little influence over the prices that their wares could command. Theirs was a sharply competitive world. Most of them operated with little margin for error.

In the emerging industrial age that profoundly unsettled many, the batch producers in some respects stood out as reassuring reminders of the antebellum economy of smaller, more locally oriented businesses. A more traditional artisanal reliance on skilled workers persisted in this sector. Moreover, these firms fitted reasonably comfortably with a number of traditional American values. As Scranton shrewdly noted, "batch capacities lay behind the aspects of national culture that resonated with constant change, suspected standardization and uniformity, and sustained the ideal of individualism expressed through purchase and display."[6] Here, in a sense, was industrialization's gentler face. The firms in these sectors seldom represented giant agglomerations of capital. They did not have great power, as J. P. Morgan did, and they did not scare people, as John D. Rockefeller's Standard Oil Company did.

Big Business

Between the close of the Civil War and the beginning of the twentieth century, Americans became acutely conscious of the appearance of something new in their lives. Initially, that new phenomenon was generally known as "the trusts," as "pools" or "combinations," and then simply as "big business." That final name, like industrialization, is a convenient summary term. It highlights similarities and masks or minimizes the infinite variety of experience in order to help us make sense of the world. The coming of big business was the most disturbing side of the new American economy. It was the harsher face of industrialization. Although they were only a tiny minority of business enterprises, it was the big firms, looming large in their industries, that attracted attention. For the first time, whole industries came to be identified with the names of the powerful individuals who dominated them—Cornelius Vanderbilt, E. H. Harriman, and James J. Hill in railroads, Cyrus McCormick in reapers, John D. Rockefeller in oil, J. P. Morgan in finance, James B. Duke in tobacco, Gustavus Swift and Philip Armour in meatpacking, Andrew Carnegie in steel. Americans felt both pride and fear as they contemplated the rise of big business. By the early years of the twentieth century, the United States could boast of having the largest, most innovative, most productive economy in the industrialized world. Its citizens enjoyed the highest standard of living on the globe. Yet, these developments profoundly worried many, and this was the focus of much of the era's political turmoil. How were the new and powerful business organizations different, and why had they come to loom so large in the economic landscape of the late nineteenth century?

Perhaps their most noticeable feature was their size. They were enormous pools of capital, undertakings so large that the modern institutions of the stock market and investment banking had to be created to make it possible to funnel so many millions into single enterprises. Even relatively large and costly antebellum businesses such as the canals, the New England textile mills, and the first railroads had not represented investments on the scale of those bound up in the later trunk or transcontinental railroads and the manufacturers that eventually came to dominate oil and steel. All that capital found form in mills, factories, refineries, and shipping and distribution facilities, which had to be planned and coordinated in such a way as to yield profits undreamed of in earlier days.

Even more important than the size of the new firms, in fact, was their structure and their management. Business historian Alfred D. Chandler, Jr., distinguished traditional from modern business by emphasizing that the modern business enterprise "contains many distinct operating units [each theoretically capable of standing alone] and it is managed by a hierarchy of salaried executives." Most traditional concerns were single units run by one or a few owners, businesses that "handled only a single economic function, dealt in a single product line, and operated in one geographic area."[7]

The railroads set the pattern and led the way. Not only were they the most potent symbol of the new industrial age and its technical achievements, but they also pioneered in the organizational innovations of big business. Furthermore, they were a primary means through which Americans came to have access to the improved transportation and communications that permitted the coordination of an enormous volume and range of economic activities across vast distances.

The railroad forged the most important link in a transportation system that created a truly national market by about the 1860s. As a large, relatively sparsely settled country, the United States had always been particularly dependent on a substantial transport infrastructure. Not only did that system move goods, information, and people to facilitate trade, but it also helped to hold the political union together. During the nineteenth century improved coastal and ocean shipping, turnpikes, canals, steamboats on inland waterways, and then the railroads had provided transportation whose speed and all-weather reliability greatly exceeded the transport capabilities of the early Republic.

Alongside the rails went the telegraph, another key element that made big business possible. Distances had always stood as an insuperable barrier to the expansion of the scale and scope of business enterprises. The advent of electronic communications through telegraphy, in combination with a fast and consistent mail delivery system, made it possible for firms to coordinate activities across great distances quickly. Once advanced transport and communications systems were in place, for the first time a firm could effectively operate and integrate many different economic functions and processes throughout a region, across the whole country, and, for a few concerns, around the world.

The railroads broke new ground in several respects. Not only did they represent and require unprecedentedly large pools of capital that called forth investment banking and the modern stock market, but they also were compelled by their circumstances to explore untried managerial methods and organizational structures. By its very nature, the business of a railroad took place over great geographic distances. This necessitated a constant torrent of information and record-keeping. Safety of operations and the efficient employment of costly equipment and numerous staff required relentless coordination, monitoring, and planning. Soon the roads grew to the point where the running of trains had to be split into several geographic divisions, each of which had much independence but all of which had to report to and be coordinated by a central office staff. The railroads thus confronted and overcame one of the key challenges in the management of giant enterprise—how to find a balance between the need for decentralized freedom of operation and centralized control.

At the same time, they confronted another problem that would soon bedevil manufacturers struggling to create regional or national concerns, the problem of destructive competition. As soon as there were two or more roads serving the same cities or locales, the temptation to grab more of the market by offering lower rates was irresistible. (In manufacturing, overproduction offered a similar temptation to cut prices.) All giant enterprises had substantial fixed costs due to the large investments tied up in physical plants and equipment as well as other overhead costs, and that put pressure on management to fight aggressively for revenues. But price-cutting

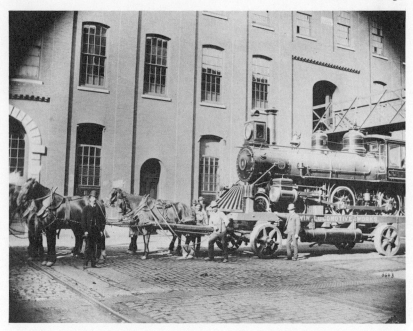

The Transportation Revolution. The Baldwin Locomotive Works' float for the 1887 Philadelphia parade celebrating the centennial of the U.S. Constitution. The steam locomotive
was a potent symbol of industry's prominence. *Courtesy Hagley Museum and Library*

could provide only brief relief. What one competitor could do,
others could mimic. Many of these price reductions were made in
secret, with large and powerful shippers quietly being given rebates or kickbacks under the table. One result was a downward
spiral of rates, to the point where the survivability of the business
was called into doubt and railroad bankruptcies became common-
place near the end of the century. Railways responded with efforts
to operate pools, which were meant to be cooperative ways to share
the business. This in turn produced a storm of political protests and
attacks on the railroads, primarily by farmers and other shippers,
and particularly by the Granger and Populist movements.

These developments brought about yet another new phenomenon for the modern economy—government regulation of industry. The great economic power of the railroads led to the creation
of state regulatory commissions intended to serve the public interest, in part by gathering and publicizing information about railroad
operations in hopes that public scrutiny would encourage the equitable use of the considerable private power represented by the rail-

ways. In 1869 the Massachusetts legislature created not the first but the most important early regulatory institution,[8] the Massachusetts Board of Railroad Commissioners. Then, in the 1870s, a number of midwestern states passed laws that sought to fix rates through the power of the state and to forbid the charging of lower rates for long hauls than for short ones (although, in fact, longer hauls were often cheaper for the railroads to provide). The constitutionality of such legislation explicitly affecting interstate commerce was unclear until the U.S. Supreme Court ruled in 1886 in the *Wabash* case that only Congress had the power to regulate commerce between the states, which, in turn, led to a national movement for a federal regulatory body. The very next year, Congress created the Interstate Commerce Commission. Because the railroads did not fit the classical economists' model of an industry that regulated itself through the invisible hand of the marketplace and because they raised grave questions of potential conflicts between private economic power and the public interest, they led the nation into new forms of competition and brought about a new and much more activist role for government.

The many-sided role of the railroads as pioneers in the rise of big business was first perceived and articulated by Chandler, the influential scholar whose life's work was to understand the appearance and the spread of the giant corporation.[9] His analysis moved the discussion of the coming of large-scale enterprises beyond the simplistic "robber barons or industrial statesmen" framework that had dominated historians' discussions of big business almost from its beginnings. Chandler and those who followed his scholarly lead paid little attention to the personalities and characteristics of the individuals who drew so much attention from the press and the politicians. Similarly, these historians spent little time explicitly considering the morality of the changes in business, although they clearly viewed the economic results of the giant corporations as substantially more positive than negative. In the Chandlerian analytical framework, technology and the nature of the markets were more significant than any other factors in accounting for where, when, and why big business arose and persisted.

There were several major routes to success as other enterprises sought to follow the railroads' lead into the world of big business. One was the strategy known as vertical integration, in which a firm combined two or more functions within a single enterprise. In the antebellum economy, it was unusual for a lone concern to engage in more than just the production of raw materials, or manufacturing, or wholesaling, or retailing. In the decades after the Civil War, however, more and more did so, particularly if they were introducing a new product. Often, they were led to move into marketing because the old, established distribution networks did not meet the needs of new products, such as Swift's dressed beef, McCormick's reapers, the electrical appliances of Westinghouse and General Electric, or Singer's sewing machines. To push the goods, to get them into the hands of customers, and to service them, it was sometimes necessary to create the manufacturing firm's own wholesale, and even retail, branches. The sewing machine, for example, was an expensive consumer durable item that had to be offered on the installment plan to reach the millions. Because it was a novelty, branch staffers also had to be prepared to teach customers how to use the new machine. They had to have replacement parts and repair personnel on hand as well. The Singer firm used a wide array of techniques including mass production, control of its own sales and service, and heavy advertising to build one of the best-known and best-managed vertically integrated firms of the era. It was also among the pioneers in multinational business; by the 1870s, Singer not only had sales operations overseas but also had even built its first factories outside North America. The ability to marry mass production and mass distribution, so well exemplified by Singer, was a key to the development of many larger firms.

Most of the early examples of successful expansion through vertical integration involved firms that grew mainly on their own rather than through mergers. Virtually all of them relied on technologies of bulk or mass production. One of the most visible of the giant businesses was Carnegie Steel, which combined mass production and vertical integration with a vengeance. The company moved backward into mining, into coke, and into the production of the pig iron that went into its giant Bessemer steel converters, which in turn supplied the firm's rolling mills. Andrew Carnegie eagerly embraced the latest technical improvements that would allow his mills to run "full and steady" at high volume and cut his per-unit production costs to the bone.

Similarly, the improvements in transportation and communications and the growth of cities opened opportunities for mass merchandising firms in the new fields of department stores, mail-order houses, and chain stores. Montgomery Ward and Sears, Roebuck & Company led the way among the mail-order firms, while distributors such as A & P and Woolworth's set new patterns in chain store retailing. They reduced or eliminated a layer of wholesalers, turned their high volumes of stock over rapidly, and reached masses of consumers through advertising and lower prices for a flood of goods. The result was successful mass distribution.

In some of the industries where large-scale output was achievable through new technologies for continuous process production (for example, oil refining, cigarette production, sugar refining, and distilling), the role of mergers was central to the rise of dominant firms. Here the pattern was set by Rockefeller's Standard Oil. The refiners were plagued by recurrent problems of overproduction and destructive competition, analogous to the competitive difficulties encountered by the railroads and by many manufacturers from the 1870s on. In industry after industry, as new techniques of mass or bulk production or continuous processing made it possible to produce goods in quantities unimaginable in earlier days, the field became crowded with contestants. Price-cutting became a widespread problem, as more productive capacity was put into place than could be profitably sustained. Manufacturers responded by forming trade associations that sought, as the railroads had, to apportion markets and fix prices. Just as the railroads had found, the manufacturers discovered that these arrangements proved extremely difficult to maintain. Rockefeller soon gave up on the association strategy and pursued instead a plan for horizontal integration, or merger. Standard Oil pressured other refiners to sell out, fighting price wars from its powerful position based on favorable railroad rebates and low production costs. Soon many refiners gave in to Standard's aggressive tactics and joined the conglomerate, often in secret. By the late 1870s, Standard accounted for about 90 percent of the country's refining capacity. In the following decade it integrated both forward and backward. It also created a formal, legal trust form for itself in which a handful of trustees held the stock of all the combined companies that had been gathered under Standard's banner. That first true trust quickly gave its name to almost any effort in the 1880s to fix prices, divide markets, or carry out mergers. An alarmed public saw on every hand the evidence of what were called "the trusts."

In 1890, Congress tried to address the public's worries by enacting the Sherman Antitrust Act, an extremely vague piece of legislation that essentially forbade all combinations "in restraint of trade." Years of litigation and court rulings would be necessary before any meaning would be given to the Sherman Act. Its long and meandering history had barely begun when, starting in 1893, the nation slid into a severe depression. In the midst of that downturn, and despite the new antitrust law, there began a massive wave of mergers.

Businesses in a wide variety of industries struggled with the falling prices and the rising competitive pressures brought by the depression. Even after the economy rebounded, the mergers continued. What was known as the Great Merger Wave lasted into 1904 as many sought to find for themselves a piece of the pie first cut by Rockefeller, Carnegie, Duke, and the other successful builders of big businesses.

The merger mania produced many failures as well as some of the largest and best-known American enterprises of the twentieth century, such as U.S. Steel, Pittsburgh Plate Glass (better known as PPG), and the National Biscuit Company (better known as Nabisco). More than eighteen hundred previously independent firms disappeared into combinations.[10] The successful corporations that emerged from the Great Merger Wave, on the whole, were those that were able to replicate the earlier strategies of role models such as Singer or Standard Oil. Companies that could utilize mass production or continuous-process methods, that could achieve mass distribution, or that met special marketing needs were likely to be the ones that lasted.[11] Efforts to create big businesses via mergers in the batch production lines and in areas subject to fashion's quick twists and turns seldom worked.

By the first years of the twentieth century the broad outlines of business in modern America had become clear. Industrialization had swept through much of the economy, and big business was established in those sectors where it would persist for many decades. The passage of time gradually made the new institution of the large corporation more familiar and less threatening than it had seemed when it first appeared on the scene. Industrialization did mean, as so many had feared, the slow atrophy of agrarian and rural influences in the culture. Most of the country, however, soon forgot such worries and embraced the pleasures of an industrial, urban, and suburban civilization. Big business at first had seemed to threaten both democracy and the opportunity for mobility that the economy traditionally had offered. The enactment of antitrust laws and the creation of a federal regulatory presence, however, served to reassure the populace somewhat. Above all, the sky never quite fell, despite the alarms raised about the dangers posed by the corporations. As the new century unfolded and the consumer carnival spilled forth its treasures, the corporation's values, methods, and influence spread into many other walks of life. Americans would never manage to love the corporation, but they certainly came to accommodate to it and to learn from it.

Notes

1. The classic volume in that literature is Matthew Josephson, *The Robber Barons: The Great American Capitalists, 1861–1901* (New York, 1934). This almost always has been the interpretive stance favored in films and television programs because its dramatic and highly personalized approach fits the needs of those media.

2. Peter Temin, "Manufacturing," in Lance E. Davis et al., *American Economic Growth: An Economist's History of the United States* (New York, 1972), 447.

3. See David A. Hounshell, *From the American System to Mass Production, 1800–1932: The Development of Manufacturing Technology in the United States* (Baltimore, 1984).

4. The manufacturer is quoted in Philip Scranton, "Diversity in Diversity: Flexible Production and American Industrialization, 1880–1930," *Business History Review* 65 (Spring 1991): 29. See also Scranton's two monographs on the textile industry in the Philadelphia region: *Proprietary Capitalism: The Textile Manufacture at Philadelphia, 1800–1885* (Cambridge, England, 1983); and *Figured Tapestry: Production, Markets, and Power in Philadelphia Textiles, 1885–1941* (Cambridge, England, 1989).

5. A few of the era's big businesses, such as General Electric and Westinghouse, mixed custom work (e.g., turbines and other power plant equipment) with mass-produced goods.

6. Scranton, "Diversity in Diversity," 32.

7. Alfred D. Chandler, Jr., *The Visible Hand: The Managerial Revolution in American Business* (Cambridge, MA, 1977), 2–3.

8. See Thomas K. McCraw, *Prophets of Regulation: Charles Francis Adams, Louis D. Brandeis, James M. Landis, Alfred E. Kahn* (Cambridge, MA, 1984), 17, and Chapters 1, 2.

9. Chandler's influence began to grow with his article, "The Beginnings of 'Big Business' in American Industry," *Business History Review* 33 (Spring 1959): 1–31. His ideas on the importance of the railroads were most fully articulated in *The Railroads: The Nation's First Big Business* (New York, 1965), and Chandler's place as the leading scholar of the history of modern business was secured through three monographs: *Strategy and Structure: Chapters in the History of the Industrial Enterprise* (Cambridge, MA, 1962); *The Visible Hand* (cited above); and *Scale and Scope: The Dynamics of Industrial Capitalism* (Cambridge, MA, 1990).

10. Naomi R. Lamoreaux, *The Great Merger Movement in American Business, 1895–1904* (Cambridge, England, 1985), 2.

11. See Chandler, *The Visible Hand*, 337–39.

Suggestions for Further Reading

Adams, Charles Francis, Jr., and Henry Adams. *Chapters of Erie*. New York, 1886.

Chandler, Alfred D., Jr. "The Beginnings of 'Big Business' in American Industry." *Business History Review* 33 (Spring 1959): 1–31.

————. *The Visible Hand: The Managerial Revolution in American Business*. Cambridge, MA, 1977.

Davis, Lance E., Richard A. Easterlin, and William N. Parker. *American Economic Growth: An Economist's History of the United States*. New York, 1972.

Galambos, Louis. "The Emerging Organizational Synthesis in Modern American History." *Business History Review* 44 (Autumn 1970): 279–90.

————. "Technology, Political Economy, and Professionalization: Central Themes of the Organizational Synthesis." *Business History Review* 57 (Winter 1983): 472–93.

Hounshell, David A. *From the American System to Mass Production, 1800–1932: The Development of Manufacturing Technology in the United States*. Baltimore, 1984.

Lamoreaux, Naomi R. *The Great Merger Movement in American Business, 1895–1904*. Cambridge, England, 1985.

Livesay, Harold C. *Andrew Carnegie and the Rise of Big Business*. Boston, 1975.

McCraw, Thomas K. *Prophets of Regulation: Charles Francis Adams, Louis D. Brandeis, James M. Landis, Alfred E. Kahn*. Cambridge, MA, 1984.

Porter, Glenn. *The Rise of Big Business, 1860–1920*. Arlington Heights, IL, 1992.

Scranton, Philip. "Diversity in Diversity: Flexible Production and American Industrialization, 1880–1930." *Business History Review* 65 (Spring 1991): 27–90.

Tilly, Louise A. *Industrialization and Gender Inequality*. Washington, DC, 1994.

Yates, JoAnne. *Control through Communication: The Rise of System in American Management*. Baltimore, 1989.

Zunz, Olivier. *Making America Corporate, 1870–1920*. Chicago, 1990.

2

Science and Technology in the Second Half of the Nineteenth Century

James Rodger Fleming

Early in the twentieth century Henry Adams wrote of himself, "The American boy of 1854 stood nearer the year 1 than to the year 1900."[1] Adams was reflecting on how poorly his education—in religion, ethics, and philosophy; in history, literature, and art; and in the concepts of science—had prepared him for the enormous upheavals (intellectual, social, cultural, and national) that he had witnessed in the second half of the nineteenth century. He was also alluding to his favorite thesis—that the pace of history was accelerating, especially in his lifetime. An editorial published in 1876 made a similar point about the complexity of the technology exhibited at the Centennial Exposition in Philadelphia as compared with that on display just twenty-five years earlier:

> Any person tolerably informed in physics and electricity, who should, in 1851, the date of the first great [Crystal Palace] exhibition, have examined the electric telegraph and apparatus, could readily comprehend and popularly describe the whole so that the general reader or listener would be entertained and, possibly, instructed; but today [1876], if a fully informed electrician and skillful mechanic were to visit one of our large telegraph offices, he would find apparatus complicated in construction to the last degree, diversified to unlimited extension, and involving in its principles of action the most subtle and abstruse problems, whose comprehension alone could only result from the closest study or the most constant experience; and any description of accuracy would fail to convey the least idea to the uninitiated, beyond the

fact of the attainment of wonderful results. Similarly the sewing
machine has now become involved in detail devoid of general
interest to readers.[2]

The vast differences in American thought and society that Adams,
the editorial writer, and their contemporaries had experienced were
in part due to developments in science and technology.[3] Surprisingly, although there are myriad specialized studies and a number
of books treating earlier periods, there are no comprehensive surveys of science or technology in the United States in the second
half of the nineteenth century.[4]

Why should a student of American history seek to understand
the history of science and technology?[5] For most of us, science was
merely an undergraduate distribution requirement whose alien concepts and esoteric experimental spaces generated abundant anxiety
and consumed a great number of hours. On the other hand, the history of science has traditionally been seen as a rather narrow and
technical branch of the history of ideas focused on the likes of Isaac
Newton, Charles Darwin, and Albert Einstein. But the history of
science and technology *in American society* is a newer field whose
leading practitioners are attempting to weave diverse strands of
cultural, intellectual, and institutional history into fully contextualized accounts of social and conceptual change. It is an important
aspect of the American story in general. Obviously, a student of
post-World War II society should know something about nuclear
power, the space program, and computing—essentially the context
and consequences of these technical developments more so than
any specific technical details.[6] Familiarity with the basic (and changing) worldviews promoted by science is also desirable, particularly
as they influence and intersect other aspects of the general culture
such as religion and social thought.

The same is true for earlier eras, including the late nineteenth
century. A study of theories, inventions, institutions, and careers in
science and technology—especially in their national context and
with particular reference to change over time—should result in a
more complete historical understanding and may lead to new and
compelling insights. For example, much has been written about the
American debate over Darwinism, especially in its religious context, but much more is yet to be learned about the evolutionary
philosopher Herbert Spencer's influence on the entire spectrum of
American social thought from the progressive platforms of the Socialist party to the conservative "Social Darwinism" of Andrew

Carnegie and William Graham Sumner.[7] Likewise, works focusing on the struggles and strategies of women scientists and their careers and institutions are now revealing new aspects of American society.[8]

Historiography and Periodization

The midnineteenth century long has been a neglected period in the history of American science, characterized by some as the "trough" between the twin "peaks" of legendary colonial glory and contemporary world leadership.[9] Throughout the century, American scientists in most fields were typically regarded at best as junior partners of their European betters. If American contributions were recognized at all, it was not until the closing decades. By the 1870s, however, as Nathan Reingold has argued, America had become a "mature but small scientific nation with many of its basic institutions and attributes in existence or in embryo"; its scientific infrastructure, as Robert Bruce has documented, had been formed and "launched" in the three preceding decades.[10]

What was called "science" in nineteenth-century America represented a broad range of activities that included basic and applied research, college teaching, and government service. In 1872, after spending a quarter of a century as the head of the Smithsonian Institution, Joseph Henry wrote to the British scientist John Tyndall about the difficulties he had encountered in promoting and advancing science in America. His letter identified three distinct aspects of the scientific enterprise: 1) the discovery of new truths; 2) the teaching of scientific principles; and 3) the application of scientific principles to useful purposes. Henry felt that while the second and third categories were widely recognized and supported, the first—the pursuit of basic research—was still suffering. Americans had yet to understand "the difference between the discovery of new truths, and the teaching of old ones."[11]

Historians of science, attempting to explain the conditions necessary for the emergence of modern science in the United States, have suggested that the American experience was similar to (if not prototypical of) other colonies that became nation-states. According to the oft-cited typology proposed by the historian George Basalla, an initial phase of exploration, during which Europeans studied the continent's natural phenomena and native populations, was followed by a period of "scientific colonialism" (ca. 1770–

1860), during which scientific activity by colonists and citizens was to a great extent (but not exclusively) dependent on European institutions and traditions.[12] Basalla concluded that the emergence of a viable domestic infrastructure in support of American science and invention depended on a number of conditions (he listed seven), including the establishment of national scientific organizations and formal channels of communication, the development of a proper technological base, government support or at least neutrality in science and technology policy matters, the effective teaching of science at all grade levels, and elevation of the social status of scientists and engineers. Most of these requirements were met, or at least took on recognizably modern forms, in the second half of the nineteenth century. Throughout the period the patrons of science and invention—government (especially the military), colleges and universities, and private industry (including philanthropists)—were establishing new forms of institutional support that promoted scientific specialization and the creation of new disciplinary and professional structures.

Consider for a moment the situation of antebellum science. Most scientists of the time were either self-educated or had been trained at eastern liberal arts colleges such as Harvard or Yale. Most had earned a B.A. degree (some had an M.D.) in a field broadly defined as "natural philosophy." Some had spent a postgraduate year in Europe studying, touring, and purchasing books and apparatus; a few had received Ph.D.s at European universities.[13] Most identified their special interests in either natural history (botany, zoology, medicine, agriculture) or the earth sciences (especially geology).

Research in antebellum America was often conducted by individual scientists with very limited resources, although some government funding existed, particularly in the earth and agricultural sciences and in natural history exploration. Most scientists conducted research in more than one specialty; for example, Elias Loomis was both an astronomer and a meteorologist. American scientists had little mathematical sophistication, few had well-equipped laboratories, and as yet no specialized journals existed for their publications. The disciplinary foundations of physics, chemistry, and biology had not yet been established. A considerable amount of research was done "out of doors" by, for example, collectors in the field or by geological surveys. Scientific papers on all subjects appeared in unspecialized journals such as Benjamin

Silliman's *American Journal of Science and Arts*, the *Journal of the Franklin Institute*, and the *Proceedings* of the American Philosophical Society. Amateurs and professionals had not yet parted ways. They worked together with organizations such as the Smithsonian Institution (1846) and the American Association for the Advancement of Science (1848) to promote and popularize science. In the minds of most people, science was most closely linked to cultural pursuits, including philosophy, religion, and literature. God and nature were still intimately related; indeed, they were parent and child.

The situation was quite different in the second half of the century. The Civil War, as historian Allan Nevins has noted, "transformed an inchoate nation, individualistic in temper and wedded to improvisation, into a shaped and disciplined nation, increasingly aware of the importance of plan and control."[14] The war was the first major conflict affected by the impact of the Industrial Revolution, and although the Union drew upon existing technology rather than generating much that was new, its organizational and administrative accomplishments resulted in a new "national consciousness."[15] According to historian Peter Hall, "the war changed everything." It transformed and revitalized the elite "culture of organization," introduced new national business networks (railroads, telegraph lines, and the banking system), and infused new technologies into American society.[16]

For example, the medical department of the U.S. Army experienced a vast increase in the scale of its operation during the war. In 1860 it was comprised of ninety-eight officers and was run on a budget of $90,000. By 1865 it had twelve thousand medical officers and an appropriation of $20 million. This last figure is larger than the budget of the entire army of 1860! Between 1861 and 1865, Union physicians treated a quarter of a million wounds and approximately seven million cases of disease. Over a million patients were admitted to its 204 hospitals. The department also established field hospitals, an ambulance corps, camp inspections, mass inoculations, and, of course, a centralized administrative structure. Although this scale of operation did not continue after the war, the experiences of this and many other military departments was not lost on the participants. A notable example of the scale and dynamic of new military scientific initiatives emerged in the field of meteorology, with the Army building on its Civil War experience to create a massive, well-funded national weather service.

Meteorology, the Military, and Modernity

In the managerial era that dawned after the war, the federal government established a national weather service with direct links to the military. Although weather observations had been made in America since colonial times, the first national service providing daily reports and forecasts was run from 1870 to 1891 as part of the War Department, under the direction of the chief signal officer.[17] Before that, meteorological and climatological observations were collected by volunteer observers and a number of federal agencies, including the Army Medical Department (1814–1882), the General Land Office (1817–1821), the Navy (1834–1837), and the Smithsonian Institution (1849–1874).[18]

The U.S. Army Signal Service, highly decorated for its successes in monitoring Confederate troop movements during the Civil War, had been mustered out with the volunteer army of 1865, leaving the chief signal officer, Colonel Albert J. Myer, a bureau chief without a bureau, in charge of one lieutenant and two clerks.[19] Myer, an aggressive administrator and founder of the service, now faced the task of rebuilding the Signal Corps and redefining its mission for peacetime service. He was grasping for a mission that would keep the corps alive when, in December 1869, a bill was introduced in Congress establishing a national storm warning service.

Because of their prior involvement in meteorological research, both the Smithsonian Institution and the Army Medical Department were considered likely candidates to organize the new system. The final version of the bill, however, named the secretary of war as the responsible party. The chief signal officer immediately called on Congressman Halbert Paine, the sponsor of the bill, to stake his claim. Paine recalled later that Myer "was greatly excited and expressed a most intense desire that the execution of the law might be entrusted to him."[20] Defining storms as the "enemy" of commerce, Myer argued that the Signal Corps could use telegraphy to track their movement and provide meteorological intelligence in advance of their arrival: "The telegraph can announce meteorological observations, statistics, and reports giving the presence, the course, and the extent of storms . . . and their probable approach, as it would, in time of war, those of an enemy."[21]

Congress was persuaded by Myer's zeal, signaling expertise, and the promise of military discipline in the system, and thus the first national weather service was established in 1870 in the War

Department under his direction. With generous support from Congress, the Signal Office budget soared from $5,000 in 1869 to $400,000 by 1874. During the same period, Myer's command expanded from three enlisted men to over five hundred college-educated observers. The Signal Office became a major military and scientific service, providing "telegrams and reports for the benefit of commerce" and daily weather predictions to the public, who had become accustomed to and had come to depend on daily weather forecasts.

By virtue of its privileged access to commercial telegraph lines, an aggressive construction program of military telegraph lines along the eastern seacoast and into the southwestern and northwestern frontiers, and, during national emergencies, a direct line to the White House, the Signal Office soon established itself as the center of an electric intelligence network that spanned the nation. The men of Myer's command served both as meteorological observers and, at times, as a military police force reporting to the chief signal officer on "peacetime" enemies such as disgruntled workers during the rail strikes of 1877, Indian uprisings in the Southwest, and natural hazards to commerce and agriculture. Signal Service observers reported on the hatching and migration of locust swarms, on frost and drought in the cotton-, corn-, and tobacco-growing regions, and on hazards to shipping along the coast. Mercantile interests were advised of weather conditions affecting the packing and shipment of perishable goods such as oysters, pork, and ice. Sailors received notice of fogs, storms, and fair winds. Insurance companies received data useful to them for setting rates for shipping, agriculture, and weather-related liabilities such as severe storm damage. River reports warned of floods and low water; railway reports announced heavy snows and track conditions; and sanitary reports charted the course of cholera and yellow fever epidemics in the interest of public health.

The fact that America now had a well-funded national weather service did not go unnoticed in Europe. In contrast to their usual disdain of "colonial" science, European scientists now expressed admiration for the huge scale of the American meteorological service, its generous funding, and its utility (if not its theoretical accomplishments). In 1873, Myer, representing the United States at the International Meteorological Congress in Vienna, proposed that the weather services of the nations of the world prepare an international series of simultaneous observations and charts to aid in the study of world climatology and weather patterns. The result was the *Bulletin of International Simultaneous Observations*, published by the Signal Office from 1875 to 1889.

The military tradition in meteorology continued after Myer's death in 1880. His successor, General William B. Hazen, was a veteran of both the Civil War and the Indian wars. Under Hazen's leadership the Signal Office established a scientific study room, published a multivolume international *Bibliography of Meteorology*, and responded to its critics in Congress on the issue of whether the military should be supporting a national weather service.[22] The Signal Office, however, did not fare well in the 1880s. Its funding was reduced slightly, and some stations were closed. In 1882, Secretary of War Robert Todd Lincoln recommended an end to meteorology in the Army. Two years later a committee of the National Academy of Sciences recommended transfer of meteorology to civilian control, and the Allison Commission began its congressional investigation of the scientific bureaus of the government, including the weather service of the Signal Office.[23] In 1885 a controversy over the handling of the Lady Franklin Bay polar expedition resulted in Hazen's court-martial. After Hazen's death in 1887, General Adolphus W. Greely, the celebrated Arctic explorer and new chief signal officer, openly advocated removing the weather service from military control.

By an act of Congress of October 1, 1890, the U.S. Weather Bureau was established in the Department of Agriculture, where it remained until 1940. Contentious relationships in the weather service continued, however. The first chief (1891–1895), Mark W. Harrington, a scientist from the University of Michigan, was deposed in a political feud with the secretary of agriculture. The next administrator (1895–1913), Willis L. Moore, was accused of mismanagement and fiscal impropriety. By World War I the Signal Corps and Weather Bureau were again cooperating, issuing military forecasts, tracing the trajectories of artillery shells, and studying the weather conditions affecting gas warfare.

As this example demonstrates, a recounting of science and technology in American society need not focus on great men with great ideas. The history of meteorology may be written largely as a political study that examines closely the part played by the military in post-Civil War society, the role of the federal government in providing scientific services to the public, and the impact of national telegraphy as a new mechanism for social control during peacetime. It may also be used to illustrate rapid modernization in the 1870s and 1880s, decades before the focus of standard accounts by Samuel P. Hays and Robert H. Wiebe.[24]

Meteorology is not unique in this respect. Increasingly, historians are incorporating the genres of political, social, and cultural history into their accounts of scientific and technical change. They are posing hitherto unasked questions about privilege and patronage, about elites and nonelites, and about mass experience of technological systems. From fields as well-cultivated as physics and astronomy to much newer specialties such as environmental history, the tendency is to weave accounts of natural knowledge, social relations, technology, and culture into unified explanations of social change.[25]

The Patrons of Science

Throughout the second half of the nineteenth century, the earth and agricultural sciences received the greatest amount of federal patronage, as they had in earlier eras. Geology, like meteorology, was largely supported by the federal government. There was no centralization of effort, however. Congress funded the Geological Survey of the Fortieth Parallel (1867), led by geologist Clarence King, in hopes of a financial return on the minerals it discovered; the Army Corps of Engineers (1869) sponsored a survey of the hundredth meridian by Lieutenant George M. Wheeler, in part for the military reconnaissance of Nevada and Utah; Congress supported John Wesley Powell's exploration of the Colorado River (1870) and his survey of the Rocky Mountain region (1874); the General Land Office sent "U.S. Geologist" Ferdinand V. Hayden into the field as head of the Geological and Geographical Survey of the Territories (1873); and the Coast and Geodetic Survey, under the direction of Benjamin Peirce, conducted surveys of the interior to connect mapping efforts on the East and West Coasts. By 1886, according to one estimate, the federal government had spent $68 million on surveys of the West, many of which were a duplication of effort.[26]

Agriculture also received significant federal appropriations late in the century. In 1862, President Abraham Lincoln established the Department of Agriculture (USDA) and signed the Land-Grant College bill. The USDA was inadequately financed for its first twenty years, receiving appropriations just shy of $200,000 in 1864 and the same amount in 1880. The department experienced something of a renaissance in the late 1880s when the Hatch Act of 1887 was passed, providing for basic agricultural research at state experimental stations. In 1889 the USDA gained cabinet-level status, and, in 1891, when the functions of the national weather service were transferred to it, the USDA's appropriation soared to over $1 million. The overarching concern motivating most of these government efforts was the role that the settlement of the West played in the national agenda. Scientists who could connect their research to that agenda, whether by stringing telegraph wires into Indian Territory, mapping rich mineral deposits, or developing new arid-land agricultural practices, were first in line for government support.

Colleges and the new research universities also became major patrons of science in the latter decades of the century. Developments at some of the older colleges set the stage for the rise in first degrees in science and engineering. Harvard's Lawrence School of Science (1847), Yale's Sheffield School of Science (1847), and the Columbia School of Mines (1864) were all founded by practically minded benefactors. The new Massachusetts Institute of Technology (1861) and the land-grant colleges (after 1862) also supported the growth of applied sciences and engineering. Between 1870 and 1900 the number of bachelor's degrees granted by colleges and universities more than tripled, rising from about ten thousand to almost thirty thousand. During the same period the American Ph.D. was invented, with the numbers granted soaring from one in 1870 to 382 in 1900.

The landmark event of this era in American higher education was the founding of Johns Hopkins University in 1876 under the leadership of Daniel Coit Gilman, a graduate of Yale's Sheffield School of Science. While the antebellum colleges had been tied to their denominational roots and had provided a liberal arts education based on mental, moral, and physical discipline, the new university model of American higher education, first unveiled at Hopkins, was self-consciously patterned on the German system of *lehr-freiheit* (freedom to teach) and *lern-freiheit* (freedom to learn) in service to a "pure science" research ideal. Professors J. J. Sylvester in math, Henry Rowland in physics, and Ira Remsen in chemistry represented the bearers of a new, rigorous discipline that was to be instilled in the laboratory and the seminar room for the advancement of knowledge and the enlightenment of society.[27]

Following the adoption of the graduate school system in American higher education at places such as Clark (1889), Harvard (1890), Stanford (1891), and Chicago (1892), scientists were able to pursue their highly specialized interests in departments organized by fields with rather well-defined conceptual boundaries. Specialization and professionalization were the dominant trends as increasingly advanced training became a prerequisite for a career in science. Institutional support structures—associations, specialized journals, advanced laboratories, and professional standards—grew up around the new divisions of knowledge being established at the academic "knowledge factories."

These influences were being felt as early as 1874 when the American Association for the Advancement of Science reorganized into special-interest sections. The first scientific society to organize around a discipline was the American Chemical Society, established in New York in 1876. It was not until a decade later, however, that a flurry of professional organization occurred. The American Physiological Society (1887), the Association of American Anatomists (1888), the American Society of Zoologists (1890), the Botanical Society of America (1894), the American Mathematical Society (1894), the American Astronomical Society (1897), the American Society for Microbiology (1899), and the American Physical Society (1899) all were founded with the intent of both raising their standards and insulating their community of discourse from nonspecialists.

The last society mentioned, that of the physicists, stands as a reminder of the distortion that may occur if the history of one scientific discipline is used to comprehend all of science. The history of physics often has been taken as a model against which the development of the other sciences is judged or through which the general history of science in America can be told.[28] However, if we read only the history of physics, we would be forced to conclude (erroneously) that not much significant science was done in this nation before the last decade or so of the nineteenth century. Compared to the glorious theoretical productions of European physicists such as James Clark Maxwell, Heinrich Herz, and Hermann von Helmholtz, the work of even the best American experimentalist, A. A. Michelson, seems rather insignificant (although he received a Nobel Prize in 1907).

A more accurate and much richer story emerges when one considers the comparative histories of other scientific specialties. The disciplinary histories of chemistry, the life sciences, the earth sciences, and the social sciences reveal crucial differences in timing, patrons, institutions, major characters, theoretical breakthroughs, the influence of social issues, and the degree of dependence on or independence from European science. The weaving together of these separate strands in such a way that one science is not cast as normative for the development of the others would be a major goal of a yet-to-be-written comprehensive survey of science and technology in the United States in the second half of the nineteenth century.

At century's end, the question of the place of intellectual elitism in a democratic society had not been resolved. In 1883, in his well-known address, "A Plea for Pure Science," the physicist (and elitist) Henry Rowland asked his colleagues to distance themselves professionally from the invention and patenting of electromechanical "conveniences" such as telegraphs and electric lights and to confront the public's disregard of abstract science and propensity for egalitarian leveling. He called for amply funded universities where great and virtuous men (like himself) could find the assistants, equipment, and financial resources they needed to devote their undivided attention to the most abstract scientific problems. A rejoinder came from Alexander Graham Bell, inventor of the telephone, member of the National Academy of Sciences, and patron of *Science* magazine: "Research is none the less genuine, investigation none the less worthy, because the truth it discovers is utilizable for the benefit of mankind."[29]

In truth, in higher education, government, and the associations, science was being practiced by elitist teachers of privileged students at the same time that it was being promoted publicly for its "democratic utilitarian" contribution to the larger social good.[30] Government scientists, as usual, insisted that they were doing "practical work for practical purposes."[31] The state colleges sought to cultivate their image as symbolic bearers of a Jeffersonian tradition of service and self-reliance, granting opportunities and benefits to the general populace. Private philanthropy, including direct giving to colleges and universities, although modest, was also growing in scale. Increasingly a portion of the wealth accumulated by entrepreneurs and the leaders of industry and banking was being directed to philanthropic goals, including the support of scientific research. In 1867 the estate of Alexander Dallas Bache, a leader of American science and former head of the Coast Survey, was used to endow a research fund of $50,000 at the National Academy of Sciences.[32] By one estimate the total endowment for science was $3 million in 1902, mostly concentrated at Harvard, Chicago, and the Smithsonian.[33] That year Andrew Carnegie endowed the Carnegie Institution of Washington with $10 million to alleviate what he termed America's "national poverty in science."

Technology and Progress

In truth, the major contribution of nineteenth-century science to the emergence of modern America lies not in the particular theoretical or experimental accomplishments of any particular discipline. Rather, it is ingrained in the scientific modes of thought that increasingly were wedded to the processes of technological innovation, in the reciprocal influences of the sciences and technologies that transformed the American economy and were infused into the general society, and in the popular expectation of and enthusiasm for continued and unlimited progress.[34]

In 1865 the first few miles of oil pipeline were laid in Pennsylvania, and Thaddeus Lowe invented a machine for producing ice. The following year a functioning transatlantic telegraph cable linked America and Europe. In 1869 the ceremonial driving of the Golden Spike at Promontory Point, Utah, completed a transcontinental railroad link, and young Thomas Alva Edison invented a stock ticker.[35] In 1876, American technology gained Bell's telephone and Edison's Menlo Park "invention factory." By the 1880s homes and offices were illuminated by electric lamps, factory production lines were driven by electric motors, and urban commuters clambered aboard electric trolleys. Such technologies of communication and transportation, natural resource extraction, and refrigeration have, to a large extent, shaped modern civilization; the many inventions of Edison—including the electric light, phonograph, moving pictures, and the creation of the invention factory itself—served to define the material culture of a new era.[36]

In 1883 four standard time zones were established across the country; the next year telephone wires connected Boston and New York; the following year George Eastman patented a machine for producing continuous photographic film. By 1890 an electrically driven punch-card reader was being used to tabulate the census of 76 million Americans, a population double in number and much more diverse than that of 1870. Six years later, Herman Hollerith,

Thomas A. Edison. The inventor in his laboratory in West Orange, New Jersey, 1888. *Courtesy Library of Congress*

the inventor of the punch-card reader, established the Tabulating Machine Company, a forerunner of International Business Machines. In the field of medicine, activities at institutions such as the Johns Hopkins, Harvard, and University of Pennsylvania medical schools were providing support for scientific research and technological innovation. In 1893 surgeon Daniel Williams performed the first open-heart surgery in America; three years later, Michael Pupin at Columbia University took the first diagnostic X-ray photograph in the United States.

By the end of the century technological innovations had either caused or supported sweeping social changes in the nation. Alan Marcus and Howard Segal write of an ongoing "systemization" of experience in the production of power, in the organization of work, and in the very fabric of American life.[37] Electrical appliances, the telephone and telegraph, the factory system, and mass transportation had transformed the lives of millions. There was no end in sight as the world paused to take note of American accomplishments, hopes, and aspirations at the Columbian Exposition in Chicago in 1893. The nation closed the century with a surge of extraordinary prosperity.

To the British evolutionist Alfred Russel Wallace, this was "the Wonderful Century." In his book by that title, Wallace expressed the spirit of the times when he described the nineteenth century as a period of unprecedented gains in knowledge and its application to human welfare. As one reviewer commented, "It is not invention and discovery and the extension of man's dominion over nature, but the establishment of the conviction that we know no limit to this movement, that is the chief distinction of our century."[38]

There is no dramatic ending point to the era of disciplinary and professional growth that began in the late nineteenth century. In the first decade of the new century developments in the boardroom and the industrial research laboratory, in the air and in the heavens, in materials science and in the reputation of American scientists, and in many other areas prefigured a coming new order in science. The achievements included the following: General Electric Company opened its industrial research laboratory and the government established the National Bureau of Standards (both 1901), the Carnegie Institution of Washington was founded with an initial bequest of $10 million (1902), the Wright brothers flew their airplane at Kitty Hawk (1903), George Ellery Hale established the Mount Wilson Observatory in California (1904), A. A. Michelson won the Nobel Prize for Physics for his earlier spectroscope studies and measurements of light (1907), and Leo Baekeland patented Bakelite, a plastic substitute for wood, ivory, and rubber (1909). Intellectuals and the general public alike believed that the key to progress was the increased application of the tools, knowledge, and methods of science and technology to all spheres of human activity.[39] Science was the harbinger of technology, and technology was the worker of wonders. Throughout the Progressive Era the vast majority of Americans remained optimistic, believing that the great engine of progress they had built was being driven ever onward and upward by the forces of science and technology.

Notes

1. Henry Adams, *The Education of Henry Adams: An Autobiography* (1918; reprint ed., Boston, 1961), 53.

2. Editorial, "The United States International Exhibition of 1876," *Journal of the Franklin Institute*, 3d ser., 71 (1876): 365–66.

3. George Wise, "Science and Technology," *Osiris*, 2d ser., 1 (1985): 229–46, examines possible models of the interrelationship. This entire issue of *Osiris*, edited by Sally Gregory Kohlstedt and Margaret W. Rossiter and reprinted as *Historical Writing on American Science: Perspectives and Prospects* (Baltimore, 1986), is a valuable historiographic source. Edward Lurie, "Science in American Thought," *Journal of World History* 8 (1965): 638–65 makes the case for science in the transformation of American culture circa 1840–1880. A broader case in

which science and technology are factors is presented by Peter Dobkin Hall, *The Organization of American Culture, 1700–1900: Private Institutions, Elites, and the Origins of American Nationality* (New York, 1982).

4. The standard period surveys are: Raymond P. Stearns, *Science in the British Colonies of America* (Urbana, IL, 1970); Brooke Hindle, *The Pursuit of Science in Revolutionary America, 1735–1789* (Chapel Hill, NC, 1956); John C. Greene, *American Science in the Age of Jefferson* (Ames, IA, 1984); and Robert V. Bruce, *The Launching of Modern American Science, 1846–1876* (New York, 1987). For a broad survey of technology see Alan I. Marcus and Howard P. Segal, *Technology in America: A Brief History* (San Diego, 1989).

5. This question is addressed in J. L. Heilbron and Daniel J. Kevles, "Science and Technology in U.S. History Textbooks: What's There—And What Ought to Be There," *Reviews in American History* 16 (1988): 173–85. Recently a team of authors has proposed to write a college-level textbook that will integrate the history of technology and science into the general American story. See Kevles, Alex Keyssar, Pauline Maier, and Merritt Roe Smith, "Prospectus for a U.S. History Textbook," unpublished document, February 23, 1994.

6. Examples of fully contextualized studies of recent technologies include Richard Rhodes, *The Making of the Atomic Bomb* (New York, 1986); and Walter A. McDougall, *The Heavens and the Earth: A Political History of the Space Age* (New York, 1985).

7. On the Darwinian debates see Ronald L. Numbers, "Science and Religion," *Osiris*, 2d ser., 1 (1985): 70–79. On Spencer see Richard Hofstadter, *Social Darwinism in American Thought* (New York, 1944); and R. Laurence Moore, "Evolution and the Sabotaging of Karl Marx in America," *Reviews in American History* 22 (September 1994): 456–60. The standard work in the field is Dorothy Ross, *The Origins of American Social Science* (New York, 1991).

8. The starting point for such studies is Margaret W. Rossiter, *Women Scientists in America: Struggles and Strategies to 1940* (Baltimore, 1982).

9. Richard H. Shryock, "American Indifference to Basic Research during the Nineteenth Century," *Archives Internationales d'Histoire des Sciences* 28 (1948): 50–65.

10. Nathan Reingold, "American Indifference to Basic Research: A Reappraisal," in *Nineteenth-Century American Science: A Reappraisal*, ed. George Daniels (Evanston, IL, 1972), 54–55; Bruce, *The Launching of Modern American Science*, 1. Although Bruce's metaphor reminds the reader of an epic rocket launch (perhaps *Sputnik* I or *Apollo* 11), recall also that many more prosaic launchings occur each day at innumerable boat landings. It is also hard to agree with him that "by 1876 modern American science and technology were fully formed and rising to their cloud-wrapped destiny" (p. 3).

11. Joseph Henry to John Tyndall, October 22, 1872, quoted in Charles Weiner, "Science and Higher Education," in *Science and Society in the United States*, ed. David D. Van Tassel and Michael G. Hall (Homewood, IL, 1966), 177. This entire volume is a valuable, if somewhat dated, survey.

12. George Basalla, "The Spread of Western Science," *Science*, n.s. 156 (May 5, 1967): 611–22. For details concerning the first two eras see I. B. Cohen, "The New World as a Source of Science for Europe," in *IX Congreso Internacional de Historia de las Ciencias*, vol. 1, *Textos de las Ponencias* (Barcelona, 1959), 65–93; and Nathan Reingold and Marc Rothenberg, eds., *Scientific Colonialism: A Cross-Cultural Comparison* (Washington, DC, 1987).

13. Bruce Sinclair, "Americans Abroad: Science and Cultural Nationalism in the Early Nineteenth Century," in *The Sciences in the American Context: New Perspectives*, ed. Nathan Reingold (Washington, DC, 1979), 35–53.

14. Allan Nevins, *The War for the Union*, vol. 1, *The Improvised War, 1861–1862* (New York, 1959–1971), v.

15. According to Woodrow Wilson, the Civil War "created in this country what had never existed before—a national consciousness." Memorial Day Address, May 31, 1915, Arlington National Cemetery, Virginia.

16. Hall, *Organization of American Culture*, 242 and 227–39.

17. Donald R. Whitnah, *A History of the United States Weather Bureau* (Urbana, IL, 1961); Joseph M. Hawes, "The Signal Corps and Its Weather Service, 1870–1890," *Military Affairs* 30 (1966): 68–76.

18. James Rodger Fleming, *Meteorology in America, 1800–1870* (Baltimore, 1990).

19. Complete documentation of this case study appears in the author's "Historical Introduction: The Signal Office and the Bibliography of Meteorology," in *International Bibliography of Meteorology: From the Beginning of Printing to 1889*, ed. James Rodger Fleming and Roy E. Goodman, 4 volumes in 1 (Upland, PA, 1994).

20. Congressman Halbert E. Paine to Duane Mowry, October 8, 1903, quoted in Eric R. Miller, "New Light on the Beginnings of the Weather Bureau from the Papers of Increase A. Lapham," *Monthly Weather Review* 59 (1931): 68.

21. Albert J. Myer to Congressman Halbert E. Paine, January 18, 1870, "Letters . . . relative to storm telegraphy," U.S. House of Representatives, Ex. Doc. 10, pt. 2, 41st Cong., 2d sess., 22.

22. Fleming and Goodman, eds., *International Bibliography of Meteorology*.

23. "Testimony before the [Allison] Commission to consider the present organization of the Signal Service," U.S. Senate, Misc. Doc. 82, 49th Cong., 1st sess. See also A. Hunter Dupree, *Science in the Federal Government: A History of Policies and Activities to 1940* (Cambridge, MA, 1957), 190, 215, et seq.

24. Samuel P. Hays, *The Response to Industrialism, 1885–1914* (Chicago, 1957); Robert H. Wiebe, *The Search for Order, 1877–1920* (New York, 1967).

25. Exemplary in these regards are John M. Staudenmaier, *Technology's Storytellers: Reweaving the Human Fabric* (Cambridge, MA, 1985); Michael L. Smith, *Pacific Visions: California Scientists and the Environment, 1850–1915* (New Haven, CT, 1987); and Ann Shelby Blum, *Picturing Nature: American Nineteenth-Century Zoological Illustration* (Princeton, NJ, 1993).

26. Carroll W. Purcell, "Science and Government Agencies," in Van Tassel and Hall, eds., *Science and Society*, 223–49.

27. On the establishment of Johns Hopkins University see Daniel Coit Gilman, *The Launching of a University* (New York, 1906); and Laurence R. Veysey, *The Emergence of the American University* (Chicago, 1965).

28. Books such as Daniel J. Kevles, *The Physicists: The History of a Scientific Community in Modern America* (New York, 1977), although well written, should not be considered normative of the overall history of science in America. He begins his account in the late nineteenth century and focuses on twentieth-century developments.

29. This account of Rowland and Bell is adapted from Kevles, *Physicists*, 43–47.

30. Weiner, "Science and Higher Education," 163–89.

31. Julius E. Hilgard, "Testimony before the [Allison] Commission to consider the present organization of the . . . Coast and Geodetic Survey," U.S. Senate, Misc. Doc. 82, 49th Cong., 1st sess., 54.

32. An additional $40,000 was added to the Bache endowment four years later. Earlier endowments for science included the Rumford Fund of the American Academy of Arts and Sciences (1796) and the Smithsonian Bequest (1830s). On Bache see Hugh R. Slotten, *Patronage, Practice, and the Culture of American Science: Alexander Dallas Bache and the U.S. Coast Survey* (New York, 1994).

33. Howard S. Miller, "Science and Private Agencies," in Van Tassel and Hall, eds., *Science and Society*, 215.

34. Essential reading on this subject is Merritt Roe Smith and Leo Marx, eds., *Does Technology Drive History? The Dilemma of Technological Determinism* (Cambridge, MA, 1994).

35. The first Edison invention, patented in 1868, was a device to record votes in Congress and was not very popular.

36. See Reese V. Jenkins, ed., *The Papers of Thomas A. Edison* (Baltimore, 1989–).

37. Marcus and Segal, *Technology in America*, 133–254.

38. W. K. Brooks, "Review of *The Wonderful Century*," *Science* (April 7, 1899): 511, quoted in Weiner, "Science and Higher Education," 180.

39. Weiner, "Science and Higher Education," 179.

Suggestions for Further Reading

Adams, Henry. *The Education of Henry Adams: An Autobiography*. 1918. Reprint, Boston, 1961.

Bruce, Robert V. *The Launching of Modern American Science, 1846–1876*. New York, 1987.

Dupree, A. Hunter. *Science in the Federal Government: A History of Policies and Activities to 1940*. Cambridge, MA, 1957.

Elliott, Clark A. *Biographical Dictionary of American Science: The Seventeenth through the Nineteenth Centuries*. Westport, CT, 1979.

Fleming, James Rodger. *Meteorology in America, 1800–1870*. Baltimore, 1990.

Hall, Peter Dobkin. *The Organization of American Culture, 1700–1900: Private Institutions, Elites, and the Origins of American Nationality*. New York, 1982.

Kevles, Daniel J. *The Physicists: The History of a Scientific Community in Modern America*. New York, 1977.

Kevles, Daniel J., Jeffrey L. Sturchio, and P. Thomas Carroll. "The Sciences in America, Circa 1880." *Science* 209 (1980): 27–32.

Kohlstedt, Sally Gregory, and Margaret W. Rossiter, eds. *Historical Writing on American Science: Perspectives and Prospects*. Baltimore, 1986. Originally published in *Osiris*, 2d ser., 1, 1985.

Marcus, Alan I., and Howard P. Segal. *Technology in America: A Brief History*. San Diego, 1989.

Oleson, Alexandra, and John Voss, eds. *The Organization of Knowledge in Modern America, 1860–1920*. Baltimore, 1979.

Ross, Dorothy. *The Origins of American Social Science*. New York, 1991.

Rossiter, Margaret W. *Women Scientists in America: Struggles and Strategies to 1940*. Baltimore, 1982.

Rothenberg, Marc. *The History of Science and Technology in the United States: A Critical and Selective Bibliography*. 2 vols. New York, 1982, 1993.

3

American Workers and the Labor Movement in the Late Nineteenth Century

Eric Arnesen

The locomotive firemen and brakemen who walked off their jobs on the Baltimore and Ohio Railroad in July 1877 could not have predicted that their actions would precipitate the largest labor uprising that the nation had ever experienced. Protesting yet another round of wage cuts, this one coming in the fourth year of a severe economic depression, they quickly learned how deeply their grievances against corporate power resonated in many working-class communities. The strike—"a protest against robbery, a rebellion against starvation" and "despotic control," as labor reformer George McNeill described it—spread spontaneously along principal railroad trunk lines over the course of the next two weeks.[1] From Martinsburg, West Virginia, and Baltimore to Pittsburgh, Chicago, Louisville, and St. Louis, workers on all major railroad lines east of the Mississippi River were on strike within the week. Soon, even Galveston and San Francisco would be affected. Not just railroaders but coal miners, longshoremen, mill hands, and domestic workers were swept up in the rebellion. Violence erupted in many cities as police and state militiamen battled angry strikers and their sympathizers. In Pittsburgh, workers even burned down the yards and depot of the hated Pennsylvania Railroad. In the fighting that followed, hundreds of militiamen imported from Philadelphia (to replace local Pittsburgh militiamen who fraternized too much with the strikers to police them effectively) shot and killed some twenty protesters.

By August 1 the strikes were over, suppressed by company guards, local police, and federal troops ordered into action by President Rutherford B. Hayes. But the memory of "the insurrection," which both the president and the *New York Tribune* called the strike, lingered on, serving as a wake-up call to politicians, economic elites, and workers alike as to the human costs of capitalist industrialization in the United States. A journalist sympathetic to employers summed up their fears: "It seemed as if the whole social and political structure was on the very brink of ruin" as thousands of workers, "alleging that they were wronged and oppressed . . . , bid defiance to the ordinary instruments of legal authority." America's middle and upper classes now stressed their belief in the need for order—for the rule of conservative law, the election of the "best men" to office, and the restraint of radical impulses. Only the "substantial, property-owning" classes could save "civilized society" from the spectre of "communism" revealed by the strike, the *Tribune* concluded.[2]

Labor activists, not surprisingly, offered a very different interpretation. The strike was but "the Beginning of a Revolution" that would, "in the future history of this country, be designated as the beginning of the second American Revolution, which inaugurated

The Great Railroad Strike of 1877. An artist's depiction of the strike violence in Baltimore, July 20, 1877, for *Frank Leslie's Illustrated Newspaper*, August 4, 1877. *Courtesy Library of Congress*

the independence of Labor from Capital," as one labor newspaper argued.[3] However contemporaries interpreted the strike, it constituted the largest labor upheaval to that time, one whose underlying causes did not promise to go away easily. The events of 1877, which included the final collapse of what was left of Reconstruction in the South, placed the "labor question" squarely and unavoidably on the nation's agenda. Over the next quarter of a century, workers and managers continued to debate and struggle over that question in the press, in local neighborhoods, at the ballot box, and at workplaces.

American workers of this period confronted an economy undergoing dramatic transformations. The last three decades of the century witnessed a sixfold increase in the nation's Gross National Product; the number of workers engaged in manufacturing quadrupled to 6 million between 1860 and 1900; and the United States emerged as the world's premier industrial power, surpassing even Great Britain as the vanguard of the Industrial Revolution. This achievement was made possible, in part, by the vast expansion of the nation's transportation system. Railroads grew at phenomenal rates, linking far-flung markets and drawing ever greater numbers of people into a unified system of commerce. New forms of business organization emerged, enabling companies to generate massive sums of capital and to expand on a hitherto unthinkable scale. This was also an era of cutthroat business competition that wreaked havoc on large numbers of firms. If laissez-faire was an official ideology, corporate leaders came to understand that competition could be more harmful than beneficial. Pooling arrangements, holding companies, and the merger movement of 1897–1904, which produced the first billion dollar corporations, were the mechanisms devised by industrial capitalists to restrain the centrifugal forces generated by the market system, which now threatened to tear it apart. By the century's end, modern corporate America was taking firm shape.

The emergence and consolidation of the new industrial order meant, first and foremost, that America was becoming a nation of wage earners for the first time. At the start of the nineteenth century, wage labor was but one of many competing forms or systems of organizing productive activity. Skilled artisans produced in small shops, textile operatives labored in large factories, rural men and women made goods at home through the putting-out system, farm families tilled their land, garment workers toiled in sweatshops,

and African and African-American slaves performed forced labor
on plantations or in rural industries and cities. While this diversity
never completely vanished, it did change dramatically over the
course of the century. According to the 1870 census, the United
States remained a predominantly rural nation, but it had become a
nation of employees. Some 67 percent of productively engaged
people (involved in gainful occupations)—a majority of the population—now worked for somebody else, dependent upon another
person or business for their livelihood. Self-employment was the
exception, not the rule. By the century's end, the "wages system,"
as labor critics called it, was dominant.

Workers living through this period of economic transformation
must have felt as if they were riding a roller coaster in slow motion. The economy grew in fits and starts in the late nineteenth century. The United States faced two major economic depressions—
from 1873 to 1877 and from 1893 to 1897—and in each crisis, unemployment rose to over 16 percent while substantial numbers of
workers faced widespread underemployment and reduced wages.
In an era before state-sponsored unemployment insurance or other
benefits, losing one's job could mean being deprived of the means
to survive. The mainstream press (not known for its sympathy for
workers' activities) at times painted a stark picture of working-
class life during periods of depression. The New Orleans *Daily Picayune*, for instance, reported an "absolute destitution—not a thing
of words but a hard reality" producing starvation among the unemployed in 1875.[4] In February 1879 the poet Walt Whitman observed
poor, unemployed tramps "plodding along, their eyes cast down,
spying for scraps, rags, [and] bones." He believed that if "the United
States, like the countries of the Old World, are also to grow vast
crops of poor, desperate, dissatisfied, nomadic, miserably-waged
populations, such as we see looming upon us of late years—steadily,
even if slowly, eating into them like a cancer of lungs or stom-
ach—then our republican experiment, notwithstanding all its
surface-successes, is at heart an unhealthy failure."[5] Unemployment
during depressions might be most severe, but even in more prosperous times workers could and often did find themselves unex-
pectedly out of jobs when businesses went bankrupt or experienced
sudden trade and production fluctuations.

The process of capitalist industrialization offered real benefits
to some workers, but it also exacted a steep human price. By most
accounts, the standard of living enjoyed by American workers rose,

Labor in the New Industrial Age. Workmen operating one of the most productive of the new technologies, the Bessemer converter, at the Pennsylvania Steel Company, Steelton, Pennsylvania, circa 1890. *Courtesy Hagley Museum and Library*

and rose significantly, in the late nineteenth and early twentieth centuries. The gains, however, were unevenly distributed. At the top of the hierarchy within the working class, skilled craft workers, most often native-born white men or immigrants from England or Germany, reaped a disproportionate share of the benefits. Those below them fared worse. Sharp economic distinctions existed between skilled and unskilled laborers, men and women, whites and nonwhites, and native-born and most immigrant workers. For all the traditional celebrations of the rising standard of living and the fruits of plenty in the American economy, poverty remained a chronic, often inescapable feature of working-class life. Much of the research into workers' living standards concludes that most lived precariously close to the prospect of poverty. As one miner on the Mesabi Range in Minnesota expressed it in the early twentieth century, "If we eat we can't dress, and if we dress we don't eat." Not all workers were subject to such economic privation but millions were. Despite an overall upward trend in living standards, poverty remained a central facet of working-class life.[6]

The conditions of work—low wages, long hours (the twelve-hour day was not uncommon), harsh conditions, abusive managers, and high accident rates on the job—sparked repeated protests at places of employment and in workers' communities across the nation. The closing decades of the nineteenth century were marked by a degree of class conflict, much of it violent, as great as any in the industrialized world. During the 1880s, according to the Bureau of Labor Statistics, the United States experienced almost ten thousand strikes and lockouts. In 1886 alone, a year that earned the title the "great upheaval," roughly seven hundred thousand workers either went out on strike or were locked out by their employers. Even larger numbers would participate in the titanic clashes of the early 1890s.

What were these industrial battles about? At issue were more than simply wages, hours of work, conditions on the job, and union recognition, although these remained of vital importance. The battles between labor and capital assumed meanings broader than the straightforward contest for economic supremacy. The new industrial order of the Gilded Age raised critical questions about the place and power of labor in a capitalist economy, the morality of capitalist industrialization, the compatibility of political democracy and economic concentration, and the very fate of the Republic. Workers offered a variety of answers to these questions, many of which sharply challenged those presented by the economic elite and the middle class. Given the high stakes, it is little wonder that these different visions and interests generated intense conflicts.

While never homogeneous, the American working class became even more diverse in the late nineteenth century. The process of capitalist industrialization required not only entrepreneurial skill, willingness to take risks, and capital investment but also a vast quantity of labor. Workers were drawn from a broad geographical spectrum. Native-born, white American men or male immigrants from northwestern Europe constituted the majority of the skilled labor force and formed the core of the craft unions in such trades as carpentry, iron puddling, locomotive engineering, glassblowing, and machine building. Yet these were years of an ethnic "remaking" of the working class. The "old" immigrants from England, Germany, Scandinavia, and Ireland were soon outnumbered by "new" ones from southern and eastern Europe and, to a lesser extent, from China, Japan, and Mexico. Some of these newcomers were fleeing religious or political persecution in Europe; others came to earn enough money to return home and purchase land (return rates for certain groups remained high); still others intended to stay and make the best of the opportunities that the United States had to offer. New immigrants performed unskilled work in basic industries (meat packing, iron and steel production, and textile manufacturing), the extractive sector (mining), common labor (railroad track work, longshoring, and construction), and domestic service, dominating the lower echelons of the expanding market economy.

Women played a growing role in the late nineteenth-century labor force. Despite a prevailing ideology that designated the home as the woman's true sphere, women worked for wages (as domestic servants, factory operatives, and as boardinghouse keepers, for example) for needed money as well as for a sense of personal independence. They constituted 14 percent of those gainfully employed in 1870 and 20 percent of this group in 1910. As historian Susan Levine has argued, aggregate percentages mask women's concentration in particular industries and communities. In 1880 in Fall River, Massachusetts, and Atlanta, Georgia, women made up 34 percent and 35 percent, respectively, of the labor force. In most cases, they were confined to textile and garment production and light manufacturing, domestic work, and, by the twentieth century, clerical work. Prior to 1900, most wage-earning women were unmarried; upon marriage, many withdrew from the paid labor market to manage the household economy. Whether or not they received wages for their efforts, women engaged in the social reproduction of the work force, performing the crucial unpaid labor of housework and child rearing.[7]

Racial minorities occupied distinct positions within the working class. African Americans, the largest group of nonwhites, remained, for the most part, a southern, rural, and agricultural people.

In the aftermath of the Civil War, a system of sharecropping replaced the institution of slavery. In exchange for little more than a modicum of personal and familial autonomy, black agricultural workers farmed the land belonging to southern whites, producing cotton in exchange for a portion of the final crop. Confronted by fraud, violence, and falling cotton prices, blacks remained trapped in poverty, enmeshed in an economic system that offered few possibilities for social mobility. Some African Americans did exchange farm labor for waged work. Many black women performed domestic service in white homes, while others found jobs in canning or tobacco factories. Excluded from most of the industrialized sectors of the economy, black men labored in southern turpentine and lumber camps, coal mines, and on the docks of port cities. In the West, Chinese immigrant workers helped construct the transcontinental railroad before immigration restrictions and white hostility reduced their numbers and limited their options. Japanese in the Pacific Northwest and Mexicans and Mexican Americans in the Southwest were agricultural and common laborers as well.

Given the diversity and continual recomposition of the American working class, it is not surprising that workers shared no common goals or understanding of their condition and advanced no single program for reform. Even in the best of times, they remained divided along cultural, national/ethnic, racial, religious, and gender lines. Undoubtedly, many believed that social mobility was a real possibility and strove hard to achieve economic success. Others struggled merely to survive, moving about the country in a constant search for security. Still others questioned the direction of economic trends, organizing associations of fellow wage earners to offer an alternative to the doctrine of laissez-faire and unrestrained corporate growth. In its place they sought to create a more humanitarian society that repudiated what reformers called the "soulless commercialism" of the Gilded Age and that overturned the "iron heel of a soulless monopoly [that crushed] . . . the manhood out of sovereign citizens."[8] While the labor movement that emerged in the 1880s and 1890s enrolled only a minority of the population (perhaps representing no more than 10 percent of the employed labor force), it nonetheless represented the aspirations, articulated the fears, and offered alternatives on behalf of large numbers of American workers.[9] The pages that follow examine the Gilded Age's two most important movements—the Knights of Labor and the

American Federation of Labor (AFL)—and its most noted industrial conflicts.

The Noble and Holy Order of the Knights of Labor was founded in 1869 by Philadelphia garment cutters. Its models were fraternal orders whose style and ritual forms appealed to midnineteenth century Americans. During its first decade of existence, the Knights of Labor was also a secret society. Initially, members were prohibited from revealing the Order's existence (to protect members from employers' retaliation), and reference to the Order was made through symbols. The notation *****, for example, represented the Knights' name. According to one 1888 historian of the Order, these five stars, placed in front of Philadelphia's Independence Hall, indicated a scheduled meeting. "This singular and mysterious sign," the author noted, "never failed to bring together thousands of the working class."[10] For much of its first decade, the organization remained small, concentrated primarily in Pennsylvania and other eastern states.

It was only with the end of the depression of the 1870s that the Knights experienced significant growth. From 1877 to 1880 the Order grew to 30,000 members in sixteen hundred assemblies. By 1885 over 100,000 workers had joined the now public Knights. Over the course of the next year, the Order exploded in size. The Knights' victory over robber baron Jay Gould's Southwestern railroad system generated tremendous publicity and enthusiasm, winning the Order a large following. By 1886 as many as 750,000 workers had joined. Those numbers translated into temporary political success at the polls. Although the Knights officially steered clear of electoral politics, independent labor parties formed in many communities; between 1885 and 1888, historian Leon Fink has discovered, workingmen fielded their own slates in two hundred towns and cities.[11] In 1886 one newspaper editorialist could declare that "never in all history has there been such a spectacle as the march of the Order of the Knights of Labor. . . . It is an organization in whose hands now rests the destinies of the Republic. . . . It has demonstrated the overmastering power of a national combination among workingmen."[12]

By the mid-1880s the Knights had emerged as the largest and most inclusive labor organization in American history. Every state, major city, and sizable town boasted local assemblies. Between 8 and 12 percent of the industrial labor force were members of the roughly fifteen thousand assemblies across the country.[13] The Order was also part of a larger, dense network of overlapping organizations and institutions. Through its sponsorship of libraries and reading rooms, lecture societies, newspapers, parades, sporting clubs, and cooperatives, it influenced a far greater number of people than just its immediate membership alone, thereby nurturing what historian Richard Oestreicher has called a broad "subculture of opposition."[14]

The Knights' membership was also extremely diverse. "There is not a branch of labor, trade or profession that exists," the historian of the Order declared in 1888, "that cannot furnish material for a Knights of Labor assembly."[15] Drawing no sharp division between workers and honest managers, the Knights welcomed all true "producers." (Only bartenders and lawyers were barred by definition.) Its social composition was extremely broad, its membership a heterogeneous lot. The Order was open to any producer over eighteen years of age regardless of race, sex, or skill. (The sole exception was Asian immigrants, for the Knights joined the chorus calling for the expulsion of the Chinese and bans on new immigrants.) This inclusiveness was unprecedented in American labor history. As many as sixty-five thousand women and sixty thousand African Americans joined the ranks.

The Knights represented many things to many people. The Order was home to solid trade unionists, middle-class reformers, various socialists and anarchists, unskilled immigrant laborers, female household workers, and black agricultural laborers in the South. With a membership so diverse, the Knights could not speak with only one voice. The Order, as one contemporary wrote, "is not a mere trade union, or benefit society; neither is it a political party. . . . Any and every measure calculated to advance the interests of the wage-workers, morally, socially, or financially, comes within the scope of the Order." Or, as one Arkansas member put it in 1886, the Knights of Labor was the "harbinger of a higher and better civilization, in which equal and exact justice shall be done all mankind—a civilization in which those who sow shall be permitted to reap the fruits of their toil, and the weary find rest and comfort as the reward of honest exertion." In historian Bruce Laurie's words, the Knights "offered a little something for just about everyone."[16]

That said, the Knights did offer a set of pragmatic and idealistic proposals for restructuring the status quo, a strong critique of existing economic and political conditions, and a broad moral vision of what labor's place ought to be in an industrializing republic. The Knights called for the establishment of cooperatives, the reserving of public lands for actual settlers (not speculators), laws that applied equally to capital and labor, the replacement of strikes by arbitration, the abolition of child and convict labor, equal pay for equal work, more leisure time, a graduated income tax, and the eight-hour day "so that laborers may have more time for social enjoyment and intellectual improvement."

As "reformist" as many of these goals sound today, they directly challenged the dominant business creed of the Gilded Age, which staunchly upheld laissez-faire economics (notwithstanding some businessmen's and workers' support for the protective tariff); condemned any interference in the "natural" workings of the economy as unwise, dangerous, and immoral (notwithstanding managers' approval of and reliance upon local police or the military to suppress strikers); and celebrated the unbridled acquisition of material wealth. The Knights went even further. They called on the government to exercise its power of eminent domain to assume ownership of all telegraph, telephone, and railroad networks and promoted cooperative institutions to "supersede the wage system" altogether. In essence, the Knights proposed a different criterion for evaluating the health of the nation, seeking to "make industrial moral worth, not wealth, the true standard of individual and national greatness."[17] In contrast to the conservative Gospel of Wealth, then, the Knights put forth a vision of cooperation and working-class mutualism. "There is much more in the labor question than mere wages and hours," one New York member insisted in 1887. "We propose that our organization shall dominate and control every institution in this country" on behalf of the "vast body of toilers."[18]

Failure to act on its agenda, many Knights believed, would result in the triumph of a system that brutalized labor and dismantled the achievements of American democracy. The Order's Declaration of Principles laid out a well-developed analysis along this line. "The recent alarming development and aggression of aggregated wealth," it predicted, "unless checked, will inevitably lead to the pauperization and hopeless degradation of the toiling masses." It was thus "imperative, if we desire to enjoy the blessings of life, that a check should be placed upon its power and upon unjust accumulation, and a system adopted which will secure to the laborer the fruits of his toil."[19] In the previous decade labor journalist John Swinton, who would become an avid Knights supporter, had put the matter directly. "The power of money," he wrote in the New York *Sun* in 1876, "has become supreme over everything," securing "for the class who controls it all the special privileges" it required for "complete and absolute domination. This power must be kept in check . . . it must be broken or it will utterly crush the people." Many Knights would agree. By 1884 the Order committed itself to "a radical change in the existing industrial system," adopting a stance that was "necessarily one of war."[20]

The extreme concentration of economic power in Gilded Age America threatened the political liberty upon which the Republic was built, certain Knights leaders argued. Their portrait of the economic and political ruin wrought by capitalism drew upon an older tradition of labor republicanism that dated back to the era of the Revolutionary War. In its working-class variant, republicanism held that the health of the democratic system rested on the virtue of its citizenry and that virtue rested on independence. Americans associated both virtue and independence with the possession or ownership of productive property. Ideally, citizens should not be dependent on the patronage or favor of the well-to-do, which could only lead to corruption. Lack of ownership of productive property and, by extension, wage-earning itself reflected an abject, dependent status. The foundation of the strong, vigorous republic rested upon the widespread distribution of property, which ensured that independent producers participated as equals in the political process. By the 1880s such notions reflected the reality of an earlier era when self-employment and property ownership were more widespread for small farmers and artisans and before wage labor had become entrenched as the dominant employment relation. By midcentury, independence was giving way to dependence as "wage slavery" became the permanent condition of even more people and not simply a temporary sojourn en route to independence.

By the 1880s dependent workers were confronting increasingly powerful employers who seemed to exercise tremendous political influence. Notwithstanding their forays into the political arena, labor activists confronted a state protective of private property, supportive of business interests, and hostile to labor's basic demands. Increasingly, governors, federal officials, and courts obliged employers by unleashing extraordinary repression against workers' movements. State militias and federal troops crushed strikes; the federal judiciary repeatedly intervened in labor relations by out-lawing crucial tactics (the citywide boycott of unfair employers, for example) and declaring unconstitutional any restrictions on employers' power, such as laws setting the working day at eight hours or banning tenement production.[21]

To labor republicans, it appeared as if a new aristocracy had replaced the earlier democratic republic of producers. Could economic concentration and political democracy be reconciled? Could unrestrained capitalist industrialization and the republican experiment coexist? Many labor reformers answered no. George McNeill, a Knights supporter, put the matter succinctly when he stated that the "extremes of wealth and poverty are threatening the existence of the government. In the light of these facts, we declare that there is an inevitable and irresistible conflict between the wage-system of labor and the republican system of government, — the wage-laborer attempting to save the government, and the capitalist class ignorantly attempting to subvert."[22] To the Knights and other labor reformers, the very meaning of America—and the future of the Republic—was at stake in the fiercely contested struggles of the Gilded Age.

The Knights' organizational success proved to be short-lived. The year 1886 was the turning point. Employers mobilized and took the offensive, resisting the Knights' demands for wage increases and the eight-hour day. This concerted counterattack by business brought the Knights' forward momentum to a crashing halt. As employers drew ample support from local and state governments, the Knights lost strike after strike. Even Jay Gould got his rematch in 1886, and this time he won. And then there was Haymarket. When a bomb exploded in Haymarket Square in Chicago in May 1886 during a labor demonstration in support of strikers for the eight-hour day, the police blamed, without evidence, the city's anarchist leaders. The national press intensified its antilabor crusade, link-ing the labor movement as a whole to the anarchists' alleged crimes and undermining its moral legitimacy. The "first major" Red Scare that followed the Haymarket explosion triggered "a campaign of radical-bating rarely if ever surpassed," in historian Paul Avrich's words.[23] By the summer of 1887 the Knights' national membership had fallen by more than half, and it continued to plummet. That autumn, some ten thousand sugar workers on Louisiana plan-tations—nine thousand of whom were black—struck under the Knights' banner in an unprecedented interracial movement to

correct long-standing abuses and raise wages. Local white planters, state politicians, the militia, and armed vigilantes fought back
with a vengeance, crushing the strike with a reign of terror that left
dozens of black strikers dead.[24] Unable to protect or secure improvements for its members, the Knights had ceased to function as
a viable labor organization. Although labor republicanism did not
die with the Order—it would influence the American Railway Union
in the 1890s and the Socialist party in the early twentieth century—
very different voices now spoke for organized labor in the decades
after the 1880s.

Even as the Knights of Labor was struggling to survive, the
American Federation of Labor emerged in 1886 to offer a competing organizational vision. In contrast to the Knights, which was
built upon an alliance of skilled and unskilled workers, the AFL
was founded on the principle of the superiority of craft unionism.
Craft unions embraced specific groups of skilled workers, whose
knowledge, experience, discipline, and solidarity enabled them to
weather strikes and hold their own in conflicts with employers far
better than could the unskilled. Their power, David Montgomery
has shown, rested on the "functional autonomy of craftsmen," that
is, the superior knowledge "which made them self-directing at their
tasks" and allowed them to exercise a "broad discretion in the direction of their own work."[25] Similarly, their adherence to their own
codes of mutualism bound them together in a network of solidarity
and prompted them to obey work rules governing the permanence
of their labor. In many industries, skilled craftsmen, not their employers or managers, knew how to carry out the process of production, and they carefully set the terms under which they would
perform their tasks, refusing to work beyond their endurance or
custom or alongside former strikebreakers or other nonunion
men.

By the 1880s and 1890s corporations began experimenting with
new forms of management aimed at wresting control, or at least
more control over the labor process from craftsmen. Toward that
end, industrialists sought to divest workers of their skills, knowledge, and power and to invest them instead in management's own
supervisory personnel. Labor activists sharply condemned the "ra-
pidity with which machinery, the subdivision of labor, and cheap
methods are displacing skilled labor and diminishing the earnings
of wage-workers," as one correspondent to the labor weekly, *John
Swinton's Paper*, wrote in 1885.[26] Whether it involved the intensifi-

cation of labor (simply forcing workers to work harder, faster, and longer), mechanization (using machinery to substitute less skilled labor for craftsmen), or the reorganization of the production process itself, the assault on the skilled craftsmen produced an ongoing battle for control of the shop floor that often would break out into large-scale battles between unions and managers in the 1890s and the early twentieth century.

Ideologically, the AFL rejected the broader social goals of the Knights and pursued what traditionally has been termed "pure and simple unionism," or "business" unionism. Samuel Gompers, who headed the Federation for virtually all of its first three and one half decades, initially led it away from the political arena. Championing the philosophy of "voluntarism," Gompers believed that his organization could best secure its goals not through legislation—he learned from bitter experience that the courts would undoubtedly strike down labor's laws—but through its own economic strength at the workplace. By the early twentieth century, however, the AFL advocated laws restraining the courts from interfering in labor-management affairs, because the judiciary increasingly undermined the AFL's ability to exercise its strength at the workplace. This campaign would lead it into an alliance with the Democratic party.[27]

The AFL also abandoned the Knights' goal of replacing the "wages system" with one based upon cooperation. Accepting the permanency of wage labor, it instead sought to secure a place for skilled labor within the parameters of industrial capitalism. Even this aim was fiercely, and often successfully, resisted by modern corporate managers, who viewed unions as unnecessary interference in their right to set wages, determine conditions, and rule the workplace as they saw fit. The Federation's rank and file, of course, was never ideologically of one mind. Substantial numbers of socialists were members of craft unions that were affiliated with the AFL, and they sought to influence its direction. In 1893 and 1894 the organization debated and narrowly rejected the socialists' political program, which would have committed it to the collective ownership of all means of production and distribution and the creation of an independent labor party. The movement's radical impulses were by no means extinguished by this defeat, however. Within the AFL a number of important unions continued to nurture strong socialist tendencies. While pockets of radical influence persisted, AFL president Gompers steered his organization, which would dominate the labor movement well into the twentieth century, toward far more limited, conservative goals.

The ideology, structure, social basis, and function of the AFL's craft unionism generated exclusionary tendencies that made participation by African Americans, new immigrants, and women difficult. Its skilled white constituency often turned a cold shoulder toward the unskilled. On the one hand, craftsmen disparaged them as undisciplined and incapable of behaving in a proper trade-union manner. On the other hand, they often ignored those unskilled immigrants, blacks, and women who did demonstrate discipline and trade-union values. A central function of the craft union was to protect its members and preserve the dignity, skills, and wages of the craft by keeping potential competitors out of the labor market. To skilled white craftsmen, new immigrants, African Americans, and women constituted potential competition that had to be resisted. More than economics was involved, for ideological assumptions about race and gender contributed greatly to the shaping of AFL membership policies.

As a federation of skilled white workers, the AFL rarely welcomed unskilled blacks into its ranks. Reflecting and refining the racial ideology of the larger white society, some white unionists actively campaigned to keep their unions and their trades white. Numerous unions within the Federation barred nonwhites explicitly or in practice. Some blacks, however, enrolled in all-black locals of longshoremen, teamsters, and coal miners and sought affiliation with the AFL by the century's end. In 1892, AFL unions formed the interracial Workingmen's Amalgamated Council, which participated in a general strike in New Orleans on behalf of black freight teamsters. Some twenty thousand workers from forty-two unions struck in what one local newspaper called a "war of classes." The threat of military intervention broke the strike, destroying many unions and the broad cooperative spirit that had motivated them. However, examples of interracial collaboration on the New Orleans waterfront or in the mining camps of Alabama's Birmingham district proved to be the exception, not the rule. By the century's end, the AFL had grown more hostile toward black workers.[28]

Women also found it difficult to secure a place within the ranks of the AFL. Male craft unionists had inherited and refined assumptions about gender that led them to disapprove of women's participation in the wage-labor market or labor movement. Since the early nineteenth century, male workers had advocated a "family wage," arguing that a man should earn a sufficient income to maintain his family without his wife or children having to work for wages. As historian Christine Stansell has argued, "The workingmen envisioned a nineteenth-century home not unlike the bourgeois ideal, a repository for women's 'true' nature as well as a refuge from the miseries of wage labor."[29] Or, as one AFL member put it, "We believe that the man should be provided with a fair wage in order to keep his female relatives from going to work. The man is the provider and should receive enough for his labor to give his family a respectable living." Belief in the "family wage" was not restricted to men alone; some female labor activists believed that, ideally, women would not have to work for wages if men received the higher compensation they deserved. The consequences of female labor-market participation, its critics charged, could be particularly harmful. Women were exposed to hazardous and immoral working conditions; they placed themselves and their families at risk; and they "invaded" previously male trades, leading to lower overall wages, a deterioration of conditions, and the displacement of male trade unionists. In AFL leaders' thinking, "Every woman employed displaces a man and adds one more to the idle contingent that are fixing wages at the lowest limit." Such assumptions led some AFL unions to attempt to bar women from entering their trades, as opposed to organizing those who made it in. Given the AFL's stance that the "great principle for which we fight is opposed to taking . . . the women from their homes to put them in the factory and the sweatshop"—in the 1905 words of the AFL's treasurer—it is not surprising that by the start of the new century only 3.3 percent of women in industrial occupations were union members, a figure that dropped to about 1.5 percent in 1910.[30]

Just as the Knights of Labor encountered fierce employer resistance in the 1880s, the American Federation of Labor similarly engaged in do-or-die battles with corporate leaders in the 1890s. During that decade, capital handed the new Federation defeat after defeat. Even before the depression that began in 1893 sent unemployment skyrocketing, wages plummeting, and labor organizers packing, the fledgling AFL lost a series of crucial strikes that resulted in the destruction of many unions. In 1892 the powerful Amalgamated Association of Iron and Steel Workers squared off against the even more powerful industrialists Henry Clay Frick and Andrew Carnegie in western Pennsylvania. The strike/lockout at Homestead "stirred the labor movement as few other single events"

had, in the 1922 words of labor economist Selig Perlman. Strikers
and sympathizers successfully defended their town against an invasion by the company's armed, mercenary Pinkerton guards. Only
the arrival of the state militia and the arrest and prosecution of strike
leaders brought Frick and Carnegie the victory they desired. The
union lay in ashes, wages and working conditions deteriorated rapidly, strikers lost their jobs, managers crushed overt dissent and
effectively dominated local politics, and unionism in steel was wiped
out for the next four decades. The debacle at Homestead, Perlman
argued, taught the labor movement the "lesson that even its strongest organization was unable to withstand an onslaught by the modern corporation."[31] Homestead was only the most famous of the
labor upheavals of 1892. From the silver mines of Coeur d'Alene,
Idaho, to the waterfront of New Orleans, from the coal mines of
East Tennessee and Birmingham to the railroad switching yards of
Buffalo, trade unionists engaged in pitched battles with their employers over wages, conditions, work rules, union recognition, the
control of the workplace, and the dignity of labor itself. In many
cases, it was the employers who emerged victorious.

The decisive blow against organized labor occurred two years
later during the Pullman boycott of 1894. The previous year, just as
the depression was beginning and numerous railroads went bankrupt, the newly formed American Railway Union (ARU), led by
the former locomotive fireman and future socialist Eugene V. Debs,
swept as many as 150,000 railroad workers from a wide range of
crafts into its ranks, thoroughly repudiating the narrow, conservative railroad brotherhoods that had previously dominated unionism
on the rails. In contrast to the AFL, the ARU endorsed the Populist
party and called for the nationalization of the railroads at its first
convention. In the summer of 1894 striking Pullman Palace Car
Company workers in the company town of Pullman, Illinois, turned
to the ARU for assistance in their fight to reinstate fired union activists and to rescind severe wage cuts. The new industrial union
responded with a vote of solidarity. When the company refused "all
attempts at conciliation and settlement of differences" (as the U.S.
Strike Commission subsequently phrased it), ARU members refused
to handle any train carrying a Pullman car. The Pullman boycott
was on.[32]

Railroad workers' solidarity, however, was no match for the
combined power of the General Managers' Association (the railroad employers' organization) and its allies in the press and in state

and federal government. As the boycott spread, tying up the nation's major railroads, the companies placed thousands of armed deputies on railroad payrolls to combat the strikers. More serious was the response of the federal government. By placing U.S. mail cars at the end of all Pullman trains, it effectively transformed an efforts to halt rail traffic into interference with the mail, a federal offense. President Grover Cleveland dispatched companies of U.S. Army troops to Chicago and other cities to protect railroad property and to disperse strikers; dozens of strikers and sympathizers were shot by police and military troops. The judiciary also became an antilabor force. Judges issued sweeping injunctions banning ARU members from interfering with railroad activities in any way, from picketing, and even from meeting. ARU leaders were arrested, their offices broken into and their records seized. Unable to convince Gompers and the AFL to join it in a nationwide sympathy strike (Gompers viewed the strike as an "impulsive vigorous protest" that placed the labor movement in a position of "open hostility to Federal authority"[33]), the ARU went down to utter defeat. In the Pullman boycott's aftermath, the union disintegrated, strike leader Debs was convicted and sentenced to prison, and hundreds of strikers permanently lost their jobs.

With the easing of the depression in 1897 the labor movement could claim few victories. The Knights and the ARU were effectively dead, and the AFL's chief accomplishment was its mere survival during the depression. At the century's end workers faced larger, ever more powerful corporations determined to resist unionization and to control the labor process. The most advanced sectors of the economy remained union free, and the state intervened aggressively on the side of capital. If the economic expansion of the postdepression years provided new opportunities for some American workers, others continued to labor in urban sweatshops and factories or undemocratic company towns. In some industries they put in a twelve-hour day, and for unskilled or common laborers, wage rates lifted few above the poverty line. From the perspective of labor republicans who feared the impact of economic concentration and political inequality, workers were the clear losers in the contest over the definition of labor's place in an industrializing republic.

The various groups drew different lessons from the crisis of the 1890s. Gompers and staunch craft unionists believed the AFL's very survival proved the wisdom of the Federation's structure and philosophy. It is noteworthy, as Gompers reported in 1899, "that while in every previous industrial crisis the trade unions were literally mowed down and swept out of existence, the unions now in existence have manifested, not only the power of resistance, but of stability and permanency."[34] In the years between 1897 and 1904 one and one half million new members joined the AFL. Although few of these workers labored in the dynamic industrial core of the economy, the addition of so many skilled craftsmen testified to the staying power of Gompers's vision. To Debs and labor radicals the 1890s crisis revealed the tremendous power of capital, the importance of industrial unionism, and the validity of a socialist critique. In the early twentieth century, the Knights of Labor slogan —"an injury to one is an injury to all"—would find supporters in the newly formed Socialist party, which championed the collective ownership of the means of production in the political arena, and in the Industrial Workers of the World, which promoted working-class solidarity and radical industrial unionism. Despite the growing power of the corporate sector, the struggle for control in the workplace and the contest over labor's rights in an industrial capitalist economy continued. As long as the fundamental sources of workers' grievances persisted, the labor question that claimed so prominent a place on the nation's agenda in the Gilded Age remained unresolved.

Notes

1. George E. McNeill, "The Problem of To-Day," in *The Labor Movement: The Question of To-Day*, ed. George E. McNeill (Boston, 1887), 459.

2. *New York Tribune*, July 25, 1877, quoted in Eric Foner, *Reconstruction: America's Unfinished Revolution, 1863–1877* (New York, 1988), 585.

3. *Labor Standard*, August 4, 1877, quoted in Philip S. Foner, *The Great Labor Uprising of 1877* (New York, 1977), 9. On the 1877 strike see also Robert V. Bruce, *1877: Year of Violence* (1959; reprint ed., New York, 1970).

4. New Orleans *Daily Picayune*, April 29, 1875.

5. Quoted in Alan Trachtenberg, *The Incorporation of America: Culture and Society in the Gilded Age* (New York, 1982), 70. See also Alexander Keyssar, *Out of Work: The First Century of Unemployment in Massachusetts* (New York, 1986).

6. Quoted in Melvyn Dubofsky, *Industrialism and the American Worker, 1865–1920* (Arlington Heights, IL, 1985), 21; see also pp. 16–25.

7. Susan Levine, *Labor's True Woman: Carpet Weavers, Industrialization, and Labor Reform in the Gilded Age* (Philadelphia, 1984).

8. McNeill, *The Labor Movement*, 460.

9. In some trades and cities, however, the percentage of unionized workers was considerably higher, exceeding 30 percent. By the early twentieth century, trade unions embraced between 20 and 25 percent of the country's industrial labor force. See William E. Forbath, *Law and the Shaping of the American Labor Movement* (Cambridge, MA, 1991), 20–21.

10. S. M. Jelley, *The Voice of Labor . . . Plain Talk by Men of Intellect on Labor's Rights, Wrongs, Remedies and Prospects* (Philadelphia, 1888), 195.

11. Leon Fink, *Workingmen's Democracy: The Knights of Labor and American Politics* (Urbana, IL, 1983), xiii.

12. Quoted in Bruce Laurie, *Artisans into Workers: Labor in Nineteenth-Century America* (New York, 1989), 157.

13. Kim Voss, *The Making of American Exceptionalism: The Knights of Labor and Class Formation in the Nineteenth Century* (Ithaca, NY, 1993), 2; David Montgomery, "Labor and the Republic in Industrial America: 1860–1920," *Le Mouvement Social* 3 (April–June 1980): 204.

14. Richard Oestreicher, *Solidarity and Fragmentation: Working People and Class Consciousness in Detroit, 1875–1900* (Urbana, IL, 1989).

15. Jelley, *The Voice of Labor*, 196.

16. Ibid.; "Our Progress: A Description in Detail of How the First Local Assembly Began in Arkansas," *Journal of United Labor*, September 25, 1886; Laurie, *Artisans into Workers*, 150.

17. Declaration of Principles, quoted in Carroll D. Wright, "An Historical Sketch of the Knights of Labor," *Quarterly Journal of Economics* 1 (January 1887): 157–59.

18. *Fifth Annual Report of the Bureau of Statistics of Labor of the State of New York for the Year 1887* (Troy, NY, 1888), 354.

19. Quoted in Terrence V. Powderly, *Thirty Years of Labor, 1859–1889* (1890; reprint ed., New York, 1967), 128; Declaration of Principles, quoted in Wright, "An Historical Sketch of the Knights of Labor," 157–59.

20. Quoted in Melvyn Dubofsky, "Labor Organizations," in *Encyclopedia of American Economic History: Studies of the Principal Movements and Ideas*, vol. 2, ed. Glenn Porter (New York, 1980), 532.

21. Forbath, *Law and the Shaping of the American Labor Movement*.

22. McNeill, *The Labor Movement*, 459.

23. Paul Avrich, *The Haymarket Tragedy* (Princeton, NJ, 1984), 215. On Haymarket see also Bruce C. Nelson, *Beyond the Martyrs: A Social History of Chicago's Anarchists, 1870–1900* (New Brunswick, NJ, 1988).

24. Jeffrey Gould, "Louisiana Sugar War: The Strike of 1887," *Southern Exposure* 12 (November–December 1984): 45–55.

25. David Montgomery, *Workers' Control in America: Studies in the History of Work, Technology, and Labor Struggles* (New York, 1979), 11.

26. "Crush of Machinery," *John Swinton's Paper*, January 24, 1886.

27. Julia Greene, " 'The Strike at the Ballot Box': The American Federation of Labor's Entrance into Election Politics, 1906–1909," *Labor History* 32 (Spring 1991): 165–92.

28. Eric Arnesen, *Waterfront Workers of New Orleans: Race, Class, and Politics, 1863–1923* (New York, 1991); Herbert G. Gutman, "The Negro and the United Mine Workers of America: The Career and Letters of Richard L. Davis and Something of Their Meaning, 1890–1900," in *The Negro and the American Labor Movement*, ed. Julius Jacobson (New York, 1968), 49–127; Paul Worthman, "Black

Workers and Labor Unions in Birmingham, Alabama, 1897–1904," *Labor History* 10 (Summer 1969): 375–407; Jacqueline Jones, *Labor of Love, Labor of Sorrow: Black Women, Work, and the Family from Slavery to the Present* (New York, 1985); Tera Hunter, "Domination and Resistance: The Politics of Wage Household Labor in New South Atlanta," *Labor History* 34 (Spring–Summer 1993): 205–20.

29. Christine Stansell, *City of Women: Sex and Class in New York, 1789–1860* (New York, 1986); Martha May, "Bread before Roses: American Workingmen, Labor Unions, and the Family Wage," in *Women, Work, and Protest: A Century of U.S. Women's Labor*, ed. Ruth Milkman (Boston, 1985), 1–21.

30. Alice Kessler-Harris, *Out to Work: A History of Wage-Earning Women in the United States* (New York, 1982), 152–53.

31. Selig Perlman, *A History of Trade Unionism in the United States* (New York, 1922), 135. Two excellent treatments of the Homestead strike are Paul Krause, *The Battle for Homestead, 1880–1892: Politics, Culture, and Steel* (Pittsburgh, 1992), and David P. Demarest, Jr., *"The River Ran Red": Homestead, 1892* (Pittsburgh, 1992). See also Arthur G. Burgoyne, *The Homestead Strike of 1892* (1893; reprint ed., Pittsburgh, 1979).

32. On the Pullman strike see Shelton Stromquist, *A Generation of Boomers: The Pattern of Railroad Labor Conflict in Nineteenth-Century America* (Urbana, IL, 1987); and Nick Salvatore, *Eugene V. Debs: Citizen and Socialist* (Urbana, IL, 1982).

33. Quoted in Laurie, *Artisans into Workers*, 209.

34. Quoted in Perlman, *A History of Trade Unionism*, 135–36.

Suggestions for Further Reading

American Social History Project. *Who Built America? Working People and the Nation's Economy, Politics, Culture, and Society.* Vol. 2. *From the Gilded Age to the Present.* New York, 1992.

Baron, Ava, ed. *Work Engendered: Toward a New History of American Labor.* Ithaca, NY, 1991.

Dubofsky, Melvyn, and Warren Van Tine, eds. *Labor Leaders in America.* Urbana, IL, 1987.

Fink, Leon. *Workingmen's Democracy: The Knights of Labor and American Politics.* Urbana, IL, 1983.

Gompers, Samuel. *Seventy Years of Life and Labor: An Autobiography.* Ed. Nick Salvatore. 1925. Reprint, Ithaca, NY, 1984.

Laurie, Bruce. *Artisans into Workers: Labor in Nineteenth-Century America.* New York, 1989.

McLaurin, Melton Alonza. *The Knights of Labor in the South.* Westport, CT, 1978.

Montgomery, David. *The Fall of the House of Labor: The Workplace, the State, and American Labor Activism, 1865–1925.* New York, 1987.

Rachleff, Peter. *Black Labor in Richmond, 1865–1890.* 1984. Reprint, Urbana, IL, 1989.

Rosenzweig, Roy. *Eight Hours for What We Will: Workers and Leisure in an Industrial City, 1870–1920.* Cambridge, England, 1983.

Stromquist, Shelton. "United States of America." In *The Formation of Labor Movements, 1870–1914: An International Perspective.* Vol. 2. Ed. Marcel van der Linden and Jurgen Rojahn. Leiden, The Netherlands, 1990, 543–77.

4

The Immigrant Experience in the Gilded Age

Roger Daniels

It has been traditional since early in the twentieth century for students of immigration to differentiate between "old" and "new" immigrants. Typically the western European "old immigration," chiefly that of Irish and other Britons, Germans, and Scandinavians, is treated as ending in the early 1880s and contrasted with the eastern and southern European "new immigration," chiefly that of Italians, Poles, Southern Slavs, Jews, and Greeks, ending in either 1914 with World War I, or during the period from 1921 to 1924 with the American quota acts.[1] This treatment of immigration in the Gilded Age, which in this volume is considered to run from 1866 to 1900,[2] ignores that essentially artificial distinction. It has been argued that the distinction was never an appropriate way to structure rational discussion of the process during the "century" of immigration from 1815 to 1924, which is marked by the beginning of the Pax Britannica at one end and American immigration legislation at the other.[3] It was, however, a useful heuristic device for those who wished to limit immigration and/or stress the cultural dominance of what we now call "Anglo-conformity." The portion of that eleven-decade "century" treated here has no intrinsic unity, although one can argue that the end of the Civil War makes a logical starting point. The terminal date 1900 is not a meaningful one in immigration history. Using Gilded Age dates to bound the story is thus, from one point of view, an imposition. However, any attempt to tell the Gilded Age tale *without* a significant treatment of immigrants would be a farce. This account should be considered a segment of a continuing process, for many of the themes begun here will have a resolution only in the twentieth century. The three most salient special characteristics of Gilded Age immigration are the great increase in its volume, the decided shift in its sources and composition, and the beginning of its effective restriction.

Any meaningful account of immigration must begin with statistics. Between 1866 and 1900, 13,259,469 immigrants were recorded as entering the United States, as indicated in Table 4.1. On the one hand, these thirty-four years saw the entry of a larger number of persons, by far, than had come to the United States and the British North American colonies in the previous two and one-half centuries; on the other hand, nearly as many persons, 12,928,517, would come in the next fourteen years. What is too often forgotten in the use of such statistics, which seem to show the United States being inundated by immigrants, is that the best single indicator of the incidence of newcomers, the percentage of foreign born recorded in the census, did not change significantly for seven censuses. From 1860 through 1920 each and every census showed that approximately one-seventh of the population had been born abroad.[4] In 1870 that one-seventh amounted to some 5.7 million persons; by 1900 it amounted to more than 10.3 million persons. Throughout the period, the foreign-born population was predominantly male. Table 4.2 shows the number and gender of foreign born recorded in each Gilded Age census.

Table 4.1 Immigration to the United States, 1866–1900

Years	Number of Immigrants
1866–1870	1,513,101
1871–1880	2,812,191
1881–1890	5,246,613
1891–1900	3,687,564
Total	13,259,469

Source: *Historical Statistics of the United States* (1975), 1:106.

Because immigration is a process rather than a discrete event, there are some recurring questions that should always be asked: Who were the immigrants? Where did they come from? Why did they leave home? How did they get to their destinations? Where did they go? What did they do when they got there? What kind of reception did they receive?[5]

Table 4.2 Foreign Born, 1870–1900

Year	Number of Foreign Born	Percent Male
1870	5,567,229	54.
1880	6,679,943	54.4
1890	9,249,547	54.8
1900	10,341,276	54.4

Source: *Historical Statistics of the United States* (1975), 1:14.

Table 4.3 shows the major sources of Gilded Age immigration. More than three-fifths of all immigrants in the period came from western Europe, most of them from Germany, Britain, Ireland, and Scandinavia. But, as the table shows, the incidence of western Europeans in the immigration stream to the United States shrank steadily during the period. To put these data in perspective, during the four decades preceding the Civil War such immigrants made up 95 percent of the total, while in the twenty years after the Gilded Age they amounted to just over two-fifths. Table 4.4 shows their broad geographical distribution for the period from 1820 to 1920.

Table 4.3 Immigration, 1866–1900, by Country or Region of Origin

Germany	Number	Percent of All Immigrants
1866–1870	554,416	36.6
1871–1880	718,182	25.5
1881–1890	1,452,970	27.7
1891–1900	505,152	13.7
	3,230,720	24.7

Ireland	Number	Percent of All Immigrants
1866–1870	239,419	15.8
1871–1880	436,871	15.5
1881–1890	655,482	12.5
1891–1900	388,416	10.5
	1,720,188	13.0

Scandinavia	Number	Percent of All Immigrants
1866–1870	109,654	7.0
1871–1880	243,016	8.6
1881–1890	656,494	12.5
1891–1900	371,512	10.1
	1,380,676	10.4

Britain	Number	Percent of All Immigrants
1866–1870	359,807	23.8
1871–1880	548,043	19.5
1881–1890	807,357	15.4
1891–1900	271,538	7.4
	1,986,745	15.0
Western Europe	**8,318,329**	**62.7**

Italy	Number	Percent of All Immigrants
1866–1870	8,277	0.5
1871–1880	55,759	2.0
1881–1890	307,309	5.9
1891–1900	651,893	17.7
	1,023,238	7.7

Poland*	Number	Percent of All Immigrants
1866–1870	1,129	0.1
1871–1880	12,970	0.5
1881–1890	51,806	0.4
1891–1900	96,720	2.6
	162,625	1.2

Austria-Hungary	Number	Percent of All Immigrants
1866–1870	6,901	0.5
1871–1880	72,969	2.6

1881–1890	353,719	6.7
1891–1900	_592,707_	16.1
	1,026,296	7.7

Russia	Number	Percent of All Immigrants
1866–1870	1,883	0.1
1871–1880	39,284	1.4
1881–1890	213,282	4.1
1891–1900	_505,290_	13.7
Total	759,739	5.7
Southeastern Europe	**2,971,898**	**22.4**

Canada	Number	Percent of All Immigrants
1866–1870	119,848	7.9
1871–1880	383,640	13.6
1881–1890	393,304	7.5
1891–1900	_3,311_	0.1
(data for 1892–		
93 missing)	900,103	6.8

China	Number	Percent of All Immigrants
1866–1870	40,019	2.6
1871–1880	123,201	4.4
1881–1890	61,711	1.2
1891–1900	_14,799_	0.4
	239,730	1.8

Source: *Historical Statistics of the United States* (1975), 1:106–7.
*For 1899 and 1900, Polish data listed under Austria-Hungary, Germany, and Russia.

The numbers, however, must be used cautiously. Only toward the end of the nineteenth century was there any considerable immigration bureaucracy, and many arrivals, particularly those who entered through minor ports or came overland from Canada, were not counted.[6] After 1882 little illegal immigration occurred, but even when immigrants were counted, as most were, what was recorded was presumed nationality, not ethnicity. It is clear, for example, that a goodly portion of the nearly two million persons recorded as entering from Britain were, in fact, of Irish ethnicity resident in Britain.[7] Similarly, the polyglot empires of Europe—German, Austro-Hungarian, and Russian—sent many nationalities. Large numbers of Poles, Italians, Southern Slavs, and Magyars came, but many, perhaps most, are not recorded as such. To take as an example two nations not included in the chart, data for the 1890s indicate that nearly sixteen thousand immigrants came from Greece and more than thirty thousand from Turkey. But Theodore Saloutos, the leading historian of Greek Americans, has argued convincingly that about two-thirds of the immigrants from Turkey were ethnically Greek, so that some thirty-five thousand Greeks actually came in the decade.[8] Moreover, until the establishment of Israel in 1948, there was no Jewish state and American immigration records did not list religion; therefore, Jews, as such, do not figure in the data at all.

Table 4.4 Immigrants by Region of Last Residence, 1820–1920

Region	1820–1860 (%)	1861–1900 (%)	1901–1920 (%)
Northwestern Europe	95	68	41
Southeastern Europe	–	22	44
North America	3	7	6
Asia	–	2	4
Latin America	–	–	4
Other	2	1	1

Source: Roger Daniels, *Coming to America* (New York, 1990), 122.

What kind of people were these 13 million immigrants? One of the great myths of American immigration is that most new arrivals were desperately poor, or, as Emma Lazarus (1849–1887) put it,

> Your huddled masses yearning to breathe free,
> The wretched refuse of your teeming shore.[9]

While it is true that few who came to America were rich, the vast majority were not the poorest of the poor in their own societies. While instances have occurred when persons totally without resources have been sent to the United States or its predecessors— one thinks of the slaves, indentured servants, and redemptioners of the colonial and early national periods, the Irish famine refugees of the 1840s, many of the Southeast Asian refugees from the war in Vietnam—Gilded Age immigrants either paid their own way to America or had their passage taken care of for them by a relative, friend, or prospective employer. In addition, they were predominantly young adults, overwhelmingly male, who had taken a calculated risk in an attempt to improve their lives. Many of those of most nationalities who entered the country came with the intention of being sojourners, that is, of staying for a season or a few years and returning home with savings that would improve their family's status. Irish and Jews were the major exceptions to this generalization; relatively few immigrants from either group ever returned or planned to. Contemporary opinion and most later scholarly discussion associate sojourning primarily with very poor immigrants from lesser developed areas, particularly Chinese, Poles, Italians, and Southern Slavs, but many skilled tradesmen regularly came to America from developed countries on a seasonal basis. English housepainters, for instance, often worked in the United States in the spring, went to Scotland for the summer, and worked in England for the rest of the year.[10] There are no statistics for return migration during the Gilded Age; the American government did not begin to record such data until 1909. Enumerating the return migrants before 1909, like tallying illegal immigrants today, is the impossible task "of counting the uncountable." Walter D. Kamphoefner's comment that return migration "data" constitute a "statistical swamp" is an appropriate one.[11] Even if we knew how many immigrants returned, we would still need to know how many came back again.

Single males or those with wives back home were more likely to return than men with families in the United States or single women. For the period for which data exist, there seems to be a direct positive correlation between the "maleness" of a given immigrant group and the propensity of its members to return.[12] Many who came planning to stay, returned; others planning to return, stayed. Much depended on what they experienced in America and what they heard and learned about conditions back home.[13]

Almost all of those who crossed the Atlantic in the Gilded Age came by steamship. The whole Atlantic traffic was transformed between the mid-1850s and the mid-1870s. In the earlier period some 95 percent of all immigrants came by sail; by the later period roughly the same percentage came by steam. This meant shorter crossing times, better—or less bad—shipboard conditions, and, usually, lower fares. In the Gilded Age the transportation of immigrants on steamships especially constructed for the trade became a modern big business. The major European steamship companies (no American line had a significant share of the trade) set up vast networks of ticket brokers in both the United States and Europe. By the 1890s the Hamburg-Amerika (HAPAG) line had more than three thousand agents in the United States, most of whom were ethnic entrepreneurs providing that and other services to their communities. By the turn of the century perhaps one steamship ticket in three was prepaid, that is, purchased in the New World for some specific immigrant in the Old. Often railroad tickets were prepaid as well, so that an immigrant's ticket, purchased from a HAPAG agent in Cleveland and picked up from a HAPAG agent in Krakow, might take him or her from Krakow to Hamburg by train, cover room and board in the line's *Auswandererhallen* in Hamburg until sailing time, steerage fare to New York, and rail fare to Cleveland.

In the Gilded Age, as in most other periods, immigrants came to America chiefly to seek employment. What was different was that, increasingly, work was in urban and industrial occupations. While some types of laborers were recruited directly—museums in Cornwall still preserve the handbills advertising the presence of "good paying jobs" in this or that American mining district—perhaps a majority of those coming to the United States were participating in what came to be called chain migration, in which successive immigrants linked by kinship or acquaintance followed one another like links in a chain, not just to America but to a particular place there where an immigrant was already established and might even have a job waiting for the new arrival. As the American consul in Naples reported in 1890, a typical explanation for emigrating heard there was: "My friend in America is doing well and he has sent for me."[14] While labor contractors, many of them immigrants themselves, were important for newcomers seeking jobs, many employers preferred referral hiring in which immigrant workers brought their own kind into the shops. Moreover, similar chains often moved them from place to place within the United States.[15] This process is important not only from an economic point of view but also from a social one. While leaving home

The Atlantic Crossing. "Emigrants Coming to the 'Land of Promise,' " photograph by
William H. Rau, 1902. *Courtesy Library of Congress*

may have been an "uprooting," most Gilded Age migrants moved
into at least semifamiliar surroundings because some of their kith
and kin were with them, and, in the majority of their communities
there were institutions, particularly ethnic churches, to help cush-
ion the shock of the new.

By the beginning of the Gilded Age, immigrants already were
concentrated heavily in certain American regions and cities. According to the 1870 census close to one-half of all immigrants lived
in the Northeast, which had less than one-third of the nation's population. Similarly, more than two-fifths of immigrants lived in the
North Central states, which had almost one-third of all U.S. inhabitants. Conversely, immigrants were less attracted to the West and

South; the former had 6.6 percent of the population and only 4.5 percent of the immigrants, while the latter, with close to one-third of the population, had just 7.2 percent of the foreign born. The same census, which showed that a little less than one-quarter of the American population lived in urban areas[16] and that immigrants constituted 14 percent of the population, reported that foreign-born persons were just about one-third of the population of the fifty-two American cities with more than twenty-five thousand people. In nine of those cities—New York; Chicago; San Francisco; Cleveland; Detroit; Milwaukee; Scranton, Pennsylvania; Lawrence, Massachusetts; and Fall River, Massachusetts—the immigrant population was more than 40 percent. The foreign born totaled more than 35 percent of the residents of all the large cities on the Great Lakes and in the Ohio and Mississippi valleys except for Louisville, whose population was about 23 percent immigrant. The only other two southern cities with more than one-fifth foreign born were New Orleans and Baltimore, each a one-time major port of arrival.

Ethnic groups tended to concentrate in different regions and cities. The two largest groups in 1870, the Irish and the Germans, comprised 14.5 and 11.5 percent, respectively, of the populations of large American cities in 1870. In New England, the Irish dominated. No large New England city had a German-born element of as much as 5 percent, while all of them were more than 10 percent Irish. Lawrence, at more than 25 percent, was the most Irish, followed by Boston, Lowell, Fall River, and Worcester, Massachusetts, and Hartford, each more than 20 percent Irish. In the Midwest the Germans were the most numerous, although the Irish also boasted a large presence there. No large midwestern city was less than 10 percent German, and three of them—Chicago, Cleveland, and St. Louis—were more than 10 percent Irish as well. Milwaukee, at about 32 percent, claimed the highest proportion of German inhabitants and was followed by Cincinnati, at about 23 percent. Six other cities of the Midwest—St. Louis, Chicago, Cleveland, Toledo, Dayton, and Detroit—were more than 15 percent German. Both groups were well represented in Middle Atlantic cities with the Irish predominant in New York; Jersey City, New Jersey; Albany; Brooklyn; Scranton; Paterson, New Jersey; Pittsburgh; and Philadelphia, while Germans were predominant in Buffalo, Newark, and Rochester. New York, with a population approximately

22 percent Irish and 16 percent German, was the only city in which each group exceeded its national urban norm.[17]

By 1900 the Census Bureau was dividing the foreign-born population into eight groups (Teutons, Irish, British Americans, British, Slavs, Scandinavians, Greco-Latins, and Asiatics) and had constructed a table showing the tremendous increase in the number of "Slavs" and "Greco-Latins"—117.3 percent and 98.4 percent, respectively, since 1890—as opposed to the other groups' modest gains, or, in the case of the British and Irish, actual declines. It also had begun to count the second generation along with the immigrant generation in what it called "whites of foreign parentage," who in 1900 were computed at just over one-third of the population, at 25,850,980, or 34 percent.[18] The Census Bureau also examined the percentage of sixteen national groups to be found in cities of twenty-five thousand or more. Natives of Russia were the most urban, at nearly 75 percent; natives of Poland, Italy, and Ireland each were recorded at more than 60 percent urban; natives of Bohemia, Austria, and Hungary were listed between 50 and 55 percent; and Germans came in right at 50 percent. At the very bottom were the Scandinavians: the Swedes at 36 percent, the Danes at 28 percent, and the Norwegians at 22 percent.[19] As only about 32 percent of the entire population lived in such cities, the growing immigrant propensity for the city is unmistakable.

The increasing urbanization and proletarianization of immigrants is clearly reflected in occupational statistics reported on landing. Table 4.5 shows that the percentage listed as having no occupation, which usually meant dependent women and children but also included unknowns, went down considerably during the Gilded Age, from a clear majority, 54.5 percent, to about two-fifths. The percentage listed as servants and laborers rose, while the number of those reporting themselves to be farmers went down. It is also noticeable that, in years of concentrated immigration such as 1888, the percentage of unskilled workers rose. In 1873, the heaviest year of the early 1870s, the unskilled were nearly 55 percent of those reporting occupation. The trends continued in the early twentieth century. In the two most intense immigration years, 1907 and 1914, about three-quarters of those reporting occupation were recorded as unskilled, but it is important to note that, throughout the Gilded Age, between one-fifth and one-quarter of those reporting occupation were skilled tradesmen, with another 5 percent or more

in the commercial and professional categories.[20] It is largely from
these substantial groups that most immigrant leaders came.[21]

Table 4.5 Stated Occupations of Immigrants, Selected Years

Year	Percent with Occupation	Professional/ Commercial Tradesmen	Skilled Laborers	Farmers	Servants/ Laborers	Misc.
1868	46.5	7.6	24.5	17.6	50.1	0.2
1878	54.8	7.9	21.8	19.6	43.3	7.5
1888	55.4	3.6	19.8	9.9	65.3	1.7
1898	60.5	5.3	23.9	11.7	54.9	4.2

Source: *Historical Statistics of the United States* (1975), 1:111.

Because Gilded Age immigrants came to work, the migration
flows were affected by economic conditions in America. As Harry
Jerome and others have demonstrated, major economic downturns
in the United States soon resulted in lower levels of immigration.[22]
Moreover, although the image of the "greenhorn" is an important
part of American folklore, in fact many, if not most, Gilded Age
immigrants had migrated within Europe—or in some cases to Latin
America or North Africa—before coming to the United States. The
kinds of work that they did was highly differentiated, although most
of it was clearly at the bottom of the economic ladder. In part because of their regional focus, in part because of chain migration,
many groups developed vocational and entrepreneurial niches,
which often had little to do with the experience or traditions of
their native lands. Certainly there were some, such as the Cornish
miners noted above, the Italian marble workers recruited to work
in Vermont quarries, and the German machinists who arrived to
work in Cincinnati mills, who brought specialized and marketable
skills with them. Likewise, the building trades were full of craftsmen who had learned their livelihood in the Old Country. Others,
however, especially entrepreneurs, found unfilled spaces within the
American economy and filled them. Chinese laundry and restau-
rant operators, Greek candy and popcorn vendors, and Italian bar-
bers were not practicing trades and skills brought from the Old
World.

Most Gilded Age immigrants had neither capital nor skills. They
filled the common labor needs of the economy at the time of their
arrival. In antebellum America, the canal system had been dug

largely by Irish labor. The midwestern railroads were largely built by Irish labor, while those in the Far West were constructed mainly by the Chinese. Toward the end of the century, much of the maintenance of right-of-way and the construction of branch lines was done by the Italians and the Southern Slavs, who superseded the Irish in the East and the Midwest as the Japanese, the Sikhs, and the Mexicans would later supersede the Chinese in the West.

The Irish and the Germans, the two dominant ethnic groups in the antebellum era, were predominantly second- and third-generation Americans in the Gilded Age, even though, as noted above, very large numbers of reinforcements arrived in each decade. A great many of the 1.7 million Irish who came were women; they actually outnumbered male Irish immigrants after 1880.[23] Heavily concentrated in eastern cities, the Irish, who came speaking English and with some experience of electoral politics, quickly came to dominate certain parts of the urban infrastructures that were being created. The Irish cop and fireman are not just stereotypes: the Irish all but monopolized those jobs when they were being created.[24] Other Irish not only laid the horsecar and early streetcar tracks, but they or their compatriots also became the first drivers and conductors. If many or most of the immigrants came without skills, first- and second-generation Irish came to dominate the building trades. By 1900, when Irish-American men made up about one-thirteenth of the male labor force, they constituted about one-third of the plumbers, steamfitters, and boilermakers. In that same year, however, 25 percent of the Irish-born men and 17 percent of the second generation had unskilled or semiskilled jobs, the latter figure slightly higher than the 15 percent rate for all native-born whites. Furthermore, there were important differences from city to city. In 1890 almost two-thirds of Boston's Irish born were in unskilled jobs, but "only" one-third of those in Chicago were. While few of the women worked outside of the home after marriage, very large numbers of them worked before marriage as domestics and in other unskilled occupations.[25]

In many Gilded Age cities the Irish came to dominate two crucial institutions: municipal politics and the Roman Catholic church. In national politics, the Irish were less influential than their numbers justified, and few of their kind of candidates were nominated for national office. Many of the concerns of national Democrats were of little or no concern to them. This author once interviewed an old Irish Tammany Hall Democrat who remembered, or claimed to remember, William Jennings Bryan campaigning in New York City with reprises of his "Cross of Gold" speech. Every time he came to the phrase "burn down your cities," the ward heeler recounted, "the son-of-a-gun would smile!" Clearly, the farmers' champion and the urban Irish politico had few interests in common.

Jay P. Dolan has recounted how the Irish began to dominate the American church in the antebellum years. By the Gilded Age the Irish dominance of the church was clear, even in many midwestern dioceses such as Cincinnati, where German Catholics predominated. Irish leadership gave the church an aggressive, embattled posture that native or other foreign-born and ethnic leadership might have mollified. Even after the second-generation Irish outnumbered the immigrants, and despite the relatively high number of vocations among the American-born Irish, large numbers of Irish clergy arrived in the United States after being trained in the seminary at Maynooth, County Kildare.

Germans, the most numerous immigrant group, made up one-quarter of all foreign born as late as 1900. Unlike the Irish, who were largely impelled by poverty and "overpopulation," the 3.2 million German immigrants during the Gilded Age were pushed by the economics of prosperity. What we now call "modernization"—industrialization, urbanization, and the whole panoply of socioeconomic changes that accompany them—was more prevalent in parts of Germany than anywhere else on the European continent. These changes in the traditional structure of society made movement of some kind a necessity for millions of Germans. Most moved within their country, largely to other cities. For many, however, emigration seemed a rational alternative, sometimes after an initial move to a German city. While large numbers remained in eastern cities (for example, New York, Newark, and Buffalo), the majority settled in what demographers came to call the "German Triangle," an area defined by the three midwestern cities of Cincinnati, St. Louis, and Milwaukee. While the majority were urban immigrants, most of the considerable minority of rural Germans also settled in this general region and immediately to the west of it, although there were occasional German-bloc communities elsewhere, such as in Anaheim, California.[26]

Most of the nearly 1.4 million Scandinavian immigrants in the late nineteenth century continued to follow patterns established in the antebellum years. The majority went to rural destinations and were heavily concentrated in the West-North Central states—Minnesota, Iowa, Nebraska, and the Dakotas—although by the end of the century second-generation Scandinavians were migrating along the lines of the Northern Pacific and Great Northern railroads to the Pacific Northwest, and there was direct Nordic immigration to that region as well. Yet, increasingly, Scandinavian immigration became urban; large Swedish settlements existed in all of the cities of the two regions noted above, as well as in Chicago and Jamestown, New York, and there was a distinct Norwegian maritime community established in Brooklyn throughout the period.[27]

Of the nearly 2 million British immigrants—some 15 percent of all who came in the Gilded Age—very few generalizations can be made. Charlotte Erickson's phrase, "invisible immigrants," is certainly appropriate. There were neither special concentrations of British immigrants in particular places nor were there special ethnic niches. Indices of regional distribution calculated by David Ward for 1870 and 1890 show the British born more approximating the median distribution of immigrants than any other major group. Some Britons were capitalists (the outlaw Billy the Kid was, in effect, a hired gun for a Scottish combine), others were tradesmen, industrial workers, and remittance men. They were clearly overrepresented in the professional/commercial and skilled worker categories.[28]

The immigrants from southern and eastern Europe who began to dominate the immigration flows in the final decade of the century had a less varied experience. The overwhelming majority of them came into the very bottom of American urban industrial society. The apocryphal comment by an Italian immigrant describes what tens of thousands of Italians expected, but surely most of them had a good notion of what was in store for them:

> We thought that the streets were paved
> with gold. When we got here we saw that
> they weren't paved at all. Then they told us
> that we were expected to pave them.

However, among Italians and other groups there were also entrepreneurs. In the Far West, Italians made a major impact in the development of viniculture;[29] the burgeoning garment industry in New York, Rochester, Philadelphia, Chicago, and elsewhere was largely the product of eastern European immigrant Jewish entrepreneurs and workers, male and female. Both Jews and Italians were centered chiefly in East Coast cities. Poles and Southern Slavs tended to be concentrated in heavy industry, and although they were well represented in New York as was almost every immigrant group, their most influential settlements were in interior cities such as Pittsburgh, Cleveland, Detroit, and Chicago.

Two important non-European groups figure significantly in the Gilded Age immigration story—the Chinese and the French Canadians.[30] The Chinese had begun to emigrate in considerable numbers in the 1850s. Almost all came from the region around the South China city of Guangzhou (Canton) and were impelled to come by the same kind of economic motives that affected the vast majority of other immigrants. Chinese workingmen—only 3 or 4 percent of Chinese immigrants were female—were crucial to the development of the Far West. They built railroads, engaged in mining, cleared land, and were pioneers in market gardening and other forms of agriculture in California and elsewhere in the West.[31] After 1880 more and more Chinese lived in large cities and followed urban pursuits. Chinese-owned laundries and restaurants—labor-intensive enterprises requiring little capital—employed more and more of them. While some laundries were family-owned-and-operated businesses, like the one described in Maxine Hong Kingston's marvelous book, *The Woman Warrior*, others employed large numbers of single men at minimal wages and under abominable working conditions. From the very first there were successful Chinese entrepreneurs, and the wealthiest merchants/labor contractors in cities such as San Francisco, Portland, Seattle, and New York were as well off as all but the richest Gilded Age magnates.

If Chinese immigrants had the longest journey in coming to America, French Canadians had the shortest; they constituted the only group whose migration was accomplished chiefly by rail. This journey is vividly described in the first (1878) French Canadian-American novel, Honoré Beaugrand's *Jeanne la Fileuse* (Jeanne the mill girl), which describes life in the largely French-Canadian metropolis of Fall River, Massachusetts.[32] The Dupuises, Jeanne's adopted family, leave Montreal at 4 P.M. one day and get to Fall River at 2 P.M. the next. Their tickets cost $10 apiece, while Chinese immigrants paid about $50 for a trans-Pacific passage and most Europeans paid somewhat less to cross the Atlantic. They have to change trains twice in Massachusetts—in Boston and in Lowell—but the railroad, operating like HAPAG and the other steamship lines, makes it simple by providing bilingual personnel to help the immigrants and delivers their baggage to the housing provided by the textile mill that will employ all but the youngest children. By 1900 what may be called the third colonization of New England[33] had put more than eight hundred thousand first- and second-generation French Canadians in the United States, most of them very close to the Great Lakes and the provinces of Quebec and Ontario where almost all the French Canadians then lived. Like the Dupuises of the novel, most immigrated as families, settled in ethnic enclaves, and assumed that they would save enough from their meager earnings—adults could earn as much as $1.22, children as little as 28 cents, per day for a six-day, sixty-hour week—to buy a good farm back home in Canada.

All Gilded Age immigrant groups shared certain experiences and problems. They benefited from the great industrial expansion that provided employment for most of their breadwinners, and they suffered from the contractions in the business cycle that convulsed each of the century's last three decades. In common with all migrants they had problems of adjustment and acculturation. However, those who entered the United States during this period were the first free American immigrants to suffer from federal restriction and regulation of immigration.

Nativism, which John Higham has defined as "intense opposition to an internal minority on the grounds of its foreign (that is, 'un-American') connections," has been present in America since at least the mideighteenth century, when Benjamin Franklin fulminated against Germans and claimed to be afraid that the German language would supersede English in Pennsylvania.[34] But the term itself was only coined about 1840 during one of several intense periods of nativist feeling in American life. The chief targets in the 1840s and 1850s were Catholic immigrants, mainly Irish and German, who seemed to the typical Protestant Know Nothing (a nativist of the time) to be the great threat to the Republic. Although political nativism made great strides and brought about the election of many congressmen and state officials in the antebellum years, the movement was never able to get its demands for the restriction of immigration and the tightening of naturalization laws onto the national statute books.[35] Its local legislative triumphs were short-lived as the U.S. Supreme Court ruled, in the *Passenger Cases* of 1849, that immigration constituted "foreign commerce" and that congressional jurisdiction was preemptive. Even in the absence of federal statutes—and there were no such statutes before 1875—

states could not enact restrictive or even regulatory legislation *except* generally in matters of health and public safety.[36]

The coming of the Civil War demonstrated, on the one hand, that the most subversive forces in American life were those who would destroy the Union, and, on the other, that ethnic soldiers and regiments were strong supporters of the nation. Perhaps nothing better exemplifies the positive attitude toward immigrants held by the Civil War Congresses than the fact that the Homestead Act of 1862 gave those who had declared their intention to become citizens the same rights as citizens. After the war the naturalization statutes were expanded to include blacks. The original 1790 law had limited naturalization to "free white persons," although a number of Asians were naturalized also. The abolition of slavery in 1865 and the establishment in 1868 of a national citizenship by the Fourteenth Amendment—"all persons born or naturalized in the United States . . . are citizens of the United States and of the State wherein they reside"—made the words "free" and "white" in the statute inappropriate. Congress passed a new naturalization statute in 1870. Senator Charles Sumner (R-MA) wanted to make the naturalization process color blind (something that would not occur until 1952), but the majority was willing only to drop the word "free" and add "persons of African descent" to the eligible class.

By 1870 an anti-Chinese movement in California, led in part by Catholic workingmen such as Dennis Kearney, had transformed Far Western politics. In addition, the use of Chinese as strikebreakers in a shoemakers' labor stoppage in North Adams, Massachusetts, and similar episodes elsewhere had converted eastern trade unions to the anti-Chinese cause. The Kearneyites and others in the West had broader goals: although the most famous slogan of the movement was "The Chinese Must GO!," it was well understood that a cessation of further Chinese immigration, rather than the expulsion of those already present, would be satisfactory to all but the most rabid "anti-coolieites."

The struggle over Chinese immigration went on for a dozen years. As was true of so many issues in the Gilded Age, support of or opposition to Chinese immigration broke pretty well along class lines. Exclusion's key advocates were workingmen, their allies, and politicians who needed their votes, while against it were chiefly the employers of labor and those missionary churchmen who wanted to convert China. Furthermore, in addition to understandable economic grievances—Chinese labor did work cheaply—the anti-

Chinese movement quickly developed variants of the racism that was already endemic in America. Not only did "John Chinaman," as he was often called, "work cheap and smell bad," but he was also subhuman.[37] Courts in California and other western states refused to accept the testimony of Chinese, municipal ordinances were passed to harass them, state legislatures tried, fruitlessly, to halt their immigration, and the California constitution of 1879 had an entire anti-Chinese section that forbade their employment by public bodies and called upon the legislature to protect "the state . . . from the burdens and evils arising from" their presence.[38] The western anti-Chinese movement was not something invented by politicians; in the words of one scholar, it "sprang from the people."[39] In an 1879 California referendum the voters opposed to Chinese immigration numbered 154,638 to 883, or 99.4 percent of those casting a ballot.

Persuading the national government to act was another matter, however. The fact that few Chinese were settled anywhere but in the West, the long tradition of free immigration, and the contrary economic interests of those who dreamed of exploiting the China market all combined to inhibit anti-Chinese legislation at the national level. A special complication was a provision in the 1868 Burlingame Treaty with China, which stated that "the United States of America and the Emperor of China cordially recognize the inherent and inalienable right of man to change his home and allegiance, and also the mutual advantage of the free migration and emigration of their citizens and subjects respectively from one country to the other for purposes of curiosity, of trade or as permanent residents."[40]

Both countries also pledged to eliminate what was usually called the "coolie trade," something that Sumner and others in Congress had long sought. The treaty, whose major purpose was to promote trade, put immigration policy and foreign policy at loggerheads. Presidents Rutherford B. Hayes and Chester A. Arthur each vetoed measures inhibiting Chinese immigration because they believed the bills violated existing treaties. A new treaty negotiated with China in 1880 gave the United States the right to "regulate, limit or suspend" Chinese immigration and residence. Finally, in 1882, Arthur signed the so-called Chinese Exclusion Act.[41] It suspended the immigration of Chinese "laborers" for ten years. (Arthur's earlier veto blocked a bill imposing a twenty-year suspension.) At the end of the ten-year period another ten years was tacked on, and in 1902 exclusion of Chinese "laborers" was made permanent. Total exclusion came in 1924 and lasted until 1943.

Although it affected only a tiny portion of American immigrants—there were perhaps 125,000 Chinese in the United States in 1882—the Chinese Exclusion Act was the hinge on which all American immigration policy turned. This first significantly restrictive legislation established a new pattern of limitation by the exclusion of this or that class of persons. Certainly, Congress had long been concerned with the dumping of convicts on American soil, with unfree labor, and, since 1875, with prostitution, but the 1882 act was the first legislation to affect law-abiding free persons. The 1882 Congress also enacted a head tax of fifty cents per incoming passenger, but this was a user fee to defray the costs of administration—such as it was—and for the aid of distressed immigrants. Those crossing land borders, like the French Canadians, were not taxed.[42] Six additional pieces of legislation in the 1880s modifying Chinese and contract-labor immigration statutes were the only other related acts of the decade.

In the meantime, anti-immigrant sentiment and agitation was growing. Labor leaders made analogies between existing tariff legislation and the restrictive immigration they desired; as Samuel Gompers expressed it, the country that kept out pauper-made goods should also keep out the paupers.[43] Even more important were the intellectual arguments against immigration of the "wrong" kinds of persons that were being formulated by many of the best and the brightest American intellectuals. Leading historians and political scientists came to believe that democratic political institutions had been developed by and could thrive only among "Anglo-Saxon" peoples, while eugenicists and sociologists argued that of all the many "races," only one—variously called Anglo-Saxon, Aryan, Teutonic, or Nordic—had superior innate characteristics. Rather conveniently for the self-esteem of what the census would categorize as "old stock" Americans, these vague terms seemed to describe most of those who had immigrated earlier.

In 1881, Carroll D. Wright (1846–1909), Massachusetts commissioner for labor statistics and a progressive reformer, launched a diatribe at one immigrant group: "The Canadian French are the Chinese of the Eastern States. They care nothing for our institutions. . . . They do not come to make a home among us . . . their purpose is merely to sojourn a few years as aliens . . . and, when they have gathered out of us what will satisfy their ends, to get them from whence they came, and bestow it there. They are a horde of industrial invaders, not a stream of stable settlers."[44] Soon other reformers, some progressive, some reactionary, were attacking what had been the whole basis of American immigration policy: unrestricted entry for free white persons. In 1891, Congress responded to some of the anti-immigrant pressures by expanding the excluded classes to include "all idiots, insane persons, paupers or persons likely to become a public charge, persons suffering from a loathsome or a dangerous contagious disease, persons who have been convicted of a felony or other infamous crime or misdemeanor involving moral turpitude, polygamists. . . ."[45] These new restrictions were largely symbolic, at least in the Gilded Age. Between 1892 and 1900 only 22,515 potential immigrants were excluded, a mere seven-tenths of 1 percent of the total. An even smaller number, 3,127, were deported in the same period.

This was very unsatisfactory to the growing forces of restriction. The most active pressure group was the Immigration Restriction League, founded by a group of Harvard graduates in 1894. The League's leaders, caught up in what its historian has called the "Anglo-Saxon complex," campaigned relentlessly for an immigration policy based on ethnocultural discrimination. Its founder, Prescott F. Hall (1868–1921), argued that the issue that Americans needed to consider was whether they wanted their country "to be peopled by British, German and Scandinavian stock, historically free, energetic, progressive, or by Slav, Latin and Asiatic races [this latter referred to Jews rather than Chinese or Japanese], historically down-trodden, atavistic and stagnant."[46]

The League and its chief political spokesman, Henry Cabot Lodge, the scholar in politics who represented Massachusetts in Congress from 1887 to 1924, eventually settled on a literacy test as the best means to bring about the desired ethnocultural balance. The House passed a literacy bill five separate times—in 1895, 1897, 1913, 1915, and 1917—and was joined by the Senate on all but the first occasion. Each bill was vetoed, by presidents as diverse as Grover Cleveland, William Howard Taft, and Woodrow Wilson; the final veto was overridden in 1917.

Cleveland's veto is of particular interest. He attacked the bill as "a radical departure," "illiberal, narrow and un-American," and argued that the nation's "stupendous growth" had been "largely due to the assimilation and thrift of millions of sturdy and patriotic adopted citizens." He reminded the nation that some "immigrants who, with their descendants, are now numbered among our best citizens" were once attacked as undesirable. Furthermore, the literacy test did not impress him, as he argued that "it is infinitely more safe to admit a hundred thousand immigrants who, although unable to read and write, seek among us only a home and an opportunity to work than to admit one of those unruly agitators and enemies of governmental control who can not only read and write, but delights in arousing by inflammatory speech the illiterate and peacefully inclined to discontent and tumult."[47]

The timing of the literacy test's successes is instructive. In 1895 and 1897 the severe depression was surely a major factor; the return of prosperity deprived it of its congressional majority for almost two decades. When, under the stimulus of progressivism and war, it was finally enacted, it had little effect. European immigration would be effectively controlled only by the ethnic quota systems instituted in the 1920s.

Immigration in the Gilded Age was clearly in a state of flux, changing as the country and its needs changed. In 1893, Frederick Jackson Turner spoke of a closed frontier. However ambiguous that notion seems to us today, it was a powerful influence on contemporary minds, persuading many that growth and opportunity would be more limited in a frontierless society, and, therefore, those of little faith wished to set boundaries on immigration. It is not surprising that Turner spent much of his last unproductive years at the Huntington Library musing about the evils of unrestricted immigration.[48] The seeds of the restrictions of the 1920s were surely planted in the 1880s and 1890s, but that the mature plants bore the bitter fruit that they did was largely due to developments in the twentieth century.

Notes

1. For a classic early treatment see Peter Roberts, *The New Immigration* (New York, 1912). John Bodnar, without using the hoary terminology, trifurcates the periodization: 1815–1861, 1865–1890, and 1890–1914 in "Immigration," in *The Reader's Companion to American History*, ed. Eric Foner and John A. Garraty (Boston, 1991), 533–38. An earlier standard reference work slotted the "old immigration" from 1843–82 and the "new immigration" from 1885–1914, in Richard B. Morris, ed., *Encyclopedia of American History* (1953; reprint ed., New York, 1965), 473–74. The pejorative thrust of this dichotomy can best be seen in the following definition from the U.S. Immigration Commission: "The old immigration movement was essentially one of permanence. The new immigration is

very largely one of individuals, a considerable proportion of whom apparently have no intention of permanently changing their residence, their only purpose in coming to America being to temporarily take advantage of the greater wages paid for industrial labor in this country." U.S. Immigration Commission, *Abstracts of Reports of the Immigration Commission*, 41 vols. (Washington, DC, 1911), 1:24.

2. Because immigration was then enumerated by fiscal years, the federal data really cover July 1, 1866–June 30, 1901.

3. Roger Daniels, *Coming to America: A History of Immigration and Ethnicity in American Life* (New York, 1990), 121–22, 183–84.

4. The figures were: 1860, 13.2 percent; 1870, 14.0 percent; 1880, 13.3 percent; 1890, 14.7 percent; 1900, 13.6 percent; 1910, 14.7 percent; 1920, 13.2 percent.

5. Such questions were propounded more than a century ago by the British social scientist E. G. Ravenstein in "The Laws of Migration," *Journal of the Royal Statistical Society* 52 (1889): 241–301.

6. The Mexican border was not a statistically significant area of ingress until after the Mexican Revolution.

7. For a discussion of the Irish in nineteenth-century Britain see Lynn H. Lees, *Exiles of Erin: Irish Migrants in Victorian London* (Ithaca, NY, 1979).

8. See Theodore Saloutos, *A History of the Greeks in the United States* (Cambridge, MA, 1964), and his essay "Greeks," 430–40, in *Harvard Encyclopedia of American Ethnic Groups*, ed. Stephan Thernstrom (Cambridge, MA, 1980).

9. Emma Lazarus, "The New Colossus" (1883). For a trenchant analysis of the poem and its impact see John Higham, "The Transformation of the Statue of Liberty," in his *Send These to Me: Immigrants in Urban America* (1975; revised ed., Baltimore, 1984), 71–80. Much the same notion was put forth by a Baptist minister the year *before* Lazarus wrote. Addressing the 1882 meeting of the Home Mission Society, the Reverend John Peddie of New York City proclaimed to Europe: "Send us your poor and degraded you would trample underfoot, and on our wide plains and prairies, under the fostering light of free institutions, of education, and religion, we will make of them such noble specimens of manhood as never grew on your crammed and narrow soil." Cited in Lawrence B. Davis, *Immigrants, Baptists, and the Protestant Mind in America* (Urbana, IL, 1973), 42–43.

10. Frank Thistlethwaite, "Migration from Europe Overseas in the Nineteenth and Twentieth Centuries," *XI Congrès International des Sciences Historiques, Rapports* (Stockholm, 1960), 5:32–60, has often been reprinted, most recently in *A Century of European Migrations, 1830–1930*, ed. R. J. Vecoli and S. M. Sinke (Urbana, IL, 1991), 17–49, with a "Postscript," 50–58.

11. Walter D. Kamphoefner, "The Volume and Composition of German-American Return Migration," 293–311, in Vecoli and Sinke, *European Migrations*, 305.

12. For an overprecise reckoning see Thomas Archdeacon, *Becoming American: An Ethnic History* (New York, 1983), 139.

13. The most recent survey of return migration argues that the "temporary migrant was in truth far different from the immigrant who planned to stay." Mark Wyman, *Round-Trip to America: The Immigrants Return to Europe, 1880–1930* (Ithaca, NY, 1993), 204. His arguments, largely sociological analogies, are not persuasive. While one can "predict" that large numbers of individual migrants in certain circumstances will return, there is no way that one can "predict" that x

and y will stay and z will return, when all three are, for example, single, young, adult male Czechs coming to Chicago in 1887.

14. Cited by Philip Taylor, *The Distant Magnet: European Emigration to the U.S.A.* (New York, 1972), 90.

15. This process is well described by June Granatir Alexander in "Staying Together: Chain Migration and Patterns of Slovak Settlement in Pittsburgh Prior to World War I," *Journal of American Ethnic History* 1 (1981): 56–83, and "Moving Into and Out of Pittsburgh: Ongoing Chain Migration," in Vecoli and Sinke, *European Migrations*, 200–220.

16. The term "urban areas" as used here is based on the definition adopted in 1940 and now used by the Census Bureau for all pre-1950 data, which calls all places of twenty-five hundred or more "urban." The 1870 census used eight thousand as the cut-off between rural and urban.

17. David Ward, *Cities and Immigrants: A Geography of Change in Nineteenth-Century America* (New York, 1971), especially the chapter, "The Cityward Movement of Immigrants," 51–83.

18. The Census Bureau definitions were often curious and irregular, as follows: "Teutons," "comprising" natives of Germany, Austria, Holland, Belgium, Luxembourg, and Switzerland; "Greco-Latins," "consisting of" natives of France, Italy, Spain, Portugal, and Greece; "Irish" were not defined; "Slavs," "include" natives of Russia, Hungary, Bohemia, and Poland; "Scandinavians" "composed" of natives of Norway, Sweden, and Denmark; "British," "including" the natives of England, Scotland, and Wales; "British Americans," "comprising" natives of Canada and Newfoundland; and "Asiatics," "including" natives of China, Japan, and other parts of Asia. Left out of this compilation were West Indians, Africans, Mexicans, and other non-Canadian natives of the New World, amounting to some 150,000 persons in 1890 and 260,000 persons in 1900. *Statistical Atlas: Twelfth Census of the United States* (Washington, DC, 1903), 50–51.

19. Ibid., plate 73.

20. In 1907 and 1914 this figure falls to about one-sixth, white collar and professional types stay at about 5 percent, and farmers, now more clearly differentiated from farm workers, are down to about 1.5 percent.

21. For the neglected topic of immigrant leadership see Victor R. Greene, *American Immigrant Leaders, 1800–1910* (Baltimore, 1987).

22. Harry Jerome, *Migration and Business Cycles* (New York, 1926).

23. For the entire Irish migration see Kerby A. Miller, *Emigrants and Exiles: Ireland and the Irish Exodus to North America* (New York, 1985); for female migrants, see Hasia R. Diner, *Erin's Daughters in America* (Baltimore, 1983), and Janet Nolan, *Ourselves Alone: Women's Emigration from Ireland, 1855–1920* (Lexington, KY, 1989).

24. James F. Richardson, *The New York Police: Colonial Times to 1901* (New York, 1970).

25. Oscar Handlin described Boston's Irish as living where "no promise dwelled" in his seminal monograph *Boston's Immigrants, 1790–1865: A Study in Acculturation* (Cambridge, MA, 1941), which set a standard for a generation of immigration historians. An examination of later studies, such as Dennis Clark, *The Irish in Philadelphia* (Philadelphia, 1974), and Miller, *Emigrants and Exiles*, suggests that Boston was a worst-case scenario. One wonders whether, if Handlin had studied a different city, his brooding masterpiece, *The Uprooted* (Boston, 1951), would have had a less gloomy and deterministic cast.

26. Kathleen N. Conzen, "Immigrants in Nineteenth-Century Agricultural History," in Lou Ferleger, ed., *Agriculture and National Development: Views on the Nineteenth Century* (Ames, IA, 1990), 303–42, is an authoritative summary.

27. See, for example, Philip J. Anderson and Dag Blanck, eds., *Swedish-American Life in Chicago: Cultural and Urban Aspects of an Immigrant People, 1850–1930* (Urbana, IL, 1992).

28. Charlotte Erickson, *Invisible Immigrants: The Adaptation of British and Scottish Immigrants in Nineteenth-Century America* (Coral Gables, FL, 1972); Ward, *Cities and Immigrants*, 67, 72.

29. Andrew F. Rolle, *The Immigrant Upraised: Italian Adventurers and Colonists in an Expanding America* (Norman, OK, 1968).

30. Mexican Americans were important throughout the Southwest—they were the majority in New Mexico territory—but they were *not* immigrants (they lived in territory that was once part of Mexico). Statistically significant immigration from Mexico is coterminous with the 1910 revolution.

31. Sucheng Chan, *This Bittersweet Soil: The Chinese in California Agriculture, 1860–1910* (Berkeley, 1986) is outstanding; for a survey see Shih-shan Henry Tsai, *The Chinese Experience in America* (Bloomington, IN, 1986).

32. Honoré Beaugrand (1849–1906) was an immigrant journalist who realistically described the conditions in the mills that were the chief source of immigrant employment. In other hands his "docudrama" could have been an indictment of the exploitative conditions, but he, and many French Canadians, treated them as an improvement over the conditions of life for the poor in Quebec.

33. Marcus Lee Hansen wrote about the coming of the Irish as "The Second Colonization of New England," in his *The Immigrant in American History* (1940; reprint ed., New York, 1964), 154–74.

34. John Higham, *Strangers in the Land: Patterns of American Nativism, 1860–1925* (1955; reprint ed., New Brunswick, NJ, 1988), 4.

35. For the best treatment of Know Nothingism see Tyler Anbinder, *Nativism and Slavery: The Northern Know Nothings and the Politics of the 1850s* (New York, 1992).

36. The Passenger Cases, *Smith v. Turner* and *Norris v. The City of Boston*, are 48 *U.S.* 283; for an account of state law before 1876 see Gerald L. Neuman, "The Lost Century of American Immigration Law (1776–1875)," *Columbia Law Review* 93 (1993): 1833–1901.

37. The standard work is Elmer Sandmeyer, *The Anti-Chinese Movement in California* (1939; revised ed., Urbana, IL, 1973); for ideology see Stuart Creighton Miller, *The Unwelcome Immigrant: The American Image of the Chinese, 1785–1882* (Berkeley, 1969), and Alexander Saxton, *The Indispensable Enemy: Labor and the Anti-Chinese Movement in California* (Berkeley, 1971). See also Roger Daniels, *Asian America: Chinese and Japanese in the United States since 1850* (Seattle, 1989), chapter 2.

38. California Constitution, 1879, Article XIX.

39. Lucille Eaves, *A History of California Labor Legislation* (Berkeley, 1910), 115–16.

40. William M. Malloy, comp., *Treaties, Conventions, International Acts, Protocols and Agreements between the United States and Other Powers, 1776–1909* (Washington, DC, 1910), 1:196–233.

41. 22 *Stat.*, 58. The welter of proposed Gilded Age immigration and naturalization legislation, much of it dealing with the Chinese, can be followed in E. P.

Hutchinson, *Legislative History of American Immigration Policy, 1789–1965* (Philadelphia, 1981), chapters 3 and 4.

42. 23 *Stat.*, 214. Two years later Congress suspended the head tax for seaborne passengers coming from Canada and Mexico.

43. Arthur Mann, "Gompers and the Irony of Racism," *Antioch Review* 13 (1953): 203–14.

44. Massachusetts Bureau of Statistics of Labor, *Twelfth Annual Report* (Boston, 1881), 469.

45. 26 *Stat.*, 1084. "Polygamists" was directed at Mormons, not Muslims. The statute stated that persons convicted of political offenses were exempt from the ban.

46. Barbara Miller Solomon, *Ancestors and Immigrants: A Changing New England Tradition* (Cambridge, MA, 1956), especially 82–151.

47. James D. Richardson, *The Messages and Papers of the Presidents, 1789–1902*, 10 vols. (Washington, DC, 1907), 9:757–61 (March 2, 1897).

48. Ray Allen Billington, "Frederick Jackson Turner and the Closing of the Frontier," in Roger Daniels, ed., *Essays in Western History in Honor of T. A. Larson* (Laramie, WY, 1971), 45–56.

Suggestions for Further Reading

Anderson, Philip J., and Dag Blanck, eds. *Swedish-American Life in Chicago: Cultural and Urban Aspects of an Immigrant People, 1850–1930.* Urbana, IL, 1992.

Berthoff, Rowland T. *British Immigrants in Industrial America, 1790–1850.* Cambridge, MA, 1953.

Brault, Gerard J. *The French-Canadian Heritage of New England.* Hanover, NH, 1986.

Chan, Sucheng. *This Bittersweet Soil: The Chinese in California Agriculture, 1860–1910.* Berkeley, 1986.

Daniels, Roger. *Coming to America: A History of Immigration and Ethnicity in American Life.* New York, 1990.

Diner, Hasia R. *Erin's Daughters in America.* Baltimore, 1983.

Dolan, Jay P. *The American Catholic Experience.* New York, 1985.

Dublin, Thomas, ed. *Immigrant Voices: New Lives in America, 1773–1986.* Urbana, IL, 1993.

Emmons, David M. *The Butte Irish: Class and Ethnicity in an American Mining Town, 1875–1925.* Urbana, IL, 1989.

Erickson, Charlotte. *Leaving England: Essays on British Emigration in the Nineteenth Century.* Ithaca, NY, 1994.

Greene, Victor R. *American Immigrant Leaders, 1800–1910.* Baltimore, 1987.

Higham, John. *Strangers in the Land: Patterns of American Nativism, 1860–1925.* 1955. Reprint, New Brunswick, NJ, 1988.

Luebke, Frederick C. *Immigrants and Politics: The Germans of Nebraska, 1880–1900.* Lincoln, NE, 1969.

Miller, Kerby A. *Emigrants and Exiles: Ireland and the Irish Exodus to North America.* New York, 1985.

Morawska, Ewa. *For Bread, With Butter: The Life-Worlds of East Central Europeans in Johnstown, Pennsylvania, 1890–1940.* New York, 1985.

Mormino, Gary, and George E. Pozzetta. *The Immigrant World of Ybor City: Italians and Their Latin Neighbors in Tampa, 1885–1985.* Urbana, IL, 1987.

Nugent, Walter T. K. *Crossings: The Great Transatlantic Migrations, 1870–1914.* Bloomington, IN, 1992.

Rischin, Moses. *The Promised City: New York's Jews, 1870–1914.* Cambridge, MA, 1962.

Saloutos, Theodore. *A History of the Greeks in the United States.* Cambridge, MA, 1964.

Thernstrom, Stephan, ed. *The Harvard Encyclopedia of American Ethnic Groups.* Cambridge, MA, 1980.

Vecoli, Rudolph J., and Suzanne M. Sinke, eds. *A Century of European Migrations, 1830–1930.* Urbana, IL, 1991.

Ward, David. *Cities and Immigrants: A Geography of Change in Nineteenth-Century America.* New York, 1971.

Yans-McLaughlin, Virginia, ed. *Immigration Reconsidered: History, Sociology, and Politics.* New York, 1990.

5

Urbanizing America

Robert G. Barrows

Booth Tarkington, a Pulitzer Prize-winning novelist who achieved distinction as an author during the first two decades of the twentieth century, was born in Indianapolis, Indiana, in 1869. The medium-sized midwestern city where he grew up often appeared as the setting in his critically acclaimed fiction. In a series of novels in which he thinly disguised his hometown as a "Midland city," Tarkington described "a deteriorating social order caused by urbanization and industrialization" and contrasted it, often unfavorably, with the city of his youth. The opening pages of *The Turmoil* (1915) set forth his view of the changes late nineteenth-century urbanization had brought to Indianapolis and, by extension, to other American cities:

> Not quite so long ago as a generation, there was no panting giant here, no heaving, grimy city; there was but a pleasant big town of neighborly people who had understanding of one another, being, on the whole, much of the same type. It was a leisurely and kindly place—"homelike," it was called. . . . The good burghers were given to jogging comfortably about in phaetons or in surreys for a family drive on Sunday. No one was very rich; few were very poor; the air was clean, and there was time to live.[1]

This rosy view of life in the Hoosier capital during the Gilded Age is clearly an oversimplification born of nostalgia. But Tarkington's lament for a simpler time also reflected a reality that readers of his generation would have accepted without hesitation—that during the previous forty or fifty years the nation's cities had undergone a profound transformation.

When the Constitution was ratified in 1788 only about 5 percent of the residents of the new nation lived in cities. Today, about 75 percent of the population lives in places defined as urban. Thus, a central theme of U.S. history has been the transition from a rural, agrarian society to one that is highly urbanized. The latter third of the nineteenth century—years when the interrelated processes of urbanization, industrialization, and immigration reached high tide— was a key period in that transition. Horace Greeley's 1850s dictum that young men should consider seeking their fortunes in the expansive West grew more urgent as he observed developments in the East during and after the Civil War. "We cannot all live in cities," the New York editor wrote in 1867, "yet nearly all seem determined to do so."[2]

Decennial census statistics demonstrate these demographic changes in a variety of ways. The first, and most obvious, change is the growth in the number and percentage of persons who lived in urban areas (see Table 5.1). In 1860, on the eve of the Civil War, the nation's urban population (defined as those living in places of 2,500 or more) stood at 6.2 million, just under one-fifth of the total. By the end of the century 30 million urbanites constituted about two-fifths of the nation's residents. Thus, in just forty years, the number of urban dwellers in the country had almost quintupled, and their proportion of the total population had doubled.

This is not to say that the nation's rural population was not also growing. It was—from 25 million in 1860 to nearly 46 million by 1900. The point, however, is that the *rate* of urban population growth was significantly greater during these years than the rate of growth for rural residents, which is how "urbanization" is defined. Between 1880 and 1890, for example, urban population increased by 56 percent, the total U.S. population by 26 percent, and rural population by only 13 percent.

Another way of measuring urban growth during the Gilded Age is simply to look at the expansion in the number of places that surpassed the threshold of 2,500 residents. Even with this rather generous definition of "urban," only about 400 localities could claim such status at the beginning of the Civil War (see Table 5.2). This number grew to 663 during the 1860s, an increase of over two-thirds. While this rate of growth slowed during the next thirty years, the overall pattern continued. By the end of the century the nation recorded some 1,737 "urban places," an increase since 1860 of a remarkable 343 percent. This growth resulted from both the

Table 5.1 Urbanization in the United States, 1860–1900

Year	Total U.S. Population (in thousands)	Total Urban Population (in thousands)	Total Rural Population (in thousands)	Percent Urban	Percent Rural	Percent Increase in Total Population	Percent Increase in Urban Population	Percent Increase in Rural Population
1860	31,444	6,217	25,227	19.8	80.2	–	–	–
1870	38,558	9,902	28,656	25.7	74.3	22.7	59.3	13.6
1880	50,156	14,130	36,026	28.2	71.8	30.1	42.7	25.7
1890	62,947	22,106	40,841	35.1	64.9	25.5	56.4	13.4
1900	75,995	30,160	45,835	39.7	60.3	20.7	36.4	12.2

Source: U.S. Bureau of the Census, *Historical Statistics of the United States: Colonial Times to 1970.* 2 vols. (Washington, DC, 1975), 1:11–12.

Table 5.2 Urban Places, 1860–1900

Year	Number of Urban Places	Percent Increase in Number of Urban Places	Number of Cities over 100,000 Population
1860	392	–	9
1870	663	69	14
1880	939	42	20
1890	1,348	44	28
1900	1,737	29	38

Source: U.S. Bureau of the Census, *Historical Statistics of the United States: Colonial Times to 1970.* 2 vols. (Washington, DC, 1975), 1:11.

development of older towns and cities and the creation of new urban places, especially in the West.

Late nineteenth-century urbanization was characterized by the growth of cities of all sizes, from small county seats to metropolitan giants. Widely remarked upon, then and now, was the growth in the number of *big* cities—those with more than 100,000 residents—that seemed to dominate the age. Only nine such places existed in the country in 1860. Two decades later the nation had twenty such cities, and thirty-eight by 1900. By 1880, New York had become the first U.S. city to claim one million inhabitants.

Smaller cities and towns were also growing. And, in spite of the economic and cultural importance of places such as New York, Philadelphia, Chicago, and New Orleans, the smaller cities were in many ways more representative of the nation's urban experience. In 1880 almost eight million Americans lived in urban areas of less than 100,000, compared to about six million in larger ones. By the end of the century the small- to medium-sized cities still claimed a slight majority of the nation's urban population: about sixteen million persons lived in cities smaller than 100,000, fourteen million in places of 100,000 or more. Between 1860 and 1900 the number of urban areas in the 10,000–25,000 range grew from 58 to 280, and the percentage of native-born residents in cities smaller than 25,000 exceeded that of larger ones throughout the late nineteenth century.[3]

While it is important to understand these broad national trends, it is equally important to recognize that summary data for the entire United States obscure significant regional differences (see Table 5.3). Throughout the late nineteenth century the northeastern section of the country was by far the most heavily urbanized. In 1860, when about one-fifth of the nation's total population lived in urban areas, more than one-third of the residents of the Northeast did so. By the end of the century the Northeast was two-thirds urban, the nation as a whole about two-fifths. At the other end of the spectrum, only about 10 percent of southerners lived in cities on the eve of secession. That figure almost doubled during the next forty years but still stood at only 18 percent—less than half the national figure—at the beginning of the twentieth century.

The North Central and West regions fell between the extremes of the Northeast and South; the urban percentages of their populations were in the midteens in 1860 and approached 40 percent by the close of the Gilded Age. As had been true in the Ohio and Mississippi river valleys earlier in the nineteenth century, cities and towns were "spearheads" in the post-Civil War settlement of the trans-Mississippi West. That is, as seats of government and centers of business, transportation, and communication they were integral parts of the settlement process, not afterthoughts that only developed once farming, ranching, mining, or logging activities were well under way.

Table 5.3 Percentage Urban by Region, 1860–1900

	1860	*1880*	*1900*
United States	19.8	28.2	39.7
Northeast	35.7	50.8	66.1
North Central	13.9	24.2	38.6
South	9.6	12.2	18.0
West	16.0	30.2	39.9

Source: U.S. Bureau of the Census, *Historical Statistics of the United States: Colonial Times to 1970*. 2 vols. (Washington, DC, 1975), 1:22–37.

States within regions also exhibited substantially different patterns of urbanization. In 1880, for example, the northeastern states of Rhode Island and Vermont recorded urban populations of 82 and 10 percent, respectively. In the North Central region, twenty years later, the population of Illinois was 54 percent urban (in part because of the rapid expansion of Chicago during the late nineteenth century), but the urban compositions of Illinois's eastern and western neighbors at the end of the century were 34 percent (Indiana) and 26 percent (Iowa). North Dakota, also in the North Central region, had a population in 1900 that was only 7 percent urban. In short, the urban population of the United States during the late nineteenth century was quite unevenly distributed and in 1900 was still concentrated in the northeastern quadrant of the country in a band extending from the Atlantic seaboard to the Mississippi River.

Where did these millions of new city dwellers come from? Some of the population growth resulted from net natural increase—an excess of births over deaths among those already situated in urban areas. The bulk of city growth during the late nineteenth century, however, came from net migration. Urban areas attracted far more new inhabitants than they lost. Roughly half of these new city residents came from rural areas in the United States, while the other half were foreign immigrants. In the words of historian Raymond A. Mohl, "The rapid urban growth of the period resulted from a tremendous release of rural population. Most of the new urbanites came from the American farm and peasant villages of the old world."[4]

Students of American land policy and agricultural history once argued that the western frontier served as a "safety valve" during the late nineteenth century, absorbing excess population from the increasingly crowded cities of the East. Historians now believe that the reverse of that hypothesis is closer to the truth. The high birth-rates of rural areas, combined with agricultural mechanization that reduced the demand for farm workers, led to a surplus of rural population. So, too, did farm failures, especially during the depressions of the mid-1870s and the mid-1890s. As the cultural and economic disparities between country and city grew wider, and as rural youth heard that (in the words of a twentieth-century Broadway song) "everything's up to date in Kansas City," many of those without good prospects at home joined the urban exodus, especially to the manufacturing cities of the Northeast and Midwest.

African Americans, particularly those from the rural South, comprised a numerically small but socially significant component of that exodus. During the 1870s roughly 68,000 southern blacks moved to the North, most to urban areas. During the final decade of the nineteenth century the number of African Americans who left the South grew to 185,000, a prefiguring of the "Great Migration" of the World War I decade and thereafter. Between 1870 and 1900 popular destinations in the North were not necessarily the largest cities. In 1900, for example, blacks constituted less than 2 percent of the population in New York, Cleveland, Detroit, and Chicago. In contrast, African Americans made up over 9 percent of the population of Indianapolis in that year, and almost 13 percent in Evansville, Indiana (the latter situated on the Ohio River and thus an easily accessible northern destination). It is important to recognize, however, and it is a point often ignored as historians focus their attention on the northward migration of southern blacks, that the urbanization of the African-American population also dramatically affected southern cities. Not all rural blacks who abandoned the land automatically decamped for the North, especially not as a first step. Thus, between 1880 and 1900, the African-American populations of Savannah and Nashville almost doubled.

In Atlanta the black population more than doubled, growing from 16,000 to 36,000, and the number of black residents in Memphis increased during the final two decades of the nineteenth century by 235 percent.[5]

The pushes that impelled some rural Americans to leave the farm, and the pulls that attracted them to the city, also affected large numbers of foreigners. "Farmers who left the country for the city," observes historian Alan M. Kraut, "were met there by the new immigrants."[6] Immigration was not, of course, a new phenomenon in the post-Civil War decades; net immigration to the United States in the 1840s had been 1.4 million persons, and about 2.6 million had arrived in the 1850s. What was new in the late nineteenth century was the increased size of this stream, as well as its origins.

Immigration, which had fallen off slightly during the Civil War decade, rebounded during the 1870s to the prewar level of 2.6 million. Then, in the 1880s, a decade of American prosperity and relative political stability in Europe, some 5 million immigrants came to the United States, almost twice as many as had arrived in any previous ten-year period. The numbers declined somewhat but were still high during the 1890s; in spite of a severe depression in the middle years of the decade, net immigration was 3.7 million.[7]

During the 1880s the so-called new immigrants from southern and eastern Europe ("new" as contrasted with the "old" prewar influx from northern and western Europe) began to appear in noticeable numbers at American ports of entry. This trend accelerated in the 1890s and continued on through the first two decades of the new century. Whereas Germans had constituted 28 percent of all immigrants to the United States in the 1880s, their proportion fell to 16 percent in the 1890s and to just 4 percent between 1900 and 1909. Italians, however, increased their proportion of the immigrant stream from 5 percent in the 1880s to 16 percent in the 1890s and 24 percent during the first decade of the twentieth century. Former residents of Poland, Russia, and Austria-Hungary recorded equally impressive gains.[8]

Not all of these newcomers stayed. Some, especially young males, were "birds of passage" who followed seasonal patterns of migration or who stayed for only a few years to acquire a nest egg before returning to their home villages. Of the millions who did remain, the great majority settled in urban areas. "By the 1880s," observes a careful student of the process, "most immigrants found that cities offered them more plentiful economic opportunities than the countryside. . . . With few exceptions most newcomers congregated in cities, many never leaving the port city in which they landed. Unlike earlier immigrants, the latest settlers soon found that their own skills and preferences, as well as the state of the [rapidly industrializing] American economy, combined to make them urban dwellers."[9] By 1890 the populations of New York and San Francisco were just over 40 percent foreign born. Interior cities were affected as well; sizable foreign-born contingents were to be found in Chicago (41 percent), Cleveland (37 percent), Minneapolis (37 percent), and Kansas City (16 percent).[10]

Their burgeoning populations, combined with advances in technology, led to striking spatial changes in American urban areas during the late nineteenth century. Cities expanded, both horizontally and vertically, in an attempt to accommodate not only their new residents but also the concomitant increase in commercial and industrial activity. Between the Civil War and the turn of the century the built environment of urban America underwent a radical transformation. The most important developments in the creation of what Mohl has called the "new city" were in the areas of transportation and construction.

In the preindustrial city of midcentury "the heaviest users of streets were not wheels or hoofs, but human feet. . . . The vast majority of people walked to their destinations, and it was this form of transportation that determined the city's size and shape."[11] The "walking city," as it has been termed, was, by later standards, remarkably compact, rarely extending much beyond two miles (a half hour's walk) from the city's center. As a consequence, there was little differentiation of land use. Commercial, residential, governmental, religious, educational, and even industrial structures were jumbled together. Different types of people were jumbled together, too. "Limited housing options in the walking city brought a degree of social integration," and only "short distances separated rich and poor, native and immigrant, white and black."[12]

The development most responsible for reshaping the walking city was probably the postwar spread of the street railway. The concept of urban mass transit did not suddenly appear on the scene in the late nineteenth century. Most major eastern cities in the antebellum decades had omnibus service (a sort of urban stagecoach from which the modern word "bus" derives), some early railroads provided local commuter operations in addition to their long-haul passenger and freight activities, and a horse-drawn street railway began running in New York City as early as the 1830s. This latter form of transportation spread slowly in the 1840s and 1850s and then much more rapidly in the years after the Civil War. Whereas the omnibus had bounced along on rutted or cobblestoned thoroughfares, the streetcar rolled smoothly on iron rails. In addition, streetcars required no more horse (or mule) power than omnibuses, yet they held more passengers and could travel faster (six to eight miles per hour). By the mid-1880s over five hundred street railway lines were operating in three hundred American cities, and they had become the country's most important form of intraurban transportation.

In urban public transit, the horse gradually gave way to other forms of motive power as the century wore on. Several cities installed cable cars. These looked much like horsecars but were propelled by a stationary engine that moved an underground cable to which the cars could be attached or detached. They were faster, larger, and more comfortable than horsecars, and they were particularly suited for hilly cities such as San Francisco or Pittsburgh. Their disadvantages included high installation and maintenance costs and frequent breakdowns that idled all the cars operated on a given cable. Most cable car systems were gradually phased out.

The principal successor to the horsecar was the electrified streetcar. These trolleys (so called because of the moving "troller" that connected the vehicle with overhead electrical wires) could cover ten or twelve miles per hour. The new technology spread rapidly following its introduction in Richmond, Virginia, in 1888. By the early twentieth century the vast majority of urban mass transit mileage had been converted to electricity.

These improvements in urban transportation signaled the demise of the compact walking city. As street railway lines extended out from the city's center—often to a "destination" site, such as a lake, amusement park, or cemetery—residential and commercial development followed. Outlying city wards, as well as areas beyond the city limits, experienced rapid population growth. It was a process that left some late nineteenth-century urban areas with the appearance of a wagon wheel—a downtown hub with radiating spokes of settlement. As Howard P. Chudacoff and Judith E. Smith observe, horsecars and trolleys "spread people into outlying areas, but because transit owners built track only where it appeared that settlement would be most dense and because subdividers and builders located their real estate projects near mass-transit lines,

Transportation in the New City. Horse-drawn wagons and carriages, an electric trolley car, and pedestrians congest a cobblestoned street in Philadelphia in 1897. *Courtesy National Archives*

outward expansion proceeded unevenly. . . . Only slowly did they fill in the vacant districts between existing fingers of settlement."[13]

As noted earlier, the social geography of the walking city was characterized by a mingling of economic classes and ethnic groups. The most desirable residences were often located very close (the shortest walk) to the city's center. Urban mass transit rearranged— indeed, inverted—that pattern. "The physical growth and expansion of the city," writes Mohl, "promoted social fragmentation and differentiation, as people sorted themselves out by class, ethnicity, and race. . . . The streetcar encouraged the wealthy and the middle class to abandon the central district of the city as a place of residence. Simultaneously, the urban working class, immigrants, and the poor began occupying vacated housing in the urban core."[14]

The late nineteenth century was thus a period not just of urbanization but also of suburbanization. Rapid population growth coupled with the expansion of reasonably priced mass transit both permitted and encouraged residential construction at the constantly retreating margins of American cities. These areas tended to be economically and architecturally homogeneous. As Sam Bass Warner, Jr., observed in his acclaimed book *Streetcar Suburbs: The Process of Growth in Boston, 1870–1900* (1962), both homeowners and speculative builders in Gilded Age Boston "sought safety for their investment by building dwellings of a type common to the area. . . . Even though there were no zoning laws and no mass builders who put up whole communities in a few years, this repetitive habit of little builders produced an effect somewhat similar to the modern class-graded residential suburbs." Paradoxically, Warner notes, the decentralized and individualized nature of late nineteenth-century suburban residential construction led to "great uniformity of behavior, a kind of regulation without laws."[15]

As the periphery of the city changed, so too did the core. Whereas the suburbs were differentiated by income and wealth, central cities developed distinct sections based on specialized economic functions. Districts emerged that were known for banking and finance (New York's Wall Street, for example), warehousing, wholesaling, transportation (any union railroad station and its environs), retailing, government, and both legal and illegal entertainment. Downtown land values, now expressed as dollars per frontage foot along the major thoroughfares, rose sharply as this process continued, as did the taxes on such property. These developments soon squeezed out any single-family residences that still existed in the city's center.

As increasing numbers of white-collar workers found employment in the central business district, most cities underwent building booms to accommodate them. Multistory office buildings began to dominate the urban skyline. By today's standards these were not very tall structures. The weight of brick and masonry construction had long placed practical limits on building heights; the higher they went (and the heavier they became), the thicker the lower walls and foundations needed to be. With a few exceptions, mainly in New York, most new commercial and office buildings erected in the immediate post-Civil War decades did not surpass five or, at most, ten stories.

New construction technologies permitted central cities to grow vertically, just as the street railway had permitted urban areas to expand horizontally for great distances. Use of a load-bearing steel skeleton sheathed with a light masonry or stone skin—"curtain wall" construction, as it became known—allowed architects to raise their sights (and thus their sites). They perfected this technique in Chicago where the ten-story Home Insurance Building (1885) became the prototype skyscraper. Day-to-day use of the new structures, which quickly rose to thirty or forty stories, became practicable with the concurrent development of high-speed electric elevators to deliver office workers to the upper floors and central heating plants to keep them comfortable once they got there. Mostly in the early twentieth century, but to some extent in the late nineteenth as well, the skyscraper was "a symbol of increasing concentration, both of people and of power[,] in the city center."[16]

Residential construction also began to extend upward. As city populations mushroomed, "vertical space became acceptable and even necessary for residential as well as business and commercial purposes."[17] Architects and builders thus began to construct multistory apartment houses for upper- and middle-class urbanites and tenement houses for poorer working-class families. The apartments ranged from large, luxurious structures built of the finest materials to small wood-frame buildings constructed by speculators seeking a quick profit.

Tenement houses evolved in antebellum New York and spread to many other cities during the last third of the nineteenth century. (Seldom, however, were tenements packed so closely together as they were in Manhattan. New York's housing density was by far the highest in the nation.)[18] While details differed from place to place, a typical tenement was 25 by 90 feet (with a 10-foot rear lot), stood four to six stories tall, and had four apartments on each floor. Depending on the number of stories, each building was intended to house sixteen to twenty-four families. Many tenants, however, sublet their small rooms, some no more than 8 feet wide, to secure additional income. A single building might thus shelter some 150 people. Privacy, obviously, did not exist. Disease, not surprisingly, was rampant.

The infamous "dumbbell" tenement (whose name refers to the shape) featured a narrow air shaft in the center of the building

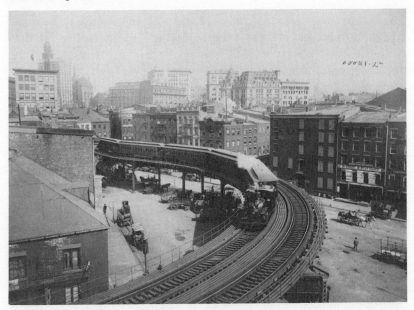

The Changing Urban Landscape. An elevated railroad train wends its way among the multistory buildings of New York City, 1894. *Courtesy Library of Congress*

intended to provide light and ventilation. As urban historians David R. Goldfield and Blaine A. Brownell note, this supposed amenity was in fact "a real health and safety hazard. The shaft was a convenient duct for flames to leap from one story to the next and a garbage dump that reeked with foul odors, especially in the hot summer months. It was also an excellent echo chamber for noise."[19] The failure of tenements as a solution for housing the working-class urban poor became increasingly apparent, especially when the conditions of New York's Lower East Side were publicized by Jacob Riis in his renowned description of *How the Other Half Lives* (1890). The New York Tenement House Law of 1901, which established more stringent criteria for multifamily dwellings, was a belated response to the tenement crisis, and its provisions were copied in statutes and ordinances across the country.

Street railways, discussed earlier, were only one part of a complex urban infrastructure that developed during the late nineteenth century. By 1900, and somewhat earlier in many places, American cities had become, in Joel A. Tarr's words, "networked" or "wired, piped, and tracked." Following the economic depression of the mid-1870s, improvements in urban infrastructure advanced steadily.

These developments went hand in hand with an increase in the quality and number of civil engineers. Quoting Tarr again: "At the turn of the century the city was the center of economic activity, and the construction of urban infrastructure, both public and private, often attracted the nation's best engineering talent."[20]

Cities hired such engineers in a quest for, among other things, safe and reliable systems to provide water and remove sewage. A typhoid epidemic in Massachusetts during the 1880s prompted the city of Lawrence to install a new type of sand filter to purify its water. Subsequent improvements in technology and increased understanding of the nature of waterborne diseases led numerous other urban areas during the next twenty years to adopt advanced methods of filtration and purification. Between 1890 and 1920 the number of waterworks increased from 1,878 to 9,850, and the population served by filtered water grew from 310,000 to over 17 million between 1890 and 1914.[21]

Water treatment and the extension of water mains throughout metropolitan areas were followed by calls for sanitary sewers. The earliest of these merely emptied into a convenient body of water. (In the case of Chicago, that meant Lake Michigan, from which the city drew its drinking water.) To avoid fouling their own nests, cities employed "a new generation of sanitary engineers [who] began in the eighties to devise filters and to build [sewage] treatment plants that incorporated new chemical and biological discoveries." By the 1890s "sanitary bathrooms and kitchens with running water became standard features in new urban homes, and plumbing was installed in the better dwellings of many older districts." The number of miles of sewers in use expanded from six thousand in 1890 to almost twenty-five thousand by 1909. Gas, electric, and telephone service also came to many American cities during the closing years of the nineteenth century. Gas was originally used primarily for lighting, although gas lamps began to be replaced by electric lights in the eighties. The nation's forty-eight thousand telephone subscribers in 1880 grew to eight hundred thousand by the end of the century, most of them in urban areas.[22]

Urbanization and industrialization can exist independently; cities obviously existed before the machine age, and early factories were often located in rural areas. In late nineteenth-century America, however, the processes were closely associated. In the decades following the Civil War the "twin forces of urbanization and industrialization now fed upon each other: each reinforced and modified the course of the other. Together . . . cities and their factories transformed the United States from an agricultural debtor nation into a manufacturing and financial power."[23]

Urban areas centralized resources that were important for industrial growth. As hubs of transportation they could most easily concentrate raw materials and disperse finished products. As centers of communication they could facilitate the rapid exchange of information that became increasingly vital as the economy became more complex. Moreover, as centers of population they provided pools of both industrial workers and consumers of manufactured goods.

During these years "the factory became a characteristic and ever-present urban institution." And as cities grew in size, so did their workplaces. The Cambria Iron Works in Johnstown, Pennsylvania, for example, employed about one thousand persons in 1860—a large force for the time. Twenty years later, however, Cambria Steel had forty-two hundred workers, and that number grew to almost ten thousand by 1900. Around the turn of the century the meat-packing plants that had grown up in Chicago, whose brutal working conditions soon shocked readers of Upton Sinclair's novel *The Jungle* (1906), employed some thirty thousand people.[24]

While urbanization and industrialization grew increasingly intertwined, factories and central business districts gradually became less closely associated. Just as residences were eventually forced out of the city center, so too were large manufacturing establishments. The cost of land in the city core, and the requirements of many industries such as steel and railroad repair for large amounts of horizontal space, drove factories to the periphery where, as Goldfield and Brownell put it, "land was cheap and municipal regulations were few."[25]

The result was the development of industrial suburbs, sometimes called "satellite cities." One of the most famous was Pullman, Illinois, a combination railroad-car factory and residential town established in the 1880s south of Chicago and the site of a violent strike in 1894. (Readily accessible from Interstate 94, Pullman is now a National Historic Landmark.) Pittsburgh's steel industry moved upriver to Allegheny and Homestead (the latter town the site of another well-known labor disturbance in the 1890s). The suburbanization of industry also encouraged residential diffusion. Factory workers, many of whom could not afford a daily commute by trolley, often located close to their place of employment. Near

Indianapolis, for example, the small industrial/residential suburb of Brightwood was platted in 1872 about two and one-half miles northeast of the city's center. Annexed into Indianapolis in 1897, the suburb-turned-neighborhood continued for many years to serve as a residential area for the workers in nearby industries.

The complexity of urban life in the late nineteenth century presented challenges that the municipal governments of the age were often unable to meet. Cities were creatures of their states, and legislatures were rarely willing to cede control of city charters or to grant municipalities a significant degree of home rule. Mayors had little authority, and their terms of office generally were limited to only one or two years. City councils were often fragmented, with members focusing attention on their own wards at the expense of broader municipal concerns. Little wonder that a visiting Englishman reported in the late 1880s that "the government of cities is the one conspicuous failure of the United States."[26]

The vacuum in governmental power and authority was filled by urban political machines (or, less pejoratively, party organizations) of which New York's Tammany Hall is perhaps the best-known example. Critics then and since have excoriated the machines and the bosses who ran them for everything from incompetence to grand larceny. There is ample evidence to support the charges. In one notorious case, the construction of a courthouse budgeted at $250,000 cost in excess of $13 million; contractors were instructed to pad their bills, and the excess payments were returned to the machine in the form of kickbacks. Less brazenly (but no less costly to the taxpayers), political bosses engaged in what Tammany district leader George Washington Plunkitt called "honest graft"— profiteering based on, for example, inside knowledge of where future public improvements were planned. Throughout the late nineteenth century there were periodic attempts to "throw the rascals out"; such efforts, while sometimes successful, were generally short-lived. Reformers, Plunkitt observed, were "only morning glories" who had little staying power.[27]

If the urban political bosses of the Gilded Age have not been quite rehabilitated by recent scholarship, they have at least been reevaluated and reassessed. The "functionalist" (as opposed to the "reformist") analysis of urban machine politics focuses on the ubiquity and longevity of the institution. How did city bosses maintain control if their activities were so scandalous? The answer, simply, is that they responded to the felt needs of many of their constituents. As Mohl summarizes this interpretation: "In an age when official municipal welfare and social services were weakly developed or administered in a bureaucratic or tight-fisted manner, the bosses and the machines provided very real and important services in the urban neighborhoods. . . . They offered a humanizing contact with a government increasingly perceived as distant and bureaucratic."[28]

This could be especially important to recent immigrants grappling with the myriad difficulties of acculturation in a strange environment. Plunkitt proudly described the operation of his system in New York's Fifteenth Assembly District:

> What tells in holdin' your grip on your district is to go right down among the poor families and help them in the different ways they need help. . . . If a family is burned out I don't ask whether they are Republicans or Democrats, and I don't refer them to the Charity Organization Society, which would investigate their case in a month or two and decide they were worthy of help about the time they are dead from starvation. I just get quarters for them, buy clothes for them if their clothes were burned up, and fix them up till they get things runnin' again. It's philanthropy, but it's politics, too—mighty good politics. Who can tell how many votes one of these fires bring me?[29]

Doing good was not, of course, the sole or even the principal motivation of the city boss or ward heeler, and the fact that charitable activity was sometimes a by-product does not excuse the bribery, graft, and general malfeasance associated with late nineteenth-century urban politics. It does, however, help to explain why the system was not only tolerated but also actively supported in immigrant and working-class districts. It also explains why, as Plunkitt observed, "reform administrations never succeed themselves."[30]

Some students of late nineteenth-century city government have gone beyond the reformist-functionalist dichotomy. As historian Jon Teaford has written, "Municipal government was no simple dualistic struggle between a citywide party boss with a diamond shirt stud and malodorous cigar and a good-government reformer with a Harvard degree and kid gloves." Teaford himself has focused attention on the activities and successes of various experts—landscape architects, civil engineers, and public health and public safety officials—who turned their departments into "strongholds of expertise." Rejecting interpretations of Gilded Age municipal governance in which "scoundrels have won much greater coverage than conscientious officials," he contends that the evolution of American city government during the years from 1870 to 1900 was in fact an "unheralded triumph." "Problems persisted" at the turn of the century, he admits, "and there were ample grounds for complaint. But in America's cities, the supply of water was the most abundant, the street lights were the most brilliant, the parks the grandest, the libraries the largest, and the public transportation the fastest of any place in the world."[31]

As the nineteenth century drew to a close, economist and statistician Adna Ferrin Weber published a pioneering study that examined the previous one hundred years of urban development. Weber introduced his book with the observation that "the concentration of population in cities" had been "the most remarkable social phenomenon" of the century. Fascinated by the processes of urbanization and the complexity of modern urban life, he described the late nineteenth-century city as "the spectroscope of society; it analyzes and sifts the population, separating and classifying the diverse elements. The entire progress of civilization is a process of differentiation, and the city is the greatest differentiator." His interest in the details of population concentration did not, however, blind him to the mixed results: "The cities, as the foci of progress, inevitably contain both good and bad."[32] Reflecting on the positive and negative developments in their cities since the Civil War, most urban Americans at the turn of the century would no doubt have agreed with Weber's assessment.

Notes

1. Booth Tarkington, *The Turmoil* (New York, 1915), 2, as quoted in Clifton J. Phillips, *Indiana in Transition: The Emergence of an Industrial Commonwealth, 1880–1920* (Indianapolis, 1968), 523–24.

2. Raymond A. Mohl, *The New City: Urban America in the Industrial Age, 1860–1920* (Arlington Heights, IL, 1985), 2–3.

3. U.S. Bureau of the Census, *Historical Statistics of the United States: Colonial Times to 1970*, 2 vols. (Washington, DC, 1975), 1:11–12; Blake McKelvey, *The Urbanization of America, 1860–1915* (New Brunswick, NJ, 1963), 63.

4. Mohl, *The New City*, 19.

5. Ibid., 21–22; David R. Goldfield and Blaine A. Brownell, *Urban America: A History*, 2d ed. (Boston, 1990), 221–26, especially Table 7.2; Darrel Bigham, *We Ask Only a Fair Trial: A History of the Black Community of Evansville, Indiana* (Bloomington, IN, 1987), 22; Lawrence H. Larsen, *The Rise of the Urban South* (Lexington, KY, 1985), 38.

6. Alan M. Kraut, *The Huddled Masses: The Immigrant in American Society, 1880–1921* (Arlington Heights, IL, 1982), 64.

7. Mohl, *The New City*, 23.

8. Kraut, *The Huddled Masses*, 20–21.

9. Ibid., 12, 63.

10. Mohl, *The New City*, 20.

11. Howard P. Chudacoff and Judith E. Smith, *The Evolution of American Urban Society*, 4th ed. (Englewood Cliffs, NJ, 1994), 79.

12. Mohl, *The New City*, 28.

13. Chudacoff and Smith, *The Evolution of American Urban Society*, 85.

14. Mohl, *The New City*, 37.

15. Sam Bass Warner, Jr., *Streetcar Suburbs: The Process of Growth in Boston, 1870–1900* (1962; reprint ed., Cambridge, MA, 1978), 76–77, 117.

16. Goldfield and Brownell, *Urban America*, 273, 300.

17. Mohl, *The New City*, 49.

18. Robert G. Barrows, "Beyond the Tenement: Patterns of American Urban Housing, 1870–1930," *Journal of Urban History* 9 (August 1983): 395–420.

19. Goldfield and Brownell, *Urban America*, 249.

20. Joel A. Tarr, "Building the Urban Infrastructure in the Nineteenth Century: An Introduction," 61–85, in *Infrastructure and Urban Growth in the Nineteenth Century* (Chicago, 1985), 61, 78.

21. McKelvey, *The Urbanization of America*, 90; Tarr, "Building the Urban Infrastructure in the Nineteenth Century," 73.

22. McKelvey, *The Urbanization of America*, 90–91 (quotations); Goldfield and Brownell, *Urban America*, 171–73; Tarr, "Building the Urban Infrastructure in the Nineteenth Century," 73.

23. Chudacoff and Smith, *The Evolution of American Urban Society*, 107.

24. Mohl, *The New City*, 57, 59; Goldfield and Brownell, *Urban America*, 187–88.

25. Goldfield and Brownell, *Urban America*, 188.

26. James Bryce, *The American Commonwealth*, 2 vols. (London, 1889), 1:608.

27. Alexander B. Callow, Jr., *The Tweed Ring* (New York, 1965), especially 198–200; idem, ed., *The City Boss in America: An Interpretive Reader* (New York, 1976); William L. Riordon, *Plunkitt of Tammany Hall*, paperback ed. (New York, 1963), 3–6, 17–20.

28. Mohl, *The New City*, 87.

29. Riordon, *Plunkitt of Tammany Hall*, 27–28.

30. Ibid., 17.

31. Jon C. Teaford, *The Unheralded Triumph: City Government in America, 1870–1900* (Baltimore, 1984), 7–8, 4, 6.

32. Adna Ferrin Weber, *The Growth of Cities in the Nineteenth Century: A Study in Statistics* (1899; reprint ed., Ithaca, NY, 1963), 1, 442–43.

Suggestions for Further Reading

Barth, Gunther. *City People: The Rise of Modern City Culture in Nineteenth-Century America*. New York, 1980.

Buder, Stanley. *Pullman: An Experiment in Industrial Order and Community Planning, 1880–1930*. New York, 1967.

Callow, Alexander B., Jr., ed. *The City Boss in America: An Interpretive Reader*. New York, 1976.

Cronon, William. *Nature's Metropolis: Chicago and the Great West.* New York, 1991.

Davis, Allen F. *Spearheads for Reform: The Social Settlements and the Progressive Movement, 1890–1914.* New York, 1967.

Doyle, Don H. *New Men, New Cities, New South: Atlanta, Nashville, Charleston, Mobile, 1860–1910.* Chapel Hill, NC, 1990.

Jackson, Kenneth T. *Crabgrass Frontier: The Suburbanization of the United States.* New York, 1985.

Kraut, Alan M. *The Huddled Masses: The Immigrant in American Society, 1880–1921.* Arlington Heights, IL, 1982.

Larsen, Lawrence H. *The Rise of the Urban South.* Lexington, KY, 1985.

———. *The Urban West at the End of the Frontier.* Lawrence, KS, 1978.

McKelvey, Blake. *The Urbanization of America, 1860–1915.* New Brunswick, NJ, 1963.

Melosi, Martin V., ed. *Pollution and Reform in American Cities, 1870–1930.* Austin, TX, 1980.

Mohl, Raymond A. *The New City: Urban America in the Industrial Age, 1860–1920.* Arlington Heights, IL, 1985.

Rosenzweig, Roy. *Eight Hours for What We Will: Workers and Leisure in an Industrial City, 1870–1920.* Cambridge, England, 1983.

Schlesinger, Arthur M. *The Rise of the City, 1878–1898.* New York, 1933.

Taylor, Graham R. *Satellite Cities: A Study of Industrial Suburbs.* New York, 1915.

Teaford, Jon C. *The Unheralded Triumph: City Government in America, 1870–1900.* Baltimore, 1984.

Thernstrom, Stephan. *The Other Bostonians: Poverty and Progress in the American Metropolis, 1880–1970.* Cambridge, MA, 1973.

Warner, Sam Bass, Jr. *Streetcar Suburbs: The Process of Growth in Boston, 1870–1900.* 2d ed. Cambridge, MA, 1978 [1962].

Weber, Adna Ferrin. *The Growth of Cities in the Nineteenth Century: A Study in Statistics.* 1899. Reprint, Ithaca, NY, 1963.

6

Women in Industrializing America

*Stacy A. Cordery**

Women were 48 percent of the population during the Gilded Age.[1]
Rather than attempting to describe the condition of women of every class, race, ethnicity, religion, and region (among the many categories possible), this essay focuses on how the origins of modern America affected women. As a near majority of the populace, women could not help being touched in tangible ways by the tensions that arose as the nineteenth century gave way to the twentieth. The determining context of Gilded Age America was the acceleration of industrialization. This process recast the ideology of woman's "separate sphere" and shaped the urban experience of migrants and immigrants. During this period, women's political campaigns, and above all the push for women's rights begun in 1848, gathered adherents and credibility. In addition, the continuing associational movement, the breakdown of the separate sphere, the increasing numbers of women in the labor force, and the westward movement affected the lives of middle- and working-class women. Many important trends evident during the Gilded Age presaged the emergence of the "new woman" of the Progressive Era.

The "typical" woman of the Gilded Age was white, middle class (broadly defined), Protestant, native born, married, and living in a small town. She was likely to be better educated than her mother and also likely to have fewer children.[2] The received wisdom about her sexuality saw her as "passionless," and the patriarchal society gave her little active control over her medical health or reproductive system.[3] She was assumed—and she assumed herself to be—

*The author wishes to thank Simon Cordery, Lewis L. Gould, Kris Lindenmeyer, Melody Smith, and the editor for their assistance with the preparation of this chapter.

morally superior to her husband and closer to God. Her husband as likely as not worked away from the home. She rarely stepped into the public sphere, confining her daily actions to the home. If she was among the small but increasing number of women who did move into public life, she did so within the supportive context of church-related or secular women's associations. Her causes ranged from the bold demand for suffrage to the popular temperance crusade, with myriad reforms in between. If she was a member of a woman's club, her children were probably grown or she had servants or she was unmarried or widowed. Her late nineteenth-century ideas about women and men were based on the "asexual nature of women and their concomitant moral superiority."[4] This dual ideology, stressing gender differences, fueled growing feminist demands among middle-class women, both white and black.[5]

Industrialization, which had begun in the United States approximately forty years before the Civil War, continued in the postwar decades to change the lives of middle-class women and reconfigure their households. The man's workplace moved out of the home and took the man with it—out of the middle-class woman's day. Instead of participating in his livelihood, she was confined to the domestic sphere, forbidden by social custom to appear in public without her husband or a chaperone (her father's representative if she was unmarried). As industrialization made deeper inroads into American society, middle-class men counted their worth in dollars and affirmed their masculinity by participating in men's rituals such as politics, fraternal associations, and sports—and both their masculine and their economic credentials were validated in the figure of the pious, pure, domestic, submissive, and leisured wife. Historian Barbara Welter termed this conception of women "the cult of true womanhood."[6]

With some exceptions, nineteenth-century Americans, both men and women, believed that a woman should be confined to the home. Her separate sphere—the domestic, female sphere—entailed certain tasks and responsibilities. She was the model wife and mother, and her highest calling was to bear and raise children. On her shoulders devolved the responsibility for rearing not only polite and well-mannered children but also children well-schooled in the precepts of Christianity. As the man returned home from the ruthless, amoral, competitive, materialistic world of work and politics—his sphere— she stood by him, gently questioning his morals or his religious habits only when they slipped from the ideal. She was to provide "a haven in a heartless world" for her besieged husband.[7] On the one hand, the social dictates of the cult of true womanhood put men and women in conflicting roles and defined the normal female life as one lived at home as a wife and mother in the company of women friends leading similar lives. On the other hand, they provided a safe, secure, and empowering space—a "female world of love and ritual"—from which women could set forth to ameliorate society's ills.[8] Nursing the spiritual and physical health of her immediate family had its analogy in serving the needs of strangers. Of course, these accepted notions of women in the nineteenth century applied most forcefully to white, middle-class women. Whether or not the notion trickled down to the working class or gained currency in all ethnic and racial communities is debatable. Even as the Gilded Age dawned, the idea of the "true woman" in her separate sphere was belied by increasing numbers of working women and those white and black middle-class women who were venturing out of the home and into the political realm.

Ironically, industrialization provided the impetus both for the creation of the separate sphere and for the effort by middle-class women to break out of it. Industrialization changed the way women worked within the home, supplying time-saving domestic appliances and often giving them greater leisure. It also created jobs outside the home for more and more women. By the turn of the century, one in seven women was employed. Most were single and fending for themselves. Some married women worked in remunerative jobs to supplement their husbands' insufficient incomes. The industrial work force dwelt in cities, and the squalor, disease, and wretched living conditions among the working poor created many social ills that middle-class women determined they should try to correct.

White and black women since the colonial era had formed organizations to provide charitable relief, but these associations multiplied during the Gilded Age as the industrializing cities filled with immigrants and rural Americans. Many nineteenth-century women's relief organizations began as study clubs—themselves a continuation of an earlier movement for women's self-improvement—but branched out to render relief to the poor, to provide assistance for immigrants, or to care for orphans and "wayward women." Reform groups used a voluntary work force to raise money, petition local and state governments, visit the objects of their charity, teach lessons in moral uplift, and make the larger community aware of the plight of the less fortunate. As they did so, they pushed against the customary boundary of the woman's sphere.

By far, the most popular women's association of the nineteenth century was the Women's Christian Temperance Union (WCTU). Founded in 1873 as a single-issue association, it soon became inextricably linked with the ideas and goals of its most prominent member and, by 1879, its president, Frances Willard. Her slogan was "Do Everything," and the women who flocked to join pursued various avenues of reform. The WCTU was managed locally and had chapters in every state. Claiming over 175,000 members by 1900, it was the largest women's organization in existence. The WCTU quickly moved past its early efforts at curtailing men's use of alcohol. From praying in saloons, the WCTU went on to run newspapers, own businesses, pay temperance speakers to preach the evils of alcohol, and care for the children of alcoholics. If nothing else, the WCTU demonstrated to women the effectiveness of their actions when organized—even across class and racial lines.[9] The leading African-American spokeswoman in the temperance fight was Frances Harper. She served as Superintendent of Colored Work in the WCTU, but labored hard, particularly in the South, to prevent white women from blaming the bulk of alcohol abuse on African-American men. While Willard welcomed black women to the WCTU, she did not run an organization free of racism. African-American women were not represented among the upper echelons of WCTU management, for example, nor were black delegates treated equally at regional or national meetings. Prominent African Americans such as Ida B. Wells and Josephine St. Pierre Ruffin supported the cause of temperance but deplored the overt racism of most of the WCTU women.

In the late 1870s, Willard converted to the cause of suffrage because she believed that the women's vote would bring about restrictions on alcohol that would help in her goal of home protection. As she threw the considerable weight of the WCTU into the suffrage fray, her support did not immediately garner votes for women. It did, however, introduce many other women to the suffrage idea from a friendly source. After Willard's death in 1898, the WCTU backed away from its militant prosuffrage position and focused again on the eradication of alcohol use.

While other groups had fewer members than the WCTU, their benefits and agendas could be just as multifaceted. Historian Anne Firor Scott credits club women with "inventing Progressivism" in the 1880s. In that decade, increasing numbers of women's clubs began "municipal housekeeping," or putting their piety, purity, and domesticity to work in the world around them. Literary and study club members became aware of the unsavory conditions of their towns and cities, usually through some unexpected personal experience. They communicated their shock, horror, and sadness at the conditions of their cities to their colleagues and then set to work. Scott's breakdown of the many types of municipal housekeeping is eye-opening. In the category of education, women engaged in political activity, promoted curricular innovations such as parent education, vacation schools, and special education for disabled children, and created structural innovations such as visiting nurses, vocational guidance, libraries, and school sanitation. Under the category of public health, women called for regulation of the water and milk supplies, pure food and drug legislation, sanitary garbage-disposal legislation, dental clinics, hospitals, well-baby clinics, school lunch programs, and public baths and laundries. Women combatted social evils by lobbying to close brothels, by setting up detention homes for delinquent girls, and by supporting vice commissions and scientific studies of prostitution and venereal disease. The category of recreation included pushing for legislation to regulate motion pictures and dance halls, and the building of playgrounds, gymnasiums, concert halls, and working-girls' clubs. Women's associations sponsored similar reforms in the categories of housing, social service, corrections, public safety, civic improvement, and assimilation of the races. The breadth of women's clubs' activities evinced the grass-roots nature of the work. The General Federation of Women's Clubs (GFWC), founded in 1890, was the umbrella organization for white women's clubs, and it was the job of the GFWC to disseminate information and assistance on these seemingly countless programs.[10]

Separate female institutions boosted women's self-esteem, turned them into expert parliamentarians, introduced them to a wider world, put them at their ease in public places, and provided them with invigorating and supportive circles of friends and coworkers. For many women, club work became their career. Anna J. H. Pennybacker, a white, middle-class southern widow with a normal-school education, supported her three children in part from the profits of some rental houses but primarily from paid lectures to women's organizations all across the United States. They were her network of friends—colleagues upon whom she called for everything from emotional support to financial donations for the Belgian orphans during World War I. She founded three women's clubs, was a member of at least eight throughout her life (she often belonged to more than one at a time), and held various elected positions in them. She was president of the Texas Federation of Women's Clubs, the GFWC, and the Chautauqua Woman's Club. Her dedication to organized womanhood, as she called it, was lifelong, and she was not atypical.

In the Gilded Age, sometimes called the nadir for African Americans, middle-class black women labored in a racist society that denied them access to politics, the legal system, and governmental support. Because they were accustomed to depending upon their own initiative, it is possible that a larger percentage of black women engaged in associational work more frequently than did white women.[11] Like their white counterparts, black women had been organizing benevolent societies, often church-related, since the colonial era, and the acceleration of industrialization with its accompanying social ills generated more associations. Middle-class African-American women combined the bourgeois ideologies of the separate sphere and the cult of true womanhood with other qualities prized by the African-American community: intelligence, racial consciousness, an emphasis on education, self-confidence, and outspokenness.[12] These qualities stood women in good stead as racial slurs and attacks on their femininity from whites grew more shrill and were published in "respectable" journals. For Gilded Age black women, race and gender could not be divided. In part, the too-often invisible charitable work that women pursued was a rebuke to racist critics.[13]

African-American women moved from study clubs to municipal housekeeping, just as white club women did. The Art and Study Club of Moline, Illinois, visited the sick and clothed the poor. The Adelphi Club of St. Paul, Minnesota, distributed food, called on the ill in the hospital, and supported a South Carolina kindergarten and a local orphanage. African-American women elsewhere organized or managed homes for the elderly, juvenile delinquents, working women, unwed mothers, and orphans. They started hospitals and public health clinics. They created employment services and programs to train kindergarten teachers and librarians, thus, as historian Stephanie Shaw points out, turning club work into community development.[14] Black women's clubs engaged in municipal housekeeping to provide the sort of social services that the white power structure denied to African Americans, particularly in the South.

Many women's clubs took advantage of networking possibilities by joining an umbrella association. The Colored Women's League was the first to organize in 1892. Three years later, the National Federation of Afro-American Women formed. In 1896 both groups combined their resources to create the National Association of Colored Women (NACW), which provided assistance on the state and local level for various women's clubs' projects. Mary Church Terrell became its first president. "Lifting as We Climb" was the motto of the NACW. It made reference to "racial uplift," always a major goal of black club women.

Another important result of women's participation in voluntary associations was their heightened political acumen. Women learned to voice their demands in front of hostile audiences and to articulate critical rebuttals. Women in associations governed themselves, kept minutes, elected officers, presided over meetings, wrote out platforms, managed finances, and lobbied male politicians. Speaking about the seven years her club spent in preparation and study before tackling the prevailing social problems, the president of the Chicago Women's Club believed that "no one acquainted with the difficulty of managing large interests by means of a body of untrained women, without business habits or parliamentary experience, can feel that these years of preparation and education were wasted. It is my firm conviction that without this preliminary training we should never have attained that steadiness of purpose and that broad habit of looking at all sides of a question which has made us a power in the community."[15] They gained a sense of pride and increased self-esteem, even as they pushed against the behavioral codes that mainstream society prescribed for them.

All of the clubs taught women about the male political system. The increasing membership and rapidly multiplying types of women's associations were two hallmarks of the era. In the Gilded Age, the older, natural-rights justification for suffrage gave way to an ideology that embraced differences between women and men. Women redefined their sphere by emphasizing the transcendent piety and purity of "true womanhood." Most late nineteenth-century women who ventured out of their sphere did so under the banner of moral superiority. Society could hardly chastise women who were simply taking care of widows and orphans. From there it was a short step to the late Gilded Age notion of women becoming more overtly political. The Texas Federation of Women's Clubs noted in January 1901 that "while it is not the desire of Texas club women to 'get into politics,' there are matters to the furtherance of which the Federation stands pledged, that can only be consummated by legislation."[16]

If politics is defined as "any action, formal or informal, taken to affect the course or behavior of government or the community," then women of the nineteenth century—black and white, native-born and immigrant—engaged in a full spectrum of political activities.[17] In traditional politics, women supported men's activities. They made the food for the party gatherings. They sewed the political banners. In some cases, they participated in political parades dressed as the Goddess of Liberty or Columbia. Nevertheless, they could not vote. Legal and ideological constraints kept women from exercising their full franchise, and the push for women's suffrage claimed only a few proponents in the Gilded Age.[18] Giving women the vote and allowing them to occupy elected positions was the proposed reform that most directly challenged the era's gendered notion of politics. Women who appropriated the privileges of the man's sphere would not only cause social disaster—because they would not be at home to care for their families—but they would lose their position of moral superiority as they stepped down into the morass of chicanery that was politics. Furthermore, voting was a man's privilege. Ever since the passage of the Fifteenth Amendment in 1870, which gave the ballot to black men, all women understood that what kept them from the polls was only their sex. The vast majority of Americans quite happily maintained a masculine body politic. Nevertheless, some intrepid women carried on the fight begun at the first women's rights conference at Seneca Falls, New York, in 1848.

The Declaration of Sentiments, adopted by the two hundred and fifty women and forty men at Seneca Falls, became the platform of the nineteenth-century women's rights movement. Suffrage was the most radical reform in a host of demands concerning education, religion, property rights, and marriage and divorce laws. While all of these reforms would find advocates, suffrage became linked with Elizabeth Cady Stanton and Susan B. Anthony. These two friends had begun to push against the woman's sphere before the Civil War when they joined the ranks of the abolitionists. In 1869, however, Stanton, Anthony, and others criticized the Fifteenth Amendment and the Republican party, which sponsored it, because it excluded women. That year, they founded the National Woman Suffrage Association (NWSA). NWSA members felt passionately about suffrage—even to the point of adopting the racist argument that many white women were more fit to vote than many black men enfranchised by the Fifteenth Amendment. The NWSA worked throughout the Gilded Age to convince Americans of the need for a federal constitutional amendment for women's suffrage. Even though agitating for the vote was controversial and demanded of its crusaders the bravery to stand untroubled in the storm of public criticism, Stanton and Anthony faced competition from a rival organization. Created the year before the NWSA, the American Woman Suffrage Association (AWSA) believed it best not to fight passage of the Fifteenth Amendment, agreeing with Frederick Douglass that it was "the Negro's hour." The AWSA's strategy was to do battle state by state, by convincing legislators to insert the word "women" into or remove the word "men" from their suffrage laws. Throughout the Gilded Age these two associations fought each other for scarce members, financial backers, and support from male politicians.[19]

While the AWSA generally limited its concern to getting the vote, the NWSA called for several reforms. In 1892, Stanton attempted to explain the interconnectedness of the reforms to members of the House Judiciary Committee, stating that "the strongest reason why we ask for woman a voice in the government under which she lives; in the religion she is asked to believe; equality in

"HOW IT WOULD BE, IF SOME LADIES HAD THEIR OWN WAY." A cartoon mocking women's bid for equality, *Harper's Weekly*, May 16, 1868. *Courtesy Library of Congress*

social life, where she is the chief factor; a place in the trades and professions, where she may earn her bread, is because of her birthright to self-sovereignty; because, as an individual, she must rely on herself. No matter how much women prefer to lean, to be protected and supported, nor how much men desire to have them do so, they must make the voyage of life alone, and for safety in an emergency they must know something of the laws of navigation."[20] Even though the AWSA and the NWSA did not share the same strategy, they did pursue the same main goal. In 1890 the two organizations merged, becoming the National American Woman Suffrage Association (NAWSA). Stanton and Anthony were the first two presidents. The impetus for the merger came from the repeated failures of either organization to gain real progress toward the vote; from the (by then) enlarged sphere of middle-class women who had been participating in many social reforms; and from the grudging acknowledgment among a few more men and women that the vote for women would not destroy the family but might instead purify the immoral political realm. Caught up in the fervor of professionalism sweeping the country, and to accommodate fairly former members of the old organizations, the NAWSA formalized its procedures. It adopted the AWSA strategy of a state-by-state ballot referendum. Although the reformed NAWSA garnered additional members in the last decade of the nineteenth century, it failed to convince the majority of Americans to eschew their firm antisuffrage sentiments.

Neither the AWSA, the NWSA, nor the NAWSA could boast any real success in the Gilded Age. Eight states held referenda on women's suffrage, but none passed. The two states that did allow women to vote, Utah and Wyoming, did so for reasons having little to do with the suffragists. Utah gave women the vote to conserve its Mormon hegemony as more "gentiles" moved in, and Wyoming hoped to encourage families to settle in its desolate and sparsely populated territory. While wary of the ballot, state legislators were more receptive to the other demands in the women's-rights pantheon. By the close of the century, several states had passed laws to end women's "civil death" upon marriage. Thanks to suffragists and other reformers, many states allowed married women to own and dispose of property, to initiate lawsuits, to enter into legal contracts, and to keep their own earnings and distribute them as they wanted. In some states women were given guardianship over their children in the wake of a divorce. Although the long struggle for the vote would not be won nationwide until 1920, these by-products of the suffrage battle were great victories in their own right.

Along with club work and suffrage, middle-class women turned to another area of reform during the Gilded Age. To share in the misfortunes of the inner-city work force and to put their Christian beliefs into action, a number of women—often college educated and unmarried—lived among the poor in settlement houses. American cities were notorious for crime, disease, unhygienic living conditions, unsafe workplaces, and unscrupulous employers who would take advantage of the newly arrived. Amidst the noise and filth, women created a safe environment that was for them an alternative to standard family life. For the people they served, settlement houses were partly training schools and partly recreation centers. Settlement workers tried in multiple ways to make life better: they set up libraries; health clinics; kindergartens; night schools; classes in English, nutrition, politics, art, music, and vocational training; boys and girls' clubs; and penny savings banks.

The most famous settlement house was Hull House, founded in 1889 by Jane Addams and her partner, Ellen Gates Starr. Patterned on Toynbee Hall in London, England, this Chicago institution became itself the model for others to follow. Originally intending to uplift local working-class immigrants, the women associated with Hull House worked with the city and state government to lobby for antisweatshop legislation, an eight-hour work day, and a minimum wage. Hull House had its own women's club and men's club, gymnasium, public bath and kitchen, and labor museum. Trade unions held meetings at Hull House. Addams and the women who lived and worked with her—Mary Rozet Smith, Florence Kelley, Julia Lathrop, Alice Hamilton, Grace Abbott—simultaneously sought to meet the needs of their neighbors and to weaken the power of the corrupt political bosses.[21] With different levels of success, hundreds of settlement houses opened across the United States. Janie Porter Barrett, a graduate of Hampton Institute, founded the Locust Street Settlement House in Hampton, Virginia, in the 1890s. This home for African Americans grew from her own charitable and informal instruction of young women at her residence. Barrett taught household management and job training skills for preparation both as wives and workers. Lillian Wald, a public-health nurse, began living among poor immigrants in New York in 1893. Her Henry Street Settlement House was established in 1895 to care for the medical, vocational, and social needs of her neighbors. Like Hull House,

Henry Street became a bastion of civic reform. It offered safe play-grounds for children, campaigned to eradicate tuberculosis, and sponsored scholarships for needy boys and girls. Women such as Eleanor Roosevelt and Amelia Earhart worked for short periods in settlement houses and considered their time there formative and enlightening.

The effect of industrialization on working-class women had little to do with voluntary action and reformulating the boundaries of the separate sphere. Females provided labor to fuel industrializa-tion. Women comprised 14 percent of the total work force in 1870 and 16 percent in 1890. At the same time, the percentage of all women who worked outside the home steadily increased through-out the Gilded Age: 15 percent in 1870, 16 percent in 1880, 19 per-cent in 1890, and 21 percent in 1900. The typical female worker was young, urban, single, and either an immigrant or the daughter of immigrants, who lived at home with her family. Her work was temporary—just until she married. The job she was most likely to hold was that of domestic servant.[22] Her labor in the homes of middle-class women allowed the latter more leisure to do their vol-untary work. By definition, female wage workers contradicted the dominant social ideology of the cult of true womanhood. Middle-class reformers, physicians, ministers, and editors warned women that they would "unfit themselves" for marriage and motherhood if they continued in the work force. Yet, most women worked not because they wanted to but because family economics demanded it.

The only consistent exceptions seem to be women who were self-employed and some farmers' daughters. The former found their precarious independence usually better than being a wife, or better than being only a wife.[23] Farmers' daughters craved the indepen-dence and excitement of a city job, but the extent to which their salary was necessary for the family's survival is unclear. Wages for women were consistently lower than those for men and, in fact, provided barely enough for an individual to live on. The average cost of living for a self-supporting female worker was estimated to be $5.51 per week, but the average wage was $5.68 per week. Em-ployers viewed women as temporary workers who labored for "pin money," not a wage necessary to support a family. Therefore, not only public sentiment but also the inequitable wage system placed laboring women in a difficult position.[24]

Prostitutes constituted a category unto themselves. While women's reform associations certainly censured this job choice,

Jane Addams. The founder of Chicago's Hull House and a leader of reform. *Courtesy of Jane Addams Papers Project, Duke University*

prostitutes frequently made a better wage than other working women, and, depending upon their situation, often enjoyed preferable working conditions. Female brothel owners could make great sums of money, but few prostitutes could acquire the necessary capital to open and run their own establishment. Married women sometimes engaged in prostitution, with or without the knowledge of their husbands, to add to the family's income. A few women were forced into it by bosses or family members. By far, the largest number of women who became prostitutes lived alone or suffered from chronically low wages, or both. Most did not stay in the field long and professed the same desire to be married and have children as other women.[25]

Domestic workers could be cooks, maids, laundresses, and nannies, in any combination. Married women and single women, immigrants, daughters of immigrants, native-born blacks, and native-born whites all worked as domestics. Numerically, foreign-born women held the most domestic positions, even though native-born white women were the most sought after by employers. Native-born servants dominated in the countryside, as did immigrants in the cities and African Americans in the South. In urban California, Mexican-American women who worked were usually domestics. Most domestics were "live-in" servants who received room and board for their work, along with a small wage. Employers preferred live-ins for various reasons, not the least of which was the round-the-clock surveillance. Daughters of immigrants and native-born servants more often lived with their employers than did African-American domestics. As the century progressed and more white women moved into factory and office work—two remunerative avenues closed to black women—African Americans led the trend to servants living outside the home. Living away more easily accommodated a married servant, and racism also played a role in black domestics living elsewhere. Many upper- and middle-class white women thought that the model of their own lives would uplift and assimilate poor immigrant servants, but for black women, that was not considered a realistic goal.

The relations between female employers and their domestic servants could be uncomfortable and fraught with tension. Domestics complained of being on call twenty-four hours a day and scrutinized at every task. They hated the tedious labor and the inherent inequality between themselves and the mistress. The job was lonely, as families usually employed just one domestic. She had no close friend nearby, nor even a sympathetic ear. If the employer was much older than the domestic, a maternal relationship might exist. This could be fulfilling for both women, or, especially if the employer was prejudiced, it could result in condescension and domineering treatment. For their part, employers complained about maids who broke and stole household goods, who wanted too much time off or were ill too frequently, and who were ignorant, lazy, forgetful, noisy, or rude. Conflict between Protestant employers and Catholic employees added to the mutual mistrust.[26]

In the urban South, nearly five times as many married black women as white women worked outside the home. Most of these wives were domestics. They were often forced into wage labor because of their husbands' low incomes. The majority of single, black female workers were domestics, too. In rural communities, African-American women in the South labored also in the cotton and rice fields, jobs that had been forced on them since slavery. Because white women would not work in someone else's fields, this backbreaking labor was reserved in the postbellum South for African Americans. Very few black women worked in factories, but their numbers increased as the century wore on. Almost none worked in white-collar jobs such as clerk and saleswoman. One of the major differences between black and white women workers was the support received at home. Black communities—although they might have glorified the domestic ideal of womanhood—conceded that economic necessity forced wives into the work force, and hence were less critical of women who worked after marriage.

Although native-born white women in early textile factories such as those in Lowell, Massachusetts, had constituted the first industrial laborers in America, by the Gilded Age the majority of the female industrial work force was comprised of foreign-born women or their American-born daughters. In immigrant communities wives and mothers took in boarders, but daughters went away from the home to work. Industry was not wide open for women. Instead, jobs were clustered in garment factories (in the manufacture both of cloth and clothing), laundries, carpet factories, tobacco factories, canneries, meat-packing plants, candy factories, and bookbinderies. These jobs were extensions of "women's work" in the home. Because most women in industry were young, unskilled, and unmarried, bosses considered them temporary hires and paid them far less than they paid male laborers. The female work force was usually tractable—a result of the expected docile nature of women and also of the general exclusion of women from labor unions whose male members perceived women's labor as a threat to their own employment. Industrial jobs had the benefit of a shorter workday than domestic service (usually ten hours or longer at the beginning of the Gilded Age and eight by the turn of the century). Factory work, however, could be dangerous, unhealthy, difficult, boring, and cyclical. Industries had no safety codes as the Gilded Age dawned and no regulations regarding breaks, vacations, retirement, workers' compensation, injury pay or time off, or sexual harassment. In the 1890s, often because of the efforts of female reformers, factory codes began to improve working conditions.

Working women did express their unhappiness with the system of labor in the United States; when they went on strike, however, their protests were tailored to the local situation. Women's strikes in the Gilded Age were rarely successful. Most trade unions were closed to them, and so they did not have the benefit of male support and sheer numbers. Men did not welcome women into trade unions because they believed that the lower-paid women's work force would displace them or force wages down. Unskilled women worked the machines that had initially put skilled male workers on the unemployment lines, and thus the introduction of women into a field often heralded a new, and unwelcome, era for an industry and for the men who had previously worked it alone. Leonara Barry led the recruitment drive on behalf of the Knights of Labor from her position as the organization's general investigator of women's work, and by the early 1880s union membership was 10 percent female. Before the decade was over, though, the Knights had lost its strength and membership declined drastically. The next major trade union to arise was the American Federation of Labor, which was hostile to women. Some female workers organized their own associations, more mutual-aid societies than unions. Many women participated in work stoppages such as the wave of strikes in the garment industry in the 1880s.[27] In the late Gilded Age the push for protective legislation began and would bear fruit in the Progressive Era, helped along by the many female reformers in the Woman's Trade Union League (founded in 1903).

Native-born white women rarely worked in factories. Instead, they took the less stressful, but hardly better paying, clerical, teaching, and sales jobs.[28] These three fields had belonged exclusively to men, but as the Gilded Age progressed, public sentiment held that women's morals and futures would not be unduly damaged by jobs in offices and stores. Consequently, working-class and middle-class women moved with alacrity into cleaner and less physically demanding jobs such as bookkeeper, typist, stenographer, and copyist.

The Gilded Age witnessed a significant increase in college-educated women. Both coeducational and women's colleges had existed before the Civil War, but more colleges opened their doors to women in the postbellum years, including Bryn Mawr, Radcliffe, and Mount Holyoke. Although opponents of women's education, particularly scientists, warned that women's brains were too small to handle the work without compromising their reproductive systems, many women took the risk. Upon graduation, they married at a lower rate than the rest of the female population. This could have resulted from the empowering taste of the homosocial circle or the liberating dose of the life of the mind that women experienced at college, or it could have to do with the shortage of men in the wake of the Civil War. Certainly it was nearly impossible for a woman in the Gilded Age to have children and a husband along with a career. Seventy-five percent of all women who earned doctoral degrees between 1877 and 1924 remained single.[29]

Many college-educated women chose to enter the few professional careers open to women in the Gilded Age. Nursing and teaching were predominantly women's fields by the mid-Gilded Age. Also in this era, some institutions began to graduate women physicians and attorneys. By the turn of the century, several medical schools across the North and Midwest admitted women, and female doctors began to practice in women's hospitals, in clinics, and from their own offices. It was relatively easier to pursue a career in medicine than in law because of the obvious differences in men's and women's bodies. Sentiment existed for women to tend to ailing women, infants, and children, just as they had always done, and the move toward professionalism in the Gilded Age assisted the entrance of women into medicine and law. One decade into the twentieth century, there were nine thousand women physicians but only fifteen hundred female lawyers in the United States. Myra Bradwell was the first woman to seek admittance to the bar. When she initially applied for a license to practice in 1869, the Illinois State Supreme Court turned her down. The U.S. Supreme Court also found against her, but on technical grounds, and the Illinois legislature allowed her to practice. In 1879, Belva Lockwood was admitted to practice before the Supreme Court. Inroads into the legal system continued but at a snail's pace.

Science remained closed to women and the ministry nearly so. No female scientist held a job in industry, and few denominations allowed women to seek ordination. Most women in science were professors in women's colleges. Teaching in college became a viable option after the Civil War as more and more institutions of higher learning opened their doors to female students. The percentage of female college students increased throughout the Gilded Age and the Progressive Era, but the number of female college professors did not rise correspondingly. To have a career in the Gilded Age, most women had to forego marriage and children and face an uncertain financial future at the very least. Probably most women also risked the displeasure of their families because of their unusual life choice as well as the loss of a peer group. This latter was one reason that Hull House and other settlements attracted so many like-minded college-educated women. There, their aspirations found a receptive audience.

As industrialization, immigration, and urbanization caused a population increase in the East, the Homestead Acts and the lure of quick riches drew a number of Americans to the West. The experience of women in the West is difficult to characterize. Some single women took advantage of the free or inexpensive land given out by the U.S. government and established their own homesteads. Others went west as prostitutes or dance hall entertainers, and many led a peripatetic life following the mining camps. Some single women sought employment in the wide open West rather than in the crowded Eastern cities. Religion played a role in settling the frontier, as zeal led female missionaries and nuns to Christianize and care for the western families. Most women who made the journey toward the Pacific Ocean did so as wives, sometimes willingly and sometimes unwillingly accompanying their farmer, rancher, miner, or businessman husbands. For most women the journey was arduous, even after the railways crossed the plains and brought the trappings of eastern civilization closer. Women worried about Indian attacks, disease, the lack of doctors, the difficulty of keeping their homes clean, the dearth of formal educational opportunities in the West, and the relatives they left behind.

In the most rural areas, women did not inhabit a separate sphere. As the family began the process of building and planting, women's labor in the fields and the barns was crucial to the family's survival. The doctrine of separate spheres, if it was part of the intellectual construct of western women and men, was at least more flexible as they shared work. A 1901 editorial from the journal *The Independent* asserted that "there is nothing essentially masculine about outdoor employment. There is in running a reaper nothing more to weaken femininity than in running a sewing machine. To drive a team of horses in a hay field will no more unsex a woman than driving a fast team in a city park. To be compelled to drudge is as demoralizing in the kitchen as it is in the garden—no more, no less."[30]

Rather than being simply "gentle tamers" of the Wild West and its men, women helped to build community structures as they had done in the East. They founded and belonged to women's clubs and to women's auxiliaries of farm and ranch societies, such as the Women's Christian Temperance Union, the Populist party, the Grange, and the Farmers Alliance. Western women dedicated themselves to municipal housekeeping in the latter part of the Gilded Age. They established orphanages, Sunday schools, libraries, museums, and other institutions. In western states and territories, many women enjoyed the vote—even as their eastern sisters fought for it. School board elections were first opened to women in the West, and by 1870 in Wyoming and Utah women held the full elective franchise. While the initial impetus for giving women the vote in Utah probably did not come from women, female members of the Church of Jesus Christ of Latter-Day Saints took advantage of it, publishing their own suffrage newspaper and pushing to extend the vote to women elsewhere in the West.[31]

Native American women did not internalize the cult of true womanhood. Few had heard of it. The ones who had were usually exposed to white Christian missionary women who were trying to convert this people religiously and culturally. Gilded Age Anglo-Americans continued to marginalize Native Americans. The U.S. government's Indian policies consigned them to reservations, where women and men suffered terrible upheaval and ignominy. A facile generalization about the lives of Native American women is bound to be erroneous in its particulars, but, broadly speaking, Indian women did not live within a separate female sphere. More likely, men and women shared work or performed tasks that the writers of the separate sphere prescriptive literature would not have recognzied as "women's work." Native American women were agricultural as well as domestic workers. They were not significantly touched by industrialization, immigration, or urbanization, except for the very few women whose home-industry products (baskets, pottery, or cloth) were sold to wealthy white women and the ever fewer women who worked as domestics (usually on the East Coast). Many Native American women were able to escape unhappy or abusive marriages with greater ease than the white majority, and in some tribes, women enjoyed a higher status because of their religious or medical skills or because of their longevity. It is possible that the ongoing pressure to assimilate into white culture robbed these women of their more nearly equal status in their communities, for by the end of the Gilded Age a larger number of white missionaries and others who believed in the cultural hegemony of European Americans sought to make Native Americans conform to the dictates of white society.[32]

Native Americans, however, were but distant figures for most middle- and working-class Americans. Politicians and editors proclaimed the might of industry, while immigrants and native-born Americans moved to the cities to seek a better future. Industry, with its promise of prosperity and progress, irrevocably altered the lives of women. Factories were the main attraction for immigrants to make the long journey to the United States, and, although many more men migrated, the women who did underwent the jarring cultural shock of discovering American social norms. Working-class women took in boarders, laundry, and piecework, while their daughters went off to factories. Labor in industry opened up for women during the Gilded Age, even though unions did not. The difficult jobs women performed belied the contemporary notion that they were fragile and domestic. Still, working-class life was an uphill struggle. Tenements, corrupt politicians, and unsanitary living conditions spurred middle-class women to their sisters' aid, but only infrequently did middle- and working-class women form partnerships in the business of cleaning up the slums and factories. More often, middle-class women pursued municipal housekeeping in voluntary associations drawn from their own social group, while they promoted the assimilation of their white domestic helpers as individuals. Women's associations and suffrage organizations provided the key for middle-class women to unlock the bonds of the cult of true womanhood, as did settlement houses, college education, and entry into professions.

As the Gilded Age ended and the Progressive Era dawned, middle-class club members and suffragists continued to ameliorate the troubles of women and children, the traditional objects of their concern. They began to appeal more and more frequently for direct governmental intervention and secured legislation on topics as broad ranging as the environment, sanitation, juvenile courts, historic preservation, education, pure food and drugs, and crime. Women such as Carrie Chapman Catt, who early in her life began work in the field of suffrage, continued the battle, finally gaining the vote for all women in 1920. The first generation of college-educated women opened the doors for others who followed in their footsteps seeking personal satisfaction in medical, legal, and governmental careers. African-American women persevered in the staggering task of "lifting as they climbed," educating whites and fighting stereotypes. The genteel activism in black women's clubs paved the way for better treatment by local and state politicians, at least in the North. Reform efforts had demonstrated the ability of women not only to survive but also to prosper outside their "proper" sphere. As a nurturing arena for action and a justification for excursions into public space, the separate sphere had buoyed women, but by the end of the Gilded Age its constraints had become obvious, its boundaries a liability. The "new woman" of the Progressive Era— educated, informed, and more free of the separate sphere—was clearly the legacy of Gilded Age activists on all fronts.

Notes

1. *Historical Statistics of the United States: Colonial Times to 1970* (Washington, DC, 1975), 6. These figures are taken from the 1890 census.

2. "The average number [of children] born to a white woman surviving to menopause fell from 7.04 in 1800, to 6.14 in 1840, to 4.24 in 1880, and finally to 3.56 in 1900." Daniel Scott Smith, "Family Limitation, Sexual Control, and Domestic Feminism in Victorian America," in *Clio's Consciousness Raised*, ed. Mary Hartman and Lois Banner (New York, 1974), 122.

3. The literature on women's sexuality in the Gilded Age is vast. See, for example, Nancy F. Cott, "Passionlessness: An Interpretation of Victorian Sexual Ideology, 1790–1850," *Signs* 4 (Winter 1978): 219–36; Carl Degler, *At Odds: Women and the Family in America from the Revolution to the Present* (New York, 1980); and John D'Emilio and Estelle B. Freedman, *Intimate Matters: A History of Sexuality in America* (New York, 1988).

4. William G. Shade, " 'A Mental Passion': Female Sexuality in Victorian America," *International Journal of Women's Studies* 1 (January/February 1978): 21. Shade cites Eliza Farnham, Antoinette Brown Blackwell, and Isabella Beecher Hooker as examples of late nineteenth-century feminists whose writings are based on a recognition of the differences between men and women, rather than on the earlier nineteenth-century beliefs of feminists such as Elizabeth Cady Stanton and Margaret Fuller, who contended that men and women, despite a few biological differences, were equal.

5. See Shirley J. Carlson, "Black Ideals of Womanhood in the Late Victorian Era," *Journal of Negro History* 77 (Spring 1992): 61–73. Carlson holds that "the ideal black woman embodied the genteel behavior of the 'cult of true womanhood.' . . . In addition, as an *African American*, her thoughts and actions exemplified the attributes valued by her own race and community" (p. 61, emphasis in text).

6. Barbara Welter, "The Cult of True Womanhood, 1820–1860," in *Dimity Convictions: The American Woman in the Nineteenth Century* (Athens, OH, 1976), 21–41. This article was first published in 1966. One of the most enduring historiographical debates in nineteenth-century women's history concerns this concept and whether the woman's homosocial sphere limited her power and influence or provided a powerful base of support from which she could pursue her social reforms. Welter and Gerda Lerner ("The Lady and the Mill Girl: Changes in the Status of Women in the Age of Jackson," *Mid-Continental American Studies Journal* 10 [Spring 1965]: 5–15) favor the former position, while the following historians argue some permutation on the latter: Carroll Smith-Rosenberg, "The Female World of Love and Ritual," *Signs* 1 (Autumn 1975): 1–29; Nancy Cott, *The Bonds of Womanhood: Woman's Sphere in New England, 1778–1835* (New Haven, CT, 1975); and Estelle B. Freedman, "Separatism as Strategy: Female Institution Building and American Feminism, 1870–1930," *Feminist Studies* 5 (Fall 1979): 512–29. For the most recent scholarship on the separate sphere see *Gendered Domains: Rethinking Public and Private in Women's History*, ed. Dorothy O. Helly and Susan M. Reverby (Ithaca, NY, 1992).

7. The phrase is Christopher Lasch's from *Haven in a Heartless World: The Family Besieged* (New York, 1977).

8. The phrase is from Carroll Smith-Rosenberg, "The Female World," p. 1.

9. On the WCTU see Frances Willard, *Glimpses of Fifty Years: The Autobiography of an American Woman* (Chicago, 1889); Barbara Leslie Epstein, *The Politics of Domesticity: Women, Evangelism, and Temperance in Nineteenth-Century America* (Middletown, CT, 1981); Ruth Bordin, *Woman and Temperance: The Quest for Power and Liberty, 1873–1900* (Philadelphia, 1981); idem, *Frances Willard: A Biography* (Chapel Hill, NC, 1986); and Suzanne M. Marilley, "Frances Willard and the Feminism of Fear," *Feminist Studies* 19 (Spring 1993): 123–46. For African-American women in the temperance movement see Patricia A. Schecter, "Temperance Work in the Nineteenth Century," *Black Women in America: An Historical Encyclopedia*, 2 vols., ed. Darlene Clark Hine (Brooklyn, NY, 1993), 2:1154–56.

10. The categories of municipal housekeeping are drawn from Anne Firor Scott, *Natural Allies: Women's Associations in American History* (Chicago, 1991), 184–89.

11. Idem, "Most Invisible of All: Black Women's Voluntary Associations," *Journal of Southern History* 56 (February 1990): 3–22.

12. Carlson, "Black Ideals of Womanhood," 61–62. For an understanding of how Christian ideals and the black churches have historically influenced the work of club women see Evelyn Brooks Higginbotham, *Righteous Discontent: The Woman's Movement in the Black Baptist Church, 1880–1920* (Cambridge, MA, 1993).

13. On the issue of the indivisibility of race and gender consult Else Barkley Brown, "Womanist Consciousness: Maggie Lena Walker and the Independent Order of St. Luke," in *Unequal Sisters: A Multi-Cultural Reader in U.S. Women's History*, ed. Vicki L. Ruiz and Ellen Carol DuBois (New York, 1994), 268–83.

14. On the myriad activities of African-American women see Stephanie J. Shaw, "Black Club Women and the Creation of the National Association of Colored Women," *Journal of Women's History* 3 (Fall 1991): 10–25 (the specific examples cited come from pp. 17 and 18); Kathleen C. Berkeley, " 'Colored Ladies Also Contributed': Black Women's Activities from Benevolence to Social Welfare, 1866–1896," in *The Web of Southern Social Relations: Women, Fami-*

lies, and Education, ed. Walter J. Fraser, Jr., R. Frank Saunders, Jr., and Jon L. Wakelyn (Athens, GA, 1985), 181–203; Scott, "Most Invisible of All," especially p. 16; and Linda Gordon, "Black and White Visions of Welfare: Women's Welfare Activism, 1890–1945," *Journal of American History* 78 (September 1991): 559–90.

15. Although almost all historians of women's clubs make this point, see particularly Karen J. Blair, *The Clubwoman as Feminist: True Womanhood Redefined, 1868–1914* (New York, 1980); Scott, *Natural Allies*; and Lori D. Ginzberg, *Women and the Work of Benevolence: Morality, Politics, and Class in the Nineteenth-Century United States* (New Haven, CT, 1990). The quote is from Scott's book, 221–22.

16. Mary Y. Terrell, president of the Texas Federation of Women's Clubs, to the membership ("Dear Club Friends"), January 7, 1901, in the Anna J. H. Pennybacker Collection, Center for American History, University of Texas at Austin. The goals of the Texas Federation of Women's Clubs were the creation of a state library commission, a law prohibiting the killing of game and song birds, industrial education for women, and legislation controlling "the sale of that deadly drug Cocaine."

17. Paula Baker, "The Domestication of Politics: Women and American Political Society, 1780–1920," *American Historical Review* 89 (June 1984): 620–47. The quote is from p. 622. See also Michael McGerr, "Political Style and Women's Power, 1830–1930," *Journal of American History* 77 (December 1990): 864–85; and Baker, *The Moral Frameworks of Public Life: Gender, Politics, and the State in Rural New York, 1870–1930* (New York, 1991).

18. The list of women's participation in traditional politics comes from McGerr, "Political Style and Women's Power," 867. See also Mary Ryan, *Women in Public: Between Banners and Ballots, 1825–1880* (Baltimore, 1990).

19. On suffrage see Eleanor Flexnor, *Century of Struggle: The Woman's Rights Movement in the United States* (Cambridge, MA, 1975); Ellen Carol DuBois, *Feminism and Suffrage: The Emergence of an Independent Women's Movement in America, 1848–1869* (Ithaca, NY, 1978); Israel Kugler, *From Ladies to Women: The Organized Struggle for Woman's Rights in the Reconstruction Era* (New York, 1987); and Aileen S. Kraditor, *The Ideas of the Woman Suffrage Movement, 1890–1920* (New York, 1981).

20. Elizabeth Cady Stanton, "Solitude of Self," speech given before the House Judiciary Committee and the National American Woman Suffrage Association convention in 1892, in *Feminism: The Essential Historical Writings*, ed. Miriam Schneir (New York, 1972), 158.

21. On Hull House see Jane Addams, *Twenty Years at Hull House* (1910; reprint ed., Urbana, IL, 1990); Mary L. Bryan and Allen F. Davis, eds., *One Hundred Years at Hull House* (Bloomington, IN, 1990); and Davis, *American Heroine: The Life and Legend of Jane Addams* (New York, 1973).

22. The information in this paragraph is taken from Lynn Y. Weiner, *From Working Girl to Working Mother: The Female Labor Force in the United States, 1820–1980* (Chapel Hill, NC: 1985), 4–5. See also Alice Kessler-Harris, *Out to Work: A History of Wage-Earning Women in the United States* (New York, 1982); and Joanne J. Meyerowitz, *Women Adrift: Independent Wage Earners in Chicago, 1880–1930* (Urbana, IL, 1988).

23. For a study of self-employed women that broaches the idea that some women preferred their independence to marriage see Wendy Gamber, "A Precarious Independence: Milliners and Dressmakers in Boston, 1860–1890," *Journal of*

Women's History 4 (September 1992): 60–88. Gamber found that there were 994 self-employed women in Boston in 1890.

24. Weiner, *From Working Girl to Working Mother*, 25.

25. Timothy J. Gilfoyle, *City of Eros: New York City, Prostitution, and the Commercialization of Sex, 1790–1920* (New York, 1992); Anne M. Butler, *Daughters of Joy, Sisters of Misery: Prostitutes in the American West, 1865–1890* (Urbana, IL, 1985).

26. Consult Fay E. Dudden, *Serving Women: Household Service in Nineteenth-Century America* (Middletown, CT, 1983); and David M. Katzman, *Seven Days a Week: Women and Domestic Service in Industrializing America* (New York, 1978).

27. For an example of women's essential role in a Knights of Labor-sponsored strike, see Susan Levine, *Labor's True Woman: Carpet Weavers, Industrialization, and Labor Reform in the Gilded Age* (Philadelphia, 1984).

28. Weiner, *From Working Girl to Working Mother*, 27–28.

29. Barbara J. Harris, *Beyond Her Sphere: Women and the Professions in American History* (Westport, CT, 1978), 101. See also Mary R. Walsh, *Doctors Wanted, No Women Need Apply: Sexual Barriers in the Medical Profession, 1835–1975* (New Haven, CT, 1977); and Gloria Moldow, *Women Doctors in Gilded Age Washington: Race, Gender, and Professionalism* (Chicago, 1987).

30. *The Independent*, July 18, 1901.

31. The information on western women comes from *The Women's West*, ed., Susan Armitage and Elizabeth Jameson (Norman, OK, 1987), particularly Elizabeth Jameson, "Women as Workers, Women as Civilizers: True Womanhood in the American West," 145–64, and Nancy Grey Osterud, " 'She Helped Me Hay It as Good as a Man': Relations among Women and Men in an Agricultural Community," 87–97, in *"To Toil the Livelong Day": America's Women at Work, 1780–1980*, ed. Carol Groneman and Mary Beth Norton (Ithaca, NY, 1987).

32. See Joan M. Jensen, "Native American Women and Agriculture: A Seneca Case Study," in *Unequal Sisters*, 70–84; and Glenda Riley, *Inventing the American Woman: A Perspective on Women's History* (Arlington Heights, IL, 1986), 142 and 175–76.

Suggestions for Further Reading

Barnhart, Jacqueline Baker. *The Fair But Frail: Prostitution in San Francisco, 1849–1900*. Reno, NV, 1986.

Buhle, Mari Jo. *Women and American Socialism, 1870–1920*. Urbana, IL, 1981.

Clinton, Catherine. *Half Sisters of History: Southern Women and the American Past*. Durham, NC, 1994.

Crocker, Ruth. *Social Work and Social Order: The Settlement Movement in Two Industrial Cities, 1889–1930*. Urbana, IL, 1992.

Davies, Margery W. *Woman's Place Is at the Typewriter: Office Work and Office Workers, 1870–1930*. Philadelphia, 1982.

D'Emilio, John, and Estelle B. Freedman. *Intimate Matters: A History of Sexuality in America*. New York, 1988.

Deutsch, Sarah. "Learning to Talk More Like a Man: Boston Women's Class-Bridging Organizations, 1870–1940." *American Historical Review* 97 (April 1992): 379–404.

————. *No Separate Refuge: Culture, Class, and Gender on an Anglo-Hispanic Frontier in the American Southwest, 1880–1940.* New York, 1987.

Fischer, Christine, ed. *Let Them Speak for Themselves: Women in the American West, 1849–1900.* Hamden, CT, 1977.

Jeffrey, Julie Roy. *Frontier Women: The Trans-Mississippi West, 1840–1880.* New York, 1979.

Marti, Donald B. *Women of the Grange: Mutuality and Sisterhood in Rural America, 1866–1920.* New York, 1991.

Matthews, Glenna. *"Just a Housewife": The Rise and Fall of Domesticity in America.* New York, 1987.

McCarthy, Kathleen D., ed. *Lady Bountiful Revisited: Women, Philanthropy, and Power.* New Brunswick, NJ, 1990.

Meckel, Richard. *Save the Babies: American Public Health Reform and the Prevention of Infant Mortality, 1850–1929.* Baltimore, 1990.

Meyerowitz, Joanne J. *Women Adrift: Independent Wage Earners in Chicago, 1880–1930.* Chicago, 1988.

Peiss, Kathy. *Cheap Amusements: Working Women and Leisure in Turn-of-the-Century New York.* Philadelphia, 1986.

Riley, Glenda. *Women and Indians on the Frontier, 1825–1915.* Albuquerque, 1984.

Rosenberg, Rosalind. *Beyond Separate Spheres: Intellectual Roots of Modern Feminism.* New Haven, CT, 1982.

Rosenzweig, Linda W. *The Anchor of My Life: Middle-Class American Mothers and Daughters, 1880–1920.* New York, 1993.

Rothman, Sheila. *Woman's Proper Place: A History of Changing Ideals and Practices, 1870 to the Present.* New York, 1978.

Scott, Anne Firor. *Making the Invisible Woman Visible.* Chicago, 1984.

Smith-Rosenberg, Carroll. *Disorderly Conduct: Visions of Gender in Victorian America.* New York, 1985.

White, Deborah Gray. "The Cost of Club Work, the Price of Black Feminism." In *Visible Women: New Essays on American Activism*, ed. Nancy A. Hewitt and Suzanne Lebsock. Urbana, IL, 1993.

7

The African-American Experience

Leslie H. Fishel, Jr.

A revolution emerged from a rebellion. The South rebelled, and for three decades after the war most corners of the country experienced a revolution in economic activity, territorial expansion, demography, class structure, education, and politics. No community felt the impact of these changes more than the colored people or Negroes, as they were known then. A young African-American activist, William E. Matthews, writing from Boston in July 1868, captured their sense of pride and promise. "The negro of today looms up and assumes an importance never before accorded him," he asserted, "and he possesses an influence and power which he but little realizes."[1]

Some of that importance, influence, and power, coupled with talent and perseverance, brought political position and, occasionally, leverage for a number of African Americans during the Reconstruction years. Blacks served in Congress and several state legislatures and in federal, state, and local governments at varying levels of authority. Their success and, in many instances, their accomplishments served to encourage the multitude of their race, North and South, for whom freedom still meant little change. The Reconstruction process slowly eroded during the 1870s and died in 1877, when President Rutherford B. Hayes withdrew the last federal troops from the South (from South Carolina and Louisiana).

In "redeeming" their states—that is, assuming control and throwing off the burdens of Reconstruction—southern white leaders had to confront, be confounded by, and control the African-American presence. In some areas, such as the black belt (named for the color of its soil, not its people), the numbers were overwhelming. While the question of how to handle a black multitude learning to live in freedom was only one of many economic and political problems that dogged the white South in the final two decades of the century, it clung like a leech to almost every issue.

A major component of that freedom for African Americans was the liberty to move to another plantation or region. Between 1870 and 1900 the South's black population jumped from 4.4 million to 7.9 million. The vast majority of them remained in the South, with substantial numbers moving within that region. Primarily seeking higher income-producing jobs, blacks generally went south and west from the border states, with Alabama, Arkansas, Georgia, Louisiana, Mississippi, South Carolina, and Texas registering large gains. They found employment in farming, building railroads, mining coal and phosphate, making turpentine, and lumbering. Black workers often contracted for short-term jobs, moving on when the contract was up. At the same time, the black population in the North and West practically doubled from about 460,000 to over 910,000, with migration accounting for over 50 percent of the increase. While the migratory pattern varied from decade to decade, the end result was the scattering of African Americans throughout the nation, which continued in greater numbers during the twentieth century.

One major thrust of the migratory pattern was a movement into cities or towns that were becoming urban centers. By 1900, 90 percent of New England's African Americans were city folk, and, in the mid-Atlantic, midwestern, and western states, from two-thirds to over three-quarters of blacks lived in cities. In the South the percentages were considerably lower, ranging from 19 percent along the Atlantic Coast to about 16 percent in the border states and the Southwest.[2]

Although whites played a role in both abetting and obstructing these migratory movements, the human implications of this diaspora are measured by its impact on African Americans. As Reconstruction petered out state by state in the 1870s, most blacks were weighed down by little political support and less economic opportunity. Job-seeking away from home was an inviting option, but it strained family ties and placed a heavy burden on the women. This "moving on" created an impression of black indolence that whites too readily accepted and to which they added charges of shirked responsibilities and disloyalty. In reality, one historian explained, blacks were merely following an entrepreneurial model, exhibiting "a rational economic response based on their ability to earn a good deal more at occasional jobs paying a daily rate than through an annual agreement."[3]

One movement had a history all its own. From March until May 1879 about six thousand African Americans left Louisiana, Mississippi, and Texas for the plains of Kansas, an exodus characterized as "the most remarkable migration in the United States after the Civil War." Kansas fever had been building in the South for three or four years, encouraged in part by two freedmen, the spiritually sensitive Benjamin "Pap" Singleton and the politically conscious Henry Adams. Emigration to Kansas before 1879 was sufficient to result in the founding of a black town, Nicodemus, and to influence Minnesota Senator William Windom to introduce a resolution asking the U.S. Senate to investigate "the expediency and practicability of encouraging and promoting . . . the partial migration" of blacks from the South. Impelled by "terrorism and poverty," the leaderless 1879 migrants had only a firm faith that God would take care of them. Despite white resistance and poor soil, most of them put down their roots in this new land.[4]

Most southern blacks were hopelessly tied to farming. After the war the slave plantation system became a "tenant plantation system" that employed black workers as tenants on a cash, credit, or share basis. The cash system required the tenant to pay rent, while the credit system advanced a loan to him for seeds and other necessities, using the unplanted crop as collateral. Sharecropping split the crop's return into shares for landlord and tenant. All three systems exploited the tenants and kept them debt-ridden and cash poor.

The major crop was cotton. By 1910 substantial percentages of improved land were planted to cotton: almost half of Mississippi's farmland; close to 40 percent of the agricultural acreage in Alabama, Arkansas, Georgia, and Louisiana; and at least one-fifth of the land in Florida, Tennessee, and Texas. While black farm families often shifted laterally and annually from one plantation to another, white pressures assured their lack of cash, credit, and good soil, thereby restricting their upward mobility to land ownership. One historian has observed tartly that the planter's control over the black worker was extensive, reaching beyond the job to "his home, his recreation, and his daily relations with others. . . . Plantation agriculture may be described as military agriculture." Remembering his parents and grandparents after slavery, one man remarked that they had freedom, but "they knew that what they got wasn't what they wanted, it wasn't freedom, really. Had to do whatever the white man directed 'em to do, couldn't voice their heart's desire."[5]

The sugar plantations of Louisiana and the tobacco farms of Virginia and North Carolina usually hired workers for wages rather than as tenants, but their freedom was circumscribed by seasonal employment and low pay. Where families or husbands and fathers migrated in search of employment, wives, mothers, and grandmothers carried the heavy burden of keeping the family clothed, fed, and together. While the husband/father was the head of the household and often authoritarian, the wife/mother worked in the field, prepared the meals, cleaned the cabin, did the laundry, mended the clothes, bore and cared for the children, and, where possible, worked for cash doing odd chores such as sewing, raising chickens, laundering, or occasional domestic service. Their aspirations for their children embraced release from oppressive conditions and focused on education. South Carolinian William Pickens, Yale Phi Beta Kappa, educator, and official of the National Association for the Advancement of Colored People (NAACP), testified out of his own experience that "many an educated Negro owes his enlightenment to the toil and sweat of a mother."[6]

If local obstructions presented baffling barriers for black mothers and families to overcome, national acts and attitudes stood as precipitous mountains. The justices of the U.S. Supreme Court in the 1880s, for example, "shared with other whites a fundamental perception of Negroes as different," vulnerable to "treatment which no classes of whites would have been expected to tolerate." The Court's 1883 decision in *The Civil Rights Cases* invalidating the Civil Rights Act of 1875 has been called "the most important decision of the decade." The Court, through Justice Joseph P. Bradley, denied that individuals' access to places of public accommodation such as hotels and theaters deserved statutory protection against racial discrimination. With reasoning that was inconsistent with previous landmark cases, such as *Prigg v. Pennsylvania* (1842) and *Munn v. Illinois* (1877), the Court held that both civil rights and the public nature of public accommodations were limited and that neither the Thirteenth nor Fourteenth Amendments permitted congressional implementation of the Act. Justice John Marshall Harlan, a southerner and former slaveholder, was the only dissenter. He maintained that the Fourteenth Amendment conferred "a new constitutional right, secured by the grant of State citizenship to colored citizens of the United States," and that this enabled Congress to enact protective legislation.[7]

While the white South rejoiced at this constitutional justification of its stance, northern states tried to rectify the situation. Massachusetts (1865), New York, and Kansas (1874) already had civil rights statutes on their books; states without civil rights laws moved into the void created by the Court's decision. In 1884, Ohio and New Jersey passed civil rights laws, and seven states followed suit in 1885. By 1895 seventeen states had civil rights legislation on their books, a consequence in most instances of African-American persistence. Unhappily, the statutes were weak, penalties a tap on the wrist, and enforcement often lax.[8]

National politics after Reconstruction showed a rapidly declining interest in African Americans on the part of the Republican party. President James A. Garfield believed that education would close the chasm between the races, but he did not live long enough to test his theory. His successor, Chester A. Arthur, had little interest in black people, Republican or otherwise, and, aside from appointing some blacks to patronage positions to maintain party support, he ignored them. Prominent Republicans, such as former Cabinet member and Senator Carl Schurz; George William Curtis, editor of *Harper's Weekly*; E. L. Godkin, editor of *The Nation*; and former abolitionist and Civil War veteran Thomas W. Higginson, came out as Mugwumps, arguing against continuing Republican support of southern black officeholders. The 1884 election victory of Grover Cleveland, a Democrat disinclined to offend the white South, contributed to the diminishing enthusiasm for racial equality.[9]

The black response to this ebbing support by the party of their choice varied by and within sections. Northern blacks, for whom Republican largesse was minuscule, toyed with the idea of leaving the party. T. Thomas Fortune, editor of the New York *Age*, the most prominent black weekly, and an early Mugwump, continued to snipe at blacks who had remained loyal to the Republicans, although he himself returned to the party after the 1884 election. Black leaders who were frustrated by "the systematic proscription of the colored citizens" in northern states, a white paper reported, contributed to "the murmurs of revolt" that were surfacing. A few blacks, hoping for recognition, supported the Prohibition party in 1886, but to no avail.[10]

In the South, white leaders wrestled with the problem of controlling, or canceling out, the black vote. Fraud and intimidation

provided some control, but, although these tactics continued beyond the end of the century, they were uncertain and incomplete.
During the 1880s, African Americans voted in measurable, if de-
creasing, numbers, while the white leadership, primarily the landed
upper-class gentlemen of the "courtly" school of southern politicians, searched for ways to eliminate the black voter by law or constitutional mandate. Georgia, South Carolina, Tennessee, and Florida
introduced the poll tax, multiple box voting, or the secret ballot in
the late 1880s. In the next decade, a flurry of laws further restricted
the franchise by requiring literacy and/or property tests and a demonstrated understanding of a clause in the state constitution. By
1908 all eleven former Confederate states had, either by statute or
constitutional amendment, removed most blacks and a considerable number of poor or illiterate whites from the electorate.

"ONE VOTE LESS." Cartoonist Thomas Nast attacks the cynicism of the *Richmond Whig*
regarding the murder of African Americans in the South, *Harper's Weekly*, August 8, 1868.
Courtesy Library of Congress

Black southern politicians loyal to the Republicans saw their influence and patronage gradually disappear by the mid-1880s. P. B. S. Pinchback of Mississippi, for example, a former lieutenant governor and U.S. Senate nominee, lost his job as surveyor of customs in New Orleans in 1885. He later moved to New York and then to Washington, where he remained influential in African-American circles. D. Augustus Straker of South Carolina, who later became a distinguished Detroit attorney and African-American leader, served for two years as a customs inspector in Charleston before moving on in 1882. These and other southern black leaders, beset by internal division, fraud and violence, and a shrinking pool of supportive voters, "played politics with a desperate air." With the cards stacked against them, they knew they were in a losing game.[11]

Out of the confusion and frustration of African Americans looking for a reassuring political home, Fortune issued a call for an Afro-American National League, which finally met in Chicago in January 1890. Proposing to act on economic issues, it flashed like a rocket over African-American skies, dying as quickly several years later, a victim of shoddy organizing and inadequate financing. In addition, a new element provided competition. The popular farmers' movement of the 1870s, the Grange, began in the next decade to foster splinter groups, which sprang up all over the South. These formed cooperatives and lobbied state legislators for a graduated income tax and railroad and telegraph regulation. In some states these groups, known as Wheels or Alliances, made peace with the Knights of Labor, a national labor union based in the North that was spreading its locals through the South.

Facing the issue of black members, the Wheels, Alliances, and Knights initially welcomed them, but, as the Farmers Alliance grew to become the dominant agricultural organization, it yielded to white majority pressure and spurned black members. Similarly, the Knights of Labor succumbed to opposition from within and from outside of its organization and drifted away from integration and, in the 1890s, into obscurity. The American Federation of Labor, founded in 1881, supplanted the Knights and in 1890 confirmed its commitment to separate unions. A few years earlier, black farmers had formed their own Colored Farmers Alliance, which spread over the South, claiming over a million members and espousing causes similar to those of the white Alliance. From 1889 to 1891, in separate annual conventions held simultaneously with its white counterpart, the Colored Alliance tried to work cooperatively with the white organization, but race-related issues created an unbridgeable gap. The whites' unwillingness to accept black voting and office-holding, added to the threat of Senator Henry Cabot Lodge's Federal Elections Bill of 1890 (which would permit federal investigation of alleged election fraud), split the two Alliances. For African-American laborers and farmers, a few years in the 1880s opened promising vistas of interracial cooperation that quickly closed in the following decade.

When the Alliance movement merged into populism, and populism into the Populist party, blacks found white men such as Tom Watson of Georgia, an outstanding leader, voicing support for their economic interests but not for social equality. The high water mark for the Populists, the presidential election year of 1892, was a trying time for southern blacks, some of whom ended up voting Democratic or Populist. The party's defeat and demise marked the end of black efforts to cooperate on economic and political issues with southern whites. One historian of African-American politics argues that "the bottom was actually reached after 1891." No political measures to assist blacks, such as elections or educational bills, he maintains, can be found between that date and World War I.[12]

The education of blacks was an issue in the late nineteenth century that would not disappear. Reconstruction legislatures dominated by African Americans established school systems that were forward-looking and nondiscriminatory, but these were largely dismantled or seriously underfunded after Reconstruction. In 1882, Senator Henry W. Blair of New Hampshire first introduced an education bill that would have provided millions of dollars to southern black and white schools. Congressional debate was heated, and although the bill passed the Senate three times during the 1880s, it failed passage in the House. On the fourth and final time, in 1890, it lost in the Senate before it reached the House, a victim of the bogey of federal control, sectional animosity, and fear of an educated black population.

The numbers of black students in school had doubled between 1877 and 1887, but still only two-fifths of eligible black children were enrolled. Schools, especially in rural areas, were often dirt-floored log houses without the bare essentials of desks and blackboards. Where cotton, tobacco, sugar, and rice culture prevailed, formal education for black children was hit or miss and brief. "You might find a school close to town somewhere that accommodated the colored," Nate Shaw recalled, "and if you did you were doin [*sic*] well. But out in the country . . . weren't much school [they] could get." When schools existed, they would stay open for a month or two and then close so the children could pick cotton. White schools had much longer terms and better financing. State subsidies for colored schools were small and inadequate; parents often had to make up the difference. Those whose resources would not stretch to include school support kept their children home and at work. Others, especially mothers, for whom their children's education loomed like a bridge to a more responsive world, moved their families to towns and cities where colored schools were better supported and better taught.[13]

For whites, the danger was the extent to which an educated black community would upset the southern caste structure and destroy its labor system. "We must have colored servants," an Alabama minister complained in 1891, "for there is no other laboring class there." A Richmond industrialist and former Confederate general, Thomas Muldrop Logan, agreed, asserting that "when the freedman regards himself qualified to earn a support by mental work he is unwilling to accept manual labor." The result was a flowering of industrial education schools modeled after Hampton Institute in Virginia and, after 1881, Booker T. Washington's Tuskegee Institute in Alabama.[14]

Industrial education meant different things to different people. Tuskegee, the first industrial school managed by blacks, offered a wide range of courses providing agricultural and manual skills. These included, according to the 1883–84 school catalog, "farming, brickmaking, carpentering, printing, black-smithing; and housekeeping and sewing for girls." To these Washington added as future offerings "tinsmithing, shoemaking, painting, and broom-making." His biographer points out that at this early day in the life of Tuskegee Institute, its founder "overstated the industrial offerings" and played down the extensive academic side of the curriculum, which included, among other courses, "Mental and Moral Science, Rhetoric, Grammar and Composition." Nevertheless, training in vocational skills was the major thrust of this and comparable institutions. The irony of industrial education was that it had little to do with the skills required by the rapidly expanding industries: iron, steel, and textiles. It focused instead on the traditional manual trades, and, in that sense, industrial education looked backward rather than forward.[15]

A more unusual and lesser-known side of industrial education was life on the western plains, a form of on-the-job training. The black U.S. 9th and 10th cavalries, known as the buffalo soldiers, policed Indian country from immediately after the Civil War until the Battle of Wounded Knee in December 1890. (The term "buffalo soldiers" is attributed to Native Americans who thought that the black soldiers' hair resembled that of the buffalo.) Tough, battle-scarred veterans, these men erected or refurbished military posts, strung wire, escorted stagecoaches and civilian working parties, opened roads, mapped unknown territories, and located water sources for new settlers. Neither angels nor demons, they were, their biographer concludes, "first-rate regiments." In addition, other African Americans were scattered around the West as lawmen, outlaws, or cowboys, an integral, and occasionally integrated, part of the westward movement.[16]

Richard Wright, the principal of the only colored high school in Georgia, probably did not have buffalo soldiers and black cowboys in mind when he testified before a congressional committee in 1883 "that these differences of race, so-called, are a mere matter of color, and not of brain." Whites in the West were often grateful for law enforcement no matter what the soldiers' color, but white southerners oppressed the race and suppressed opportunities for its development, while white northerners closed their eyes and their minds to race needs. Yet there was plenty of evidence to support Wright's contention that the color issue obscured the race's intellectual and economic potential.[17]

Southern whites justified violence against African-American men and women, for example, out of a fear of color and a denial of brain. The year before Wright testified, the Chicago *Tribune* began to publish statistics on lynching, the most dramatic crime. Between 1882 and 1899 over 2,500 black men and women were lynched, almost half of them between 1889 and 1899. Of the victims 2 percent were women. Accusations of rape, attacks on white women, and occasionally murder were the usual excuses for a lynching, along with a host of lesser allegations. Ida B. Wells, a black newspaperwoman in Memphis, castigated the lynching fever in 1892 in a black newspaper, defending black males against a rape charge and exposing the lawlessness of lynching. She was run out of town for her article, and a mob destroyed the newspaper's office. That year marked the highest number of recorded lynchings, but the practice continued through World War I.[18]

Southern violence against African Americans also occurred in ostensibly legal ways. As the law enforcement system trapped more blacks, prisons expanded, the number of black inmates multiplied, and costs escalated. To offset expenses and occupy prisoners' time, states and counties began leasing convicts to railroad builders, planters, and mine owners for a pittance. "Such a system bred . . . terrible scenes of inhumanity . . . mass sickness, brutal whippings, discarded bodies, near starvation, rape,"[19] and made wealthy capitalists of the lessees. As rumors spread about violence and mistreatment, investigations were mounted, reported, and forgotten. The anxieties of white citizens, stirred by newspaper reports of expanding black crime, made this exploitation of prison labor palatable during the last part of the century.

Toward the end of the century, urban violence erupted on a large scale with an antiblack riot in Wilmington, North Carolina. While federal patronage appointments to postmasterships were an initial irritant, the extremist element in North Carolina whipped up white supremacy sentiment based on protecting white women from black men allegedly intent on ravaging them. Following a heated racist election campaign in November 1898, the victorious Democrats could hardly wait to expel Republican officeholders and frighten a black editor into leaving. When communications between negotiating whites and blacks broke down, the lid blew off. Two days after the election, whites turned their guns on blacks and blood flowed.

Powerless to retard the hysteria or retaliate in kind, blacks depended upon friends to speak up and out. Ten days later the Reverend Francis J. Grimke, the eminent African-American pastor of Washington, DC's, Fifteenth Street Presbyterian Church, preached what a constituent called a "vigorous, courageous and manly denunciation" of the riot and other outrages. Shortly thereafter, he published a pamphlet of four sermons on white oppression. On receipt of a copy, George T. Downing, a black former abolitionist and successful caterer, wrote Grimke that his sermons "bristle all over with the needful, with truth, with proper denunciation, with encouragement."[20]

The Wilmington explosion was the first antiblack urban outburst after the Civil War. It was followed by a series of city riots, all nurtured by a mix of black assertiveness and virulent white hostility and fear. New Orleans boiled over in 1900, Atlanta in 1906, and Springfield, Illinois, two years later. It was the Springfield riot that led the journalist William English Walling to suggest a new interracial organization that would become the NAACP.

Violence was a way of life that surrounded the black community after the Civil War and called for defensive mechanisms other than counterattack. Two such devices, growing naturally out of African-American culture, were a maturing social stratification and an expanding adherence to the church. Even before the war, some northern blacks had developed strong class structures in major cities. Philadelphia was perhaps the prototype, followed by New York and Boston. In Philadelphia a number of families that had amassed wealth—not on the scale of white tycoons, but at a comfortable level—set the pattern. Robert Purvis, a former abolitionist and long-time gentleman farmer, used his talents to expand black opportunities. William Still pulled himself up by his bootstraps to become a leading entrepreneur, primarily in the coal and lumber business. Jacob White, Jr., managed a black cemetery, "the biggest single enterprise run by blacks in Philadelphia." In Boston, three generations of the Ruffin family held sway in black society, with a handful of other similarly light-skinned families. The pattern was comparable in New York, Chicago, and smaller cities such as Cleveland and Pittsburgh.[21]

Major southern cities, including Baltimore, Charleston, and New Orleans, each had its slice of African-American aristocracy, men and women who were sufficiently well-to-do to pay attention to class symbols and society. Sometimes with pre-Civil War roots, the families were headed by physicians, attorneys, bankers, civil servants, or politicians. Wives set the social rules, but many participated as activists in such reform movements as women's rights or education. Smaller southern cities such as Atlanta, Memphis, Augusta, and Little Rock copied their larger sisters; the black elite celebrated their status and the family ties that bound them together.

The city at the apex of black wealth and influence was both southern and national. After the Civil War, Washington attracted politicians and civil servants because of the federal government, educators because of black schools and Howard University, ministers because of the plethora of churches, and business people because of the potential African-American market. Aptly called the "Capital of the Colored Aristocracy," Washington had a population of seventy-five thousand African Americans in 1900, of which fewer than one hundred families could be considered part of the social elite. The family of Senator Blanche K. Bruce of Mississippi was an arbiter of social activity, along with James Wormley, proprietor of the well-known hotel that carried his name, and the Cook brothers, both Oberlin College graduates, one the head of the black school system in the district, the other a District of Columbia tax collector. Grimke, longtime minister of the Fifteenth Street Presbyterian Church, and his wife, Charlotte Forten, of the distinguished Philadelphia family, were notable members of black Washington society.[22]

Black society often took the lead in organizing literary clubs that flourished for a time and then faded, but the impulse for intellectual pursuits persisted. The Grimkes and Anna J. Cooper, an educator with a Sorbonne doctorate, met regularly with others at the Grimke home for discussions of previously assigned books, followed by "small talk and general conversation around Mrs. Grimke's tea table." Dances and cotillions, elaborate weddings, and banquets were common among the elite in all cities. Wisconsin's Senator Timothy Howe was one of four white senators to attend an elaborate dinner at former Lieutenant Governor Pinchback's New Orleans home in 1876. Howe's grudging admiration for the guests ("Some were very dark. Others were very light"), the women's appearance ("All were well dressed and some overdressed"), the entertainment of vocal and instrumental music ("Both showed severe culture"), and the dancing ("Some was very good") also characterized his appreciation of the conversation. "I talked for some time with a sister of James Kennedy, not yet eighteen. I have rarely seen a girl of her years so interesting."[23]

Howe's observation about the guests' light and dark skin confirms scholarly doubts that only light-colored blacks comprised the social elite, while their darker brothers and sisters made up the rank and file. Some evidence in these post-Reconstruction decades suggests that the mixed-blood blacks, or mulattoes, often played leadership roles, especially in the North, but a recent study of five southern cities found "little evidence of color as a badge of special status." White southerners, increasingly appalled by the products of black-white liaisons (for which they or their forebears were largely responsible), gradually tightened state legal strictures against intermarriage, a process that may have slowed down, but could not stop, racial mixing. On the other hand, many northern states, either weary of hostile race legislation or aware of its statutory impotence, repealed their anti-intermarriage laws. Whatever the legal condition, uncounted light-colored blacks continued to pass as white for a first-class train ticket, a hotel room, a job, or, in some cases, for life.[24]

One phenomenon of the African-American class structure before World War I was the absence of a middle class. One could argue that the black elite, for the most part composed of men and women in barbering, teaching, government service, small business, and agriculture or at the lower income end of the professions, was in economic terms a middle class, but those who formed the black elite did not believe that. The underclass, South and North, were the unskilled and semiskilled. In the South they were flattened by lack of cash and credit, lack of upward opportunity, lack of education, and white oppression. In the North, black males held service jobs in restaurants and hotels, drove cartage vehicles and hacks, and were hod carriers, janitors, and miners. Women were cooks, maids, washerwomen, seamstresses, and nursemaids. Factories hired black men for the lowest-paid, lowest-skilled jobs and withheld promotions. Like their southern counterparts, northern blacks lacked access to cash, credit, and upward mobility.

Northern educational opportunities improved as the decades moved toward the new century: schools integrated, black colleges strengthened their offerings, white colleges became more open to blacks, and university graduate schools grew more willing to accept qualified black candidates. The northern underclass, however, faced a double threat from whites; one was an increasing apathy about race matters (what W. E. B. Du Bois called "negative indifference, positive prejudice"), and the second was intense competition from southern European immigrants who flooded the country from the 1880s to just after World War I. Slowly but surely in that period, immigrants took over barbering, waiting, domestic service, and other menial positions in which blacks had once been dominant.

As the northern black underclass was slowly pushed aside by European immigrants, the northern black urban elite felt threatened by black migrants from the South. The fragile stability and substance, as well as the limited advancement and promise that the black elite had achieved in cities such as Detroit, Boston, Philadelphia, and New York, began to dissipate and destruct with the increasing influx of southern blacks who were less educated, farm-oriented, and often darker in color, with different speech, home life, and religious patterns. Black society was "a small group growing by accretions from without," Du Bois affirmed in 1901, "but at

the same time . . . overwhelmed by [the migrants]." This undermining of the black elite's carefully constructed modus operandi vis-à-
vis the white community and within the black community
undoubtedly contributed to the urban chaos that accompanied the
influx of masses of southern black migrants during and after World
War I.[25]

If there was a tie that binds for the African-American community, it was the fiber of religious belief, worship, and institutions.
The church, before and immediately following the Civil War, was
an incubator for African-American leaders. Men such as Peter Williams, Henry Highland Garnet, J. W. C. Pennington, and Lott Cary
stood out in public as well as in the pulpit. "Churches were the
largest and most elaborate economic, social, and political institutions organized by African-Americans" before World War II, one
historian recently asserted. Their "ritual behavior"—that is, what
blacks did in church, at camp meetings, and in prayer groups—was
not, as another scholar has demonstrated, "an ecstatic jumble," although countless white contemporaries and some black clergymen
thought so. Rather, black liturgy from slavery onward was a rich
meld of African tradition, black American experience, and white
American practices, varying from region to region, from denomination to denomination, and from church to church.[26]

The African-American church began before American independence, splintering over the decades into about nine major
denominations and myriad smaller sects. By the end of the nineteenth century the Negro Baptists had the most members, over two
million, followed by the most prominent Methodist Episcopal (ME)
denominations (African ME [AME], AME Zion, and Colored ME)
with slightly over one million members. The Presbyterians, Epis-
copalians, Congregationalists, Catholics, and the miscellany of
smaller independent denominations attracted many fewer commu-
nicants. Most mainstream bodies organized separate divisions for
their black churches but retained control over clergy appointments
and influenced financial and church building decisions. The black
Baptist congregations, however, were autonomous, reporting to no
higher administrative authority. This was one major reason for their
popularity.[27]

Church liturgy in this period roughly divided according to economic class. The upper-class blacks tended to deprecate emotional
outbursts, although their services were considerably more partici-
patory and warmer in feeling than those of their white counterparts.

The underclass, as a general rule, was more open and more inclusive: sermons invited responses, hymns were sung with abandon. The ring shout, traceable to African practice, was a popular camp meeting or after-the-service ritual, marked by men and women chanting religious songs as they moved in a circle, slowly increasing the pace, the tempo, and the volume until exhaustion and ecstasy set in.[28]

While the service was central to their belief, African Americans depended on the church for other activities. The minister, poorly paid and sometimes not well educated, was a key figure who often moved his church into secular education (reading and writing), fund-raising for both the church and the black community, sickness and burial benefit societies, and, quietly, occasional political activity. The multiple organizations that emerged in black communities, North and South, were generated by or connected to the church: the Odd Fellows, the Masons, literary clubs, sewing groups, and social gatherings. It was in the church and these related activities that African Americans just out of slavery learned how to organize, handle meetings, resolve internal conflict, persuade the outside public, and protect the rights of their community. For the most part excluded from white associations, African Americans had to be self-taught by experience, and they proved to be able learners. "The church," Du Bois concluded in 1899, "is a centre of social life and intercourse; acts as newspaper and intelligence bureau, is the centre of amusements—indeed, is the world in which the Negro moves and acts." Although Du Bois was writing about Philadelphia, his conclusion could apply to most black churches, North and South.[29]

The decade of the 1890s was a crucial period in determining the future of race relations, in both the North and the South. In the North, states slowly responded to black pressures for civil rights acts. Segregated schools could be found in some northern cities, large and small, although by 1900 most northern states had prohibited separate schools based on race. City neighborhoods that were loosely defined by race after the Civil War were tightening into black enclaves and restricted white areas. In larger cities, by 1900, some enclaves had begun to take on the character of ghettos. In the South, segregation became the common pattern for schools, housing, and businesses. Encouraged by a series of Supreme Court decisions, states gradually segregated transportation facilities.

The key case was *Plessy v. Ferguson* in 1896 in which a majority found a Louisiana segregation law constitutional. The law required separate accommodations on railroads for blacks and whites, and the Court's opinion, written by Justice Henry B. Brown, a native of Massachusetts, held that this restriction did not infringe upon the liberty of black people enunciated by the Thirteenth Amendment or their rights as citizens guaranteed by the Fourteenth Amendment. Justice Brown denied that the law would lead to an expansion of segregation statutes and practices (he was wrong) and claimed that segregation would be "a badge of inferiority" only if "the colored race chooses to put that construction on it." The lone dissenter, Justice Harlan, demolished the majority argument in a stirring and brilliant opinion that correctly labeled as a "thin disguise" the belief that separate could be equal. In a memorable sentence, he declared that "our Constitution is color-blind and neither knows nor tolerates classes among citizens."[30]

The year before the *Plessy* decision, Frederick Douglass died. His fame as an abolitionist carried him into Republican politics after the Civil War, and he became a guiding star for many African Americans. Douglass held several federal posts and served as marshal of the District of Columbia (1877–1881), recorder of deeds of the District of Columbia (1881–1886), and minister to Haiti (1889–1891). He used his prominence, along with a skillful pen, superb oratory, and access to government officials, to advance his ideas, often in the face of younger, quite vociferous critics. He stood for trying to work with whites and against the "go-it-alone" approach of some black leaders. He deplored the Kansas exodus of 1879, denounced the Supreme Court's 1883 civil rights decision, accepted the election of Democrat Grover Cleveland, and decried the formation of the Afro-American National League. Although he wanted blacks to speak and act for themselves, he firmly believed in racial cooperation and integration. After his wife's death, he married a white woman who had worked for him in the Recorder's Office. "The most prominent Negro of the day," a biographer noted, "his words carried weight on both sides of the color line."[31]

Several months after Douglass's death, Booker T. Washington, destined to be the best-known black leader prior to World War I, delivered a speech before a predominantly white audience at the Atlanta Cotton Exposition, urging racial separation in social matters and cooperation in economic spheres. Do not "permit our grievances to overshadow our opportunities," he counseled his race, reminding whites that the black millions could help by "pulling the load upward or they will pull against you the load downward." The speech, later called the Atlanta Compromise, became a rationale for justifying segregation, disfranchisement, and limited educational opportunities. Born into slavery and educated at Hampton Institute in Virginia, Washington was appointed principal of Tuskegee Institute in 1881, before it opened. Slowly but steadily, with the help of black and white supporters, he made Tuskegee a model for black industrial education schools. He frequently traveled north as a fundraiser and public speaker, offering wealthy northerners an opportunity to let their gifts to Tuskegee and other black schools substitute for substance in the fight for equality. Behind the scenes, Washington advised President Theodore Roosevelt on appointments, worked for black enfranchisement, fought discrimination where he could, and subsidized a network of black journals and politicians who fed him information and responded to his instructions about what to write, whom to praise, whom to attack, and what strategy to use in national, state, and local issues.[32]

The year of the *Plessy* decision, 1896, also saw the awarding of the first Harvard Ph.D. to a black person, W. E. B. Du Bois, whose scholarly talents bore fruit immediately with the publication of his dissertation, *The Suppression of the African Slave Trade* (Cambridge, 1896); a detailed historical and sociological study, *The Philadelphia Negro* (Philadelphia, 1899); and a groundbreaking series of race studies published by Atlanta University (1898–1911). After the turn of the century, he opposed Washington's accommodationist philosophy, took a leading role in organizing the NAACP, and became the first editor of its magazine, *The Crisis*.

While black men occupied an 1890s spotlight, the women of the race were moving on stage. Ida B. Wells's antilynching crusade continued into the next century. Victoria Earle Matthews organized the White Rose Mission and Industrial Association in New York City in 1897 to assist new black arrivals. "Our women," Fannie Barrier Williams, a member of Chicago's black elite, told the World's Congress of Representative Women in 1893, "have the same spirit and mettle that characterize the best of American women." They asked only for the same opportunity to acquire knowledge that was available to other women, after which, she promised, "the exceptional career of our women will yet stamp itself indelibly upon the thought of this country."[33]

Even as Williams was speaking—and she would go on to establish a commendable career encouraging black women to stand up for their rights—others were organizing to defend their character and capabilities. Josephine St. Pierre Ruffin of Boston, Mary Church Terrell of Washington, and Mary Margaret Washington of Tuskegee were working on behalf of women in their local areas when the need for a national organization became clear. In 1896 they and others established the National Association of Colored Women (NACW), combining "the resources and energies of scores of local and regional clubs into one strong organization in order to attack the prevailing negative image of black womanhood." It grew rapidly, defying the image of inferiority attached to black women and aggressively describing their potential, as Terrell defined it in her 1897 presidential address, to "become partners in the great firm of progress and reform." The women of the race were preparing to battle against a pernicious pair: racism and sexism.[34]

Two Ohio literary figures contributed significantly to the decade of the 1890s. Paul Laurence Dunbar's third book of poetry, *Lyrics of Lowly Life* (New York, 1897), achieved national notice. His dialect poems were superb renditions of a widespread patois, which appealed to whites but confirmed their racial condescension. His short stories, according to one critic, mirrored "the white man's definitions of reality." Not above writing lyrics for minstrel shows and "music-hall entertainments familiarly known as 'coon shows,' " Dunbar also wrote undeniably moving protest poetry. "I know why the caged bird sings, ah me," he intoned, ". . . when he beats his bars and would be free." Dunbar died of tuberculosis in his thirty-third year, his short life torn by the tension between popularity and protest.

While Dunbar was struggling for and with recognition, Charles W. Chesnutt was publishing short stories in national magazines, taking subtle stands against plantation life and racial discrimination. In 1899, "a banner year," Chesnutt published two books of short stories and a brief biography of Frederick Douglass. His second novel, published in 1901, "prompted" by the Wilmington riot, "was an angry protest" against southern disfranchisement of blacks. In the 1890s the literary accomplishments of a race still "caged" began to get national attention.[35]

The late nineteenth century has been described by one eminent historian, Rayford W. Logan, as the "nadir" for blacks in *The Negro in American Life and Thought: The Nadir, 1877–1901* (New York, 1954). For a generation this view has held sway, but it is a skewed perspective. Looking at southern and northern whites who perpetrated the physical violence, economic repression, political exclusion, and social ostracism, one could call the period a low point in their existence. Whites created and sustained the conditions and the atmosphere that deprived African Americans of their rights as citizens and human beings. The term "nadir" applies to white communities, North and South, that constructed and enforced a containment barrier around the black community.

For blacks, the late nineteenth century witnessed elements of success in a struggle against great odds. In spite of the oppression, the black community developed a faithful and fruitful life for itself, keeping family ties whole, making do with less than enough money, nurturing male and female leaders, preparing to organize to defend its rights, improving educational opportunities, and fostering literary and artistic achievement. This was no small accomplishment in the face of blanketing, breath-denying opposition; in this sense, the "nadir" term does not fit the black community.

Du Bois emerged in the early twentieth century as a major proponent of the counterattack against white deprivations. His book *The Souls of Black Folk: Essays and Sketches* (Chicago, 1903) is still a classic. In one essay he praised Booker T. Washington for preaching "thrift, patience, and industrial training," and then criticized him harshly when Washington "apologizes for injustice," concedes disfranchisement, minimizes the effect of "caste distinctions," and "opposes the higher training and ambition of our brighter minds."

Du Bois set the tone for the century to come. "One ever feels his two-ness," he admitted, "an American, a Negro . . . two warring ideals in one dark body." His confession was not so much personal as communal; he spoke for his race. And he went on to prophesy with amazing accuracy. "The problem of the twentieth century," he wrote, "is the problem of the color line" all over the world.[36]

The last decades of the nineteenth century set the stage for the next one hundred years: an obdurate white attitude in conflict with a growing black aggressiveness and maturing appreciation of self, family, traditions, and the creative instinct. These are contributions of the Gilded Age to posterity.

Notes

1. *The Christian Recorder*, July 18, 1868. The *Recorder* misprints his middle initial as "B." For a biographical sketch of Matthews see William J. Simmons, *Men of Mark: Eminent, Progressive, and Rising* (Cleveland, 1890), 167–74.

2. U.S. Bureau of the Census, *Negro Population, 1790–1915* (Washington, DC, 1918), 43–44 (Table 13), 92 (Table 9), 93 (Table 10), 95–105 (Table 12). For an explanation of the complexity of using demographic data see William Cohen, *At Freedom's Edge: Black Mobility and the Southern White Quest for Racial Control, 1861–1915* (Baton Rouge, LA, 1991), Appendix A, 299–300. The 50 percent figure is derived from his Table 4, p. 93.

3. Cohen, *At Freedom's Edge*, 127.

4. The substance of this paragraph comes from Nell Irvin Painter's superb study, *Exodusters: Black Migration to Kansas after Reconstruction* (New York, 1977). The quotations are on pp. 185, 176, and 190.

5. Jay R. Mandle, *Not Slave, Not Free: The African American Experience since the Civil War* (Durham, NC, 1992), 33–35, 37–40 (Tables 5, 6). For the "military agriculture" quotations see Edgar T. Thompson, *Plantation Societies, Race Relations, and the South: The Regimentation of Populations* (Durham, NC, 1975), 217. The man's quotation is in Theodore Rosengarten, *All God's Dangers: The Life of Nate Shaw* (New York, 1975), 8. T. Thomas Fortune, the brilliant but erratic black journalist, put the issue succinctly in 1884: "To tell a man he is free when he has neither money nor the opportunity to make it, is simply to mock him." *Black and White: Land, Labor, and Politics in the South* (1884; reprint ed., New York, 1969), 36.

6. Jacqueline Jones, *Labor of Love, Labor of Sorrow: Black Women, Work, and the Family from Slavery to the Present* (New York, 1985), chapter 3, 79–109. Quotation is on p. 96.

7. J. R. Pole, *The Pursuit of Equality in American History* (Berkeley, 1978), 188–94. Quotations are on pp. 188, 191, and 194.

8. Leslie H. Fishel, Jr., "The Genesis of the First Wisconsin Civil Rights Act," *Wisconsin Magazine of History* 49, no. 4 (Summer 1966): 326.

9. This is a very brief summary of events chronicled in several books, notably Stanley P. Hirshson, *Farewell to the Bloody Shirt: Northern Republicans and the Southern Negro, 1877–1893* (1962; reprint ed., Gloucester, MA, 1968), 88–135. The term "Mugwump," derived from a New England Indian word, was applied first to Republicans in 1884 who came out against presidential nominee James G. Blaine, and then to all independent Republicans.

10. Leslie H. Fishel, Jr., "The Negro in Northern Politics," *Mississippi Valley Historical Review* 42, no. 3 (December 1955): 480–81.

11. J. Morgan Kousser, *The Shaping of Southern Politics: Suffrage Restriction and the Establishment of the One-Party South, 1880–1910* (New Haven, CT, 1974), 247, for "courtly"; Edward L. Ayers, *The Promise of the New South: Life after Reconstruction* (New York, 1992), 34–53; see p. 42 for "desperate." The secret

ballot, considered an election reform in northern urban centers, was used in the South to exclude voters who had difficulty in deciphering a complicated ballot in the isolation of a voting booth.

12. For a full account of the Afro-American League see Emma Lou Thornbrough, *T. Thomas Fortune: Militant Journalist* (Chicago, 1972), chap. 4. The literature on the Farmers' Alliances and Knights of Labor is extensive. I have used the excellent summaries in Ayers, *Promise of the New South*, chaps. 9, 10. The quotation is from Hirshson, *Farewell to the Bloody Shirt*, 251.

13. James M. McPherson, *The Abolitionist Legacy: From Reconstruction to the NAACP* (Princeton, NJ, 1975), 128–31; Rosengarten, *All God's Dangers*, 25; Jones, *Labor of Love*, 97–99.

14. Leslie H. Fishel, Jr., "The 'Negro Question' at Mohonk: Microcosm, Mirage, and Message," *New York History* 74, no. 3 (July 1993): 296 (1891 quotation); James D. Anderson, *The Education of Blacks in the South, 1860–1935* (Chapel Hill, NC, 1988), 27–28 (General Logan's quotation).

15. Louis R. Harlan, *Booker T. Washington: The Making of a Black Leader, 1856–1901* (New York, 1972), 140; August Meier, *Negro Thought in America, 1880–1915: Racial Ideologies in the Age of Booker T. Washington* (Ann Arbor, MI, 1963), 85–99, has an able summary of the growth of industrial education.

16. William H. Leckie, *The Buffalo Soldiers: A Narrative of the Negro Cavalry in the West* (Norman, OK, 1967), 260.

17. Anderson, *The Education of Blacks*, 30.

18. Ida Wells-Barnett, *On Lynchings* (New York, 1969) (reprints of her pamphlets published in 1892, 1895, and 1900), "Southern Horrors," 4–24, "Mob Rule in New Orleans," 46–47. Ida B. Wells married in 1895 and took the name Wells-Barnett. She became an influential leader in Chicago and a founding participant of the NAACP.

19. Ayers, *Promise of the New South*, 154.

20. Joel Williamson, *The Crucible of Race: Black-White Relations in the American South since Emancipation* (New York, 1984), 195–201; M. M. Smith to Grimke, November 20, 1898, and Downing to Grimke, February 22, 1899, in Francis J. Grimke, *The Works of Francis J. Grimke*, ed. Carter G. Woodson (Washington, DC, 1942), 4:52, 54–55. Several other prominent men and women of both races acknowledged with pleasure the Grimke pamphlet, ibid., 55–69.

21. Roger Lane, *William Dorsey's Philadelphia and Ours: On the Past and Future of the Black City in America* (New York, 1991), 107 (quotation), 98–133; Elizabeth H. Pleck, *Black Migration and Poverty: Boston, 1865–1900* (New York, 1979), 93–94. See also Roi Ottley and William J. Weatherby, eds., *The Negro in New York: An Informal Social History, 1826–1940* (New York, 1967), 133–35; and Allan H. Spear, *Black Chicago: The Making of a Negro Ghetto, 1890–1920* (Chicago, 1967), 51–70.

22. The most informative source on the black aristocracy is Willard B. Gatewood, *Aristocrats of Color: The Black Elite, 1880–1920* (Bloomington, IN, 1990). The quotation is from a chapter heading, p. 39. The traditional account of blacks in the District of Columbia is Constance M. Green, *The Secret City: A History of Race Relations in the Nation's Capital* (Princeton, NJ, 1967).

23. Anna J. Cooper, *Personal Recollections of the Grimke Family* (n.p.: Anna J. Cooper, 1951), 1:11–12; Timothy O. Howe to Grace, December 25, 1876, Timothy O. Howe Papers, Box 2, The State Historical Society of Wisconsin, Madison. See also Maggie Riechers, "The Herndons: The Black Upper Class at

the Turn of the Century," *Humanities* 14, no. 5 (September/October 1993): 24–27.

24. Howard N. Rabinowitz, *Race Relations in the Urban South, 1865–1890* (New York, 1978), 249. See also Joel Williamson, *New People: Miscegenation and Mulattoes in the United States* (New York, 1980), 82, 92–96, 100–103.

25. W. E. B. Du Bois, *The Black North in 1901: A Social Study* (New York, 1969 [originally appeared as a series of articles in the *New York Times*, November/December, 1901]), 43, 39; Robert Gregg, *Sparks from the Anvil of Oppression* (Philadelphia, 1993), 23–24, disputes Du Bois and argues that Philadelphia blacks adjusted to the pre-World War I influx, but points out (n7) that Detroit was not able to. The southern migration to Boston created class division and tension, and although migrants did eventually join fraternal organizations and sororities, they generally lived in separate neighborhoods, according to Pleck, *Black Migration*, 75–85.

26. Gregg, *Sparks from the Anvil*, 1; Walter F. Pitts, *Old Ship of Zion: Afro-Baptist Ritual in the African Diaspora* (New York, 1993), 8.

27. U.S. Bureau of the Census, *Negroes in the United States, 1920–1932* (Washington, DC, 1935), Table 11, 551–52. The data are from 1906, the year of the first religious census. The total black church membership, adults and children, in that year was 3,691,844, out of a total black population of about 9,300,000.

28. Ellen Southern, "The Religious Occasion," in C. Eric Lincoln, ed., *The Black Experience in Religion* (Garden City, NY, 1974), 60–63.

29. Lincoln, *The Black Experience*, 65; W. E. B. Du Bois, *The Philadelphia Negro: A Social Study* (Philadelphia, 1899), 201.

30. Otto H. Olsen, *The Thin Disguise: Turning Point in Negro History, Plessy v. Ferguson, A Documentary Presentation (1864–1896)* (New York, 1967), 111–12, 117, 120. Olsen's "Introduction" is helpful (1–28) but should be read with Andrew Kull, *The Color-Blind Constitution* (Cambridge, MA, 1992), which argues that an arbitrary color-blind reading of the Constitution is inaccurate and fails to account for legislative, judicial, and administrative rulings which, both favorably and unfavorably, are based on racial classifications.

31. Benjamin Quarles, "Frederick Douglass," in Rayford W. Logan and Michael R. Winston, *Dictionary of American Negro Biography* (New York, 1982), 181–86. The quotation is on p. 185.

32. The quotations are in Booker T. Washington, *Up from Slavery: An Autobiography* (1901; reprint ed., Garden City, NY, 1937), 220, 222. For other biographical details see Harlan, *Washington*.

33. Fannie Barrier Williams, "The Intellectual Progress of the Colored Women of the United States since the Emancipation Proclamation," in Bert James Loewenberg and Ruth Bogin, eds., *Black Women in Nineteenth-Century American Life: Their Words, Their Thoughts, Their Feelings* (University Park, PA, 1976), 273.

34. Darlene Clark Hine, "Lifting the Veil, Shattering the Silence: Black Women's History in Slavery and Freedom," in Hine, ed., *The State of Afro-American History: Past, Present, and Future* (Baton Rouge, LA, 1986), 236–37.

35. Robert Bone, *Down Home: A History of Afro-American Short Fiction from the Beginning to the End of the Harlem Renaissance* (New York, 1975), 52, 79. The poetry lines are from "Sympathy" in Lida Keck Wiggins, *The Life and Works of Paul Laúrence Dunbar* (New York, 1907), 207.

36. Du Bois, *Souls of Black Folk*, 59, 3, 13.

Suggestions for Further Reading

Anderson, James D. *The Education of Blacks in the South, 1860–1935.* Chapel Hill, NC, 1988.

Ayers, Edward L. *The Promise of the New South: Life after Reconstruction.* New York, 1992.

Burton, Art. *Black, Red, and Deadly: Black and Indian Gunfighters of the Indian Territory, 1870–1907.* Austin, TX, 1991.

Cohen, William. *At Freedom's Edge: Black Mobility and the Southern White Quest for Racial Control, 1861–1915.* Baton Rouge, LA, 1991.

Durham, Philip, and Everett L. Jones. *The Negro Cowboys.* New York, 1965.

Foner, Philip S. *Organized Labor and the Black Worker.* New York, 1974.

Fredrickson, George M. *The Black Image in the White Mind: The Debate on Afro-American Character and Destiny, 1817–1914.* New York, 1971.

Gatewood, Willard B. *Aristocrats of Color: The Black Elite, 1880–1920.* Bloomington, IN, 1990.

Harlan, Louis R. *Booker T. Washington: The Making of a Black Leader, 1856–1901.* New York, 1972.

Hirshson, Stanley P. *Farewell to the Bloody Shirt: Northern Republicans and the Southern Negro, 1877–1893.* Gloucester, MA, 1968.

Jones, Jacqueline. *Labor of Love, Labor of Sorrow: Black Women, Work, and the Family from Slavery to the Present.* New York, 1985.

Leckie, William H. *The Buffalo Soldiers: A Narrative of the Negro Cavalry in the West.* Norman, OK, 1967.

Lewis, David Levering. *W. E. B. Du Bois: Biography of a Race, 1868–1919.* New York, 1993.

Mandle, Jay R. *Not Slave, Not Free: The African-American Experience since the Civil War.* Durham, NC, 1992.

McFeely, William S. *Frederick Douglass.* New York, 1991.

Meier, August. *Negro Thought in America, 1880–1915: Racial Ideologies in the Age of Booker T. Washington.* Ann Arbor, MI, 1963.

Montgomery, William E. *Under Their Own Vine and Fig Tree: The African-American Church in the South, 1865–1900.* Baton Rouge, LA, 1993.

Pitts, Walter F. *Old Ship of Zion: Afro-Baptist Ritual in the African Diaspora.* New York, 1993.

Rabinowitz, Howard. *Race Relations in the Urban South, 1865–1890.* New York, 1978.

Shapiro, Herbert. *White Violence and Black Response: From Reconstruction to Montgomery.* Amherst, MA, 1988.

Thornbrough, Emma Lou. *T. Thomas Fortune: Militant Journalist.* Chicago, 1972.

Williamson, Joel. *The Crucible of Race: Black-White Relations in the American South since Emancipation.* New York, 1984.

————. *New People: Miscegenation and Mulattoes in the United States.* New York, 1980.

Woodward, C. Vann. *The Strange Career of Jim Crow.* 3d rev. ed. New York, 1974.

8

Native American Resistance and Accommodation during the Late Nineteenth Century

Edmund J. Danziger, Jr.

Long ago the Arapahoes had a fine country of their own. The white man came to see them, and the Indians gave him buffalo meat and a horse to ride on, and they told him the country was big enough for the white man and the Arapahoes, too.

After a while the white men found gold in our country. They took the gold and pushed the Indian from his home. I thought Washington would make it all right. I am an old man now. I have been waiting many years for Washington to give us our rights.

—Little Raven, Arapaho
Vanderwerth, *Indian Oratory* (p. 144)

If the Great Spirit had desired me to be a white man he would have made me so in the first place. He put in your heart certain wishes and plans, in my heart he put other and different desires. Each man is good in his sight. It is not necessary for eagles to be crows. Now we are poor but we are free. No white man controls our footsteps. If we must die we die defending our rights.

—Sitting Bull, Sioux
Armstrong, *I Have Spoken* (p. 112)

I know that my race must change. We can not hold our own with the white men as we are. We only ask an even chance to live as other men live. We ask to be recognized as men. We ask that the same law shall work alike on all men. . . . Whenever the white man treats the Indians as they treat each other, then we will have no more wars. We shall all

be alike—brothers of one father and one mother, with one sky above
us and one country around us, and one government for all.

—Chief Joseph, Nez Percé
Moquin and Van Doren, *Great Documents* (p. 251)

Unbridled greed, exploitation of natural resources, enormous business profits, bloody racial conflict, cultural repression, and despair
characterized the three decades following the Civil War when the
American West was transformed. U.S. citizens and their families
surged like a tidal wave across the Great Plains and beyond, home-
steading farms, exterminating millions of buffalo and replacing them
with herds of white-faced cattle, digging gold and silver from the
mountainsides, and binding the Mississippi Valley to the West Coast
with iron rails. These momentous events overwhelmed some aboriginal peoples. "When the buffalo went away," remarked the aged
Crow, Chief Plenty-Coups, "the hearts of my people fell to the
ground, and they could not lift them up again."[1] Other leaders, such
as Sitting Bull and Chief Joseph, fought on, either militarily or using accommodation strategies. Their story is the subject of this essay, which also examines how federal Indian policymakers tried to
improve conditions among displaced Native peoples. Sadly, by the
1890s the reservation scene suggested the unfulfilled hopes of both
aboriginal leaders and altruistic "Friends of the Indian."

Post-Civil War America alarmed Native peoples of the trans-
Mississippi West, many of whom maintained their nomadic and
seminomadic hunter-gatherer life-styles. The U.S. Census Bureau
estimated in 1870 that of the 383,712 Indians, 234,740 still freely
roamed the western territories and states. Most nomads lived in
Alaska (70,000), Arizona (27,700), Nevada (16,220), Montana
(19,330), Dakota Territory (26,320), and in present-day Oklahoma
(34,400).[2] What threatened their world was the rapid influx of pioneers with eyes fixed on aboriginal lands suitable for farming, ranching, lumbering, mining, town sites, and railroad rights-of-way.
Settlers expected federal Indian Office agents and U.S. Army troops
to support their countrymen by cajoling or forcing Native inhabitants off most of the land. At this point the often cordial relations
between Indians and newcomers, referred to by Little Raven, turned
sour and then bloody as many Indian families and their leaders tenaciously fought to save their homelands.

When confronted with "Indian trouble," federal policymakers
usually believed that they had no choice but to remove Native im-

pediments to the nation's expansion. Congress's initial strategy was to dispatch peace commissioners, including Civil War hero William T. Sherman, in hopes of concentrating nomadic tribes in either present-day South Dakota or Oklahoma, away from the major overland trails and railroad routes. Kiowa, Comanche, Kiowa-Apache, Cheyenne, Arapaho, and Sioux leaders negotiated a series of treaties in the mid-1860s that promised to restore peace and pledged the Natives to make way for white settlers. Neither side, however, listened carefully and respectfully to the views of the other, nor were the Indians convinced about the need to alter their traditional ways of life.[3] At the Medicine Lodge Treaty Council in October 1867, for example, Comanche Chief Ten Bears asserted:

> You said that you wanted to put us upon a reservation, to build us houses and to make us Medicine lodges [schools and churches]. I do not want them.
>
> I was born upon the prairie, where the wind blew free, and there was nothing to break the light of the sun. I was born where there were no enclosures, and where everything drew a free breath. I want to die there, and not within walls. I know every stream and every wood between the Rio Grande and the Arkansas. I have hunted and lived over that country. I lived like my fathers before me, and like them, I lived happily.[4]

With many Indians holding this kind of attitude, sporadic fighting thus persisted across the Plains and beyond the Rockies.

Crazy Horse, Sitting Bull, Geronimo, Cochise, Chief Joseph— their names resounded down through the decades and became symbols of Indian determination to control their hunting grounds and retain established ways of life. Their struggle with U.S. military forces during the late nineteenth century comprises one of the best-known chapters in American history.

Triggered by white encroachment on Indian lands, cultural differences, and the federal government's determination to use force if necessary to concentrate the tribes on small reservations, the Indian wars lasted well into the 1870s. U.S. soldiers, conditioned by formal warfare on eastern Civil War battlefields, had difficulty coping with the semiarid western terrain and the martial skills of elusive, unorthodox fighters who often had no permanent villages to attack or crops to destroy. To elude the blue coats, hostiles sometimes found sanctuary and sustenance among peaceful fellow tribesmen living on reservations under the jurisdiction of civilian Indian agents. Yet time was on the Army's side as railroads crisscrossed the West, more and more settlers appropriated Indian resources, and buffalo—the Plains Indians' staff of life—were slaughtered by the millions. Individualistic Native societies also had difficulty uniting as tribes or forming intertribal alliances against the white invaders with their superior numbers, Indian scouts, railroads, telegraph lines, and mass-produced tools of war.[5]

Until the collapse of armed resistance, the Natives, who had much at stake, fought back stubbornly and often brilliantly, considering the odds. On the southern Plains, for example, reservation life galled the Kiowas, Comanches, Southern Cheyennes, and Southern Arapahoes. Farming failed to feed the warriors' families, Washington sent inadequate supplementary rations, whiskey hucksters sowed discontent, and whites nibbled at the edges of Native lands and slaughtered the buffalo for their hides, leaving the carcasses to rot. These circumstances provoked aboriginal peoples, who hungered for the old ways and were willing to fight rather than endure more reservation life. Kiowa Chief Satanta spoke for many when he said that "I love the land and the buffalo and will not part with it. . . . I have heard that you intend to settle us on a reservation near the mountains. I don't want to settle. I love to roam over the prairies. There I feel free and happy, but when we settle down we grow pale and die."[6] Partly out of desperation, the tribes sent hunting/raiding parties into Texas, Kansas, and Nebraska. Led by Satanta and other recalcitrant warrior-buffalo hunters, the southern Plains tribes fought against Washington's concentration policy for nearly a decade. The largest outbreak of hostilities was the Red River War of 1874–75. The Indians, finally overpowered, surrendered their weapons and horses and saw their leaders shipped off to prison in Florida.[7] Peace returned to the Plains south of the Platte River but at great cost to the aboriginal inhabitants.

Meanwhile, in the Southwest, reservation life together with further land losses drove many Apaches to take to the warpath rather than surrender their freedom and homeland. "This is the country of the Chiricahua Apaches," Chief Cochise once asserted. He continued:

> This is the country where the Chiricahua Apaches belong. The mountains and the valleys, the days and the nights belong to the Chiricahua Apaches. It was so from the memory of the oldest man, and that memory comes from the oldest man ahead of him. There was none but the Indian here and the land was filled with food. The Indians could make a living for themselves. The men

with steel came and tried to take it from us and we defeated them. Now the Americans—and none is more treacherous than the Americans, and none more arrogant. The Americans think they are better than other men. They make their own laws and say those laws must be obeyed. Why?[8]

Led by Cochise, Victorio, Nana, and Geronimo, the Apaches fought intermittently until the mid-1880s, but their fate was similar to that of the southern Plains tribes: military power forever broken and leaders imprisoned.[9] The Apaches thus resigned themselves to reservation life as had their Navajo and Pueblo neighbors.

The story repeated itself with some variations in the Pacific Northwest and on the northern Plains, where reservation conditions, slipshod federal management, and charismatic Native leaders encouraged some groups to resist militarily. On the California-Oregon border, for instance, the Modocs refused to share a reservation with the Klamaths, and under Captain Jack the Modocs kept escaping back to their former home at Tule Lake. Following a brief war in 1872, Washington removed the tribe to the Quapaw Agency in Oklahoma. The Modocs' exile lasted until 1909.[10] In another example, the refusal of some Nez Percés to settle on the Lapwai reservation and their subsequent 1,300-mile flight toward Canada is well chronicled. Following Chief Joseph's surrender in 1877, his people were also held as prisoners of war in Oklahoma.[11] Joseph's famous surrender speech (to General Nelson A. Miles in Montana's Bear Paw Mountains) and subsequent remarks to American audiences and policymakers reflected the Indians' frustration as wards of the government.

I have heard talk and talk, but nothing is done. Good words do not last long unless they amount to something. Words do not pay for my dead people. They do not pay for my country, now overrun by white men. . . . Good words will not give my people good health and stop them from dying. Good words will not get my people a home where they can live in peace and take care of themselves. I am tired of talk that comes to nothing. . . . You might as well expect the rivers to run backwards as that any man who was born a free man should be contented when penned up and denied liberty to go where he pleases.[12]

Many Sioux and northern Cheyennes also resisted being penned up on reservations that were poorly managed, ill suited to agriculture, and constantly encroached upon by land-hungry whites. Under the leadership of Red Cloud, Crazy Horse, Sitting Bull, and others, they fought for their freedom and their hunting grounds. First the white man promised "that the buffalo country should be left to us forever," Sitting Bull claimed. "Now they threaten to take that away from us. My brothers, shall we submit or shall we say to them: 'First kill me before you take possession of my Fatherland.' "[13] Not until 1877 did peace return to the northern Plains, and with the Indian barrier breached, white settlers quickly spread across the grasslands.[14]

The Indian wars, sparked by Washington's determination to concentrate all Native peoples on restricted reservations, were full of significance. They opened vast natural resources to non-Natives, although the cost was high. Between 1866 and 1891 regular U.S. troops fought 1,065 "actions" with Indians, and the War Department kept an average of 16,000 officers and men on active duty.[15] Concerns about the frontier Indian danger had been an integral part of the nation's story since its founding a century earlier. Now the country faced an equally perplexing problem: what role should former warriors and their families play in American society? From their perspective, the Sioux, Nez Percés, Modocs, Apaches, and other tribes—militarily humbled and stripped of their livelihoods—must have wondered, too, about their future as Uncle Sam's wards. The answers came quickly. Once gathered onto reservations, America's Native peoples found themselves caught up in a new struggle for their children, for their identities, and for their souls.

Mark Twain astutely observed that "soap and education are not as sudden as a massacre, but they are more deadly in the long run."[16] During the late 1870s, U.S. Indian policymakers set as their goal the cleansing and Americanization of "savage" reservation residents in preparation for their integration into mainstream society. Advocates of "civilizing" the Indians obviously believed that aboriginal peoples were capable of learning the English language and of adopting an alternative, superior mode of life if they were brought under the influence of honest and capable Indian agents, Christian missionaries, farmers, and teachers. To "allow them to drag along year after year . . . in their old superstitions, laziness, and filth . . . would be a lasting disgrace to our government," wrote Commissioner of Indian Affairs Hiram Price, but to transform the Indians into self-sufficient and productive citizens would be "a crown of glory to any nation."[17]

Assimilation of Native Americans into the dominant society required specific strategies in the judgment of Washington officials and humanitarian reformers. These included the promotion of Indian self-sufficiency through farming and stock raising, the formal education of their young, the allotment of Indian land in severalty, and the conferring of U.S. citizenship on Indians who had abandoned traditional ways.[18] How to deal with America's aboriginal people, President Rutherford B. Hayes confided to his diary, "is a problem which for nearly three centuries has remained almost unsolved. . . . Let all our dealings with the Red man be characterized by justice and good faith, and let there be the most liberal provision for his physical wants, for education in its widest sense, and for religious instruction and training. To do this will cost money, but like all money well expended it is wise economy."[19] With the western Indians peaceful and concentrated on secluded and often infertile reservations, the time had come to test fully these techniques.

By 1890 the Office of Indian Affairs supervised fifty-eight agencies scattered from New York to California. Washington charged each federal agent, who was responsible for one or more reservations, with destroying tribal customs and beliefs, replacing them with mainstream American life-styles and values, and encouraging Indian integration into the dominant society. At that point reservations (dubbed "virtual open-air prisons" by historian Donald J. Berthrong) would no longer be necessary. Agents' specific responsibilities included: administering agency as well as tribal moneys and property; controlling the chiefs; fostering farming by the men and instructing the women in household skills; safeguarding the health of the inhabitants; aggressively restricting Indian dress, language, and other "vicious habits"; advancing Christianity; and educating children. The agency staff (usually a clerk, farmer, medical doctor, blacksmith, and one or more teachers) also played key roles in this Americanization process.[20]

Two of the agents' biggest challenges were educating Indian youth and maintaining law and order. Considered "as bright and teachable as average white children of the same ages," Native youngsters were the key to Washington's "civilization" program. Congress therefore took back control of Indian education from Christian missionaries and between 1877 and 1900 created its own educational system and increased the level of annual funding from $20,000 to $1,364,368.[21] More than 20,000 Indians attended an elaborate federal school system by the close of the century. English was the language of instruction, and teachers emphasized the vocational application of knowledge. As with adults, this meant farming plus a knowledge of common trades for the boys and domestic arts for the females. Native self-sufficiency and Americanization remained the government's objectives.[22]

To make sure that reservation economic development and cultural change took place in an orderly environment, Congress in 1878 authorized experimental police units to fill the power vacuum created by the withdrawal of military troops from the West and the weakened authority of tribal chiefs. The system proved so successful that within three years it operated on forty-nine reservations and included 84 commissioned officers and 786 noncommissioned officers and privates.[23] To the Indian Office, a disciplined and well-trained police force also served as a "perpetual educator" for fellow Natives who would walk the white man's road. "Indian police became more than law enforcers," Berthrong noted; "they slaughtered issue beefs, returned truants to boarding schools, carried messages for agents, took tribal censuses, and built roads and agency buildings."[24] The courts of Indian offenses, established by the Interior Department in the early 1880s, formed another weapon in the federal government's acculturation arsenal. Soon, ninety-three Native judges staffed courts at twenty-eight agencies. They heard cases against Indians charged with theft, destruction of property, drunkenness, and trafficking in intoxicating liquors. The courts also enforced Indian Office rules that forbade various practices of medicine men, polygamy, and the sun, scalp, and war dances.[25]

Tribal sovereignty came under attack in the late 1800s as did traditional Indian customs, languages, and political structures. After 1871 the U.S. Congress legislated policies and programs, with or without Indian consultation. No longer would the government negotiate treaties with Native political groups. Tribal sovereignty, implied by earlier treaties, seemed inappropriate for the 1870s. Indians had become wards of the government. Congress also enacted the Major Crimes Act in 1885, which made Indians who committed certain infractions on reservations subject to federal government jurisdiction rather than tribal authority. The U.S. Supreme Court upheld the act's constitutionality in *United States v. Kagama*.[26] In another case the Court determined that the Fourteenth Amendment did not give U.S. citizenship to Native persons born on reservations.[27]

As vulnerable subject peoples hemmed in on reservations, Indians ironically suffered at times at the hands of the very persons charged with protecting them. Historian Francis Paul Prucha concluded that the "Indian service, upon which rested much of the responsibility for solving the 'Indian problem' of the post-Civil War decades, was itself a large part of the problem."[28] Opportunities for fraud corrupted many federal agents who were paid meager salaries yet annually handled large amounts of Indian money, annuity goods, and farm equipment "in isolated areas away from civilized restraints and comforts." Agents also supervised the leasing of reservation lands and negotiated contracts for agency improvements. Sioux Chief Red Cloud once asked an audience in New York City, "I wish to know why Commissioners are sent out to us who do nothing but rob us and get the riches of this world away from us! I was brought up among the traders, and those who came out there in the early times treated me well and I had a good time with them. . . . But, by and by, the Great Father sent out a different kind of men; men who cheated and drank whiskey; men who were so bad that the Great Father could not keep them at home and so sent them out there. . . . I want to have men sent out to my people whom we know and can trust."[29]

Reform proposals were many but the results modest. Three times the House of Representatives approved transfer of the Indian

"THE REASON OF THE INDIAN OUTBREAK." A cartoon critical of allegedly rapacious Indian agents, *Judge*, December 20, 1890. *Courtesy Library of Congress*

Office from the Interior Department, where the spoils system governed appointments, to the War Department, but the bills got no further. Ulysses S. Grant's administration tried to improve Indian Office field operations by using inspectors and replacing political patronage appointees with more honest and competent agents nominated by religious denominations. The latter experiment failed miserably. Not enough qualified Christian men wished to become Indian agents, patronage pressures emanating from Congress and the White House undermined the process, and interdenominational competition degenerated into "flagrant bigotry," according to Prucha. Also ineffective was the Board of Indian Commissioners, a group of Christian philanthropists appointed to advise the government on Native affairs and serve as a watchdog over the Indian service. Hayes's secretary of the interior, Carl Schurz, reformed Indian Office operations and purged it of many dishonest officials, but the service did not fully eradicate the political spoils system until the next century.[30]

The reservation environment, as overseen by federal Indian agents, elicited mixed responses from Natives of the prairies, plains, mountains, and deserts of the West. Their eastern cousins, introduced to reservations earlier in the century, felt much the same way. Historian Arrell M. Gibson claimed that for many American Indians the reservation "matched, and in some cases exceeded, the somber 'Trail of Tears' for needless, agonizing want, unthinkable suffering, and personal and group decline to the brink of destruction."[31]

Reservation factionalism sprang from these mixed responses. Indian agents of the period quickly and conveniently categorized bands or tribal factions as "progressive" or "traditional," yet historian David Rich Lewis cautions that communities contained many interest groups that were sometimes in flux because of the variety of issues they faced. Furthermore, individuals, as Lewis discovered in his study of northern Ute leader William Wash, "frequently transcend the bounds of static factional categories."[32] Nevertheless, a few of the popular options available to reservation individuals and groups after the Civil War should be discussed, albeit with caution.

Some aboriginal leaders and their followers, believing that further military resistance was foolish, abandoned hope of ever restoring traditional life-styles and pragmatically tried to make the best of reservation life. They took up farming, sent their children to school, attended church services, adopted "citizen's dress," cooperated with the local Indian agent, and generally tried to walk the white man's road. The rural isolation of most reservations limited work opportunities, but by the turn of the century the U.S. Census Bureau calculated that 60 percent of Native American males able to hold jobs were "gainfully employed." Nearly 90 percent of the women, on the other hand, remained at home.[33]

For those willing to adjust to the white man's expectations, reservations offered chances for economic self-sufficiency. Most were in farming. Historian Donald L. Parman argues that prior to allotment restrictions in the 1880s and the decline of Indian agriculture (discussed below), "many Indians were making the adjustments necessary for successful agriculture. . . . On thirty-three unallotted reservations, eighteen increased the acreage under cultivation over 10 percent annually and thirteen raised production levels over 10 percent." Although nearly three-fourths of the Indian men worked as farmers or farmhands in 1910, other opportunities existed within reservation boundaries. Some contracted to carry supplies for the agency or, as noted above, worked as Indian police and judges.[34]

Others found off-reservation jobs. Most notable were Native performers who toured with the Wild West shows. Buffalo Bill hired between seventy-five and one hundred Indians during the 1880s, for example. They thrilled audiences in the United States and Europe and in return saw new sights, savored the appreciative crowds, and earned a livelihood. Less dramatic were the traveling medicine shows and their Native employees. Aboriginal dances and crafts attracted large crowds who were then sold a variety of quack medicines. In the late nineteenth century, thirty troupes of the Kickapoo Medicine Company, each employing ten or more Indians, traveled American roads. Indian scouts (often Apaches, Pawnees, Osages, and Delawares) employed by the U.S. Army also traveled for a living. Less glamorous was the hard work performed off-reservation by western Indians who hired out to local ranchers, for instance, and by Chippewa Indians of northern Michigan, Wisconsin, and Minnesota who worked in white towns, lumber camps, sawmills, and mines, and for railroad companies.[35]

Among the Natives who stayed closer to home, the old ways of life still beckoned, and many disregarded Indian Office prohibitions to keep such customs alive: courtship practices and polygamy, clan ceremonies, and sacred rituals such as the sun dance. Reservation residents also used two mind-altering drugs, alcohol and peyote,

which Washington had forbidden.[36] These Natives massively resisted Washington's Americanization program. Parents withheld
their children from government schools and their cooperation from
officials who would change other aspects of the old ways. In some
cases, the government seemed to ask the impossible. Farming, for
example, ran counter to hunter-warrior traditions; furthermore, reservation lands often were semiarid or, in the north, had too short a
growing season. When favorable agricultural conditions prevailed,
the poverty-stricken Indians frequently lacked the equipment, livestock, and seeds to farm profitably. Constant white encroachment
on Native lands also hurt the chances for economic self-sufficiency.
Perhaps the most subversive force was the Indians' distrust, based
on bitter experience, of the supposedly superior American way of
life.[37] In 1875 an aged Navajo chief explained why he would not
send his people's children to the agency school: "I do not believe
in the white man or his ways. . . . The white man makes our young
men drunk. He steals away our daughters. He takes away their hearts
with sweet drinks and clothes. He is a wolf."[38]

Reservation living conditions in the late 1800s also prompted
widespread despair and drunkenness and a leadership crisis. "Our
men had fought hard against our enemies, holding them back from
our beautiful country by their bravery," lamented Pretty-Shield, a
Crow medicine woman. "But now, with everything else going
wrong, we began to be whipped by weak foolishness. Our men, our
leaders, began to drink the white man's whisky, letting it do their
thinking. . . . Our wise-ones became fools. . . . But what else was
there for us to do? . . . Our old men used to be different; even our
children were different when the buffalo were here."[39] In 1881, when
Sitting Bull ended his Canadian exile and surrendered to the commander at Fort Buford in Dakota Territory, he spoke with disdain
about reservation life and Indian accommodationists, stating that
"I do not wish to be shut up in a corral. It is bad for young men to
be fed by an agent. It makes them lazy and drunken. All agency
Indians I have seen were worthless. They are neither red warriors
nor white farmers. They are neither wolf nor dog. But my followers are weary of cold and hunger. They wish to see their brothers
and their old home, therefore I bow my head."[40]

Amid such resignation and despair on the reservations, Indian
messiahs emerged offering some hope. Most influential was the
Paiute Wovoka, who preached the Ghost Dance religion. It assured
Indians that if they practiced the ritual Ghost Dance and behaved

properly, their white antagonists would disappear and the old days would return—including the buffalo. Ghost Dancers would also be reunited with their ancestors. Washington's resolve to overcome such religious resistance to reservation acculturation plans climaxed with the notorious clash between federal troops and Sioux Ghost Dancers at Wounded Knee in South Dakota in 1890.[41] But more subtle, and far more devastating in the long run to Uncle Sam's wards, were federal Indian policy changes in the 1880s.

These changes resulted in part from the advocacy of the Women's National Indian Association of Philadelphia, the National Indian Defense Association, the Indian Rights Association, and other reform organizations established in the late nineteenth century and known collectively as "Friends of the Indian." Building on the reform traditions of Christianity and the antebellum era, these groups shared a belief that past federal Indian programs had failed miserably. Beginning in 1883 their representatives convened annually, along with professional educators and government officials, at Lake Mohonk, New York, to discuss Indian affairs and promote reform efforts.[42] The Indian was clearly not being prepared for American citizenship by his reservation—"that hot-bed of barbarism," as Commissioner of Indian Affairs John H. Oberly called it, "in which many noxious social and political weeds grow rankly."[43] Instead, Natives, demoralized by dependence on the government dole, remained communal in their thinking and followed too many of the old ways. To save the aborigines, the reservation system must be dismantled. The Indian Rights Association urged Congress to provide the "three foundation stones" that Natives must have to become industrious and self-sufficient members of American society: education, a protected individual title to land, and U.S. citizenship.[44]

Native education greatly needed reform. In 1880, Congress appropriated a mere $75,000 to support aboriginal schools, and the Indian Office reported that only fifteen of its sixty-six agencies could adequately educate their children.[45] Reformers saw the greatest obstacle to their goals in the overpowering influence of the children's families to whom the youngsters returned each day and relapsed "into their former moral and mental stupor."[46] During the 1880s and 1890s, Friends of the Indian encouraged the building of more boarding schools on reservations as a partial solution to these problems. Here, the children learned academic subjects as well as "industrial training." For the boys, this included instruction in farming, stock raising, and gardening, plus such trades as carpentry, masonry, and blacksmithing. Girls learned competencies appropriate to their domains: the kitchen and dining room, dormitory, laundry room, and sewing room. The on-reservation boarding facility, like the day school, was still subject to strong reservation influences, particularly the pervasive Indian languages and the proximity of the children's parents.[47]

To improve education, that is, to detribalize the children and prepare them for integration into American life, Friends of the Indian involved students with two off-reservation institutions. In 1879, Richard Henry Pratt started a boarding school on an experimental basis in Carlisle, Pennsylvania. The school drew its first eighty-four students, a mixture of boys and girls, from the Rosebud and Pine Ridge Agencies in Dakota Territory.[48] By the mid-1890s, Carlisle enrolled 769 pupils whose education was similar to that offered by reservation residential schools except that students were under tighter discipline and totally cut off from home influences for years at a time. English was the only language of instruction.[49] So successful was the Carlisle experiment in the eyes of white reformers that the Indian Office created eighteen similar institutions by 1895. The number of Indians enrolled in nonreservation boarding schools that year was 4,673.[50]

Beginning in 1890, Commissioner of Indian Affairs Thomas J. Morgan advocated a second off-reservation educational experience. He observed how effective public schools were at "Americanizing our foreign population" and hoped that these institutions might do the same for Native children. Thus, he began contracting with selected school districts.[51] Within five years 487 children attended public schools in California, Oregon, Washington, Utah, Nebraska, Oklahoma, Wisconsin, and Michigan. By 1895 the Indian Office educational network had thus grown to include 19 off-reservation boarding schools, 75 reservation boarding schools, 110 reservation day schools, and 62 institutions (operated by churches or secular groups) with whom the government contracted. That year Congress appropriated $2,060,695 for Indian education. In the 1890s, Washington also required that all Indian children attend school and placed Indian Office educational personnel under Civil Service Act provisions.[52]

It is hard to generalize about Indian response to these educational reforms. Certainly many learned English and some of the ways of American society, including job skills. However, the lack of employment opportunity on their home reservations, to which most Indian students returned, meant that a large percentage "simply returned to camp life," as Berthrong has noted. Luther Standing Bear, a Sioux who attended Carlisle, took a different view of these relapses:

> According to the white man, the Indian, choosing to return to his tribal manners and dress, "goes back to the blanket." True, but "going back to the blanket" is the factor that has saved him from, or at least stayed, his final destruction. Had the Indian been as completely subdued in spirit as he was in body he would have perished within the century of his subjection. But it is the unquenchable spirit that has saved him—his clinging to Indian ways, Indian thought, and tradition, that has kept him and is keeping him today. The white man's ways were not his ways and many of the things that he has tried to adopt have proven disastrous and to his utter shame. . . . many an Indian has accomplished his own personal salvation by "going back to the blanket."[53]

No comprehensive studies exist about the lives of boarding school graduates, yet scholars agree that young Indian men and women who returned to their home reservations often ended up working for the paternalistic Bureau of Indian Affairs in menial capacities. Instead of converting their families and friends to Christian civilization, which the off-reservation boarding school system expected to happen, large numbers of graduates reverted to their community's lifeways.[54]

Besides education, reformers saw a second means for assimilating Indians into national life in the granting of land in severalty, that is, individual possession rather than tribal ownership. Throughout the 1880s, Friends of the Indian thus advocated an allotment program to break up reservation land holdings into individual family tracts. Indian farmers would learn how to compete in a market economy alongside their white neighbors. Allotment would also weaken tribal ties. Severalty was not a new program; the Indian Office had applied it to selected tribes with mixed results.[55] Massachusetts Senator Henry L. Dawes, chair of the Senate Committee on Indian Affairs and a leading light at the Lake Mohonk conferences, led the lobbying effort for a general Indian allotment act. Not only reformers but also the railroads, white settlers, and other entrepreneurs favored severalty legislation because over sixty million acres of surplus reservation lands would be for sale following allotment.[56]

Success came in 1887. The Dawes Act provided 160-acre allotments to reservation families plus all the "rights, privileges, and
immunities" of other U.S. citizens. Following a quarter-century trust
period, Washington would issue fee-simple titles to the new owners.[57] According to historian Frederick E. Hoxie, the Dawes Act
"was the first piece of legislation intended for the general regulation of Indian affairs to be passed in half a century, and it remained
the keystone of federal action until 1934, when the Indian Reorganization Act replaced it. . . . [S]upporters of the Dawes Act hailed it
as the 'Indians' Magna Carta.' "[58] This sense of satisfaction seemed
justified. Communal reservations, so long an impediment to the
acculturation process, were soon dismantled by allotment, which
reformer Merrill E. Gates described as "a mighty pulverizing engine for breaking up the tribal mass."[59]

Understandably, Indians were less sanguine about the prospects
of allotment. In the past, a paternalistic federal government rarely
sought Native input into policy decisions, which usually led to more
Indian land loss and removals. Delaware Chief Charles Journeycake
shared this perspective with the Indian Defense Association in 1886:
"We have been broken up and moved six times. We have been de-
spoiled of our property. We thought when we moved across the
Missouri River and had paid for our homes in Kansas we were safe.
But in a few years the white man wanted our country. We had good
farms. Built comfortable houses and big barns. We had schools for
our children and churches, where we listened to the same gospel
the white man listens to. The white man came into our country from
Missouri. And drove our cattle and horses away." As for the prospects of allotment farming following the Dawes Act, Shoshone Chief
Washakie made this pronouncement to Indian Office officials: "God
damn a potato!"[60]

From the Indian perspective, the paternalistic allotment program "hung like a millstone" around their necks. The aboriginal
land base had shrunk from 139 million acres to 34,287,336 acres
by 1934, when Washington abandoned the program. Native communities lost not only "surplus" lands but also many individual allotments. Farmers lacked proper training and access to credit
because they could not use their allotments as collateral. In 1888,
Congress appropriated only $30,000 for Indian farm machinery,
livestock, seeds, and other agricultural assistance. Fledgling Native farmers, under these circumstances, often leased or sold their
lands rather than compete with non-Indian neighbors. Some land

sales occurred without Native approval. The amount of Indian farm-land in the eleven major states where reservation land had been allotted declined from 3.1 to 2.4 million acres between 1910 and 1930. As they became an increasingly landless minority, aboriginal peoples' dependence on the federal government was perpetuated rather than eliminated.[61]

Nevertheless, Friends of the Indian persisted after 1887 in open-ing "surplus" Native land to non-Native settlers. "The greatest dan-ger hanging over the Indian race," Schurz had warned in 1881, "arises from the fact that, with their large and valuable territorial possessions which are lying waste, they stand in the way of what is commonly called 'the development of the country.' "[62] During the 1890s, Congress abolished tribal governments in the Indian Territory, forced allotment upon the Natives there, thus open-ing the area to white settlement, and paved the way for Oklahoma statehood.[63]

To the north the Great Sioux reservation was reduced radically in 1889, triggering a tragic reaction. Here, as well as elsewhere in the West, thousands of Indians were prompted by the reservation ordeal, and even more by land loss, to join the messianic Ghost Dance movement. Once the Indians were a happy people, recalled the Paiute prophet Wovoka; then the white man came. "He dug up the bones of our mother, the earth. He tore her bosom with steel. He built big trails and put iron horses on them. He fought you and beat you, and put you in barren places where a horned toad would die. He said you must stay there; you must not go hunt in the moun-tains."[64] Chief Red Cloud revealed something of the Sioux's de-spair and why they reached out to the Ghost Dance for salvation:

> We had no newspapers, and no one to speak for us. We had no redress. Our rations were again reduced. You who eat three times each day, and see your children well and happy around you, can't understand what starving Indians feel. We were faint with hun-ger and maddened by despair. We held our dying children, and felt their little bodies tremble as their souls went out and left only a dead weight in our hands. . . . There was no hope on earth, and God seemed to have forgotten us. Some one had again been talking of the Son of God, and said He had come. The people did not know; they did not care. They snatched at the hope. They screamed like crazy men to Him for mercy. They caught at the promises they heard He had made.

The white men were frightened and called for soldiers. Indian provocation and resistance once again led to confrontation and bloodshed—this time at Wounded Knee, with the deaths of over two hundred Sioux men, women, and children.[65]

To summarize the post-Civil War era: as eastern Indians coped peacefully with reservation life, the western tribes battled fiercely to safeguard their homelands and traditional ways. Chiefs such as Sitting Bull, Joseph, and Geronimo became legends, but the consequences of 1,065 military engagements with U.S. troops meant that defeated Native nations would be confined to reservations, where altruistic Friends of the Indian tried to "civilize" and assimilate Indian wards through a battery of programs, including farming instruction, formal education of the young, and the allotment of aboriginal holdings. Some Natives accepted these initiatives, believing they had no choice but to walk the white man's road. Others continued to resist, militarily and in other more subtle but equally determined ways, as the Ghost Dancers showed in 1890.

At the turn of the century, America's 267,905 Indians, not including Native groups living in Alaska, had made their initial adjustment to life on widely scattered reservations. In 1899 the Indian Office had vital statistics for 187,319 of its wards and claimed that 13 percent resided in permanent homes, 28 percent spoke English for everyday purposes, and 23 percent could read. Schools enrolled 23,615 students.[66]

Aboriginal peoples were not thriving, but at least Indian adaptability and fortitude enabled them to survive the transition and establish permanent homes on restricted land bases. Native peoples had forged a new set of relationships with whites on and off the reservations by 1900. No longer free-wheeling nomads who controlled vast resources, the Indians led lives that revolved around island communities.

Non-Indian Americans who surrounded the reservations assumed that their neighbors would soon vanish into the dominant society; so, too, did Washington policymakers. A century later we realize how wrong they were. Native Americans, employing resistance and accommodation strategies and with help from generations of new leaders, have regained much numerical, cultural, and political strength.[67] Geronimo and Sitting Bull would be pleased.

Notes

1. Frank Linderman, *Pretty-Shield: Medicine Woman of the Crows* (1932; reprint ed., New York, 1972), 248.

2. "Census of 1870," in U.S. Bureau of the Census, *Report on Indians Taxed and Indians Not Taxed in the United States (Except Alaska) at the Eleventh Census: 1890*, 25 vols. (Washington, DC, 1894), 7:21–22. Other Indians were peacefully settled on reservations or at Indian agencies in the eastern states or the western states of Arkansas, California, Iowa, Kansas, Missouri, Nebraska, Nevada, Oregon, and Texas.

3. Thomas W. Dunlay, "Fire and Sword: Ambiguity and the Plains War," in Philip Weeks, ed., *The American Indian Experience: A Profile, 1524 to the Present* (Arlington Heights, IL, 1988), 137–39; William T. Hagan, "United States Indian Policies, 1860–1900," in William C. Sturtevant, ed., *Handbook of North American Indians*, 15 vols., vol. 4, *History of Indian-White Relations*, ed. Wilcomb E. Washburn (Washington, DC, 1988), 52–53. Hagan notes that the peace commissioners were much more successful in moving to Oklahoma the prairie tribes of eastern Nebraska and Kansas. These included the Sauk and Fox, Potawatomis, Osages, Iowas, Pawnees, and the Poncas.

4. Quoted in W. C. Vanderwerth, ed., *Indian Oratory: Famous Speeches by Noted Indian Chieftains* (Norman, OK, 1971), 161.

5. Robert M. Utley, "Indian-United States Military Situation, 1848–1891," in Washburn, *Handbook*, 170–73; Hagan, "United States Indian Policies," 55; idem, "How the West Was Lost," in Frederick E. Hoxie, ed., *Indians in American History: An Introduction* (Arlington Heights, IL, 1988), 181–84; Dunlay, "Fire and Sword," 140–51; Philip Weeks, *Farewell, My Nation: The American Indian and the United States, 1820–1890* (Arlington Heights, IL, 1990), 160–91.

6. Quoted in Virginia Irving Armstrong, comp., *I Have Spoken: American History through the Voices of the Indians* (Chicago, 1971), 86.

7. *Annual Report of the Commissioner of Indian Affairs to the Secretary of the Interior, 1873* (Washington, DC, National Cash Register Microfiche Edition, 1969), 200 (hereafter cited as ARCIA); ARCIA, 1874, 10–11; Francis Paul Prucha, *The Great Father: The United States Government and the American Indians*, 2 vols. (Lincoln, NE, 1984), 1:535–36; Arrell M. Gibson, *The American Indian: Prehistory to the Present* (Lexington, MA, 1980), 408–12; Weeks, *Farewell*, 160–69.

8. Quoted in Armstrong, *I Have Spoken*, 87–88.

9. Prucha, *Great Father*, 1:539; Hagan, "How the West Was Lost," 187–89; Gibson, *American Indian*, 418–22; Utley, "Indian-United States Military Situation," 178–80.

10. ARCIA, 1871, 297–309; ARCIA, 1873, 12–14; Gibson, *American Indian*, 351, 417–19.

11. Prucha, *Great Father*, 1:541–42, 574–77; Gibson, *American Indian*, 419.

12. Quoted in Armstrong, *I Have Spoken*, 116.

13. Quoted in T. C. McLuhan, ed., *Touch the Earth: A Self-Portrait of Indian Existence* (New York, 1971), 90.

14. ARCIA, 1873, 5–6; ARCIA, 1874, 6–8; ARCIA, 1875, 6–9; ARCIA, 1876, xiv–xv; Utley, "Indian-United States Military Situation," 174–76.

15. U.S. Bureau of the Census, *Report on Indians Taxed*, 7:637, 643.

16. Quoted in James Axtell, *The Invasion Within: The Conquest of Cultures in Colonial North America* (New York, 1985), 329.

17. "Annual Report," October 24, 1881, in Wilcomb E. Washburn, ed., *The American Indian and the United States: A Documentary History*, 4 vols. (New York, 1973), 1:300.

18. Carl Schurz, "Present Aspects of the Indian Problem," in Francis Paul Prucha, ed., *Americanizing the American Indians: Writings by the "Friends of the Indian," 1880–1900* (Cambridge, MA, 1973), 14; "Report of Commissioner of Indian Affairs J. Q. Smith," October 30, 1876, in Washburn, *Documentary History*, 1:217; "Report of Commissioner of Indian Affairs Hiram Price," October 24, 1881, ibid., 300–301; Gibson, *American Indian*, 428; Prucha, *Great Father*, 1:593–94; Weeks, *Farewell*, 217–18.

19. T. Harry Williams, ed., *Hayes: The Diary of a President, 1875–1881* (New York, 1964), 148.

20. "Report of Commissioner of Indian Affairs Edward P. Smith," November 1, 1875, in Washburn, *Documentary History*, 1:210–11; Gibson, *American Indian*, 429–31; Prucha, *Great Father*, 2:645; Donald J. Berthrong, "Nineteenth-Century United States Government Agencies," in Washburn, *Handbook*, 261–63; idem, "The Bitter Years: Western Indian Reservation Life," in Weeks, *American Indian Experience*, 155; ARCIA, 1890, cxxix.

21. U.S. Bureau of the Census, *Report on Indians Taxed*, 7:74; David Wallace Adams, "From Bullets to Boarding Schools: The Educational Assault on the American Indian Identity," in Weeks, *American Indian Experience*, 220–21; Brian W. Dippie, *The Vanishing American: White Attitudes and U.S. Indian Policy* (Middletown, CT, 1982), 112; "Report of Commissioner E. A. Hayt," November 1, 1879, in Washburn, *Documentary History*, 1:249. For a discussion of Christian mission schools among the Indians see Prucha, *Great Father*, 1:141, 146–48, 597, and 2:693–94, 707–11.

22. Hagan, "United States Indian Policies, 1860–1900," 58–59; Prucha, *Great Father*, 2:689, 692–93; Gibson, *American Indian*, 431–32; Adams, "Bullets to Boarding Schools," 220–21.

23. ARCIA, 1873, 4–5; "Report of Hiram Price," October 10, 1882, in Washburn, *Documentary History*, 1:336–37; "Report of Price," 1881, in ibid., 1:307.

24. "Report of Price," 1881, in Washburn, *Documentary History*, 1:307; *Report on Indians Taxed*, 7:76; Berthrong, "Bitter Years," 158.

25. "Report of Hiram Price," October 10, 1883, in Washburn, *Documentary History*, 1:348–49; "Report of Commissioner of Indian Affairs T. J. Morgan," September 5, 1890, in ibid., 1:470–71. The sun dance, writes historian Arrell Gibson, was "the most important Teton Sioux ritual. . . . It was a time for giving thanks, for renewing national solidarity, and for gaining personal strength and status," Gibson, *American Indian*, 70.

26. Gibson, *American Indian*, 439–40; Walter L. Williams, "American Imperialism and the Indians," in Hoxie, *Indians in American History*, 235–37; *U.S. Statutes at Large*, 33:385; *United States v. Kagama*, 118 U.S. 375 (1886).

27. *Elk v. Wilkins*, 112 U.S. 94 (1884).

28. Prucha, *Great Father*, 1:582.

29. ARCIA, 1876, iii–iv; Gibson, *American Indian*, 430; Prucha, *Great Father*, 1:586–89; Red Cloud quoted in Armstrong, *I Have Spoken*, 93.

30. Paul Stuart, *The Indian Office: Growth and Development of an American Institution, 1865–1900* (Ann Arbor, MI, 1979), 5, 13, 20; Weeks, *Farewell*, 156, 197–204; Prucha, *Great Father*, 1:523.

31. Gibson, *American Indian*, 443, 451–55. Gibson noted, too, that by 1890 "the Indian population of the United States had been reduced from an estimated original 1,500,000 to less than 250,000."

32. David Rich Lewis, "Reservation Leadership and the Progressive-Traditional Dichotomy: William Wash and the Northern Utes, 1865–1928," in Albert L. Hurtado and Peter Iverson, eds., *Major Problems in American Indian History* (Lexington, MA, 1994), 420–34.

33. Gibson, *American Indian*, 472; Weeks, *Farewell*, 231; Berthrong, "Bitter Years," 167; C. Matthew Snipp, "Economic Conditions," in Mary B. Davis, ed., *Native America in the Twentieth Century: An Encyclopedia* (New York, 1994), 176.

34. Donald L. Parman, *Indians and the American West in the Twentieth Century* (Bloomington, IN, 1994), 9–10; Snipp, "Economic Conditions," 176.

35. Gibson, *American Indian*, 470–71; Edmund J. Danziger, Jr., *The Chippewas of Lake Superior* (Norman, OK, 1978), 94–97.

36. Weeks, *Farewell*, 231–32.

37. Gibson, *American Indian*, 466–69.

38. Quoted in Armstrong, *I Have Spoken*, 98.

39. Linderman, *Pretty-Shield*, 251.

40. Quoted in Armstrong, *I Have Spoken*, 126.

41. Ibid., 472–82; Utley, "Indian-United States Military Situation," 183.

42. Robert W. Mardock, "Indian Rights Movement until 1887," in Washburn, *Handbook*, 303–4; Hazel Whitman Hertzberg, "Indian Rights Movement, 1887–1973," in ibid., 305–6; Gibson, *American Indian*, 457–59, 494.

43. "Report for December 3, 1888," in Washburn, *Documentary History*, 1:421.

44. Prucha, *Great Father*, 2:656; "Statement of Objectives" (1885) in Prucha, *Americanizing the American Indians*, 43–44.

45. Table 10, ARCIA, 1895, 16; "Report of Acting Commissioner of Indian Affairs E. M. Marble," November 1, 1880, in Washburn, *Documentary History*, 1:283.

46. "Report of Morgan," 1890, in Washburn, *Documentary History*, 1:445; "Report of Commissioner of Indian Affairs J. D. C. Atkins," September 28, 1886, in ibid., 1:396.

47. "Report of Price," 1882, in Washburn, *Documentary History*, 1:330–31; "Report of Morgan," 1890, in ibid., 1:444–45.

48. "Report of Marble," 1880, in Washburn, *Documentary History*, 1:284.

49. ARCIA, 1895, 5; "Report of Morgan," October 1, 1889, in Washburn, *Documentary History*, 1:429–31; "Report of Price," 1882, in ibid., 1:333–34.

50. ARCIA, 1895, 5.

51. "Report of Morgan," 1890, in Washburn, *Documentary History*, 1:445–46.

52. ARCIA, 1895, 3–16; Frederick E. Hoxie, *A Final Promise: The Campaign to Assimilate the Indians, 1880–1920* (Lincoln, NE, 1984), 65. The trend toward educating Indians in the public schools continued, and by 1930 over half the enrolled native students attended these institutions. Margaret Connell Szasz and Carmelita Ryan, "American Indian Education," in Washburn, *Handbook*, 293.

53. Berthrong, "Bitter Years," 161–64; quoted in McLuhan, *Touch the Earth*, 104.

54. Berthrong, "Bitter Years," 162–64; Prucha, *The Great Father*, 2:699–700; Adams, "Bullets to Boarding Schools," 236–37; Robert A. Trennert, "Educating Indian Girls and Women at Nonreservation Boarding Schools, 1878–1920," in Hurtado and Iverson, *Major Problems in American Indian History*, 389–91.

55. "Report of Price," 1882, in Washburn, *Documentary History*, 1:336; "Report of Hayt," November 1, 1878, in ibid., 1:225–29. Objections to severalty

during the 1880s are reviewed in the House Committee on Indian Affairs, "Minority Report on Land in Severalty Bill" (1880) in Prucha, *Americanizing the American Indians*, 122–28; and Hertzberg, "Indian Rights Movement," 306.

56. *Report on Indians Taxed*, 7:67; Gibson, "Indian Land Transfers," in Washburn, *Handbook*, 226–27.

57. *U.S. Statutes at Large*, 24:388–91. For a discussion of those tribes initially exempted from the Dawes Act see Gibson, *American Indian*, 497–98.

58. Hoxie, *Final Promise*, 70.

59. Merrill E. Gates, "Addresses at the Lake Mohonk Conferences," in Prucha, *Americanizing the American Indian*, 337, 342.

60. Quoted in Armstrong, *I Have Spoken*, 127–28.

61. Weeks, *Farewell*, 221–22; Wilcomb E. Washburn, ed., *The Assault on Indian Tribalism: The General Allotment Law (Dawes Act) of 1887* (Philadelphia, 1975), 30–31; Leonard A. Carlson, "Allotment," in Davis, *Native America in the Twentieth Century*, 29; Parman, *Indians and the American West in the Twentieth Century*, 3, 9–10.

62. Schurz, "Present Aspects of the Indian Problem," in Prucha, *Americanizing the American Indian*, 25. For a detailed analysis of how the idealistic purpose of the Dawes Act was subverted see Janet A. McDonnell, *The Dispossession of the American Indian, 1887–1934* (Bloomington, IN, 1991).

63. Gibson, *American Indian*, 502.

64. Quoted in Armstrong, *I Have Spoken*, 129.

65. Red Cloud quoted in Wayne Moquin and Charles Van Doren, eds., *Great Documents in American Indian History* (New York, 1973), 265–66. For a thorough account of Wounded Knee see Robert M. Utley, *The Last Days of the Sioux Nation* (New Haven, CT, 1963).

66. Berthrong, "Nineteenth-Century Government Agencies," 263.

67. Davis, *Native America in the Twentieth Century*, xi.

Suggestions for Further Reading

Armstrong, Virginia Irving, comp. *I Have Spoken: American History through the Voices of the Indians*. Chicago, 1971.

Gibson, Arrell M. *The American Indian: Prehistory to the Present*. Lexington, MA, 1980.

McLuhan, T. C., ed. *Touch the Earth: A Self-Portrait of Indian Existence*. New York, 1971.

Moquin, Wayne, and Charles Van Doren, eds. *Great Documents in American Indian History*. New York, 1973.

Prucha, Francis Paul. *The Great Father: The United States Government and the American Indians*. 2 vols. Lincoln, NE, 1984.

Sturtevant, William C., ed. *Handbook of North American Indians*. 15 vols. Vol. 4, *History of Indian-White Relations*, ed. Wilcomb E. Washburn. Washington, DC, 1988.

Vanderwerth, W. C., ed. *Indian Oratory: Famous Speeches by Noted Indian Chieftains*. Norman, OK, 1971.

Weeks, Philip. *Farewell, My Nation: The American Indian and the United States, 1820–1890*. Arlington Heights, IL, 1990.

9

The Political Culture: Public Life and the Conduct of Politics

Charles W. Calhoun

The last third of the nineteenth century is the most misunderstood and disparaged period in the political history of the United States. For the better part of the twentieth century, historians painted the era in the darkest hues imaginable, arguing that spoilsmen and corruptionists ruled its political life and that obtaining office for its own sake was the primary motivation for politicians more devoted to partisan advantage than the public good. According to this interpretation, issues and principles counted for little in political contention, and few real differences existed between the Republicans and the Democrats, who dominated elections and office-holding. Over the years scholars sought to outdo one another in censuring the Gilded Age in the most derogatory terms; it was, they said, an age of "negation," "cynicism," and "excess"—a "huge barbecue" for politicos and robber barons that excluded poor farmers and laborers.[1]

Like most stereotypes, this negative image has some validity. The roster of politicians in the late nineteenth century did include some brazen spoilsmen who seemed to crave office for its own sake or for the money it might bring. Some corruption did occur, especially in the 1870s during the general lowering of moral restraints that characterized the post-Civil War period. But during the 1960s and after, a new generation of scholars challenged this interpretation, arguing that traditional historians had overemphasized these unsavory aspects to the point of distorting the political reality. These "revisionist" historians did not deny that venality and office mongering had occurred, but they sought to shift the scholarly focus to matters of public policy whose long-term impact was ultimately more significant than the seamier side of politics. Analyzing the era on its own terms, these scholars concluded that political leaders of the late nineteenth century were generally hard-working public servants, serious about issues and governance. In this view, significant differences over policy, not mere rhetorical shadow-boxing, separated Democrats from Republicans. What leaders said mattered to voters, and what they did affected the well-being of the nation.[2] But even though this newer judgment rests on thorough research, it has not won complete acceptance among historians. One author, for example, recently portrayed Gilded Age presidential elections as "invariably . . . corrupt," the two major parties as "nearly identical," and election results as "not decided by the issues." Another says that "the leading statesmen of the period showed as little interest in important contemporary questions as the party hacks who made up the rank and file of their organizations."[3]

What caused traditional historians and some modern scholars to take such a dim view of Gilded Age politics? To a considerable degree, this negative assessment originated in the jaundiced observations of late nineteenth-century critics who were outside the political system. In trying to explain the period, many historians have paid closer attention to these commentators' biting criticisms than to the words and accomplishments of politicians themselves. The very name that scholars assign to the period, the Gilded Age, derives from an 1873 novel of that title by Mark Twain and Charles Dudley Warner, which satirized politics as rife with corruption and fraud committed by self-seeking politicians. Historians have also been fond of quoting Henry Adams, whose insufferable arrogance doomed his own quest for a political career. Late in life Adams used his autobiography to strike back at the system that overlooked him, charging that "one might search the whole list of Congress, Judiciary, and Executive during the twenty-five years 1870 to 1895, and find little but damaged reputation." He could have added that his own prejudiced diatribes had done much to damage the reputations of others.[4]

One of the most influential critics was the Englishman James Bryce, whose 1880s trip to the United States, resulting in his two-volume study, *The American Commonwealth,* led some Americans to label him the Gilded Age Alexis de Tocqueville. Bryce alleged that neither the Republican nor the Democratic party "has anything definite to say on . . . issues; neither party has any principles, any distinctive tenets. . . . All has been lost, except office or the hope of it." In reaching these conclusions, however, Bryce had come under the sway of Edwin L. Godkin, editor of the Mugwump journal *The Nation*, whose disdain for his contemporaries in politics was boundless and not altogether rational. Taking their cue from Adams, Bryce, Godkin, and other hostile contemporaries, many twentieth-century historians looked back with distaste at the politics of the last three decades of the nineteenth century.[5]

Other historical sources, such as newspapers, have contributed to slanted interpretations. Most Gilded Age dailies and weeklies were intensely loyal partisans of one party and had nothing good to say about the politicians of the other. Their "news" pages as well as their editorial columns served up mixtures of vituperation, trumped-up charges of fraud and corruption, and downright falsehoods about the opposing party. Ohio Governor Joseph B. Foraker exaggerated only somewhat when he complained in 1885 that for some newspapers it was a "common thing to call the man with whom they do not happen to agree, a liar, a thief, a villain, a scoundrel, a Yahoo, a marplot, a traitor, a beast, anything and everything they may be able to command in the way of an epithet." One study shows that a movement for "independent" journalism in the 1870s led zealous reporters to produce stories about politicians that were often scurrilous and sometimes wholly imaginary. Scholars' later reliance on these biased journals as sources contributed to their overall negative impression of politics in the period.[6]

Investigations in Congress had a similar effect. At times the party in control of the House or the Senate used committee hearings or other legislative reports to discredit actions or doctrines of the opposing party. As an American diplomat in Paris wrote home to a senator in 1876, "The fury of 'investigation' in Washington has reached such a stage that it is something like the days of the French Revolution when it was enough to cry 'suspect' and the man was ruined." Often rooted more in partisanship than reality, these inquiries seemed to lend an official authentication to charges that, when taken together, have led historians to see the period's politics in the worst possible light.[7]

This problem of skewed sources has been compounded by the tendency of some scholars to read back into the period modern values concerning government activism. In the words of Geoffrey

Blodgett, such historians exhibit "a profound impatience with the Gilded Age for having not yet discovered the Welfare State." Today the idea that the government is responsible for the nation's economic growth and the citizens' well-being is widely accepted, but in the late nineteenth century most people clung to the traditional notion that good government meant limited government. Its main purpose was to maintain order and protect persons and property. Most citizens would have resisted the redistributive tendency of many twentieth-century economic policies as a perversion of governmental power. Moreover, allegations of corrupt purposes by government officials, whether true or not, evoked calls for retrenchment and aroused suspicion of government in general that inhibited the espousal, let alone the enactment, of positive programs. The cry of "Job!" greeted many legitimate and worthwhile proposals, particularly those involving subsidies or other expenditures of money. The resulting climate of distrust reinforced among voters a small-government notion that restrained leaders who might have taken more aggressive action but who also wished to win elections. As one congressman who lost reelection in 1868 stated, "My opponent is . . . a popular because a negative man." In 1890 the Republican majority in Congress passed an extraordinary number of important laws, with the result that the party lost overwhelmingly in the congressional elections that year. Lack of achievement is one of the principal failings that scholars have alleged about Gilded Age governance. In reality, leaders accomplished more than historians used to give them credit for, but they often did so in spite of the limitations placed on them by an essentially conservative electorate.[8]

Divided control of the national government also slowed the formulation and adoption of policy. Between 1875 and 1897 each major party held the presidency and a clear majority in both houses of Congress for only a single two-year period, the Republicans in 1889–1891 and the Democrats in 1893–1895. During most of this era, Congress was divided, the Democrats more often than not controlling the House of Representatives and the Republicans usually holding a majority in the Senate. These divisions made the passage of legislation difficult. Each of the seven Congresses between 1875 and 1889, on the average, enacted only 317 public laws. But in the 51st Congress (1889–1891), when Republican President Benjamin Harrison worked with a Republican majority in both the House and the Senate, the number of laws passed shot up to 531, representing an unprecedented level of legislative accomplishment unequalled until Theodore Roosevelt's second term.[9]

The balance between the parties in Congress mirrored an equilibrium between Republicans and Democrats in the national electorate. Except for Democrat Grover Cleveland's two terms, Republicans typically sat in the White House, but in four of the five presidential elections from 1876 to 1892 the Democratic nominee wound up with more popular votes than his Republican opponent. In 1880 defeated Democrat Winfield Scott Hancock trailed Republican James A. Garfield by less than half of 1 percent. A considerable portion of the Democratic votes came from former slave states which, after the end of Reconstruction, witnessed a widespread suppression of voting by African Americans, who nearly unanimously supported the Republican party. To take the two most egregious examples, in Louisiana the black population grew by 33 percent between 1870 and 1880, but from the presidential election of 1872 to that of 1880 the number of Republican votes decreased by 47 percent. In Mississippi the black population growth was 46 percent, and the Republican vote decline was 59 percent. Because of this denial of the suffrage, by 1880 the conservative, white Solid South had emerged, assuring the Democrats of a large bloc of electoral votes that year and in future presidential elections.[10]

To counterbalance the South the Republicans could depend almost as surely on winning several states in the Northeast and the upper Midwest, but neither of these two blocs of sure states by itself held enough electoral votes to win the presidency. Hence, election results usually turned on the outcome in a half-dozen swing or "doubtful" states, the most important of which were New York and Indiana. During campaigns, party leaders and committees focused their efforts in these states, enlisting the aid of the party's best speakers and expending the largest proportion of campaign funds. In addition, the parties often chose residents from doubtful states for their national tickets. Between 1876 and 1892 the two major parties selected twenty nominees for president and vice president; eight were from New York and five from Indiana.

One of the criticisms traditional historians leveled against Gilded Age politics was that no real substantive differences divided Republicans from Democrats. Here again, the equilibrium in party strength offers some explanation. With the outcome of elections in doubt, party leaders and spokesmen saw the need to exercise caution in articulating party positions and were wary of getting too far ahead of public opinion. Taking too strong a stand, even on a minor issue, might offend just enough members of some group to bring defeat at the next election. In 1884, for instance, the Republicans lost the presidential election after trailing in pivotal New York by about one thousand votes out of one million. Contemporaries and historians alike could cite many factors, both ideological and organizational, any one of which could have tipped the balance.

When scholars charge that Gilded Age Republicans and Democrats were largely indistinguishable, they tend to apply an inappropriate standard. Historically, American political parties have not been like those of European countries, with starkly differentiated groupings of left and right. Instead, largely because victory in the electoral college requires a majority rather than a plurality, major parties in the United States seek broad consensus and try to make their appeals as wide as possible, with the result that a considerable area of agreement often exists between them. In the Gilded Age the even balance between Republicans and Democrats simply reinforced their perceived need to avoid the fringes of political assertion.

Despite this need for caution, the major parties were not like Tweedledum and Tweedledee, as some traditional historians have alleged. As several of the revisionist scholars have shown, important ideological distinctions existed between Republicans and Democrats. Certainly, each party had its internal disagreements and inconsistencies, but overall they espoused philosophies and policies that clashed in significant ways and offered voters real choices at the polls. Generally speaking, Republicans placed greater stress on government activism, especially at the national level, with the primary aim of fostering economic development. They welcomed the nation's burgeoning industrialization and believed the federal government should assist the process. In the words of Senator John P. Jones, "One of the highest duties of Government is the adoption of such economic policy as may encourage and develop every industry to which the soil and climate of the country are adapted." As the period progressed, the protective tariff emerged as the centerpiece of the Republicans' economic program. Democrats, on the other hand, tended to cling to their party's traditional belief in small government and states' rights. They criticized elements in the Republicans' program as favoring special interests. With its low-tariff wing from the agrarian, largely preindustrial South still looming large, the Democratic party continued its decades-old opposition to tariff protectionism. In pursuit of their goals Republicans read the Constitution broadly to find sanction for national government action; Democrats' interpretation viewed federal power as more restricted. In the past generation modern scholars have begun to recognize the differences between parties that Gilded Age politicians knew instinctively. As the Maine statesman James G. Blaine put it (in a somewhat partisan fashion) in his book *Twenty Years of Congress*, late nineteenth-century Democrats and Republicans displayed the same "enduring and persistent line[s] of division between the two parties which in a generic sense have always existed in the United States;—the party of strict construction and the party of liberal construction, the party of State Rights and the party of National Supremacy, the party of stinted revenue and restricted expenditure and the party of generous income with its wise application to public improvement."[11]

At the state and local levels Republicans again were more willing to resort to government action for what they perceived to be the good of society. They were more likely than Democrats to advocate restrictions on the consumption of alcohol, although many Republicans approached the question warily, fearful of repelling blocs of voters, such as German Americans or Irish Americans, who resented such interference in their personal lives. Similarly, Republicans were more inclined to favor measures to hasten the assimilation of immigrants, such as requiring the use of the English language in parochial schools. Again, Democrats tended to oppose such paternalism. In the past few decades several historians, using quantitative methods to measure voter reaction to such issues, have argued that ethnic and religious distinctions lay at the root of party affiliation. In this view, voters from pietistic, evangelical Protestant denominations tended to favor the moralistic stewardship associated with the Republicans, while liturgical, ritualistic sects, especially Roman Catholics, found comfort in the Democrats' defense of individuals' private lives.[12]

Not all citizens felt well-served by either of the two major parties, and the period witnessed occasional third-party campaigns. In 1872 a group of Republicans, primarily well-educated, economically independent professionals and businessmen, bolted their party. Disenchanted with the policies and administrative style of President Ulysses S. Grant, these self-proclaimed Liberal Republicans mounted an effort to block his reelection. Their nominee, Horace Greeley, won endorsement by the Democrats, but he met the fate of most third-party candidates, a crushing defeat. The Prohibitionists, another group drawn mostly from Republican ranks, fielded presidential tickets every year starting in 1880. They reached their high-water mark in 1888 with just under 2.2 percent of the popular vote. The Greenback-Labor or National party, whose chief policy objective was the inflation of the currency, ran nominees for president from 1876 to 1884. They garnered their largest vote in 1880 with 3.36 percent of the total. They did manage to elect a few congressmen, their greatest success coming in 1878 with fifteen members of the House out of a total of 293. Occasionally these third parties were able to upset the calculations of major party leaders, especially in closely contested states. As Senator Benjamin Harrison noted in 1885, "I have little hope of making Indiana a Republican state with 4,000 Republican Prohibitionists and 8,000 Republican Greenbackers voting separate tickets." Even so, the possibility of such parties achieving power themselves remained virtually nonexistent, and fringe groups, such as the Socialists, had even less chance.[13]

The third party that came closest to moving into major party status was the People's party, or the Populists, in the 1890s. Historians disagree over the degree to which economic distress or other causes moved farmers to become Populists, but the party's rhetoric was heavily freighted with economic issues. Farmers found themselves increasingly caught up in a world market structure with volatile prices for farm commodities. A general downward trend in prices magnified the debt burden of farmers, many of whom had overextended themselves into regions of dubious agricultural productivity. Blaming their troubles on a variety of scapegoats, including railroads, manufacturing trusts, bankers, and the monetary system, many farmers were disappointed when the two-party system seemed unwilling to adopt their various proposals for relief. In 1892 the Populist presidential candidate, James B. Weaver, won over one million popular votes (out of twelve million cast) and twenty-two electoral votes. The Populists elected some members of Congress and achieved momentary success in some individual states and parts of states. In the nation as a whole, however, most voters, even in many farming regions, stuck with the two major parties.

Indeed, throughout the late nineteenth century the vast majority of voters stood by the Republicans or the Democrats, in congressional and state elections as well as in presidential contests. Moreover, whatever their motivation, party supporters went to the polls in huge numbers. In presidential election years over 75 per-

The Republican Ticket in 1872. A Currier & Ives campaign poster playing on the candidates' working-class origins as well as the party's tariff protectionism. *Courtesy Library of Congress*

cent of eligible voters typically cast ballots, a turnout rate far in excess of twentieth-century averages. In this sense the active political community in the Gilded Age was much broader than its modern-day counterpart. In another sense, however, the political community was narrower, for virtually everywhere women were denied the ballot, and in the South, after the end of Reconstruction, conservative white Democrats employed a variety of means to block voting by African Americans. But even with these egregious exclusions from the suffrage, politics remained a consuming interest to people throughout the nation, engaging the enthusiastic participation of millions of citizens.

What kind of leader emerged in this popular political culture? Among the most enduring stereotypes from the period is that of small-minded, grasping politicians who used public office mostly to serve their own interests, and often for their own financial gain, with little real concern for matters of policy or the public good. Recent research reveals a strikingly different portrait of the people who led the two major parties, especially at the national level. Certainly, the idea of conflict of interest was underdeveloped and some politicians took bribes or otherwise engaged in corrupt practices, but in all likelihood no higher percentage did so than during most other times in the nation's history. Indeed, the zealous partisan quest for scandalous material about political opponents probably resulted in allegations of questionable conduct regarding behavior that in other eras might have been winked at or overlooked.

In reality many men who rose to be party leaders considered politics much more a financial burden than a boon. The pay of a congressman or cabinet member, for instance, while considerably above the wages of the average American, fell far short of what most such men could earn in private life. Moreover, the expenses that accompanied politics and government service diminished their finances still further. Typically, a congressman discovered that campaign costs ate up about a year's worth of his salary. Once in office, his expenses continued, including the maintenance of a second home in costly Washington, DC, during much of the year. In March 1874, for example, an Illinois congressman wrote home to his wife that he was "in debt [for] board for a month and must wait for the 3rd of April before I can make ends meet." During another session a senator found an apartment on K Street with only three rooms and no private bath for a rent of $250 per month, 60 percent of his monthly salary. In 1873, Congress voted a much-needed pay raise for its members and other federal officers, but a politically unwise provision to make the raise retroactive to the beginning of the current congressional term sparked a press outcry. Quickly the Senate and House returned their members' pay to its former level, where it remained for the rest of the period.[14]

During this so-called salary grab controversy one Massachusetts constituent wrote his congressman that "if we would preserve our republican institutions in their simplicity and purity, the salary of no officer within the gift of the people should be an inducement to any man to seek it." Such an attitude on the part of the public regarding government salaries had unfortunate consequences. Low pay certainly enhanced the attractiveness of bribes or other illicit gain. More important, it sometimes deterred able individuals from seeking public office. As one Illinois lawyer argued when he refused to run for the House, a seat in Congress often took "honorable, self-respecting gentlemen . . . and kept them in a state of shabby genteel pauperism all their lives." The result too frequently was that only men of independent means or substantial wealth could afford or would accept such service. If, by the end of the century, Americans complained that the Senate had become a "millionaires' club," to some degree they had themselves to blame.[15]

One compensation for congressional service was supposed to be the patronage power, the privilege of placing one's political friends and supporters in subordinate offices. Typically, senators and representatives from the party in power sent the president and other executive-branch officers recommendations of people to fill federal offices in their own states and in Washington. As a personnel program for the federal bureaucracy with its one hundred thousand-plus positions, this so-called spoils system was not without its own internal logic. With respect to governance, the system's defenders maintained that the president's policy aims would best be served by employees recruited from his own party and that he should gladly take the advice of senators and representatives who better knew the qualifications of applicants from their localities. On the political level, they argued, elections were won through the interested labor of a committed cadre of party workers, and rewarding such labor by the bestowal of appointive office was essential to the recruitment and maintenance of these cadres.

To many political leaders, however, dealing with patronage seemed more a punishment than a power. Yes, one might build a loyal core of backers from those who received appointments, but for each office, ranging from postal clerk to cabinet officer, a dozen or more applicants might press their claims, and as Senator John Sherman noted, "however wise may be the selection there will be many disappointments." Disappointing an office seeker might be politically damaging, but it could also be personally wrenching. As one Interior Department official wrote during the depression of the 1890s, "I have hungry men and women by the score coming to see me in the hope and belief that I can give them employment, and this has made my office here a burden. I cannot refuse to see them, and my inability to help them has come to be a kind of torture." On top of it all, politicians who recommended or who made appointments found themselves severely denounced by a growing civil service reform lobby that called for merit considerations over partisanship in the selection and promotion of government employees.[16]

From the politicians' standpoint, the worst drawback of the spoils system was the enormous loss of time and energy devoted to dealing with office seekers and pushing recommendations. Former President Harrison looked back on his years in the White House and noted that during the first eighteen months of his term a president typically spent four to six hours per day on patronage matters. Congressman Garfield called it "the most intolerable burden I have to bear." In 1883, Congress began to remedy the problem with passage of the Pendleton Civil Service Act, an important step in the creation of a professionalized bureaucracy. The law initially brought only a portion of the offices under the merit system, but successive presidential administrations expanded the classified list. The pressure for office eased somewhat, but applications still flooded in at the beginning of a presidential term and also during times of high unemployment. Both these conditions existed in the spring of 1897, when, during the first four months of William McKinley's administration, Senator John C. Spooner of Wisconsin received and answered over seven thousand letters—more than 130 on July 4 alone—most of them about offices. Whatever civil service reformers might say, in dealing with patronage, as one congressman put it, he and his colleagues considered themselves "more the oppressed than the oppressors."[17]

National political leaders faced other vexations, not least of which was the sheer physical discomfort of working in Washington much of the year. "It is so terribly hot here that we can hardly live," one congressman wrote his wife in 1870. During the summer the mercury inside the House of Representatives frequently topped ninety degrees, even after sundown. In September 1888, Spooner described the poorly ventilated Senate chamber as "a box within a box." "I have been pretty nearly laid up with a headache for a week or ten days," he complained. "Hardly a man in the Senate feels well." Moreover, although committee chairmen had the use of their committee rooms as quasi-offices, most members of Congress received no office space beyond their small desks in the crowded chamber. They were thus forced to rent offices at their own expense or do most of their work in their living quarters. Similarly, a committee chairman enjoyed the assistance of the committee's clerk, but the typical member had no staff unless he hired and paid a clerk out of his own pocket.[18]

Even with the help of a clerk, a member frequently felt overwhelmed by the work. In addition to the patronage burden, constituent correspondence was often heavy, and a member could delay answers to letters only at his political peril. Citizens expected their representative or senator to serve as their agent whenever they had business before the government, with the result that congressmen spent much time prowling the executive departments tracking down veterans' pensions, pushing claims, or otherwise advocating constituents' causes. Furthermore, with rare exceptions, members of Congress researched and wrote their own speeches, sometimes several hours in length. The work did not stop once a speech was given; a congressman who delivered a major speech or extended remarks during a day's session might stay up until two or three o'clock the next morning correcting the text for the *Congressional Record*. "It is up hill work all of it," one wrote to his wife in 1872, "and last night when I came home I could hardly draw one foot after another."[19]

Over in the executive branch conditions were hardly better. In 1891 the second in command of the Post Office Department begged for another assistant, telling Congress, "I average at my desk—without a moment's absence from the building—more than ten hours a day, besides night work." Two months after leaving the White House, Harrison confessed, "There is nothing further from my mind or thought or wish than the resumption of public office. I was thoroughly tired and worn out." Possibilities for achievement by politicians did, of course, exist, and many posted creditable records. "But," as Senator George F. Edmunds noted, "whether their own lives have been the happier for such labor, with such inevitable trials and exposures, may be greatly doubted."[20]

Grueling work, pay unequal to the labor, uncertainty of tenure—who would want such a job? Why would men pursue careers in national politics? Explaining the mystery of ambition lies perhaps more with the psychologist than the historian, but it seems clear that, like most successful politicians, men who attained positions of leadership in the late nineteenth century simply took immense satisfaction from being at the center of action and power. Garfield, a man of intellect with wide interests, frequently thought of leaving politics but could never quite bring himself to do it. After reading poet Ralph Waldo Emerson's book *Society and Solitude*, the Ohio congressman mused that "the calm spirit which [Emerson] breathes around him, makes me desire greatly to get up and out of the smoke and dust and noise of politics into the serene air of literature. Still," he confessed, "I suppose, if I were there, I should grow weary of the silence." In the words of Senator Spooner, "There is in public life . . . much that is burdensome and distasteful to a man of sensibility," and yet, "with it all there is a fascination about public life which I hardly know how to define but the existence of which is unmistakable."[21]

In large measure, the attractiveness of political life, especially for leaders at the national level, lay in the sense of accomplishment public service offered them. Despite the frustrations they endured, most remained convinced that their labors sustained and promoted firmly held principles. Hence, even such a senator as Indiana's Oliver P. Morton, often dismissed as a blatant spoilsman interested only in officemongering, could write an eight-page letter to the president discussing the intricacies of the currency question. The same issue was near the heart of Illinois Senator John A. Logan, whose letters to his wife chronicled his fierce struggle for the Inflation Bill in 1874:

> [January 21:] To tell you the truth I have not been in 4 hours any night for one week I have been so busy on my speech.
>
> [February 21:] I have been up again last night and am nearly worn out but will get some rest soon. This fight in the Senate equals any ever made as is said by every person here. We are fighting against all the large papers, all the bankers, all the importers, and aristocrats [and] for the people.
>
> [April 4:] I am nearer a worn out man than I ever have been in my life. My mind has been on such a stretch for months that I am nearly exhausted but hope soon to be all right again as our great fight is practically at an end.

Two weeks later Mrs. Logan wrote the senator and showed how much she shared his anxiety: "I could not keep from crying this evening when I read the telegram announcing that the President had vetoed the 'Finance Bill.' " Evidence of this deep sense of commitment could be multiplied many times over, but one more example will suffice. A half year after leaving office, former cabinet member Jeremiah Rusk wrote a friend: "It makes me sick to see my old department—the agricultural—shrink and wither as though it had been struck by an August frost. I felt as though the foundation had been laid for the greatest department of the Government—by its enlargement and by increasing its usefulness to the agricultural classes—but [now] it seems the policy has been changed to see how little can be done."[22]

For most Gilded Age political leaders, their commitment to principle, as well as their personal ambition, was inextricably linked to devotion to party. They could not achieve their goals unless they gained power, which they could not do except through the agency of one of the two major parties. Leaders high and low, and many voters as well, displayed a dedication to party that bordered on zealotry. Even so level-headed a politician as Treasury Secretary John Sherman once confessed to a friend that the idea of the opposing party coming to power "haunts me like a nightmare."[23]

Parties were nearly as old as the Republic. The emergence of mass politics earlier in the nineteenth century had led to the creation of partisan structures and methods that were well established by the beginning of the Gilded Age. In a general sense, party organizations served as the essential link between leaders, who formulated policy and governed, and the voters, who, with their own beliefs and notions, sought guidance and inspiration. In an age when politicians had no independent means for reaching masses of voters (such as television in the late twentieth century), the party constituted the essential vehicle for communicating with the electorate.

In both major parties the structure was pyramidal, resting on a broad foundation at the precinct or ward level and moving up through town, city, county, legislative and congressional districts, state, and nation. At each level the periodic convention was the basic governing unit for the party. Gatherings of leaders and interested activists, these conventions served several purposes. Those in attendance selected nominees for public office and issued platforms promulgating party beliefs, they chose delegates to attend subsequent conventions up the pyramid, and they created various committees to conduct the ensuing campaign and to carry on party business until the next convention.

As this structure suggests, the national party was in reality little more than a confederation of state and local parties, with only a weak national committee structure holding it together between presidential election years. Even so, the quadrennial national convention was in many ways the crowning event in the party's cycle. Here, delegates on the platform committee from throughout the nation hammered out a statement of shared ideals, and here, delegates sought to choose a presidential ticket that would win the confidence and votes of party members everywhere. Although local issues and battles remained important to voters, the national convention and the following campaign proved to be powerful forces for the renewal of party identification.

Responsibility for organizing and conducting the national campaign lay with the national committee (chosen by the national convention), and especially its executive committee and officers: chairman, secretary, and treasurer. These officials had no power to dictate to state or local committees but tried to coordinate their activities as best they could. The national committee was assisted by a congressional campaign committee, which in off-years as well as in presidential years aided party candidates for Congress.[24]

The traditional interpretation of Gilded Age politics held that in conducting their campaigns, politicians relied mostly on organizational techniques and machine management to win elections. Indeed, one important study labeled the era's political culture as "the triumph of organizational politics." Certainly, party managers perfected remarkably accurate advance polling schemes and created elaborate get-out-the-vote mechanisms, but close examination of politicians' behavior reveals that, in fact, they also placed great stress on the discussion of issues. The late nineteenth century saw a decline in the significance of parades, picnics, bonfires, rallies, and similar devices to ignite the emotions of the party faithful. More and more, political leaders turned to what they called the "campaign of education," appealing to voters on questions of government policy, especially those that affected citizens' economic well-being in an industrializing society. In the words of one campaign official in 1868, who was sending out tens of thousands of pamphlets to voters each day, "The people are intelligent and want something different from 'horrible caricatures and sensational trash.' "[25]

Successful politicians came to realize that winning or retaining power rested largely on the flow of information to the electorate. Because communications technology had advanced little beyond the telegraph, they could reach voters only through public speeches or in print. Hence, in the months before elections, hundreds of state and national party leaders took to the hustings, speaking to audiences day after day for weeks on end, laying out their party's doctrines and appealing for support. For these men, the campaign season was a punishing time, filled with poorly ventilated halls or huge outdoor crowds, endless miles in jostling, dirty railroad cars, sleep deprivation, and indigestion. One campaigner reported to the Republican national committee in 1872 that "breathing railroad dust every day and speaking in the open air every night has played havoc with my voice. I am very hoarse and must lay up a day or two for repairs." By midcampaign that year the seemingly tireless James G. Blaine confessed that eight weeks of speechmaking had left him "completely worn out." Still, he and others returned to the task year after year, because they were convinced of the continuing need to appeal to what Blaine called the "will of the Sovereign People."[26]

The parties and their leaders did not depend solely on personal speaking. An effective orator might convey his message to several thousand listeners, but a printed version of his address could expand his audience many times over. Indeed, the production and distribution of such speeches and other printed matter played a pivotal role in late nineteenth-century electioneering. Printed campaign material included congressional speeches, other addresses, statistical tables, reproduced newspaper items, and other brief broadsides. In Blaine's words, "little tracts" carrying the party's message were "exceedingly effective, short enough to read, and read by everybody."[27]

Party committees in New York and Washington dispatched pamphlets in huge quantities for local distribution. In 1872, for instance, before the end of September, the Republican congressional campaign committee had sent out more than seven million tracts in addition to a circular three times per week to three thousand rural newspapers. Typically, in election years the committees also published so-called campaign textbooks, that is, collections of documents, speeches, and similar material, to aid state and local speakers and editors as they composed their appeals to voters in their own localities. Through most of the period, congressional incumbents had the added advantage of being able to mail campaign literature as documents under their "frank," or free postal privilege. In addition, the parties counted on the help of special interest groups. In the first eight months of 1888, for example, the American Iron and Steel Association distributed over 1,100,000 of its *Tariff Tract* pamphlets in support of the Republican party's protectionist position.[28]

The conventional wisdom among most contemporary politicians (and later historians) was that a party's main objective was simply to poll its full vote, that is, that there was not much chance of winning converts from the opposing party. With party identification strong among the electorate and party switching relatively rare, the principal aim in campaigns was to inspire the party faithful to get to the polls rather than to persuade others to come on board. Yet, at times, political leaders seemed to forget this maxim and urged workers and speakers to try to attract wavering voters from the enemy camp. In 1888, for instance, one state party chairman instructed organizers of campaign speech events to "invite, especially, moderate men of the opposition who are likely to be influenced by sound arguments and persuasive appeals." Particularly in doubtful states, such as Indiana and New York, attracting even a few defectors from the opposing party could spell the difference between victory and defeat.[29]

The closeness of elections heightened the possibility that vote buying or other forms of corruption could influence the outcome. It was a rare election that did not bring a barrage of allegations of fraud leveled by the two major parties against each other or by self-styled reformers and third-party losers against one or both major parties. Substantiating the myriad charges is difficult, however, and modern scholars disagree about the amount or the impact of election corruption in the period. According to one study, citizens who took money for their votes were relatively few in number and selected candidates from their own party anyway; those who sold their vote to the party that paid them more for it were an even smaller minority of purchased voters. Of course, in a close election even a small number of purchased "floating" votes could contribute to the result, but it is equally true that all the unpurchased votes—usually the vast majority—influenced the result as well. "The majority of

James G. Blaine. The Republican nominee for president in 1884, in a photograph from 1892. *Courtesy Library of Congress*

voters," this study asserts, "were not bribed but, rather, voted for their party out of deep and long-standing loyalty."[30]

Much more than bribery, legitimate campaign outlays represented a consistent and pervasive drain on party resources. Such expenses included the salaries of paid party officials and workers, travel expenses for campaigners, polling, outfitting headquarters rooms and public lecture halls, advertising, office supplies, postage, printing and distributing documents and textbooks, financial support for party newspapers, and on and on. In 1888, *Irish World* editor Patrick Ford itemized his expenses for organizing the Irish-American voters in New York City for the Republican party. Most of the funds went for salaries (district organizers, assistant directors, clerks, messenger boys, and so forth), but his list also included "Fitting Up 30 Ward Rooms" with such items as three thousand chairs at 35 cents each, banners and signs for each room at $25.00, and gaslight for each room at $3.00 per week for fourteen weeks. The total came to $73,465, and this was for only one portion of the population in a city usually carried by the opposing party.[31]

Campaigns were costly. The responsibility for raising the necessary funds lay with party executive committees or separate finance committees, which often found their task difficult. Traditionally, committees expected state and federal officeholders to contribute a portion of their government salaries to the party cause. This source was not available to the party out of power, however, and the Civil Service Act of 1883 made federal officials less vulnerable to this kind of political assessment. By 1892 one state party chairman was complaining that "postmasters who receive from $600 to $1000 [per year in salary] send in contributions of from $3.00 to $5.00."[32]

As the period progressed, parties looked increasingly to other sources of revenue, including economic interests that stood to benefit from the enactment of party policies. Traditional historians have referred to this sort of fund-raising as "frying the fat" from large capitalists who, in turn, expected subservience from the politicians, especially on issues affecting their businesses. In reality, the relationship was more complex. For one thing, there was no certainty that such contributions would be forthcoming. After narrowly losing his race for the presidency in 1884, Blaine complained, "I was beaten in New York simply for the lack of $25,000 which I tried in vain to raise in New York in the last week of the campaign. With all the immense interests of the tariff at stake, I don't think a single manufacturer gave $20,000. I doubt if one gave $10,000." Four years later, however, when the tariff issue dominated the campaign, the national committee amassed a war chest in excess of $1.2 million. Yet in 1890 tariff beneficiaries seemed asleep again; when congressional Republicans sought reelection after passing the highly protective McKinley Tariff Act, campaign officials complained that "money comes in slowly & in small amounts." In 1896, when the tariff steward McKinley himself ran for president against William Jennings Bryan, whose economic ideas many businessmen considered dangerous, Republican campaign manager Mark Hanna had millions in campaign funds at his disposal.[33]

Raising funds from business sources thus met with erratic success, and even when the party received such contributions, they did not automatically lead to businessmen getting what they wanted. James M. Swank, general manager of the American Iron and Steel Association, a strong backer of the protective tariff and always a big contributor to the Republican party, complained about the party's poor performance in the passage of the Tariff of 1883. "It is unfortunate," he wrote the chairman of the Senate Finance Committee, "that your Committee, in considering the Tariff Commission's schedules, did not invite a few leading representatives of the most important industries of the country to appear before it. The new tariff does not give satisfaction in many quarters." Swank and the iron and steel interests had to wait seven years, until the McKinley Act, for a tariff they found fully satisfactory.[34]

Swank had been on hand in Washington for the hectic final days of congressional debate on the 1883 tariff, only to return home to Philadelphia disappointed and suffering from a severe cold and "physical prostration." His experience was not unusual and belies the stereotype of the overbearing lobbyist whipping politicians into line. The negative reputation of lobbyists notwithstanding, there was nothing inherently corrupt or even unreasonable in a legislator's listening to the recommendations of constituents and others affected by legislation. It was not unusual for a congressman to turn to such individuals as the only available source of information about a particular industry or interest. Moreover, politicians and business lobbyists frequently subscribed to the same basic views anyway. Senate Finance Committee leaders such as Justin Morrill, John Sherman, and Nelson Aldrich did not need Swank to convince them of the importance of tariff protection to further the nation's industrial development, although circumstances did not always permit them to enact their ideas.[35]

More problematic were those instances in which congressmen came under pressure from conflicting interests. What was a senator to do, for instance, when woolen manufacturers urged a decrease in import duties on raw wool and sheep farmers demanded an increase? Consider the case of New York Senator William M. Evarts who, while Congress was considering the Interstate Commerce Act, received pleas from a Buffalo coal wholesaler "to render all the aid you possibly can to the passage of the Reagan Bill," and from a Seneca Falls pump manufacturer to "use your very best endeavors in killing this suicidal bill." American business interests, or "capitalists," were not a monolith, and a congressman obviously could not have a "sweetheart relationship" with both sides of diametrically opposed interests.[36]

While some legislators were undoubtedly in the pocket of large business interests, most had the opportunity to hear a variety of voices: rich, middle class, and poor—farmers, laborers, small factory owners, importers, academics, clergymen, lawyers, and merchants, as well as bankers and leaders of large corporations. In the absence of the twentieth century's sophisticated opinion survey techniques that track Americans' attitudes on public issues, Gilded Age political leaders paid close attention to the often numerous letters they received from constituents and others. The surviving papers of congressmen and senators give unmistakable evidence of a broad citizen interest in national issues. In 1888, for instance, an Ohio farmer of uncertain literacy wrote his senator: "Do No Let a free traid bill pass if Can be *helped* because it will be a injury to the farmer in the Contry. We Cant Compeate with Foran Labor at 30 cents a day or less." On the free silver question Brooklynite Thomas Edge wrote the Senate Finance Committee chairman, "I am a poor working man but I want and mean to have the best money this nation can give for my work." "For God['s] sake," wrote a Wisconsin insurance agent to his senator, "and for the sake of suffering humanity, hurry up the tariff bill. The whole business of the country is hung up in suspense." Such letters might not carry as much weight as those from a James Swank, but they were not ignored. Most congressmen read all such correspondence and wrote replies or told a clerk to send a specific response along with an appropriate printed speech or document.[37]

Illustrations of this ardent citizen engagement, especially concerning economic questions, could be multiplied almost infinitely, demonstrating that political debate was not an empty or "false" argument among the elite but in some measure an ongoing dialogue between leaders and the led. Such evidence also suggests that voters' preferences and actions were not motivated solely or perhaps even principally by local or ethno-religious considerations. Clearly, they gave rational consideration to the economic issues that dominated national political debate, issues whose outcome would affect their own well-being. Party leaders understood that political reality; as the Republican vice chairman weighed his party's tariff strategy in 1888, he observed that "the masses may be wrong, of course, but they are going to furnish the votes that will decide this election." Conversely, citizens had more faith in the politicians' willingness and ability to act for the public good than many later historians gave them credit for. As one contemporary journalist wrote, "The politicians, after all, are the ones who inspire the people. It may be a humiliating confession for an American but it is a fact."[38]

In assessing the Gilded Age political universe as a whole, one might well ask: Was it wrong for citizens to have faith in their leaders? If not, why did not government accomplish more, especially at the federal level? In one sense, Americans got the government they asked for. With the major-party electorate evenly divided between Republicans and Democrats—leading to divided party control of the national government—stalemate often resulted. Yet, it would be wrong to dismiss the era as a whole as one of little accomplishment. The decades after the Civil War saw a shift in political concern away from the dominance of sectional issues toward questions of economic policymaking, with important implications for the evolution of government's role in the following century. When Gilded Age politicians tried to cope with the vexing and divisive currency issue, for example, they implicitly recognized that the government had a part to play in determining the country's money supply and, hence, the level of economic activity, a role that would be the essence of twentieth-century fiscal and monetary policy. The tariff issue had the power to touch people all across economic lines, and Congress's grappling with it was at its core a debate over what the government should do to promote prosperity—a question that continues to dominate policy debate to this day. Subsidies to railroads or other enterprises, often criticized as the quintessence of

Gilded Age misfeasance, could be seen as an innovative approach to government/business cooperation in creating and modernizing the infrastructure of an industrializing nation. The late nineteenth century also witnessed the beginning of serious government regulation of business with the foundations laid down by the Interstate Commerce Act and the Sherman Antitrust Act, and the government began to police itself with the Pendleton Civil Service Act. Some scholars even see the government's pension program for Union veterans as an important antecedent for twentieth-century welfare policies.[39]

Among the most important developments in the late nineteenth century was the growing strength and importance of the office of president. Having recovered from the blows struck by the attempted impeachment of Andrew Johnson and the scandals of the Grant administration, the presidency, by the end of the century, had become the center of the national political system. Historically, policy-making had been the province of Congress, but, more and more, presidents went beyond their traditional administrative role to act as legislative leaders on behalf of their policy objectives. By the end of the century, much legislation was being originally drafted in the executive branch. As with much else in American life, the 1890s brought an extraordinary transformation in presidential activism. At the beginning of the decade, Harrison employed a variety of means to achieve his ends: veto threats to influence the shape of legislation, well-timed messages and public statements to garner support, and informal dinners and other consultations with congressmen at the White House to push them in the right direction. Harrison's successor, Grover Cleveland, was in many ways a strong executive, but his ham-handed efforts to pressure Democrats in Congress frequently backfired and left him isolated from much of his party. McKinley picked up where Harrison left off. As a smoother, more skillful politician who saw the importance of cultivating good press relations, McKinley proved so effective as an administrator and legislative leader that recent scholars consider him the first modern president.

A strong national executive, with the president voicing citizens' concerns from the "bully pulpit," emerged as a defining feature of the Progressive Era that followed. In other ways as well the Gilded Age foreshadowed the Progressive Era, including the increasing emphasis on government activism to address economic problems and other issues and in the impulse toward reform. Progressivism was not merely the discovery of new purposes for government; it also represented the release of government activism from the restraining effect of the previous era's two decades of political equilibrium. One of the main reasons the Progressive Era started when it did was that the stalemate had been broken. Because the Republicans had established themselves as the majority party in the mid-1890s, President Theodore Roosevelt was freer than his predecessors of worries about perpetuating his party in power. Less fearful of frustration at the hands of historically obstructionist Democrats (many of whom were now taking on progressive ways of thinking), Roosevelt could move toward governing much more boldly.

The late nineteenth century witnessed profound changes in the United States. Scholars once treated its political life almost as an historical embarrassment, in Henry Adams's words, "poor in purpose and barren in result." Most historians now realize how inadequate that judgment was to describe this complex and portentous time, bridging the age of Abraham Lincoln and that of Theodore Roosevelt. In a rapidly evolving society, political leaders confronted problems of unprecedented intricacy and scope. That they were locked in partisan stalemate much of the time and frequently hamstrung by one of the major parties, the Democrats, who believed that Americans wanted less government, not more, often prevented vigorous action. Yet, they were able to post some modest success in reaching solutions to the society's problems. More important, leaders of a more activist inclination, including Republicans such as John Sherman, Benjamin Harrison, and William McKinley, glimpsed, if they did not fully appreciate, the broader possibilities for energetic government. In important ways they helped lay the groundwork for the twentieth-century American polity.[40]

Notes

1. Charles A. Beard and Mary R. Beard, *The Rise of American Civilization*, vol. 2, *The Industrial Era* (New York, 1930), 341; Richard Hofstadter, *The American Political Tradition and the Men Who Made It* (1948; reprint ed., New York, 1951), 164; Ray Ginger, *Age of Excess: The United States from 1877 to 1914* (New York, 1965); Vernon Louis Parrington, *Main Currents in American Thought: An Interpretation of American Literature from the Beginnings to 1920*, 3 vols. (New York, 1927, 1930), 3:23; Matthew Josephson, *The Politicos, 1865–1896* (New York, 1938); idem, *The Robber Barons: The Great American Capitalists, 1861–1901* (New York, 1934).

2. See, for example, H. Wayne Morgan, *From Hayes to McKinley: National Party Politics, 1877–1896* (Syracuse, NY, 1969), and idem, ed., *The Gilded Age*

(Syracuse, NY, 1970), 129–48, 171–87; Richard E. Welch, Jr., *George Frisbie Hoar and the Half-Breed Republicans* (Cambridge, MA, 1971); idem, *The Presidencies of Grover Cleveland* (Lawrence, KS, 1988); Allan Peskin, *Garfield* (Kent, OH, 1978); R. Hal Williams, *Years of Decision: American Politics in the 1890s* (New York, 1978); Lewis L. Gould, *The Presidency of William McKinley* (Lawrence, KS, 1980); Robert S. Salisbury, "The Republican Party and Positive Government, 1860–1890," *Mid-America* 48 (1986): 15–34; Ari Hoogenboom, *The Presidency of Rutherford B. Hayes* (Lawrence, KS, 1988); and Joanne Reitano, *The Tariff Question in the Gilded Age: The Great Debate of 1888* (University Park, PA, 1994). For historiographic treatments see Vincent P. De Santis, "The Political Life of the Gilded Age: A Review of the Recent Literature," *The History Teacher* 9 (1975): 73–106, and idem, "The Gilded Age in American History," *Hayes Historical Journal* 7 (1988): 38–57.

3. George Donelson Moss, *America in the Twentieth Century* (Englewood Cliffs, NJ, 1993), 12; John A. Garraty, *The American Nation: A History of the United States*, 8th ed. (New York, 1995), 575.

4. Mark Twain and Charles Dudley Warner, *The Gilded Age: A Tale Of Today* (Hartford, CT, 1874); Henry Adams, *The Education of Henry Adams: An Autobiography* (Boston, 1918, 1961), 294.

5. James Bryce, *The American Commonwealth*, 2 vols. (London, 1889), 1:653; William M. Armstrong, "Godkin's *Nation* as a Source of Gilded Age History: How Valuable?" *South Atlantic Quarterly* 72 (1973): 482–83.

6. Joseph B. Foraker to James V. Gluck, November 13, 1885, Joseph Benson Foraker Papers, Cincinnati Historical Society, Cincinnati, Ohio; Mark Wahlgren Summers, *The Press Gang: Newspapers and Politics, 1865–1878* (Chapel Hill, NC, 1994).

7. Robert R. Hitt to Oliver P. Morton, April 21, 1876, Robert R. Hitt Papers, Library of Congress, Washington, DC.

8. Geoffrey Blodgett, "A New Look at the Gilded Age: Politics in a Cultural Context," in Daniel Walker Howe, ed., *Victorian America* (Philadelphia, 1976), 96; J. M. Ashley to William E. Chandler, September 5, 1868, William E. Chandler Papers, Library of Congress, Washington, DC.

9. *The Statistical History of the United States: From Colonial Times to the Present* (New York, 1976), 1081, 1083.

10. Ibid., 28, 30, 1073, 1079.

11. *Congressional Record*, 51st Cong., 1st sess., 767; James G. Blaine, *Twenty Years of Congress: From Lincoln to Garfield. With a Review of the Events Which Led to the Political Revolution of 1860*, 2 vols. (Norwich, CT, 1884, 1886), 1:180.

12. See, for example, Paul Kleppner, *The Cross of Culture: A Social Analysis of Midwestern Politics, 1850–1900* (New York, 1970); idem, *The Third Electoral System, 1853–1892: Parties, Voters, and Political Cultures* (Chapel Hill, NC, 1979); Richard J. Jensen, *The Winning of the Midwest: Social and Political Conflict, 1888–1896* (Chicago, 1971); Samuel T. McSeveney, *The Politics of Depression: Political Behavior in the Northeast, 1893–1896* (New York, 1972); Melvyn Hammarberg, *The Indiana Voter: The Historical Dynamics of Party Allegiance during the 1870s* (Chicago, 1977); and Paul Kleppner et al., *The Evolution of American Electoral Systems* (Westport, CT, 1981), chap. 4.

13. *Statistical History of the United States*, 1073; Benjamin Harrison to Louis T. Michener, January 13, 1885, Louis T. Michener Papers, Library of Congress, Washington, DC.

14. John Sherman, "Elections of 1882," manuscript speech, John Sherman Papers; John A. Logan to Mrs. John A. Logan, March 22, 1874, John A. Logan Papers; Benjamin Durfee to Nelson Aldrich, November 11, 1884, Nelson Aldrich Papers, all in Library of Congress, Washington, DC.

15. M. Warner to Henry L. Dawes, December 12, 1873, Henry L. Dawes Papers, Library of Congress, Washington, DC; James A. Connally to Richard Oglesby, February 9, 1878, Richard Oglesby Papers, Illinois State Historical Library, Springfield, Illinois.

16. John Sherman, undated speech manuscript, Sherman Papers; Benjamin Butterworth to John C. Spooner, June 8, 1897, John Coit Spooner Papers, Library of Congress, Washington, DC.

17. Benjamin Harrison, *This Country of Ours* (New York, 1897), 168; James A. Garfield, *Diary*, ed. Harry James Brown and Frederick D. Williams, 4 vols. (East Lansing, MI, 1967–1981), 2:103 (October 17, 1872); John C. Spooner to H. B. Van Slyke, July 4, 1897, Spooner Papers; S. Z. Bowman to Henry L. Dawes, July 25, 1881, Dawes Papers.

18. John A. Logan to Mrs. John A. Logan, June 18, 1870, Logan Papers; John C. Spooner to H. C. Payne, September 17, 1888, Spooner to W. E. Gardner, September 29, 1888, Spooner Papers.

19. Henry L. Dawes to Mrs. Henry L. Dawes, April 28, 1872, Dawes Papers.

20. S. A. Whitefield to N. P. Banks, February 16, 1891, Nathaniel P. Banks Papers, Library of Congress, Washington, DC; Benjamin Harrison to D. S. Alexander, May 4, 1893, Benjamin Harrison Papers, Library of Congress, Washington, DC; George F. Edmunds, "Politics as a Career," *The Forum* 14 (1892): 451.

21. James A. Garfield, *Diary*, 2:7 (January 14, 1872); John C. Spooner to H. C. Cameron, November 26, 1891, Spooner Papers.

22. Oliver P. Morton to the president, March 22, 1874, Ulysses S. Grant Papers, Library of Congress, Washington, DC; John A. Logan to Mrs. John A. Logan, January 21, February 21, April 4, 1874, Mrs. Logan to Logan, April 22, 1874, Logan Papers; J. M. Rusk to L. T. Michener, October 3, 1893, Michener Papers.

23. John Sherman to Richard Smith, June 14, 1880, Sherman Papers.

24. For discussions of political party structure see Robert D. Marcus, *Grand Old Party: Political Structure in the Gilded Age, 1880–1896* (New York, 1971); Joel H. Silbey, "Party Organization in Nineteenth-Century America," in L. Sandy Maisel, ed., *Political Parties and Elections in the United States*, 2 vols. (New York, 1991), 2:769–777.

25. Morton Keller, *Affairs of State: Public Life in Late Nineteenth-Century America* (Cambridge, MA, 1977), chap. 7; Thomas L. Tullock to William E. Chandler, September 17, 1868, Chandler Papers. See also Michael E. McGerr, *The Decline of Popular Politics: The American North, 1865–1928* (New York, 1986).

26. W. S. Hillyer to William E. Chandler, September 27, 1872, James G. Blaine to Chandler, September 16, October 16, 1872, Chandler Papers; Blaine, *Twenty Years of Congress*, 1:551.

27. James G. Blaine to E. B. Washburne, July 11, 1868, Elihu B. Washburne Papers, Library of Congress, Washington, DC.

28. James Harlan to William E. Chandler, September 24, 1872, Chandler Papers; James M. Swank, printed statement, "1,101,887 TARIFF TRACTS DISTRIBUTED," September 1, 1888, William B. Allison Papers, State Historical Society of Iowa, Des Moines, Iowa.

29. Charles Beardsley to "Dear Sir," 1888, Allison Papers. See also Republican State Central Committee, Confidential Circular No. 10, September 1884, Eugene G. Hay Papers, Library of Congress, Washington, DC.

30. John F. Reynolds and Richard L. McCormick, "Outlawing 'Treachery': Split Tickets and Ballot Laws in New York and New Jersey, 1880–1910," *Journal of American History* 72 (1986): 850. See also James L. Baumgardner, "The 1888 Presidential Election: How Corrupt?" *Presidential Studies Quarterly* 14 (1984): 416–27; Peter H. Argersinger, "New Perspectives on Election Fraud in the Gilded Age," *Political Science Quarterly* 100 (1985–1986): 669–97.

31. Patrick Ford, "Expenses for Organizing New York City," [1888], Matthew S. Quay Papers, Library of Congress, Washington, DC.

32. Charles W. F. Dick to John Sherman, October 12, 1892, Sherman Papers.

33. Josephson, *Politicos*, chap. 11; James G. Blaine to Whitelaw Reid, January 26, 1888, Whitelaw Reid Papers, Library of Congress, Washington, DC; "Nat'l Campaign–1888 Subscriptions," Quay Papers; James S. Clarkson to Sherman, October 20, 1890, Sherman Papers; Morgan, *From Hayes to McKinley*, 509.

34. James M. Swank to Justin S. Morrill, November 23, 1883, May 8, 1891, Justin S. Morrill Papers, Library of Congress, Washington, DC; Swank to William B. Allison, September 26, 1888, Allison Papers.

35. George W. Cope to Edward McPherson, March 7, 1883, Edward McPherson Papers, Library of Congress, Washington, DC.

36. A. J. Hoole to William M. Evarts, July 31, 1886, The Goulds Manufacturing Company to Evarts, December 30, 1886, William M. Evarts Papers, Library of Congress, Washington, DC.

37. M. W. Ganyard to John Sherman, January 1, 1888, Sherman Papers; Thomas G. Edge to Justin S. Morrill, February 25, 1896, Morrill Papers; Isaac Bull to John C. Spooner, April 10, 1897, Spooner Papers.

38. James S. Clarkson to William B. Allison, September 24, 1888, Allison Papers; William Henry Smith to Whitelaw Reid, March 12, 1869, Reid Papers.

39. On the government's pension program see Theda Skocpol, *Protecting Soldiers and Mothers: The Political Origins of Social Policy in the United States* (Cambridge, MA, 1992), 102–51.

40. Adams, *Education*, 294.

Suggestions for Further Reading*

Blodgett, Geoffrey. "A New Look at the Gilded Age: Politics in a Cultural Context." In *Victorian America*, ed. Daniel Walker Howe, 95–108. Philadelphia, 1976.

De Santis, Vincent P. *Republicans Face the Southern Question: The New Departure Years, 1877–1897*. Baltimore, 1959.

Doenecke, Justus D. *The Presidencies of James A. Garfield and Chester A. Arthur*. Lawrence, KS, 1981.

Gould, Lewis L. *The Presidency of William McKinley*. Lawrence, KS, 1980.

Hirshson, Stanley P. *Farewell to the Bloody Shirt: Northern Republicans and the Southern Negro, 1877–1893*. Bloomington, IN, 1962.

*See also Suggestions for Further Reading following Chapter 10.

Hoogenboom, Ari. *Outlawing the Spoils: A History of the Civil Service Reform Movement, 1865–1883*. Urbana, IL, 1968.

———. *The Presidency of Rutherford B. Hayes*. Lawrence, KS, 1988.

Keller, Morton. *Affairs of State: Public Life in Late Nineteenth-Century America*. Cambridge, MA, 1977.

Kelley, Robert. *The Transatlantic Persuasion: The Liberal-Democratic Mind in the Age of Gladstone*. New York, 1969.

Kleppner, Paul. *The Third Electoral System, 1853–1892: Parties, Voters, and Political Cultures*. Chapel Hill, NC, 1979.

Marcus, Robert D. *Grand Old Party: Political Structure in the Gilded Age, 1880–1896*. New York, 1971.

McGerr, Michael E. *The Decline of Popular Politics: The American North, 1865–1928*. New York, 1986.

Morgan, H. Wayne. *From Hayes to McKinley: National Party Politics, 1877–1896*. Syracuse, NY, 1969.

Peskin, Allan. *Garfield*. Kent, OH, 1978.

Reeves, Thomas C. *Gentleman Boss: The Life of Chester Alan Arthur*. New York, 1975.

Reitano, Joanne. *The Tariff Question in the Gilded Age: The Great Debate of 1888*. University Park, PA, 1994.

Socolofsky, Homer E., and Allan B. Spetter. *The Presidency of Benjamin Harrison*. Lawrence, KS, 1987.

Summers, Mark Wahlgren. *The Press Gang: Newspapers and Politics, 1865–1878*. Chapel Hill, NC, 1994.

Thompson, Margaret Susan. *The "Spider Web": Congress and Lobbying in the Age of Grant*. Ithaca, NY, 1985.

Unger, Irwin. *The Greenback Era: A Social and Political History of American Finance, 1865–1879*. Princeton, NJ, 1964.

Welch, Richard E., Jr. *George Frisbie Hoar and the Half-Breed Republicans*. Cambridge, MA, 1971.

———. *The Presidencies of Grover Cleveland*. Lawrence, KS, 1988.

10

Party Conflict: Republicans versus Democrats, 1877–1901

Lewis L. Gould

During the last quarter of the nineteenth century, Republicans and Democrats waged one of the most intense partisan struggles for political power in U.S. history. The two major parties competed on even terms before the American public for most of this period. The elections of the era attracted eligible male voters at turnout rates that have not been equaled in the ensuing century. At a time before the spread of the mass media and pervasive professional sports, politics was a national obsession, with the fate of the Republicans and Democrats at the center of public attention. "We love our parties as we love our churches and our families." commented one politician. "We are part of them."[1]

The people who fought the party battles of the Gilded Age believed that large issues hung in the balance when votes were cast. In its 1880 platform, the Republican party charged that the Democrats exhibited "the habitual sacrifice of patriotism and justice to a supreme and insatiable lust for office and patronage." The Grand Old Party (GOP) warned against their rivals who sought "to overthrow the existing policy under which we are so prosperous, and thus bring distrust and confusion where there is now order, confidence, and hope." Four years later in their 1884 platform, the Democrats responded that "the Republican party, during its legal, its stolen, and its bought tenures of power, has steadily decayed in moral character and political capacity."[2]

The two major parties differed over the extent to which Americans should look to government at all levels for assistance in promoting the growth and expansion of the national economy. The

Republicans believed that the authority and strength of the government could be used to broaden the nation's wealth. The Democrats asserted that the role of the government should be confined and minimal. They saw unrestricted economic competition without government intrusion as the best guarantee of prosperity. While both parties condemned the growth of trusts, and the Republicans favored the use of federal power to enforce civil rights in the South, at least up to 1890, neither political organization contended that the federal government should increase its size and power to regulate the economy and pursue social justice.

The major economic and cultural issues that divided the Republicans and Democrats reflected the philosophical gulf. The question of economic policy that stood at the top of the Republican agenda was the protective tariff. Republicans argued that an active national government should employ high customs duties to ensure that foreign competition did not injure agriculture and industry. In the process, the theory went, American workers would gain secure jobs and earn wages higher than those paid to their foreign counterparts. As a result, labor groups provided extensive support for tariff protection and Republican candidates. Although many segments of the business community endorsed this Republican creed, a simple identification of the party with big business did not exist.

The tariff appealed to patriotism and nationalism. The Republicans asserted that government power could be wielded to build a more prosperous nation. "We should be slow to abandon that system of protective duties," said President Benjamin Harrison in 1892, "which looks to the promotion and development of American industry and to the preservation of the highest possible scale of wages for the American workman." Moreover, because Great Britain was the largest free trade country, Republicans often emphasized how protectionism would enhance independence from British influence.[3]

In the Democrats' view, the tariff was nothing more than a burdensome tax on the income of consumers. The government, they said, should be kept neutral and limited. Taxes should be held down to pay only for the absolutely necessary services of the government. The protective policy, said the Democrats, "is shifting sand" and an unjust levy against the American people.[4] They did not endorse free trade as an idea, speaking instead of tariffs "for revenue only" to finance a small government. At the same time, while most Democrats wanted lower tariffs, not all did. Those party members who represented areas that faced foreign competition resisted any lowering of duties on the products that their constituents made or grew. Any other course would have risked political defeat. The tariff issue divided the Democrats and unified the Republicans.

Cultural and religious ideas also affected party allegiances among the voters. The Republicans advocated moralistic policies based on Protestant values. These proposals included restrictions on the sale and use of alcohol and limits on the right of businesses to be open on Sundays. Churches, such as those of the Methodists and Baptists, the members of which believed in evangelical Protestantism and the need for the state to promote a godly society, furnished Republican voters in the Northeast and Midwest.

Democrats, on the other hand, contended that it was wrong to wield the power of the government to regulate individual behavior or to advance religious ideas. They were "in favor of the largest individual liberty consistent with public order" and opposed to laws that coerced Americans on behalf of a particular creed.[5] As a result, Democrats found supporters among Roman Catholics, German Lutherans, and other Christians who were not as evangelical and who wanted to block government from interfering with their cultural practices in the name of religious goals.

The other divisive questions of the Gilded Age did not result in clear partisan positions during the 1870s and 1880s. The country experienced economic deflation, that is, a downward trend in prices. As a result, government monetary policy aroused intense controversy. The best economic thought of the day maintained that every dollar in circulation had to have behind it an equal amount of gold metal. Because the world's supply of gold was static and the population of the globe was increasing, the value of the dollar rose. Those who had debts found it difficult to meet their financial responsibilities. One answer was to increase the amount of money in circulation.

Advocates of silver urged that the white metal should be coined into money at a fixed ratio to gold of sixteen to one, as the United States had done before 1873. Because the world's supply of silver was increasing rapidly, the actual value of the metal on currency markets by the 1890s was about half the level that the sixteen-to-one policy would have established. Those who had debts, such as southern and western farmers who disliked paying their debts in dollars of increasing value, believed that inflation was a better answer than continued contraction. Creditors who lived in the

industrial regions of the nation were unhappy with the idea of getting their payments in dollars that had a shrinking value. Neither
the Republicans nor the Democrats had a clear policy about gold
and silver before 1890, but the issue had the potential to become
quite divisive if the economic health of the nation worsened.

Finally, the question of the civil service plagued both parties.
Government was small during the late nineteenth century. The character of the people who held office revealed much about the expectations that Americans held for their government at every level.
Politicians operated under the traditional spoils system that awarded
appointments to the party faithful. Believing in the legitimacy of
partisanship, Republicans and Democrats used patronage to sustain their organizations and maintain discipline within the parties.
Gaining selection as a postmaster, U.S. marshal, or consul overseas served as a badge of distinction for the citizen thus favored.

By the 1870s, however, the patronage system had come under
attack. Critics asserted that in appointment to government positions
official ability took second place to party loyalty. Voices called for
a professional work force to do the government's business—a civil
service. The Civil Service Reform League agitated for these changes
but encountered stern resistance from politicians who saw reform
as a way of shrinking their power.

The electoral arena in which the major parties fought out these
issues during the Gilded Age reflected the even balance between
Republicans and Democrats. After Ulysses S. Grant led the Republicans to success in 1872, his party won three of the next five presidential contests. That supremacy was deceptive. The three victories
in 1876, 1880, and 1888 came even though the GOP never won a
majority of the popular vote. James A. Garfield squeezed out a thin
plurality over his Democratic rival in 1880. In the two elections
that the Democrats won in 1884 and 1892, Grover Cleveland
achieved pluralities over the Republicans but did not command a
popular majority in either.

The equilibrium extended to Congress as well. In the House of
Representatives, the Democrats were ascendant. Between 1874 and
1894 they controlled the lower house for all but four years. The
Senate was more Republican; during the same period, the GOP
controlled the upper house for all but four years. It was rare for a
party to control both houses of Congress and the presidency. The
Republicans achieved this feat only once, from 1889 to 1891. The
Democrats likewise attained supremacy just once, from 1893 to

1895. Late nineteenth-century American politics experienced a deadlock similar to the "gridlock" of the late twentieth century.

Balance did not produce apathy among the voters. At all levels, eligible voters turned out to cast their ballots during the frequent elections. Restrictions on voting blocked women, African Americans, and other minorities from the polls. On the other hand, eligible white males cast ballots at very high turnout rates. In 1896, for example, almost 80 percent of the male electorate voted when William McKinley, the Republican nominee, faced off against William Jennings Bryan, the Democratic hopeful. Participation in congressional and state races occurred at lower rates, but the figures stood well above twentieth-century percentages. The task for politicians was to bring out their own partisans. Independent voters received comparatively little attention.

The Republicans and Democrats confronted each other from electoral bases that reflected their contrasting characters as political parties. The Democrats were strongest in the states of the Old South where tradition and the memory of the Civil War weakened the GOP. The Democratic party was the defender of white supremacy, and its leaders warned southern whites that a Republican vote meant the return of Reconstruction and black rule. Despite these obstacles, pockets of Republicanism persisted, but these enclaves did not produce electoral votes for the GOP cause. Democrats could count on 135 electoral votes from the South in a presidential election, and that proved true in every race between 1876 and 1900.

The Democratic party also had support outside of the South. In the Northeast and along the border states between the sections, Democrats appealed to those Americans who wanted government to stay out of their lives and leave the economy alone. "Government is a power to protect and encourage men to make the most of themselves, and not something for men to make the most out of," said one Massachusetts Democrat.[6]

In the final analysis, however, broad support for Democratic ideas did not translate into an effective, cohesive organization. Internal divisions plagued the party, and it had difficulty in developing national leaders. As a result, it was more inclined to oppose what the Republicans did than to advocate ideas of its own.

The Republicans confronted electoral problems of their own during the Gilded Age. In the South they had no real base in presidential elections and had to establish coalitions in other regions.

While the party was strong in the Midwest, it did not dominate the Democrats in that section. Only in the Northeast did the Republicans have an advantage. By the 1870s, moreover, the issues that had carried the GOP to power during the Civil War era had lost much of their force. Popular concern with civil rights and sectional disputes was receding.

Nonetheless, the Republicans believed that their program and hold on the voters would win for them the national majority of Americans that they pursued throughout the late nineteenth century. The GOP still identified itself with the nationalism that had preserved the Union during the 1860s. "The Republican party stands for right and justice, more liberty and equality, greater humanity and Christianity, than any other party that ever existed," said a party orator in 1900.[7] They saw themselves as a disciplined, positive organization that sought to use the authority of the government to shape society toward its goals. The protective tariff symbolized to Republicans the energy and activist temper of their party.

The political task that the Republicans faced after the election of 1876 was a formidable one. Rutherford B. Hayes had defeated Samuel J. Tilden by a single electoral vote in a disputed election that left the victor under a cloud. In office, Hayes achieved greater success during his single term than many politicians had anticipated, and won a good deal of respect for the moderate and cautious way in which he governed. He sought to establish a base for the Republicans in the South, a campaign that largely failed. In battles with Republican leaders in Congress, however, he began the slow restoration of presidential authority when he secured victories over those who sought to limit his right to make his own appointments to federal offices. When in 1878 he vetoed the Bland-Allison Act, which broadened the use of silver in the money system, Congress overrode his veto, but for the most part Hayes governed in a manner that restored his party's morale after the scandals and bitterness of the early 1870s. For example, in 1879 he used a series of vetoes to block Democratic attempts to repeal the election laws that safeguarded black rights in the South.

Because Hayes had pledged to serve only one term, the Republicans had to find a new candidate to confront the Democrats in the 1880 presidential contest. The Democrats had made gains in the congressional elections of 1878, but they failed to agree on an attractive presidential nominee. Their convention turned to Winfield Scott Hancock, who had a good military record as a Civil War general but few political skills; he did not conduct a persuasive campaign. The Republicans chose Congressman Garfield of Ohio and balanced their ticket with Chester A. Arthur of New York. During the campaign, Garfield and other Republicans, including James G. Blaine of Maine, stressed the issue of the tariff which, in Garfield's words, "so deeply affects the interest of manufacturers and laborers."[8] The race produced a very tight result. Garfield emerged with a 10,000-vote plurality over Hancock and a majority in the electoral college of 214 to 155.

Garfield's presidency never really got started. Blaine became the secretary of state, and he agreed with Garfield about the need for a more activist foreign policy, especially in Latin America. First, however, Garfield had to regain the power of the president to make appointments without excessive interference from Republicans in Congress. The president won some early battles with Capitol Hill, but then was shot on July 2, 1881. He died two months later.

Few observers anticipated much from the new president, but Arthur surprised Washington and, given his previous experience, perhaps himself, when he governed with competence. Garfield's murderer had been an insane office seeker. The tragedy moved Congress to enact the Pendleton Civil Service Act in 1883. The Republicans also produced a tariff measure that same year. It became known as the "Mongrel Tariff" because it made only small reductions in customs rates and satisfied neither party. The Democrats benefited from the turbulence that the transition from Garfield to Arthur produced within the GOP; in the 1882 elections, they picked up House seats and expected to return to the White House in 1884.

Arthur was ill by 1884 and few Republicans wanted to see him as their nominee. Instead, the party chose the charismatic Blaine, the most popular political figure of the period. He was a gifted speaker, especially when talking about the tariff. For all of his talents, however, Blaine faced nagging questions about his personal honesty and his financial ties to business. Some upper-class northeastern Republicans, primarily from New York and Massachusetts, who took the name of Mugwumps (from an Indian word meaning "big chief") made it clear that they would defect to the Democrats if Blaine was selected to run on the Republican ticket.

For their candidate, the Democrats picked a fresh face in national politics, Governor Cleveland of New York. He had been elected mayor of Buffalo in 1881 and won the governorship of New

Grover Cleveland. The Democratic nominee for president in 1884, 1888, and 1892, who was victorious in 1884 and 1892. *Courtesy Library of Congress*

York the following year. Cleveland soon established a reputation as a conservative leader who was both honest and independent in his views. After his selection by the national convention, however, the public learned that a decade earlier Cleveland had accepted responsibility for being the father of a child born to an unmarried woman. There was a popular outcry, but Cleveland made a full admission of what had happened that satisfied his supporters. Blaine conducted a hard-hitting campaign that stressed the tariff issue, but he fell short in the key state of New York. In a close election, Cleveland emerged the victor with a popular plurality of 29,000 votes and a 219-to-182 electoral vote count over Blaine. Jubilant Democrats celebrated their return to national power on March 4, 1885.

During his first term, Cleveland showed that his party could govern the nation in spite of Republican taunts about Democratic incompetence. Many party members disliked the president's erratic use of patronage, however, and there were internal strains among Democrats as the 1888 presidential election approached. The late 1880s seemed politically quiet, but tensions in the nation were rising. In the Southwest, railroads experienced strikes, and urban violence erupted in Chicago's Haymarket riot of 1886. The major legislative event of the first Cleveland administration was passage in 1887 of the Interstate Commerce Act, which created the first national regulatory agency to supervise a major industry. However, because it passed with bipartisan votes and only tepid support from the White House, it added little political credit to Cleveland's record.

The Democrats came into the 1888 election with promising prospects. The Republicans had gained some House seats in the 1886 elections, but the basic Democratic coalition that had won in 1884 still appeared intact. President Cleveland set the theme for the campaign when he used his annual message in December 1887 to call for revision of the protective tariff policy. He charged that the nation's budget surplus eliminated the need for high tariff rates, and he held out the prospect of lower consumer prices resulting from reduced customs duties.

The Republicans leaped at Cleveland's challenge. Free trade, said Senator Orville H. Platt of Connecticut, means "first, financial disaster" and then "the degradation of American labor."[9] The opportunity to make a campaign on the issue of protection united the GOP. Democrats, however, were divided on the tariff issue, and they failed to develop a coherent campaign strategy. Cleveland's initiative did not get out of Congress. The president, meanwhile, observed the informal custom that an incumbent did not make an active race for reelection, and, as a result, the Democrats were disorganized and leaderless.

Benjamin Harrison of Indiana won the Republican nomination. He proved to be a very effective campaigner for his party. He conducted the race from his front porch and allowed the voters to come to see him. The pithy speeches that he gave provided the keynote for the Republicans. "We believe it to be one of the worthy objects of tariff legislation to preserve the American market for American producers," he said when he accepted the nomination.[10] Cleveland won the greater number of popular votes because of the Democratic strength in the South where African-American men were restricted from voting. In the rest of the nation, the Republicans and Harrison ran well, their ticket receiving 233 electoral votes to 168 for Cleveland and the Democrats. The GOP also controlled both houses of Congress after the ballots were counted.

"JOHN BULL AND HIS FRIEND CLEVELAND." An 1888 Currier & Ives campaign poster depicting the president befriending England with free trade, to the detriment of American working people. *Courtesy Library of Congress*

Over the next two years, the Republicans demonstrated their belief in an activist government with an ambitious program to reorder national priorities. The 51st Congress (1889–1891) enacted the McKinley Tariff, which raised customs duties, the Sherman Silver Purchase Act to respond to inflationary pressures from the South and West, and the Sherman Antitrust Act to break up concentrated monopolies. The lawmakers also expanded veterans' pensions and increased expenditures on the navy.

Republicans endeavored to push through a federal elections bill, which would restore the voting rights of African Americans in the South. That measure fell victim to opposition from Democrats, especially southerners, and to defections from the Republican ranks. One major agent of Republican energy in Congress was Speaker of the House Thomas B. Reed, who instituted new rules that made it easier for a majority to work its will.

Republicans wielded government power with equal vigor on the state and local levels during the Harrison years. In the Midwest, the party endorsed legislation to require all private schools to meet state standards and conduct their classes in the English language. This policy produced a reaction against the GOP from German Lutherans and Catholics who decried what they called "paternalism." Another Republican cause involved restricting the use of alcohol. Temperance laws in the Midwest threatened the liberty of Catholics and other nonevangelical denominations to follow their traditional life-styles. These cultural crusades by the GOP produced an adverse voter reaction.

As a result, Republicans suffered in the 1890 congressional election. Groups with grievances targeted the GOP for retaliation at the ballot box. The Democrats contended that the McKinley Tariff raised consumer prices while the Republicans were spending tax revenues recklessly. The outcome of the election was a Democratic sweep. They came out of the contest with 235 House seats to 88 for the Republicans. The prospects for the Harrison administration in the election of 1892 seemed bleak.

The two-party system in the United States faced another challenge as the 1890s opened. Falling prices for farm commodities in the South and West had eroded the economic position of those who worked the land. Many farmers could not meet their payments on farm mortgages and loans, much less make a profit on what they raised. They banded together in Farmers Alliances and called for reforms to address their complaints. Candidates for public office appeared in the states where conditions were most difficult in 1890, and they ran with the avowed support of the men of the Alliances.

The election results in 1890 attested to the impact of this farm protest. In Kansas, five Alliance candidates won seats in Congress while one house of the state legislature came under agrarian dominance. Farm candidates made gains in South Dakota, Nebraska, Minnesota, and Tennessee. Democrats staved off further Alliance victories in the South through control of the election machinery. In the affected areas of the country, discussions began about the need to establish a third party, based on Alliance voters. By early 1892 the People's party, or Populists, were ready to challenge the Republicans and Democrats.

For the Republicans the choice was the incumbent president, but they renominated Harrison without any real enthusiasm. The Democrats saw victory as likely, and they selected Cleveland to make a third race for the White House. The Populists held their national convention at Omaha, Nebraska, on July 4, 1892; their nominee was James Baird Weaver. The third party assailed the Republicans and Democrats. For more than a quarter of a century, they charged, the nation had witnessed "the struggles of the two great political parties for power and plunder, while grievous wrongs have been inflicted upon the suffering people."[11] Most voters disagreed, however. The two-party system withstood the Populist challenge in 1892.

Cleveland easily defeated Harrison and Weaver. The Democratic candidate compiled 277 electoral votes to 145 for his Republican opponent and 22 for Weaver. The margin in the popular vote for Cleveland was 400,000, the largest since Grant's reelection in 1872, and the Democrats controlled both houses of Congress. The electoral arithmetic looked bleak for the Republicans after their setbacks in 1890 and 1892. Unless the Populists could escape their sectional base, their chances to emerge as a major party also seemed small.

Democratic optimism proved temporary. The onset of the financial panic of 1893 shortly after Cleveland's second term began sparked one of the most painful economic depressions of the nineteenth century. As banks failed, railroads filed for bankruptcy, and the unemployment lines lengthened, Americans blamed the Democratic party for the prolonged crisis. Although the causes of the depression preceded Cleveland's return to power, he and his party became the targets for public discontent as the hard times persisted into 1894. A Pennsylvania Republican in 1893 told his coworkers that "on every hand can be seen evidences of Democratic times: the deserted farm, the silent factory and workshop, and in the large cities soup societies (the only industry created by the Democratic party) abound."[12]

The policies of the Cleveland administration added to the difficulties of the Democrats. Deep rifts over the silver issue remained after the 1892 elections. Democrats from the South and West favored inflationary actions as the best solutions to the agricultural depression that their regions faced. Party members from the Northeast recoiled from any abandonment of the gold standard. Cleveland lined up with the pro-gold wing of his party. He called Congress into special session during the summer of 1893 to repeal the Sherman Silver Purchase Act of 1890. The president blamed that law for triggering the Panic of 1893. By deferring action on tariff reform, an issue on which most Democrats were unified, he committed a crucial error. Cleveland achieved repeal, with the help of Republican votes in Congress, but the bitter debate over the subject ate away at Democratic cohesion.

The tariff came next. The Democrats had control of the Senate by only a few votes, and every member was crucial to the president's chances of tariff reform. The outcome was a political fiasco. Although a House bill called for lower duties, the senators pushed rates upward and refused to enact many of the promises the administration had made about revenue reform. The resulting bill became known as the Wilson-Gorman Tariff of 1894. Because it did not meet the goals of President Cleveland, he allowed it to become law without his signature in August 1894. The depression continued, the Democrats were split, and the tariff had been botched.

The woes of the party in power continued. Unemployed workers came to Washington as part of Coxey's Army (led by Jacob Coxey) to call for government action to relieve the depression. When workers walked off their jobs at the Pullman Palace Car Company in Chicago, it led to a nationwide railroad strike. The president called out soldiers to break the union that had started the walkout. Labor turned against the Democrats. The Republicans, meanwhile, claimed that Democratic tariff policies prolonged the economic distress. The Populists assailed Cleveland as an archenemy of silver. The opposition parties expected to oust the Democrats from their control of Congress. The Republican leader in the House, Thomas B. Reed of Maine, forecast that "the Democratic mortality will be so great next fall that their dead will be buried in trenches and marked 'unknown.' "[13]

The election of 1894 proved to be a turning point in American political history. The Republicans gained the most from the voters' repudiation of the Cleveland administration. They picked up 117 seats in the House of Representatives while the Democrats dropped 113 seats. The largest transfer of strength from one party to another in the history of the United States had taken place. In the Senate the GOP added five seats to its total. Even these figures disguised the extent of the Democratic disaster. In twenty-four states, no Democrat won election to a national office.

The election of 1894 produced one of the most crucial results in a nonpresidential race in the history of the country. The outcome put an end to the stalemated politics that had emerged during the 1870s. In fact, the Republicans had established an ascendancy with the American voter outside the South that would endure for a generation, until Franklin D. Roosevelt and the New Deal.

Victory for the Republicans in 1894 also meant defeat for the Populist hope of supplanting one of the two major parties. The People's party increased its vote over what it had won in 1892, but it did not emerge as a credible rival to either the Democrats or the Republicans. Democrats in the South used harassment and fraud against the Populists to keep the agrarian protest out of power. Most important, however, outside the agricultural regions, the appeal of free silver was limited. Those on fixed incomes had little love for inflation. The Populists discovered how strong the two-party system was, despite the turbulence and violence of the 1890s.

The politicians of that era did not know that 1894 marked a watershed in American electoral history. They turned their thoughts to the impending presidential election of 1896. For the Republicans, the choice was their most popular leader of the decade. William McKinley of Ohio had emerged as the spokesman for the protective tariff. His victories in races for governor in 1891 and 1893 showed that he could carry his own state in a presidential race. His campaign had the support of a close, wealthy friend, Mark Hanna, an Ohio steelmaker. In this political alliance, McKinley was the dominant personality.

In the race for the nomination, McKinley swept to a first-ballot victory at the national convention in June 1896. His vice presidential candidate was Garret A. Hobart of New Jersey. The Republicans adopted a platform that came out strongly for the gold standard. Their campaign strategy was to portray McKinley as "the Advance Agent of Prosperity."[14]

Contrary to Republican expectations, the Democrats did not cooperate by naming someone identified with the Cleveland administration. After the elections of 1894 the Democratic parties in states outside the Northeast turned to free silver as their rallying cry for 1896. The gold forces in the party were largely leaderless by this time. President Cleveland did not intend to challenge the tradition that barred presidents from a third elected term. In any event, his popularity was so low that another candidacy would have been doomed. As a result, the Democrats faced an uncertain situation when their national convention met in Chicago in July 1896.

Few political observers paid much attention to a former congressman from Nebraska. William Jennings Bryan was just thirty-six years old, but he had a plan to win the nomination. Since 1894 he had been on the speechmaking circuit in southern and western states arguing for free silver. On these trips, he told potential supporters that the friends of silver should have a second-choice candidate in mind if any of the Democratic front-runners should collapse. Bryan had a great deal of hidden strength among the delegates when the proceedings got under way. He took part in the debate about the language in the platform regarding silver. It was his great opportunity, and he made the most of it. Bryan delivered the "Cross of Gold" speech with its stirring conclusion: "Thou shalt not crucify mankind upon a cross of gold."[15] The delegates exploded in cheers and celebration. The next day, on the fifth ballot, Bryan became the Democratic nominee for president.

The results of the Republican and Democratic conventions left the Populists in a dilemma. They had hoped to run the only true free-silver candidate in the presidential race. Bryan had now preempted their basic message. If they endorsed Bryan, as many Populists wished to do, they would be saying that their party was irrelevant. If they put their own ticket into the election, the silver forces would split and guarantee McKinley the White House. After a turbulent convention, the Populists nominated Bryan and their own vice presidential choice. Most Populists supported Bryan and his running mate, Arthur M. Sewall of Maine. In the aftermath of the Chicago convention, Bryan's candidacy floated on a wave of popular enthusiasm. "Bryan buttons on Republican coat lapels are still distressingly frequent," reported a western Republican to the McKinley headquarters in late July.[16]

The Republicans responded to Bryan's nomination with an array of effective tactics. GOP chairman Mark Hanna collected several million dollars from businessmen fearful of the results of the Bryan triumph. The money went for hundreds of millions of pieces of campaign literature that made the Republican arguments against free silver and for the protective tariff. McKinley joined in the campaign of education that his party was waging, stating that "this is a year for press and pen."[17] Rather than try to match Bryan's personal tours, McKinley stayed at home in Canton, Ohio, and spoke to the delegations that visited him each day. This "front porch campaign" enabled McKinley to address three quarters of a million people in circumstances that he controlled. He delivered short, powerful talks about the tariff and the gold standard that set the tone for the Republican counterattack against Bryan.

Short of money and deserted by many of the conservative leaders of his party, Bryan took to the campaign trail in what became a true whistlestop campaign tour. He gave himself with great energy to the effort, but it proved difficult to sustain the appeal of free silver throughout the entire country. He had strength in his original base in the South and West, but his inflationary doctrines aroused less support in the industrial areas of the nation. Hanna said that Bryan was "talking silver all the time and that's where we've got him."[18] The Democratic candidate found that a single issue, however appealing, could not carry his party to the White House.

The victory of McKinley in 1896 represented the most decisive result since the 1872 presidential contest. He had 7 million popular votes and 271 electoral votes to 6.5 million ballots for Bryan and 176 electoral votes. Americans turned out in large numbers. In the North some 78 percent of the eligible participants went to the polls. The election of 1896 confirmed the significance of what had happened in 1894 to shift political dominance to the GOP.

McKinley's administration added to the Republican success of the 1890s. He was an effective executive who broadened the powers of his office. The war with Spain in 1898 enabled him to use the president's authority as commander in chief to direct foreign policy into new channels overseas. Under McKinley, Congress enacted the Dingley Tariff of 1897, which raised customs duties. The return of prosperity after 1898 provided the GOP with the opportunity to claim that their policies had restored good times to the economy. The issue of silver faded away and the passage of the Gold Standard Act in 1900 confirmed that the monetary question was a dead letter. Meanwhile, the Republicans experienced only modest losses in the congressional elections of 1898.

After 1896 the Populist party withered away as farm discontent receded. The Democrats could not overcome the divisions between the Bryan wing of the party in the agricultural regions and the more conservative, business-oriented section centered in the Northeast. Bryan's renomination in 1900 was an accepted fact among party faithful, but his chances of victory seemed remote as McKinley's popularity grew.

The only major concern for the Republicans in 1900 was the selection of McKinley's running mate. Vice President Hobart died in November 1899, and the administration could not decide which candidate it favored. As a result, the party turned to the popular war hero and governor of New York, Theodore Roosevelt. McKinley did not campaign in observance of the tradition that an incumbent president did not actively seek his own reelection. Bryan and the Democrats first tried to make imperialism an issue. When that did not catch on, they turned to the growth of trusts and business consolidation. Even free silver reappeared briefly in Bryan's remarks. None of it worked. Roosevelt gave most of the major campaign speeches for the Republicans, and he was very effective.

McKinley's victory in 1900 was more decisive than his success in 1896. He received 292 electoral votes to 155 for Bryan. The president also achieved a 900,000-vote margin of victory in the popular vote. During the summer of 1901 there was talk of a third term for McKinley, but the White House quickly said that the president would honor the two-term tradition. In the remainder of his administration, McKinley planned to pursue trade treaties to reduce the tariff, legislation to deal with the trusts, and travel outside the continental United States, which would have made him the first president to do so.

None of these plans was fulfilled. An assassin's bullet wounded McKinley on September 6, and he died eight days later. Roosevelt became the twenty-sixth president and soon put his own stamp on the White House and American history. There was more continuity between the presidencies of Roosevelt and McKinley than was realized at the time, but the symbolic shift of power from a Civil War veteran to the hero of the Spanish-American War was genuine. By 1900 the issues that had dominated politics in the Gilded Age, the protective tariff, free silver, and the civil service, were giving way to new problems. While promoting the growth of the economy, should the national government regulate business to produce a more just and equitable society as well? Would such a change mean greater power for the federal and state governments than had been true during the nineteenth century? Should the role of political parties be curbed to reduce the amount of corruption and inefficiency in public life?

The Republicans and Democrats had fought out the old questions for a generation during the Gilded Age. In that battle the two-party system had survived the challenge of Populism and witnessed the triumph of the Republicans as the nation's majority party during the 1890s. Looking back at the Gilded Age from the vantage point of the twentieth century, many Americans concluded that politics between 1877 and 1901 had been about irrelevant and obsolete matters. That was not the view of those who entered the political arena at the time. Gilded Age politicians were convinced that they fought over the destiny of the nation for stakes that mattered as much as those that engaged the leaders who preceded and followed them. A century later, as the Republicans and Democrats contest for power over issues of trade (tariffs), budgets (the monetary system), and political reform (civil service), the persisting relevance of the Gilded Age to the long sweep of American politics has been amply confirmed.

Notes

1. Richard J. Jensen, *The Winning of the Midwest: Social and Political Conflict, 1888–1896* (Chicago, 1971), 3, n. 7.

2. *The Republican Campaign Text Book for 1880* (Washington, DC, 1880), 174–75. See also *The Campaign Text Book of the Democratic Party of the United States for the Presidential Election of 1888* (New York, 1888), 6, which has the 1884 platform.

3. *Nuggets and Crystals from the Public Speeches and Official Papers of Benjamin Harrison, President of the United States* (New York, 1892), 20.

4. *Tariff Aspects with Some Special Reference to Wages: Speech of D. H. Chamberlain of New York City before the Reform Club of New York, August 24, 1888* (New York, 1888), 4.

5. The Ohio Democratic platform for 1881 is quoted in Morton Keller, *Affairs of State: Public Life in Late Nineteenth-Century America* (Cambridge, MA, 1977), 554.

6. H. Wayne Morgan, *From Hayes to McKinley: National Party Politics, 1877–1896* (Syracuse, NY, 1969), 268.

7. *Speeches and Addresses of E. J. Burkett from 1896 to 1900* (Lincoln, NE, 1900), 9–10.

8. Ellis Paxson Oberholtzer, *A History of the United States Since the Civil War*, 5 vols. (New York, 1931), 4:98, n. 1.

9. *Is the President of the United States a Free-Trader? Speech of O. H. Platt of Connecticut in the Senate of the United States, February 6 and 7, 1888* (Washington, DC, 1888), 40.

10. *Nuggets and Crystals*, 22.

11. John D. Hicks, *The Populist Revolt: A History of the Farmers Alliance and the People's Party* (Lincoln, NE, 1961), 440.

12. B. F. Gilkeson to "My Dear Sir," October 30, 1893, Lewis L. Gould Political Collection, Center for American History, University of Texas at Austin.

13. William R. Robinson, *Thomas B. Reed: Parliamentarian* (New York, 1930), 321.

14. Morgan, *From Hayes to McKinley*, 519.

15. William Jennings Bryan, *The First Battle: A Story of the Campaign of 1896* (Port Washington, NY, 1971), 206. This work is a modern reprint of the book Bryan wrote after the 1896 campaign.

16. Francis E. Warren to Moses P. Handy, July 29, 1896, Francis E. Warren Papers, American Heritage Center, University of Wyoming, Laramie.

17. Joseph P. Smith, comp., *McKinley's Speeches in September* (Canton, OH, 1896), 172.

18. Thomas Beer, *Hanna* (New York, 1929), 153.

Suggestions for Further Reading*

Blodgett, Geoffrey. *The Gentle Reformers: Massachusetts Democrats in the Cleveland Era*. Cambridge, MA, 1966.

Clanton, O. Gene. *Populism: The Humane Preference in America, 1890–1900*. Boston, 1991.

Gould, Lewis L. *The Presidency of William McKinley*. Lawrence, KS, 1980.

Hicks, John D. *The Populist Revolt: A History of the Farmers Alliance and the People's Party*. Lincoln, NE, 1961.

Jensen, Richard J. *The Winning of the Midwest: Social and Political Conflict, 1888–1896*. Chicago, 1971.

Jones, Stanley L. *The Presidential Election of 1896*. Madison, WI, 1964.

Keller, Morton. *Affairs of State: Public Life in Late Nineteenth-Century America*. Cambridge, MA, 1977.

Kleppner, Paul. *The Cross of Culture: A Social Analysis of Midwestern Politics, 1850–1900*. New York, 1970.

Kousser, J. Morgan. *The Shaping of Southern Politics: Suffrage Restriction and the Establishment of the One-Party South, 1880–1910*. New Haven, CT, 1974.

Marcus, Robert D. *Grand Old Party: Political Structure in the Gilded Age, 1880–1896*. New York, 1971.

McGerr, Michael E. *The Decline of Popular Politics: The American North, 1865–1928*. New York, 1986.

McSeveney, Samuel T. *The Politics of Depression*. New York, 1972.

*See also Suggestions for Further Reading following Chapter 9.

Morgan, H. Wayne. *William McKinley and His America*. Syracuse, NY, 1963.

——. *From Hayes to McKinley: National Party Politics, 1877–1896*. Syracuse, NY, 1969.

——, ed. *The Gilded Age: Revised and Enlarged Edition*. Syracuse, NY, 1970.

Reitano, Joanne. *The Tariff Question in the Gilded Age: The Great Debate of 1888*. University Park, PA, 1994.

Skowronek, Stephen. *Building a New American State: The Expansion of National Administrative Capacities, 1877–1920*. New York, 1982.

Welch, Richard E., Jr. *The Presidencies of Grover Cleveland*. Lawrence, KS, 1988.

Williams, R. Hal. *Years of Decision: American Politics in the 1890s*. New York, 1978.

Woodward, C. Vann. *Origins of the New South, 1877–1913*. Baton Rouge, LA, 1951.

11

Farmers and Third-Party Politics

Worth Robert Miller

In August 1896, William Allen White, editor of the Kansas *Emporia Gazette*, penned an editorial that made him an overnight celebrity with the nation's political and social elite. The Sunflower State, he claimed, had "an old mossback Jacksonian who snorts and howls because there is a bathtub in the State House; we are running that old jay for Governor. We have another shabby, wild-eyed, rattle-brained fanatic who has said openly in a dozen speeches that 'the rights of the user are paramount to the rights of the owner'; we are running him for Chief Justice, so that capital will come tumbling over itself to get into the state. . . . Then, for fear some hint that the state had become respectable might percolate through the civilized portions of the nation, we have decided to send three or four harpies out lecturing, telling the people that Kansas is raising hell and letting the corn go to weed." White caught the eye of the nation's movers and shakers with the venomous sarcasm of his editorial, which he titled "What's the Matter with Kansas?" His target was the upstart People's, or Populist, party, which they considered a major threat to respectability and order.[1]

The tone of White's remarks betrayed not only his exasperation at the heresies of the "ordinary clodhoppers . . . [who] know more in a minute about finance than [former treasury secretary] John Sherman," but also the fear that such rabble might actually win the crucial election of 1896. The Republican National Committee immediately reprinted White's tirade. It became the most widely used circular in William McKinley's bid for the presidency against Democrat William Jennings Bryan, whom Populists had also nominated. All of the forces of ridicule would be brought to bear against this threat to the establishment's right to set the nation's political, economic, and intellectual agenda.[2]

By 1896 the equilibrium that characterized Gilded Age politics had dissolved into a fluid three-way struggle for survival. The People's party had become a major contender for power in the South and West. In turn, the Democratic party had collapsed in the West. Its gubernatorial candidate in Kansas carried less than 10 percent of the vote in 1894. In the South the GOP shared the same fate, garnering only 13 percent of the vote for governor of Texas the same year. Which of the three contenders would survive the 1890s was uncertain, particularly to those living in the South and West. Voters had flocked to the new party, which claimed to address the common people's real problems, while the old parties engaged in electoral battles over what Populists alleged were meaningless issues.

Populists were hardly the rabble that mainstream party spokesmen claimed. Most were rural, middle-class property owners with a moralistic bent to their politics. They claimed to represent the America of the Founding Fathers as it had been refined through the democracy of Thomas Jefferson, Andrew Jackson, and Abraham Lincoln. It was the old parties, they claimed, that had adopted the alien ideologies that were subverting the promise of America— namely, laissez-faire capitalism, Social Darwinism, and the Gospel of Wealth. The Populist revolt was a major challenge to the socioeconomic elite precisely because it was a thoroughly American response to the dislocations caused by Gilded Age development, particularly in the South and West.

Rapid economic growth brought forth a revolutionary new America during the late nineteenth century. Industry expanded as never before. Railroad mileage grew fivefold between 1860 and 1890, making commercial agriculture possible in the West and upland South. Consequently, Americans brought 430 million new acres of land under cultivation between 1860 and 1900. The machinery that allowed American farmers to become the most efficient producers of the age also became widely available in this era. Agricultural production soared. Despite the material advances, however, almost all historical accounts characterize the Gilded Age as a period in which farming went into decline. Farmers' share of gross domestic product dropped from 38 to 24 percent from the 1870s to the 1890s. Millions lost their status as independent farmers and either became tenants or joined the urban working poor. By the end of the century, a vocation championed by the nation's greatest public figures as the quintessence of Americanism was rapidly being swept away.[3]

To millions of late nineteenth-century Americans, farming was a way of life infused with honor and patriotism. They remained loyal to an idealistic set of concepts inherited from the Founding Fathers that modern scholars have labeled republicanism. Creating a republic when all the rest of the world adhered to some form of institutionalized privilege committed the nation to an egalitarian society. The Founding Fathers also believed that history was a never-ending struggle between the forces of power and liberty. They associated power with oppression and liberty with social advance. Because wealth brought power, and poverty made men dependent upon others, liberty became contingent upon widespread equality. This commitment to both equality and liberty led Americans to develop a freehold concept that held that all men had a natural right to the land. Agricultural pursuits, they believed, encouraged frugality, industry, and community spirit. According to the Revolutionary Fathers, only an independent citizenry could defend their liberties and thus be the bulwark of the Republic.

After the Civil War, settlers flooded onto the Great Plains in search of freehold tenure and the independence it would give. Eastern Kansas and Nebraska received enough rainfall to continue the corn-hog cycle, which provided marketing options and required relatively little machinery. But as settlers moved westward, the climate grew drier. To encourage rapid settlement, boosters disseminated the fallacious idea that "rain followed the plow." Beyond the thirty-inch rainfall line, however, new techniques would have to be developed. Between 1865 and 1895 improved methods reduced the time to produce twenty-seven different crops by 48 percent. By 1900 one man using machinery to harvest wheat could do the work that twenty had accomplished in 1860. Thus, farmers found it desirable to buy machinery, fertilizer, and more land—all on credit.[4]

As the American farmer became a part of the world economy, the vagaries of feast or famine in Australia or the Ukraine also came to affect his life. His agricultural production vastly outpaced the capacity of the nation, and even the world, to purchase. Between 1870 and 1896 the wholesale price index for farm products declined by 50 percent, but railroads and other middlemen took their profits despite the farmer's plight. Soon, it cost Plains farmers a bushel of grain for every bushel they shipped to the East Coast. Critics complained that farmers had overproduced. Farmers who lived in a world of underclothed and underfed people considered this nonsense. With an equitable distribution of wealth, they believed, everyone would have the purchasing power to buy their products.[5]

Americans have long believed that the industrious should get ahead. As the condition of farmers worsened, many began a determined inquiry into the causes of their plight. Middlemen, such as commission agents, futures speculators, and wholesalers, appeared to make a profit without laboring. Railroads' freight charges seemed to be the product of monopoly control rather than the value their services added to farm products. For instance, railroads usually had reasonable rates in markets served by more than one line, but where only a single line existed, the road often gouged shippers. Thus, carrying crops on longer routes between major terminals frequently cost less than shorter routes to or from a minor depot. When farmers turned to politics, they complained bitterly about this long haul-short haul differential.

The social life of nineteenth-century rural America has long been misunderstood. Few farmers lived in physical isolation. Complaints of loneliness usually referred to loved ones left behind, not social insularity. Many settlers migrated in groups seeking to replicate familiar communities. Farmers met neighbors at church, camp meetings, fraternal orders, and literary societies. They also visited one another's homes. Frequently, farmers helped each other with swap-work and came together at barn raisings and to shuck corn. The resulting social connections greatly facilitated the creation of farmer cooperatives and political organizations.[6]

The Patrons of Husbandry, or Grange, was the first major farmers' organization of the late nineteenth century. Founded in 1867, the order grew slowly until the Panic of 1873. To circumvent middlemen the Grange founded cooperatives for buying and selling, mills for grinding grain, manufacturing establishments, and even banks. To enhance members' social lives, it also sponsored fairs, picnics, dances, and lectures. Politically, the Grange was nonpartisan, but it promoted state railroad and grain elevator regulation with significant effect in the Midwest. The U.S. Supreme Court, however, ruled such "Granger laws" unconstitutional in 1886. After the depression of the 1870s the Patrons of Husbandry went into decline.

Still, Grangers provided an organizational model for later farm orders.[7]

Plains farmers found credit harder to obtain and more expensive than did those back east. Harsher conditions made the chances for profitable agriculture uncertain, and the general deflation of the period raised interest rates. When the speculative land boom of the 1880s busted, numerous bankruptcies caused credit to dry up completely. Between 1889 and 1893 creditors foreclosed on more than eleven thousand Kansas farms. As crop prices dropped below the cost of production, farmers used their crops as firewood. By 1890, Kansas, Minnesota, Nebraska, and the Dakotas had more farm mortgages than families. Thus, western farming was in desperate straits by the last decade of the nineteenth century.[8]

While the major problem western farmers faced was holding on to the land, most cotton-belt farmers of the South did not even own the land they tilled by 1900. With emancipation, freedmen usually refused to work in gangs under the supervision of overseers. It was too reminiscent of slavery. Because former slaves associated commercial agriculture with slavery, most hoped to become yeoman farmers with the "forty acres and a mule" that Radical Republicans had advocated. Although land reform failed, necessity quickly broke up most plantations. Ownership of the resulting small plots, however, usually did not pass to the operators. Emancipation had liquidated substantial capital, making money scarce. Thus, planters agreed to take a share of the crop as rent. They also frequently became merchants and provided their tenants with seed, tools, and other necessities on credit. As collateral, the tenants signed a lien, or mortgage, on their crop. Merchants usually required farmers to produce only cotton, the most profitable crop grown in the region. Because cotton could not be eaten, farmers became dependent upon the local store for food. In the fall, farmer and merchant met at the local gin to sell the crop. Because cotton prices plummeted after 1870, farmers usually did not earn enough to pay their debts. Merchants then forced them to sign a lien on the next year's crop.[9]

Southern merchant-planters purchased their goods from northern wholesalers, also on credit. To pay their own debts, they tried to squeeze every nickel they could out of tenants. Thus, the price of goods sold on credit was considerably higher than the cash price. Interest rates on such debts also reached astronomical proportions.

Because the mortgaged crop was the farmer's only asset, no other merchant would allow additional credit. By 1900 merchants dominated credit, land use, and the marketing of crops in the South, and only 25 percent of blacks had risen to the status of landowner.[10]

White yeomen farmers of the upland South increasingly found themselves in the situation of tenants, too. In antebellum days they engaged in semisubsistence agriculture, raising mostly corn and hogs. Their animals usually ran wild in the woods, and sometimes through planters' fields. It was the farmers' responsibility to fence in their crops rather than their animals in the South. This "open-range" system made all unfenced areas common pasture. As in the West, other habits of mutuality, such as swap-work, had also developed. Yeomen grew only enough cotton to pay taxes and buy a few minor luxuries such as sugar and tobacco. During the Civil War, however, both Union and Confederate armies devastated the yeomen's herds. Railroad expansion after the war made commercial agriculture seem a quick way to recoup their losses. Thus, many expanded their commitment to cotton without any intention of remaining in the commercial world. This required credit, which merchants extended, taking farm mortgages as security. The rapid decline in cotton prices kept many farmers in debt until they lost their land and became tenants, frequently on the land they formerly had owned. In the meantime, planter-controlled state governments closed the open range. By 1900 cotton acreage had doubled, but 36 percent of white farmers had joined blacks in tenancy.[11]

Falling into tenancy was doubly catastrophic to the psyche of southern white farmers. It was a status popularly associated with blacks at a particularly racist period of history, and it signified the loss of liberty that accompanied the degeneration from republicanism to autocracy. Many attempted to start over farther west. When they left, they wrote "GTT," meaning "Gone to Texas," on their front doors to notify friends of their migration. The Southern Farmers Alliance, the immediate precursor to the Populist party, originated on the Texas frontier when tenancy appeared in the region.[12]

Southern farmers also suffered from problems common to the West. Credit was nearly impossible to obtain, except through the crop-lien system. The South had few skilled laborers and declining prices impeded capital accumulation. Both hindered industrialization. Poor consumer purchasing power drove transportation costs up because railroads passed on to the farmer the cost of moving empty cars into the region at harvest time. Both South and West retained vestiges of colonial-debtor economies well into the twentieth century.[13]

Although farmers in the Midwest and Northeast suffered from some of the same problems as those in the South and West, such as declining crop prices, their lot was significantly different. The inflation of the Civil War era allowed many northern farmers to pay off their mortgages. Their more intensive railroad network discouraged long haul-short haul differentials. Lower rail costs made less productive land profitable for grain, and proximity to growing urban centers made the supplying of perishables profitable. Dairy farming, for instance, became especially attractive where intensive cultivation had worn out the land. Longtime residency and familiarity with local agricultural conditions also made credit easier to obtain.

Federal monetary policy played a major role in the farmer's credit problems during the Gilded Age. Before the Civil War, Americans relied on a metal standard of currency. The government set the legal ratio between silver and gold at 16 to 1 in 1834. To finance the Civil War, however, the federal government suspended the redemption of paper currency with metal and printed $450 million in fiat money, called greenbacks. The result was inflation, commercial liquidity, and general prosperity.

Creditors and orthodox financial circles demanded the redemption of greenbacks with specie after the Civil War. The Public Credit Act of 1869 pledged the federal government to adopt such a policy. This caused deflation, which raised interest rates and made the money that creditors owned more valuable. Naturally, they wrapped their self-interest in a blanket of moralistic slogans. Honest money, they claimed, was necessary to convince capitalists of the long-term stability of the dollar. Otherwise, investor timidity would stunt the nation's growth. Debtors, especially in the cash-poor South and West, complained that deflation forced them to sell more products to make the dollar they had borrowed, in addition to paying higher interest rates because money was scarce.

When federal authorities revised the coinage list in 1873, they eliminated silver from the schedule of metals to be coined. Because silver had been worth more on the open market than the government's official 16-to-1 ratio, it generally had been used for purposes other than coinage anyway. But large-scale silver strikes in the mid-1870s lowered its value. If silver had remained on the coinage list, deflation would not have been as severe. Debtors and

silver interests labeled its removal the "Crime of '73." The free
(untaxed) coinage of silver and gold at 16 to 1 would have expanded
the currency while overcoming the fears many had about fiat money.
This refocused the currency issue from greenbacks to silver. Congress authorized the limited coinage of silver with the Bland-Allison
Act of 1878. Then, in 1890, the Sherman Silver Purchase Act directed federal authorities to buy up to 4.5 million ounces of silver
per month—approximately the entire domestic output. The Treasury Department, however, continued to redeem all certificates with
gold until the Panic of 1893.

The proto-Populist Greenback and Union Labor parties of the
1870s and 1880s made monetary policy one of their premier issues. Supporters considered labor to be the only legitimate source
of value. Thus, money was simply a means of keeping account of
one's labor. It needed only government fiat, not intrinsic value.
Greenbackers argued that the federal government should maintain
stable values by adjusting the money supply to match changes in
population and production. The federal government could easily
do this with greenbacks, but the supply of gold and silver could not
be controlled. Commitment to intrinsic money caused deflation,
which automatically increased the purchasing power of anyone who
possessed money. Greenbackers considered this illegitimate because
it allowed the rich to amass wealth without labor. Leo Vincent, a
prominent Populist of the 1890s, claimed that a government-owned
banking system, which circulated the greenbacks "that freed the
chattel slave" during the Civil War, would some day "free the wage
slave" as well. His father, an abolitionist in both England and
America, labeled the labor conflict of the 1880s his "third anti-
slavery struggle" but prophetically noted that it was "the most hopeless of all."[14]

Granger political activities spawned a number of state-level third
parties in the Midwest in the 1870s. In November 1874, Indiana
Independents founded the National Independent, or Greenback,
party. Greenbackers nominated Peter Cooper of New York for president in 1876. Their platform called for repeal of the Specie Resumption Act of 1875 and the issuance of legal tender notes.
Drawing voters away from the mainstream parties, however, proved
difficult in this era of highly partisan politics. For many, political
affiliation was almost akin to church membership. Thus, Cooper
polled a minuscule vote, mostly from the Midwest, in 1876.[15]

Greenbackers received a badly needed boost when a wave of labor unrest struck the nation in 1877. Wage reductions provoked numerous railroad strikes. State legislation outlawing strikes, plus the use of militia and federal troops, mobilized workers politically. Greenbackers absorbed the National Labor Reform party in 1878, creating the Greenback-Labor party. Its platform called for greenbacks, free silver, a graduated income tax, reduced working hours, abolishing convict labor, and land reform. The party received more than one million votes in the 1878 congressional races and sent fifteen men to Congress. Again, its vote was strongest in the Midwest, although the party gained substantially in the Northeast and Southwest.[16]

The Greenback-Labor party declined rapidly after 1878. Western agrarians advocated fusion (coalition) with mainstream parties. They gained control of the party in 1880 and nominated General James B. Weaver of Iowa for president. When Weaver forced fusion in some eastern state races, many laborers withdrew from the party, and its vote dropped by two-thirds. The results were even worse in 1882 and 1884, but the Greenback-Labor party developed a cadre of leaders and a list of platform issues that Populists would later inherit.[17]

Egalitarian third parties of the Gilded Age grew out of nominally nonpartisan producer groups such as the Grange. The growth of the Knights of Labor in the mid-1880s led to the next major third-party effort. Members refused to accept the permanency of their wage status or the capitalist system. Instead, they applied Jeffersonian values to the industrial setting by looking to a cooperative industrial system in which each producer would remain independent by becoming his own employer. In 1884 the Knights of Labor began lobbying Congress for an end to the importation of foreign contract laborers, many of whom had been used as strikebreakers. The order grew from one hundred thousand members in 1885 to seven hundred thousand in 1886 and soon became the nerve center of numerous boycotts and strikes. In 1886 local labor parties polled sixty-eight thousand votes in New York City and twenty-five thousand in Chicago. Their most spectacular showing, however, was in Milwaukee where they outpolled the Democratic and Republican parties combined.[18]

The Knights of Labor accepted all producers as members, even farmers. They founded the National Union Labor party in February

1887, whose platform called for reform in land, transportation, and money, a trinity of issues that Populists would later adopt. Events connected with the Knights of Labor, however, limited the new party's growth. The railroads crushed the Great Southwestern Strike of 1886, leaving the union with an aura of defeat. Knights also received blame for a bomb thrown at Chicago policemen when they attempted to break up a labor rally at Haymarket Square the same year. A severe decline in Knights membership ensued. Thus, the Union Labor party did poorly in the election of 1888. Thirty-one percent of its national vote, however, came from Kansas, where farmers made up a majority of the party's supporters. Western agrarians obviously were ripe for third-party action.

Historians have long debated why Gilded Age farmers adopted third-party politics. In 1931, John D. Hicks identified hard times as the cause. But the vast majority of all who have ever lived have been poor. Most have simply accepted their fate or worked within the established political parties. In the wake of the McCarthy scare of the 1950s, Richard Hofstadter argued that farmers' declining status in America had manifested itself as a nostalgic, conspiracy-minded scapegoatism rather than forward-looking, economically pragmatic reform. Most historians, however, have maintained that farmers' complaints in this era were valid, and the evidence for scapegoatism probably was stronger for Populism's enemies. With the civil rights, antipoverty, and anti-Vietnam War movements of the 1960s, scholars began to focus on the third party's notions of justice. Hard times alone could not explain the Populist revolt, but the presence of widespread poverty among virtuous and hardworking producers, while allegedly unethical manipulators amassed fortunes, convinced those who would become Populists that their situation was unfair and that contemporary trends posed danger for the Republic.[19]

During the year before the Great Southwestern Strike, the Knights of Labor formed a warm friendship with the Texas-based Southern Farmers Alliance, whose major purpose, one of its founders later stated, was to "educate ourselves in the science of free government" to resist the day that "is rapidly approaching when the balance of labor's products become concentrated into the hands of a few, there to constitute a power that would enslave posterity." The Alliance and Knights held joint meetings, picnics, and barbecues. Alliancemen also supported the Knights' boycotts and provided aid during the Great Southwestern Strike.[20]

The Southern Farmers Alliance had been founded in 1877. It had struggled along without much consequence until 1884 when S. O. Daws became a traveling lecturer. Armed with a cooperative message and the power to appoint organizers and establish suballiances, Daws and his subordinates spread the Alliance throughout Texas in the next two years. In their wake came trade agreements with local merchants, cooperative stores in areas where merchants proved intransigent, and Alliance yards for the bulk sale of cotton. The organization appealed mostly to small landowners. Middlemen, creditors, and the business community proved hostile. These circumstances caused Alliancemen to view themselves as an oppressed economic group, and they experienced a growing class consciousness. Pivotal to farmer radicalism was the conviction that nonproducers had rigged the economic system in order to amass wealth into their own hands. Members believed that only the mobilization of independent producers could counter such a threat to American traditions.[21]

Although Alliance cooperative economic efforts were successful for a while, most eventually went bankrupt. Many members were ready for political action when delegates met in Cleburne, Texas, in August 1886. The meeting produced a list of demands calling for the incorporation of unions and cooperative stores, fair taxation of railroads, railroad regulation, outlawing trade in agricultural futures, greenbacks, and several prolabor items. Conservative Alliancemen, however, could not abide such government intervention and immediately formed a rival group. Dr. Charles W. Macune averted a potentially fratricidal war with a proposal to establish a state alliance exchange. He argued that centralizing cooperative efforts would improve the association's buying and selling power. The Texas Alliance Exchange handled cotton, implements, dry goods, groceries, and general supplies at a savings to farmers in middlemen fees, but it was severely undercapitalized and extended credit too freely. Bankruptcy came in the summer of 1889. Similar exchanges in other states also eventually failed. Alliance leaders subsequently ascribed the failures to banker and merchant hostility.[22]

The Alliance committed itself to organizing the rest of the South at Cleburne. Lecturers from Texas blanketed Dixie in 1886, leaving thousands of suballiances in their wake. They succeeded primarily because organizers focused upon areas of their former residence. This gained them easy access to already existing social networks. When the producers of jute bagging (which farmers used to bale cotton) raised prices 60 percent in 1888, the Alliance was strong enough to sponsor a successful boycott. Texan Richard M. Humphries, who had been active in the Union Labor party, led a separate Colored Farmers Alliance, which also spread throughout the South at this time.[23]

In 1889 the Southern, Northern, and Colored Farmers Alliances met with the Farmers Mutual Benefit Association and Knights of Labor in St. Louis with an eye toward unification. The race issue and the secrecy of the tightly organized Southern Alliance eventually caused its northern counterpart to decline formal affiliation. Still, the platforms produced by both orders were strongly antimonopoly. The Northern Alliance's Kansas and Dakota delegations subsequently defected to the more radical southern organization, which immediately began organizing in the Plains and the West.

At the St. Louis conference, Macune unveiled a plan to solve the problem of underfinanced cooperatives. It called for the federal government to establish warehouses (called subtreasuries) to store farmers' crops. Instead of dumping their crops on the market at harvest time when it was glutted, farmers could store their crops in a subtreasury and use them as collateral for government loans of up to 80 percent of the market value of their crop. The resulting warehouse receipts could be used to pay debts. This would expand the money supply at harvest time when more money was needed and contract it as receipt holders sold their crops. The subtreasury plan rapidly became something of an article of faith with Alliancemen. Historian Lawrence Goodwyn has contended that the cooperative-subtreasury efforts of the Alliance created a distinctive culture of protest that led to Populism, but farmer dissidence had been grounded in the protest culture of republicanism long before the 1880s.[24]

Although the Alliance was formally nonpartisan, many of its demands could be realized only through political action. Republican leaders in the Plains states responded in an antagonistic and demeaning fashion. Kansas Senator John J. Ingalls, for instance, proclaimed that "the purification of politics is an iridescent dream." Even so, Kansas Alliance president Ben Clover called upon farmers to "close up ranks . . . (to save) the America given into our keeping by the Revolutionary Fathers with the admonition that 'eternal vigilance is the price of liberty.' " Alliance leaders told farmers that "it is just as essential for you to send men of your own kind to

represent you as it is for you to go out and cultivate your own crops."
No farmer expected a lawyer or merchant to help in the fields. Why
should one expect them to represent the farmer's interest in government? Replacing an alleged political elite with true representatives of the people is a theme common to all so-called populistic
movements.[25]

In opposition to the Republican party (GOP), third parties appeared in the Plains states in 1890. In Kansas they swept the House
of Representatives, carried five of seven congressional seats, and
named farm editor William A. Peffer to replace Ingalls in the U.S.
Senate. The holdover Kansas Senate, however, remained Republican and blocked Populists' proposals. Third parties also won the
legislature in Nebraska and elected another U.S. senator, James H.
Kyle, in South Dakota. In the South, Democrats proved decidedly
more conciliatory toward Alliancemen, who thus attempted to work
within Dixie's dominant party. They claimed to have elected four
governors, nineteen U.S. congressmen, and majorities in eight state
legislatures in 1890.[26]

When the Southern and Colored Alliances met in Ocala, Florida,
in December 1890, westerners advocated immediate third-party
action. Southerners, however, wanted to give reform within the
Democratic party a chance. Southern Farmers Alliance president
Leonidas L. Polk declared "education" to be the Alliance's most
immediate need. As historian Robert C. McMath recently noted,
the textbook trust presented "a politically correct version of history and economics . . . that celebrated the rise of industrial capitalism." Thus, the Ocala meeting founded the National Reform Press
Association to provide an alternative source of news and information to sympathizers. It would dispense ready-print literature on
economics, history, and politics along with original cartoons and
classroom lessons to hundreds of newspapers nationwide. It took
only $150 to establish a weekly newspaper in the 1890s. At Ocala,
Macune successfully proposed that the decision on forming a third
party be put off until 1892.[27]

Anxious westerners called a May 1891 conference in Cincinnati. With few southerners in attendance, however, they decided to
wait until the Alliance-called St. Louis convention of February 1892
to form a national party. Although southerners also proved reticent
at St. Louis, westerners went ahead with founding the People's party
and adopted a platform similar to the Ocala document. Afterward
they scheduled a national nominating convention for July in Omaha,

Nebraska. By that date the 1891 state legislatures' inadequate commitment to reform had readied southern Alliancemen for the third-party movement.[28]

More than thirteen hundred delegates met in Omaha in July 1892 to nominate a national ticket and write a platform for the People's Party of America. Polk was expected to receive the convention's highest honor. Unfortunately, he died just before the convention. Federal Judge Walter Q. Gresham, who had flirted with Populist doctrines, seemed to be the next best choice, but declined. In the end the presidential nomination devolved upon Weaver of Iowa, the 1880 presidential candidate of the Greenback-Labor party. As his running mate the convention chose former Confederate General James G. Field of Virginia. The "blue-gray ticket" of Civil War veterans symbolized the party's attempt to transcend the old issues inherited from the Civil War and Reconstruction and to face the problems that Gilded Age development had produced.

Party leaders scheduled the presentation of the platform for the Fourth of July. It quickly became the bible of Populism. The preamble, written by novelist Ignatius Donnelly, charged that the nation was "rapidly degenerating into European conditions." "Governmental injustice," it claimed, "bred two great classes—tramps and millionaires." This was attributed to "a vast conspiracy against mankind . . . if not met and overthrown at once it forebodes terrible social convulsions, the destruction of civilization, or the establishment of an absolute despotism." The great issue, the preamble charged, was "whether we are to have a republic to administer."[29]

The Omaha platform called for reform in land, transportation, and money. Populists demanded that public land be set aside for actual settlers rather than speculators. They called for government ownership of railroads, telephones, and telegraphs; "the railroad corporations will either own the people or the people must own the railroads." On finance, Populists demanded that the National Banking System be replaced by postal savings banks directly responsible to elected officials. They also demanded a flexible currency that could be maintained at $50 per capita. This meant greenbacks, although the platform also called for free silver. Populists likewise endorsed the subtreasury plan and expressed sentiments sympathetic to labor, favoring the democratization of politics and endorsing a graduated income tax. Except for the subtreasury plan, reformers had worked actively on behalf of all of these issues for decades. Whereas laissez-faire advocate Adam Smith had feared the power

James B. Weaver. Nominated for president by the Greenbackers in 1880 and by the Populists in 1892. *Courtesy Library of Congress*

of government, Populists feared the power of the wealthy and looked to popular control of an active government as their savior.[30]

Weaver spread the Populist message with a cross-country speaking tour in 1892. On election day he received 1,029,846 popular votes and 22 electoral votes. It was the first time a third party had broken into the electoral college since 1860. Populism was strongest among western farmers and miners. Other reformers supplemented their ranks in urban areas. Antimonopoly provided the unifying theme. In many western states, Democrats supported Populists to keep their states' electoral votes out of the GOP column. The People's party elected a governor and state Senate in Kansas, but Republicans disputed returns that would have given them the House. Populist Governor Lorenzo D. Lewelling, a Quaker and pacifist, eventually backed down in the potentially violent "Kansas Legislative War" of 1893.[31]

In the South, Populists arranged fusion tickets with Republicans in Alabama and Louisiana, but formal association with the party of Reconstruction was unacceptable to Populists in most southern states. Serious efforts, however, were made to wean blacks from the GOP. In Texas third-party leaders named two blacks to their state executive committee. Democrats consequently attempted to blunt the third-party appeal by endorsing some Populist issues in the Carolinas, Georgia, Florida, and Texas. In South Carolina, Democratic Governor Ben Tillman even endorsed the subtreasury plan, which left the third party stillborn in his state. Populists did best in Alabama, where fraud probably carried the day for Democrats. Fraud also accounted for the defeat of Alliance Democrat-turned-Populist congressman Tom Watson's reelection bid in Georgia. He had made a public appeal for African-American support for the People's party in *The Arena*, a reform journal with a national readership.[32]

Probably only one-half of the Alliance's southern membership voted the Populist ticket in 1892. Many Alliancemen were unwilling to desert the white man's party less than a generation after Reconstruction. Democratic demagoguery, fraud, and violence also took their toll. But southern Populists did even worse among black voters, who were hesitant to relinquish their power base in the GOP. In addition, the Populist economic program spoke primarily to the interests of landowners, not tenants. Still, where white Populists provided physical protection to blacks (a major concern in this era), biracial coalitions frequently proved successful.[33]

Populists fared badly in the Midwest and Northeast where close rivalries between mainstream parties provided alternatives within the traditional two-party system. Likewise, the Populist appeal failed to attract large numbers of northeastern and midwestern laborers. Alliance-Knights of Labor solidarity in the South and West translated into farmer-labor unity partly because both generally came from the same ethnic group. But recent immigrants in the Midwest

and Northeast frequently were not unionized and viewed evangelical, white, Anglo-Saxon Protestant reformers such as Populists with
suspicion. Fatefully, many suballiances, which had provided a politically neutral setting for educating prospective Populists, transformed themselves into Populist clubs in 1892. Thus, they would
no longer provide a nonpartisan educational way station from old
party to new.[34]

In 1892, Grover Cleveland and the Democrats captured the
presidency and Congress for the first time since 1856. Soon afterward financial disaster struck. The Panic of 1893 and the depression that followed clearly were the worst crisis during America's
early industrial period. At its nadir, economic activity declined about
25 percent. By the end of 1893, five hundred banks and fifteen
thousand business firms had closed. Eventually, unemployment
reached almost 20 percent of the work force, and the prices for
most farm products dropped below the cost of production.[35]

The economy of Gilded Age America suffered from several
major flaws. Railroads had expanded during the 1880s in order to
secure regional markets from penetration by competitors. Track laid
where future traffic never materialized, however, brought debt-
ridden lines to their knees in the 1890s. Industries linked to rail
expansion, such as steel, consequently found their operations overextended. In addition, America suffered the ripple effect of a European depression that had begun in 1890. The collapse of a London
banking house in that year brought a substantial call on collateral
that could not be met by 1893 in the United States.

Northeastern fiscal conservatives attributed the panic to uncertainty about the currency resulting from the Sherman Silver Purchase Act of 1890. Between 1890 and 1893 the redemption of
treasury certificates caused federal gold reserves to decline by nearly
$132 million. As reserves dropped near $100 million, entrepreneurs
questioned the soundness of the currency and became timid in their
investments. Hence, Cleveland called a special session of Congress
and, after an acrimonious debate, secured repeal of the Sherman
law in 1893.

Repeal of the Sherman Silver Purchase Act provided Populists
with a dramatic issue to promote. Because easterners dominated
both mainstream parties, only the People's party had endorsed free
silver in its national platform. Since the Civil War, the nation's
volume of business had tripled, while money in circulation had increased less than 50 percent. Populists argued that the American

economy had run out of money. Reducing the volume of money further by repeal of the Sherman Act would only aggravate an already desperate situation.[36]

With the Panic of 1893, millions came to know genuine privation. This appeared to create a greater empathy for the underdog and broader currency for the humane ideals of Populism. In his inaugural address, Populist Governor Lewelling of Kansas charged that "survival of the fittest was the government of brutes and reptiles." He further outraged the Republican party establishment by requesting that men "guilty of no crime but that of seeking employment" not be arrested for vagrancy. Opponents labeled his appeal "the Tramp Circular."[37]

In 1892, Populist Jacob S. Coxey had proposed that the federal government issue $500 million in greenbacks to state and local governments for the construction of roads. With no progress on his proposal by mid-1894, Coxey decided to "send a petition to Washington with boots on." Western farmers and silver miners proved to be his strongest supporters. The obvious sympathy that the armies of Coxey supporters inspired frightened respectable society. Borrowing trains and pilfering chicken coops, however, proved to be their most egregious offenses. When Coxey attempted to deliver his petition to Congress, police arrested him for walking on the Capitol grounds lawn. Authorities expeditiously dispersed other "armies" as well.[38]

As the excitement over Coxey began to subside, new storm clouds appeared. George M. Pullman operated a railroad sleeping-car factory outside Chicago. In late 1893 and early 1894 he laid off 40 percent of his work force and cut the wages of those remaining by 25 percent. In May 1894 his employees went on strike. When he brought in strikebreakers, the strikers turned to the American Railway Union for help. Its president, Eugene V. Debs, asked Pullman to agree to arbitration. When he declined, the class-conscious American Railway Union voted a sympathy boycott. Union members sidetracked all Pullman cars. Railroad companies countered by proclaiming their contracts with Pullman inviolate and refusing to let their trains move without Pullman cars. This stalled most rail traffic west of Chicago, including the U.S. mail. Attorney General Richard Olney then obtained a court injunction against the strikers, and President Cleveland ordered federal troops into Chicago to break the strike. The violence, which had been slight up to that point, then became spectacular. Mobs destroyed railroad cars and the switching yard. They also put part of the nearby Columbian Exposition to the torch. Although men not associated with the union did most of the damage, the strikers were saddled with the blame. The strike was quickly broken, participants blacklisted, and Debs packed away to prison.[39]

Coxey's movement and the Pullman Strike provided Populists with a dramatic opportunity to assess what ailed the nation. Many believed they were witnessing the triumph of the liberty-killing autocracy that the Founding Fathers had warned about. Visions of catastrophe if contemporary trends persisted, and of utopia if citizens took hold of their own destinies, found expression in protest literature. Between 1888 and 1900 cataclysmic and utopian political novels flooded America. Most of these works openly speculated about the future of the Republic. The vast majority of the authors were Populists.[40]

Populists hoped that the events of 1894 would bring a massive influx of urban laborers to their ranks. They believed that a union of interests existed among farmers, Coxeyites, and laborers. Debs became a major third-party spokesman overnight. Embracing Populist rhetoric, he charged that the old parties "are controlled by the money power and both are equally debauched by its influence." Along with Coxey and Lyman Trumbull, a cofounder of the Republican party, Debs came to symbolize the rapidly growing fortunes of the People's party.[41]

In the congressional races of 1894, Populists increased their vote 41 percent over their 1892 poll, despite the lower voter turnout of an off-year election. However, the third party lost a large number of offices in the West where Democrats and Populists failed to fuse. In the South, Democrats again won through fraud in Alabama and Georgia, but a Populist-Republican fusion carried North Carolina. Democrats defeated Watson's bid for Congress, this time by methods so outrageous that even prominent Democrats publicly denounced them. In Congress, Republicans gained control of the House and Populists held the balance of power in the Senate. With the election of 1894 the People's party became one of the two largest parties throughout the South and West. This gave it major-party status in one-half of the states of the Union.[42]

In the wake of the 1894 election, Democrats and Republicans in the South and West began a crusade to bring their national parties into line with popular sentiment in their regions. The silver mine owner-dominated American Bimetallic League financed their campaign. It sponsored several conferences as well as the publication of William H. ("Coin") Harvey's *Coin's Financial School*, which quickly became the *Uncle Tom's Cabin* of free silver. Silver advocates from all parties promoted it and many other monetary tracts during the mid-1890s.[43]

Despite their increased 1894 ballot, the third party's loss of offices appeared to make the chances for corrective legislation more remote. At this point, the apocalyptic times seemed to transform the evangelical justice orientation of early Populism into the expedient calculations of an established political party. In January 1895 national chairman Herman Taubeneck announced that the People's party would henceforth downplay the more radical planks in the Omaha platform and concentrate on the financial question. Party leaders subsequently promoted free silver as an entering wedge to gain control of government. The decision brought a chorus of howls from those committed to the entire Omaha platform. They feared that focusing on silver would divert the movement from issues that they considered more important. The arguments of both sides, however, also revealed a pragmatic manifestation. Democrats in the South and West had been going over to silver in droves. Fusion with Democrats meant power in the West. Emphasizing an issue that the local elite embraced, however, would destroy the third party's rationale for existence in the South.[44]

In January 1896 the Populist national committee set the date for their party's national convention after those of the Democrats and Republicans. They believed that neither old party would nominate a free silver candidate—particularly the Democrats, who had a two-thirds rule for nominations. Populists thus could expect to pick up a number of bolting mainstream party silverites. Republicans obliged by nominating William McKinley for president on a pro-gold platform, but the Democratic national convention proved a debacle for Populists. President Cleveland had offended so many elements of his party that his opponents overcame the two-thirds rule and nominated William Jennings Bryan on a free silver platform. Bryan was a dynamic speaker and close to Populists in his native Nebraska. Thus, the Populist party, which had boldly agitated for the issues and constructed the organization that had brought forth one of the largest electoral mobilizations in American history, suddenly lost its position as the leader of reform to a representative of one of the old parties.

Western Populists went to the 1896 Populist National Convention committed to giving Bryan and his Democratic running mate, Maine banker Arthur M. Sewall, their party's nominations. Many had already agreed to fusion deals at home. Southern Populists, however, did not trust the Democrats and advocated a straight Populist ticket. A compromise group proposed nominating Bryan but replacing Sewall with a southern Populist. Eventually, Bryan's opponents got the order of nominations reversed with the help of the compromise group and named Watson for vice president. They hoped that saddling Bryan with an unacceptable running mate would force him to withdraw. But Bryan needed Populist votes and remained silent. Pro-Bryan delegates then claimed that Democrats had promised to withdraw Sewall, and so the compromise group joined them in giving Bryan the presidential nomination. The whole affair seriously divided the People's party. Southern Populists had been the victims of the worst imaginable outrages by the very same Democrats whom their western brethren now embraced. Texas delegates even had drawn their guns to prevent their state standard from being included in a Bryan celebration at the national convention. In the end, Democrats did not withdraw Sewall (and may have never promised to do so). Although party officials later worked out fusion deals for presidential electors where they mattered, the trust between western and southern Populists that was necessary to sustain a national party evaporated in the wake of the convention.[45]

Bryan stumped the nation on behalf of free silver in 1896. Reformers of many schools rallied to his cause. But business interests poured millions into the McKinley campaign. On election day, McKinley, the Republican party, and the gold standard triumphed. Bryan carried the South and West but was unable to crack the Northeast or Midwest. Free silver had little appeal to industrial workers who feared inflation would increase the price of necessities. They also placed little trust in evangelical, white, Anglo-Saxon Protestant reformers such as Bryan. His candidacy, however, did save the Democratic party from going the way of the Whigs. Had easterners controlled the Democratic party and committed it to gold in 1896, the massive defections of silverites would have given the People's party a serious chance of eclipsing it as the major rival to the GOP nationally.

The People's party sent its largest contingent, thirty-one men, to Congress in 1897. They accomplished very little. Republicans controlled the presidency and both houses of Congress. In Kansas, Populists finally took control of the state government and passed a number of reform measures. Republicans, however, regained power two years later. In the South, Democrats probably stole elections in Louisiana and Texas. Although a GOP-Populist fusion carried North Carolina again, Democrats retook the state with a reign of terror in 1898. Violence also marked the end of interracial Populist coalitions elsewhere in the South about 1900.[46]

Populism as an organized political movement met its demise quickly after 1896. As Watson put it, "The sentiment is still there, the votes are still there, but confidence is gone, and the party organization is almost gone." The People's party split into acrimonious pro- and antifusion factions that spent more effort on recriminations than evangelizing. Massive gold strikes in the late 1890s increased the volume of money without the legislation that Populists had demanded. The nationalistic fervor of the Spanish-American War of 1898 likewise diverted attention from what was wrong with America to what was right. Many historians also credit Populism's demise to an overdose of prosperity as the depression of the 1890s waned. But cotton prices did not improve until after the 1898 elections when the third party met universal disaster in the South. Fusion with Democrats masked its dissolution in the West for a few years, but it was every bit as real. Diehard Populists nominated national tickets in 1900, 1904, and 1908, but electoral support for the once powerful People's party was minuscule; Congress contained no Populists after 1903.[47]

Populism was the last stand of freeholders and independent workers before they were proletarianized. Unfortunately for the movement, many laborers had already been trapped in wage slavery by the 1890s. As the People's party died, many of the disillusioned dropped out of politics. This is part of the reason that voter turnout in presidential races dropped 30 percent between 1896 and 1924. Others continued the egalitarian struggle by joining Debs in the Socialist party. Many, however, returned to the reform wings of their old parties. Several farmer demands became law during the Progressive Era—namely, monopoly regulation, banking/currency reform, and the graduated income tax. The Warehousing Act of 1916 even bore some resemblance to the Alliance's subtreasury plan. Populists also had advocated direct democracy with reforms such as the initiative and referendum, but reduced voter participation made a mockery of these reforms. America adopted the reforms agitated by Populists selectively and piecemeal. The result was hardly the egalitarian vision of Populism in its heyday.[48]

In 1906, William Allen White published in the *Emporia Gazette* an apology to the nearly forgotten Populists of Kansas. He stated, "Ten years ago this great organ of reform wrote a piece entitled 'What's the Matter with Kansas?' In it great sport was made of a perfectly honest gentleman of unusual legal ability [Populist Frank Doster] . . . because he said in effect that 'the rights of the user are paramount to the rights of the owner.' Those were paleozoic times." White admitted, "Judge Doster was right. But he was out too early in the season and his views got frost bitten."[49]

Notes

1. *Emporia Gazette* (Kansas), August 15, 1896. The editorial is reproduced in William Allen White, *The Autobiography of William Allen White* (New York, 1946), 281–82. White's comment about corn was a reference to the most famous quote of the Populist revolt, Kansan Mary Elizabeth Lease's admonition to farmers that they "raise less corn and more hell."

2. *Emporia Gazette*, August 15, 1896.

3. U.S. Bureau of the Census, *Historical Statistics of the United States: Colonial Times to 1957* (Washington, DC, 1960), 141, 278, 427.

4. As quoted in Robert C. McMath, Jr., *American Populism: A Social History, 1877–1898* (New York, 1993), 20; Fred A. Shannon, *The Farmer's Last Frontier: Agriculture, 1860–1897* (New York, 1945), 135–36, 144.

5. U.S. Bureau of the Census, *Historical Statistics of the United States*, 115, 117.

6. Gilbert C. Fite, *The Farmer Frontier, 1865–1900* (New York, 1966), 217–22; McMath, *American Populism*, 41. Willa Cather, *My Antonia*, is the finest description of this social aspect of farmers' lives in our literature.

7. McMath, *American Populism*, 58–62. The U.S. Supreme Court ruled the Granger Laws unconstitutional in *Wabash, St. Louis & Pacific Railway v. Illinois* (1886).

8. John D. Hicks, *The Populist Revolt: A History of the Farmers' Alliance and the People's Party* (Minneapolis, 1931), 24, 84.

9. Harold D. Woodman, "Post-Civil War Southern Agriculture and the Law," *Agricultural History* 53 (January 1979): 322–24.

10. U.S. Bureau of the Census, *Historical Statistics of the United States*, 278.

11. Steven Hahn, *The Roots of Southern Populism: Yeoman Farmers and the Transformation of the Georgia Upcountry, 1850–1890* (New York, 1983), 139, 269–89.

12. As quoted in Lawrence C. Goodwyn, *Democratic Promise: The Populist Moment in America* (New York, 1976), 31.

13. Samuel P. Hays, *The Response to Industrialism* (Chicago, 1957), 126–29.

14. *Guthrie Oklahoma Representative*, December 12, 1895 (first quote); *American Nonconformist and Kansas Industrial Liberator* (Winfield, Kansas), April 14, 1887 (second quote).

15. Paul Kleppner, "The Greenback and Prohibition Parties," in Arthur Meier Schlesinger, ed., *History of United States Political Parties* (New York, 1973), 1551.

16. Ibid., 1559–60.

17. Ibid., 1560–65.

18. The "Principles of the Knights of Labor" were reproduced in the *Oklahoma War Chief* (Arkansas City, Kansas), March 11, 1886; Gerald N. Grob, "The Knights of Labor, Politics, and Populism," *Mid-America* 40 (January 1959): 10.

19. See Worth Robert Miller, "A Centennial Historiography of American Populism," *Kansas History: A Journal of the Central Plains* 16 (Spring 1993): 54–69.

20. As quoted in Goodwyn, *Democratic Promise*, 33 ; McMath, *American Populism*, 75.

21. Lawrence C. Goodwyn, *The Populist Moment: A Short History of the Agrarian Revolt in America* (New York, 1978), 26–33 (this is an abridgement of *Democratic Promise*); McMath, *American Populism*, 72, 89–91.

22. Goodwyn, *The Populist Moment*, 42–58; George B. Tindall, "The People's Party," in Schlesinger, *History of United States Political Parties*, 1710–11.

23. McMath, *American Populism*, 95–96.

24. Goodwyn, *Democratic Promise*, 313–16.

25. Topeka *Advocate*, April 30, 1890 (first quote); *American Nonconformist*, July 4, 1889 (second quote); Purcell (Chickasaw Nation) *Territorial Topic*, June 5, 1890 (third quote).

26. Jeffrey Ostler, *Prairie Populism: The Fate of Agrarian Radicalism in Kansas, Nebraska, and Iowa, 1880–1892* (Lawrence, KS, 1993), 9–10. The Alliance claimed to have elected governors in Georgia, South Carolina, Tennessee, and Texas. They also claimed majorities in the Alabama, Florida, Georgia, Missouri, North and South Carolina, and Tennessee legislatures.

27. McMath, *American Populism*, 148–49. See also Theodore Mitchell, *Political Education in the Southern Farmers Alliance* (Madison, WI, 1989).

28. The Ocala, Cincinnati, and St. Louis platforms are reprinted in Hicks, *The Populist Revolt*, 430–39.

29. The Omaha platform is reprinted in Hicks, *The Populist Revolt*, 439–44.

30. Ibid., 229–37, 439–44.

31. For more on the 1893 Kansas Legislative War see O. Gene Clanton, *Kansas Populism: Ideas and Men* (Lawrence, KS, 1969), 131–36.

32. Goodwyn, *Democratic Promise*, 290–91; Tindall, "The People's Party," 1717; Thomas E. Watson, "The Negro Question in the South," *Arena* 6 (October 1892): 540–50.

33. O. Gene Clanton, *Populism: The Humane Preference in America, 1890–1900* (Boston, 1991), 96–97; Goodwyn, *The Populist Moment*, 121–24; McMath, *American Populism*, 172–73.

34. In 1902 former Alliancemen founded the Farmers Union as a deliberate resurrection of the Farmers Alliance. This time they promised to keep the farm order strictly nonpartisan and to work within the mainstream parties. It still operates today as a representative of small farmer interests. See Worth Robert Miller, "Building a Progressive Coalition in Texas: The Populist-Reform Democrat Rapprochement, 1900–1907," *Journal of Southern History* 52 (May 1986): 176–77.

35. John Spalding, *Great Depressions: 1837–1844, 1893–1897, 1929–1939* (Glenview, IL, 1966), 58–59.

36. Walter T. K. Nugent, "Money, Politics, and Society: The Currency Question," in H. Wayne Morgan, ed., *The Gilded Age* (Syracuse, NY, 1970), 125–26.

37. Lewelling's inaugural address and the Tramp Circular are reprinted in Norman Pollack, *The Populist Mind* (Indianapolis, 1967), 51–54, 330–32.

38. As quoted in H. Wayne Morgan, *From Hayes to McKinley: National Party Politics, 1877–1896* (Syracuse, NY, 1969), 466. Coxey had named his movement "The Commonweal Army of Christ." For more on Coxey's Army see Carlos A. Schwantes, *Coxey's Army: An American Odyssey* (Lincoln, NE, 1985).

39. For more on the Pullman Strike see Nick Salvatore, *Eugene V. Debs: Citizen and Socialist* (Urbana, IL, 1982), 126–39; or Stanley Buder, *Pullman: An Experiment in Industrial Order and Community Planning, 1880–1930* (New York, 1967), 147–210.

40. H. Roger Grant, "Populists and Utopia: A Neglected Connection," *Red River Valley Historical Review* 2 (Winter 1975): 482. See also Kenneth M. Roemer, *The Obsolete Necessity: America in Utopian Writings, 1888–1900* (Kent, OH, 1976). Edward Bellamy's *Looking Backward* was the first and most important novel of the utopian genre. Ignatius Donnelly's *Caesar's Column* was one of the most popular of the catastrophic novels. Both men were active in the Populist movement.

41. Alva *Review* (Oklahoma Territory), August 18, 1894.

42. Tindall, "The People's Party," 1719–20.

43. Ibid., 1721.

44. McMath, *American Populism*, 199–200.

45. Tindall, "The People's Party," 1723–24.

46. Lawrence C. Goodwyn, "Populist Dreams and Negro Rights: East Texas as a Case Study," *American Historical Review* 76 (December 1971): 1435–56; Roscoe C. Martin, *The People's Party in Texas* (Austin, TX, 1933), 137.

47. As quoted in C. Vann Woodward, *Tom Watson: Agrarian Rebel* (New York, 1938), 330.

48. Theodore Saloutos, *Populism: Reaction or Reform?* (New York, 1968), 2.

49. *Emporia Gazette*, December 14, 1906.

Suggestions for Further Reading

Argersinger, Peter H. *Populism and Politics: William Alfred Peffer and the People's Party*. Lexington, KY, 1974.

Cantrell, Gregg, and D. Scott Barton. "Texas Populists and the Failure of Biracial Politics." *Journal of Southern History* 55 (November 1989): 659–92.

Clanton, O. Gene. *Populism: The Humane Preference in America, 1890–1900*. Boston, 1991.

———. " 'Hayseed Socialism' on the Hill: Congressional Populism, 1891–1895." *Western Historical Quarterly* 15 (April 1984): 139–62.

Dethloff, Henry Clay, and Worth Robert Miller, eds. *A List of References for the History of the Farmers' Alliance and Populist Party*. Rev. ed. Davis, CA, 1989.

Gaither, Gerald H. *Blacks and the Populist Revolt: Ballots and Bigotry in the "New South."* University, AL, 1977.

Goodwyn, Lawrence C. *Democratic Promise: The Populist Moment in America.* New York, 1976; abridged as *The Populist Moment.* New York, 1978.

———. "Populist Dreams and Negro Rights: East Texas as a Case Study." *American Historical Review* 76 (December 1971): 1435–56.

Hahn, Steven. *The Roots of Southern Populism: Yeoman Farmers and the Transformation of the Georgia Upcountry, 1850–1890.* New York, 1983.

Hicks, John D. *The Populist Revolt: A History of the Farmers' Alliance and the People's Party.* 1931. Reprint ed., Lincoln, NE, 1961.

Hofstadter, Richard. *The Age of Reform: From Bryan to F.D.R.* New York, 1955.

Holmes, William F., ed. *American Populism.* Problems in American Civilization Series. Lexington, MA, and Toronto, Canada, 1994.

———. "Populism: In Search of Context." *Agricultural History* 68 (Fall 1990): 26–58.

Larson, Robert W. *Populism in the Mountain West.* Albuquerque, 1986.

McMath, Robert C., Jr. *American Populism: A Social History, 1877–1898.* New York, 1993.

Miller, Worth Robert. *Oklahoma Populism: A History of the People's Party in the Oklahoma Territory.* Norman, OK, and London, England, 1987.

———. "A Centennial Historiography of American Populism." *Kansas History: A Journal of the Central Plains* 16 (Spring 1993): 54–69.

Pollack, Norman. *The Populist Mind.* Indianapolis, 1967.

Tindall, George B. "The People's Party." In *History of United States Political Parties*, vol. 2, ed. Arthur Meier Schlesinger, 1701–31. New York, 1973.

Woodward, C. Vann. *Origins of the New South, 1877–1913.* Baton Rouge, LA, 1951.

12

Phases of Empire: Late Nineteenth-Century U.S. Foreign Relations

Joseph A. Fry

Several of the most important overviews of late nineteenth-century U.S. foreign relations have examined such themes as the "transformation" of American foreign policy, the "old" versus the "new" diplomacy, America's "outward thrust," the "emergence of America as a great power," and the "new empire."[1] These themes reflect historians' efforts to explain the nation's assertive role abroad in the 1890s, which culminated in the acquisition of an island empire. Some scholars contend that the annexation of Hawaii, the Philippines, and Puerto Rico, as well as the establishment of a protectorate over Cuba, constituted a break from previous American practices; others consider these steps reflective of a long tradition of aggressive expansion. Some deem this imperial gulp the accidental outcome of the nation's reluctant involvement in the Spanish-Cuban conflict; others portray it as the predictable result of a national ideology that emphasizes the racial inferiority of non-whites and the American mission to obtain greatness and of a committed search for economic and territorial opportunities abroad. Some emphasize the mass psychological, domestic political, or strategic bases of U.S. policies, while others accentuate economic or material motives.[2]

To address these conflicting interpretations meaningfully requires both a long and broad historical viewpoint and a working definition of imperialism. A long chronological perspective helps in determining whether or not U.S. actions in the late 1890s were comparable to earlier foreign policy involvements. A broad conception of foreign relations incorporates the actions of not only political and military officials but also nonstate actors, such as businessmen and missionaries, and provides a more inclusive understanding of interactions with other nations and societies. This broader approach also facilitates the most meaningful definition of imperialism. The key considerations are power, control, and intent. Imperialism, and hence empire, exist when a stronger nation or society imposes or attempts to impose control over a weaker nation or group of people. This control may be formal (via annexations, protectorates, or military occupation) or informal (via economic control, cultural domination, or threat of intervention). The informal species of empire often involves businessmen, missionaries, or other nonstate actors. When viewed from these historical perspectives and definitions, Gilded Age motivation, processes, and imperial results demonstrated much continuity with prior U.S. foreign relations.[3]

As with virtually all other aspects of American life, the remarkable economic growth of the late nineteenth century provided a critical backdrop to the formulation of foreign policy. Between 1865 and 1898 wheat production rose by 256 percent, corn by 222 percent, sugar by 460 percent, coal by 800 percent, and steel rails by 523 percent. In newer industries, crude petroleum production shot up from three million barrels in 1865 to more than fifty-five million in 1898 and steel ingots and castings from less than twenty thousand long tons to almost nine million.

This phenomenal growth carried multifaceted implications. In the broadest sense, economic and technological power of this order vaulted the United States into the company of the west European countries (and ultimately Japan) as the world's most modernized and economically powerful nations, and the United States assumed a position among those "metropolitan" nations possessing the power to impose their will on less-developed, agricultural or "peripheral" societies. The historian Paul Kennedy has observed that the "prime losers" as a result of the global economic, industrial, and technological changes of the nineteenth century were "the nonindustrialized peasant societies of the extra-European world, which were able to withstand neither the industrial manufacturers nor the military incursions of the West."[4] By 1900 the United States clearly stood alongside Britain, Germany, and France as one of the winners.

The development of "tools of empire" demonstrated this differential in power between the United States and less industrialized and less technologically advanced societies. Although the United States failed to keep pace with Europe in military technology following the Civil War, the arms produced by Winchester, Colt, and the Springfield Armory were easily superior to those available to Hawaiians, Filipinos, or Sioux opponents.[5] While such arms were important, the resurrection of the U.S. Navy after 1880 was the most significant military adjunct to extracontinental U.S. diplomacy. This process began in 1883 with congressional authorization of the "ABC" cruisers, the *Atlanta, Boston,* and *Chicago.* Over the remainder of the decade, another thirty steam-driven, armor-plated steel ships were authorized; in 1890, Congress appropriated the funds for the nation's first three battleships; and by the turn of the century, the United States ranked sixth in the world in the number of battleships commissioned or under construction. While the navy continued to perceive its peacetime mission to be the promotion and protection of American commerce, its strategic doctrine changed from the historic job of coastal defense and commerce raiding to commanding the seas through the deployment of capital ships in major fleet engagements. By adopting the latter approach, the United States moved into great-power naval competition with Great Britain, Germany, and Japan.[6]

Not only did the nation's economic growth produce the power and the tools essential for completing the continental empire and moving abroad, but it also stimulated America's involvement in international commerce. Total exports grew from $281 million in 1865 to $1.2 billion in 1898, while imports increased from $239 million to $616 million. Not coincidentally, the Gilded Age witnessed the expansion abroad of important U.S.-based multinational corporations such as Singer Sewing Machine, Eastman Kodak, McCormick Harvester, New York Life Insurance, and Standard Oil.[7]

With the onset of periodic economic depressions after 1873, numerous observers concluded that American productivity had far surpassed domestic demands and that even greater exports were needed to dispose of the "glut" of agricultural and industrial goods. Speaking for the agricultural sector in the mid-1880s, Representative Roger Q. Mills of Texas asked, "What is to become of this surplus? . . . Our crops are now far beyond the requirements of our home consumption." His answer was that "we must either have the foreign market or none."[8] Without ignoring agriculture, Secretary of State James G. Blaine added in 1890 "that the United States has

. . . developed a volume of manufacturers which, in many departments overruns the demands of the home market. . . . Our great demand is expansion. I mean expansion of trade with countries where we can find profitable exchanges."[9]

Historians have disagreed over the influence of this search for markets. Despite such forceful expressions, most Gilded Age policymakers and businessmen gave priority to the domestic market; at no time during the era did exports constitute more than 7.2 percent of the gross national product. The most successful exporting companies, such as Singer Sewing Machine or Standard Oil, achieved that status primarily through superior organization, marketing, and advertising rather than through crucial government support, and the bulk of American exports went to Europe and North America rather than to Latin America, Asia, or Africa—the focus of most expansionist rhetoric.[10]

Still, viewing the domestic market as primary did not preclude businessmen or policymakers from simultaneously regarding foreign commerce as important to overall profit margins, especially in certain important sectors of the economy. By the turn of the century the nation exported 15 percent of its iron and steel products, 25 percent of its sewing machines, 57 percent of its illuminating oil, 70 to 80 percent of its cotton crop, and nearly 25 percent of its wheat. Moreover, hard trade statistics did not deter Americans from coveting and pursuing *potential* profits in China and Latin America. Such persistence in the face of actual trade patterns spoke to the long-standing place of commercial expansion in the nation's foreign policy outlook. Americans from the time of Thomas Jefferson had looked abroad for markets, and historian David Healy has observed that in the debate over empire at the turn of the century "virtually no one seriously questioned the need for American trade expansion overseas."[11] Furthering foreign commerce neither took precedence in nor dictated all Gilded Age foreign policy decisions, but over the thirty years after 1870 this objective was a consistent impetus toward a more assertive world view.

This belief in the necessity of enlarging overseas markets in order to sustain national prosperity and growth was only one facet of a larger imperial ideology. Race had long been at the "center" of this American "world view."[12] From the time of the revolt against Great Britain, American policymakers had deemed nonwhites inferior and therefore less able to govern or to use land and other resources productively. These assumptions were manifest in the antebellum treatment of African Americans, Native Americans, and Mexicans and other Latinos. Following the Civil War, Social Darwinism, with its emphasis on competition and survival of the fittest, provided an ostensibly scientific rationale both for the U.S. experience on the North American continent and for prospective ventures abroad. Further refining the doctrine of white superiority, late nineteenth-century Americans also adhered to the concept of Anglo-Saxonism which alleged that they and the British possessed exceptional intelligence, industry, morality, and governmental aptitude.

Domination of others was thought to be the inevitable fate of such a superior race; still, Americans consistently and sincerely argued that their expansion was benign. By furthering liberty in the form of liberal, republican governmental institutions, morality through Christianity, and prosperity via trade and investment, American hegemony would aid those being dominated and instructed. Summarizing these collective attitudes, Senator Albert Beveridge of Indiana declared that Americans were "a people imperial by virtue of their power, by right of their institutions, by authority of their Heaven-directed purposes." God had made the United States "adept in government that we may administer government among savage and senile peoples. . . . He has marked the American people as His chosen nation to finally lead in the regeneration of the world."[13]

Considerations of national security reinforced this vision of national greatness and imperialism. From the Louisiana Purchase through the Mexican War, Americans had consistently justified expansion by insisting that territorial acquisitions were necessary to prevent strategic areas from falling under the control of strong, potentially hostile nations. During the Gilded Age the makers of American foreign policy increasingly worked within a "world of empires" as the European nations extended their dominion over Africa and Asia. These conquests had a dual influence in the United States. First, Americans worried that the Europeans might also attempt to extend their imperial reach into the Western Hemisphere. Most of this apprehension focused on the British, who controlled as much of North America as did the United States, had possessions throughout the Caribbean, and dominated commerce with South America. As the century ended, however, numerous observers came to discern an even greater threat from a rising and assertive Germany. In 1895, Senator Henry Cabot Lodge of Massachusetts warned that a failure to confront the British would embolden Germany and other European nations. Allowing "South America [to] pass gradually into the hands of Great Britain and other European powers and to be hemmed in by British naval posts and European dependencies" would leave "nothing more to be said."[14] Ironically, while resenting and apprehending potential European incursions into the Western Hemisphere and warning that European empires might preclude commercial access to Africa and Asia, those Americans who envisioned an international standing consistent with the United States' heightened economic power increasingly identified European imperialism with great-power status. Joining the company of the elite European nations appeared to require the acquisition of empire.[15]

Not all Americans endorsed such attitudes. Instead, a well-established critique questioned the wisdom and utility of an imperial foreign policy. Echoing many arguments propounded in the 1840s, dissenters in the1870s and 1890s emphasized that by imposing its power on others the United States violated professed beliefs in self-determination and liberty. Carl Schurz, sometime Republican politician and editor, warned that a republic that disregarded its principles would "morally decay."[16] Yale sociology professor William Graham Sumner added that "adventurous policies of conquest or ambition" would yield greater executive power, a bloated and otherwise unnecessary military establishment, and burdensome taxes—all of which imperiled republican government. Schurz also objected to incorporating additional, allegedly inferior, nonwhites into the body politic; acquiring "tropical countries with indigestable, unassimilable populations would be highly obnoxious" to republican government and would "greatly aggravate" the nation's already serious racial problems.[17] Others impeached the strategic rationale. They argued that annexing far-flung and militarily vulnerable possessions would neutralize the country's "compact continental stronghold" and thrust the United States into international rivalries and ultimately into the "hell of war."[18] Finally, several anti-imperialists incisively criticized the economic rationale for a more assertive policy. Schurz contended that colonies were not a prerequisite to increased trade because both Germany and the United States, which owned no colonies prior to 1898, were overtaking commercial rival Great Britain, "the greatest colonial Power in the world." Businessman Edward Atkinson added astutely that the great bulk of American exports went to Europe and Canada rather than to Asia, Latin America, or Africa, all areas of markedly less purchasing power.[19]

Acting variously out of agreement with such positions and from domestic economic and partisan political calculations, Democrats were generally less enthusiastic about an aggressive foreign policy than their Republican rivals. Southern Democrats frequently denounced territorial expansion and the imposition of control over unwilling subjects as the equivalent of Reconstruction. Most southerners were also apprehensive of any policy that might incorporate nonwhites, strengthen the central government or military, or increase agricultural imports that competed with the region's staple crops.[20] Many northern Democrats, especially Grover Cleveland, the party's only president during the era, sought to limit the nation's political, military, and territorial commitments; this objective, together with domestic political considerations, prompted him to reverse or attempt to change prior Republican policies concerning a Nicaragua canal (1885), involvement in the Congo (1885), the annexation of Hawaii (1893), and control of Samoa (1894).

In view of these dissenting perspectives and Democratic proclivities, there existed neither a unanimously held "grand imperial design"[21] nor an unbroken chain of events leading unalterably to insular empire at the turn of the century. Nevertheless, U.S. policy and actions in Samoa, Guam, Puerto Rico, Cuba, Hawaii, and the Philippines were grounded solidly on an imperial ideology with roots extending deep into the American past. In the 1890s, as in the 1840s, proponents of effective anti-imperialism remained in a minority position, unable to divert the proponents of U.S. expansion or to overcome the image of national greatness associated with this growth.

Just as American attitudes toward race, national mission, and greatness; fears of European incursions; and dreams of commercial expansion were long-standing, the nation also had established clear precedents by the 1890s for the use of superior power for imperial purposes. The attitudes and processes that yielded empire at the turn of the century had been readily apparent in U.S. suppression of Native Americans. Despite various and conflicting Supreme Court pronouncements and the self-serving explanations of white officials, the essence of these interactions took the form of foreign affairs and imperialism. The final military defeat of the Sioux on the Central Plains and the Apaches in the Southwest was only the latest manifestation of U.S. landed expansion at the expense of Native Americans. Indeed, white Americans settled more land from 1870 to 1900 than in the preceding three hundred years combined. Together with utilizing warfare, a traditional extension of diplomacy, the United States had concluded more than 350 treaties with Native American nations from 1776 to 1871. Indistinguishable in format from contemporary agreements with foreign countries such as France, these treaties were directed at the same objective as military pressures. The governor of Georgia offered a succinct explanation in 1830: "Treaties were expedients by which ignorant, intractable, and savage people were induced without bloodshed to yield up what civilized people had a right to possess."[22]

The governor's explanation revealed both the goal of white America and the key racial assumptions on which the United States constructed its continental empire. Native Americans (and Mexicans) were viewed as inferior beings and as obstacles to progress. A "few miserable savages" could not be allowed to impede the march of superior white civilization, and removing them could require drastic measures.[23] General William T. Sherman, who played a key role in the Indian wars of the late nineteenth century, contended in 1868 that "the more we can kill this year, the less will have to be killed the next war, for the more I see of these Indians the more convinced I am that all have to be killed or be maintained as a species of pauper. Their attempts at civilization are simply ridiculous."[24]

The depiction of Native Americans at public exhibits after 1876 further illustrated these imperial attitudes. Indians were portrayed as strange curiosities, as the inferior peoples over whom white American civilization had triumphed, and as inhabiting cultures at the other end of the developmental ladder from a superior white America. An official guidebook to the Buffalo Pan-American Exposition of 1901 captured these messages while describing the Native Americans on display as "long haired painted savages in all their barbaric splendor." Significantly, an earlier proponent of an Indian exhibit at the 1898 Omaha Trans-Mississippi and International Exposition had asserted that the display would demonstrate that Americans were hardly novices at imperialism because U.S. Indian policy could be applied to "aborigines" abroad.[25]

In addition to the racial attitudes that characterized U.S. insular imperialism, several other facets of U.S.-Native American relations were clear harbingers of the 1890s and beyond. The customary differential in power that characterized other imperial ventures, such as the contemporary British triumph over the Zulus or the French repression of the Indochinese, was manifest. Employing more advanced technology in the form of repeating rifles, railroads, and the telegraph, the U.S. Army gradually asserted control. The destruction of the buffalo, white diseases, and the sheer number of Anglos were crucial to achieving dominance. Still, the military played a key role, and the ties to turn-of-the-century imperialism were direct. Eighty-seven percent of the American generals who fought in the campaign to suppress Filipino insurgents following annexation of the archipelago in 1899 had battled Indians in the West, and most of the soldiers viewed the Philippine campaign as just another Indian war and dismissed the "Filipinos as savages no better than our Indians."[26]

The colonial treatment of Native Americans was also prescient. The historian John Wunder has distinguished between an "Old Colonialism" by which the United States acquired Indian lands and physically confined the Native peoples to reservations and a "New Colonialism" which "attacked every aspect of Native American life—religion, speech, political freedoms, economic liberty, and cultural diversity." The transition from the old to the new came in the 1870s when the United States stopped making treaties with Native Americans and officially and unilaterally began to legislate for them as subjects. This action sought to effect forced acculturation and Anglo conformity. English and Christianity were to replace Indian languages and religion. Individual plots of property and farming were to supplant communal ownership and hunting or gathering. Rule by government-appointed Indian agents and Native collaborators was to supersede traditional leaders and forms of governance. Denied the protection of the Bill of Rights and forbidden to leave the reservations without permission, Native Americans were described by a federal court in the 1890s as "little better than prisoners of war."[27]

Having observed the plight of the American Indian, the historian Albert Bushnell Hart in 1899 pronounced reservations the equivalent of European "colonies" and likened "Indian agents" to "British residents in the native states of India." Given this treatment of Native Americans, Hart concluded that "for more than a hundred years" the United States "has been a great colonial power." Other contemporaries equated imperialism abroad with domination of Native Americans. Confident that acquisition of the Philippines was "no new departure," Theodore Roosevelt compared Sitting Bull to Aguinaldo, the Filipino insurgent, and contended that the Florida "Seminoles . . . rebelled and waged war exactly as some of the Tagals have rebelled and waged war in the Philippines." While advocating acquisition of an island empire, Senator John Tyler Morgan of Alabama asserted that the United States' experience with Indians furnished the "most conclusive proofs of our capacity to civilize, Christianize, and enlighten the wildest of races and to elevate the most obdurate savagery . . . into enlightened citizenship."[28]

Some historians will dispute whether U.S.-Native American relations should be treated as foreign relations and therefore as a precedent for insular imperialism, but none can object to examining the American presence in Hawaii as an example of the imperial process. Such an examination is particularly useful because the growing American dominance after 1820 was accomplished primarily by missionaries and businessmen rather than the U.S. military or government. This dominance demonstrated the workings of "cultural" and "economic" imperialism and established "informal" empire prior to the official annexation of the islands in 1898.

Congregational missionaries first arrived in the islands in 1820. Their instructions from the American Board of Foreign Missions were far reaching: not only were the missionaries to raise "up the whole people to an elevated state of Christian civilization" but also "to turn them from their barbarous courses and habits" toward the "arts and institutions and usages of civilized life and society."[29] As was true with American missionaries in Asia, "these sojourners abroad were not just passive cultural intermediaries; they were, rather, conscious agents of change, of radical transformation. They came to Asia *to do something* to Asia and Asians, to reshape foreign societies."[30]

In no other area of the Pacific were they so successful. Working from the assumption that native Hawaiian culture, language, and religion were inferior, the missionaries enlisted converts ("collaborators") among local interpreters, teachers, exhorters, and even Hawaiian rulers. In 1840 the missionaries' tireless efforts, together with crucial local aid, led to a new constitution declaring Hawaii a Christian nation. The missionaries also dominated educational institutions. This was only an intermediate step. By the 1850s, English had become the principal language for business, government, and diplomacy, and it subsequently replaced the Hawaiian language in the public schools. With Americans serving as the first two ministers of public instruction, the schools were designed to promote mainland values and aspirations. Interestingly, these objectives looked toward making Hawaiians individual landowners and farmers—a vision hauntingly similar to what Wunder labeled the "New Colonialism" over Native Americans. In addition, the white presence resembled the interaction with Native Americans by inadvertently introducing devastating diseases against which the Hawaiians had no immunity. A population of at least two hundred thousand Hawaiians in the 1770s had been reduced by 1853 to about seventy thousand, and by 1886 Hawaiians had become a minority in their own land.[31]

The Americanization of the islands extended well beyond culture, as the descendants of the missionaries also came to dominate the archipelago economically. This dominance was centered in the growth and processing of sugar, which expanded dramatically after the conclusion of the Reciprocity Treaty of 1875 with the United States. The latter granted Hawaiian sugar duty-free entry onto the mainland, and sugar acreage shot up from 12,000 acres in 1876 to 125,000 in 1891. The white American minority secured control over the bulk of this land. Constituting only 5 percent of the population in 1893, they, together with Europeans, owned 65 percent of all Hawaiian land and were clearly the most powerful economic and political force in Hawaii. When the McKinley Tariff of 1890 ended Hawaiian sugar's preferential position under the reciprocity agreements and threatened the industry's prosperity and when the influx of Asian laborers and the assertiveness of Queen Liliuokalani, the Hawaiian monarch, threatened white control, the planter-missionary group instigated the "revolution" of 1893. This coup deposed the queen and established a white-dominated "republic" that ruled the islands until their annexation by the United States in 1898.[32]

Annexation made official the informal imperial control that had evolved after 1820. White American missionaries and businessmen, that is, nonstate actors, had been primarily responsible for this imperial process, but the U.S. government's role was also significant. As early as the 1840s, President John Tyler had warned other nations not to attempt to annex the islands, a position that was maintained for the ensuing forty-five years. Characteristically, in 1881, Secretary of State Blaine declared that Hawaii occupied "in the western sea much the same position as Cuba in the Atlantic. . . . [U]nder no circumstances can the United States permit any changes in the territorial control of either which would cut it adrift from the American system."[33] Even President Cleveland, who declined to annex the islands in 1893, declared them off limits to the British, Russians, and Japanese. In effect, the Monroe Doctrine's prohibition against European colonization in the Western Hemisphere had been extended to Hawaii. Behind this protective shield, the United States had tightened its control with the 1875 reciprocity agreement. The latter not only bound the islands to the mainland economically but also precluded Hawaii from extending similar economic concessions or territorial arrangements to any other nation. When reciprocity was renewed in the 1880s, the United States acquired an exclusive lease on the use of Pearl Harbor, and when the white-led revolution occurred in 1893, the American minister to Hawaii deployed a delegation of U.S. Marines from the USS *Boston* to ensure that the queen and her supporters could not reassert control. In short, state intervention at crucial junctures had reinforced and safeguarded the cultural and economic Americanization of Hawaii and in 1898 would formally incorporate the islands into the U.S. insular empire.

In sum, as the United States embarked on the decade of the 1890s the nation possessed the ideology, the power, and the experiences that provided a solid foundation for constructing an insular empire in 1898–99. Still, particular circumstances and events in the 1890s served to meld ideology, power, and experience into the actions that led to this latest nineteenth-century imperial phase. Without these circumstances, both domestic and international, turn-of-the-century imperial growth could not have taken the form it did. The severe depression of 1893 to 1897 helped focus domestic attitudes. The nation's economic plunge was precipitous: more than fifteen thousand businesses failed in 1893; 25 percent of the nation's railroads, comprising forty thousand miles of track, fell insolvent; and unemployment reached nearly 17 percent in 1894 and hovered between 12 and 14 percent through 1898. Accompanying protests seemed to threaten social and political order. More than 160,000 soft-coal miners struck in 1894, the same year that 125,000 railroad workers supported the American Railway Union's boycott of the Pullman Company. Farmers voiced similar dissatisfaction by flocking to the Populist movement. Having suffered chronic hard times throughout the late nineteenth century, more than one million disgruntled agrarians had voted for James B. Weaver, the Populist presidential candidate, in 1892, and far greater numbers supported William Jennings Bryan in 1896. The depression had disrupted the U.S. economy, politics, and society, and these protests alarmed many conservatives. The prominent New York attorney Francis Lynde Stetson warned President Cleveland that "we are on the eve of a very dark night unless a return of commercial prosperity relieves popular discontent."[34]

Such fears coincided with other accumulated uncertainties that one historian has aptly termed a "social malaise." This abrupt "decline in popular confidence" had resulted from an array of startling changes during the Gilded Age including unprecedented immigration and population growth, the development of a much more ethnically and religiously diverse society, an increasingly urban environment, and the growth of big business and organized labor. For a society that had been much more rural and agrarian, much more Protestant, and much more north European in derivation, such changes were unsettling. When combined with the depression, they prompted Americans to pay greater heed to a variety of publicists advocating an imperial foreign policy.[35]

From a wide variety of sources, Americans were bombarded with the message that national welfare involved, if not required, an assertive foreign policy. Admiral Alfred Thayer Mahan, the director of the Naval War College, the principal publicist for the "New Navy" in the early 1890s, and a confidant of Lodge and Roosevelt, argued forcefully for a powerful navy, strategic island bases such as Hawaii, and an isthmian canal. All were presented as necessary for national defense and commercial expansion. Citing the U.S. Census Bureau's 1890 declaration that the American frontier was closed and that new land was no longer available, Frederick Jackson Turner, a brilliant young historian, agreed with Mahan and asserted that the nation's ongoing westward movement necessitated a new frontier marked by "an interoceanic canal, . . . a revival of our power upon the seas, and . . . the extension of American influence to outlying islands and adjoining countries." Accentuating the superiority of America's governmental institutions and Protestant Christianity, the Congregationalist minister Josiah Strong urged American missionaries "to move down upon Mexico, down upon Central and South America, out upon the islands of the sea, over Africa and beyond." "The result," he assured doubters, "of this competition of races will be the 'survival of the fittest.' "[36] Moreover, from all segments of the political and economic spectrum, proponents of commercial expansion echoed established arguments for disposing of the agricultural and industrial surplus. Charles R. Flint, a New York industrialist, declared representatively, "We cannot remain wholly dependent for an active industrial life upon the home demand, and the markets of the world are open to us, ready to absorb the surplus products of our manufacturing capacity."[37]

Even as the decade dawned, this more aggressive policy was discernible; it featured a decided assertion of dominance over the Western Hemisphere, a much more expansive conception of legitimate strategic interests, and a heightened concern for safeguarding access to export markets. The latter two considerations prompted the United States to go to the brink of naval war with Britain and Germany over the Samoan port of Pago Pago in the late 1880s. In 1891 the Benjamin Harrison administration meddled in a Chilean revolution in a futile effort to neutralize British influence and intervened in a Haitian civil war to counter European interests and to pursue (without success) domination over the fine harbor of Môle St. Nicholas. In 1889, Secretary of State Blaine presided over the First International American Conference and unsuccessfully sought to convince the Latin American nations in attendance to join a hemispheric custom union and to accept a common currency. The following year Blaine helped fashion the reciprocity feature of the McKinley Tariff that was aimed similarly at augmenting trade with America's southern neighbors. Finally, in 1893, Harrison attempted to annex Hawaii.

Cleveland and his secretary of state, Walter Q. Gresham, were less assertive. Subscribing to many of the anti-imperialist positions, they quashed the Hawaiian annexation treaty, attempted to restore the queen to her throne, and recommended that the United States abandon the joint protectorate over Samoa. Even while adopting this more restrained approach, they continued the strategic perspective that precluded European or Japanese advances into Hawaii. Moreover, with the failure of the monarchial restoration project, the U.S. economic and cultural control that had evolved after 1820 was left undisturbed. Limiting British influence in the Western Hemisphere was also a major objective in the administration's response to a revolution in Brazil in 1893–94 and to the issue of sovereign control over the Mosquito Reserve in Nicaragua in 1894. In both instances Gresham emphasized that the United States was pursuing a neutral policy relative to contending factions and was respecting Brazilian and Nicaraguan sovereignty; but in both cases the Cleveland administration perceived the need to intervene and even its more reserved actions influenced outcomes that were favorable to American interests. The pro-American government retained power in Brazil; Nicaragua did not disturb U.S. economic and political influence on the Mosquito Coast or an American canal concession; and British influence was reduced in both countries.[38]

Significantly, Gresham's policies occasioned harsh criticism. At his death in 1895 the *Literary Digest* observed that his work had been "denounced as un-American, unpatriotic, and treacherous" and his tenure as secretary "represented as humiliating and unsuccessful." According to Gresham's biographer, his policies commanded little support beyond the State Department and other close associates and "ill comported with the increasingly perfervid nationalism of the 1890s."[39] While Gresham's declarations and actions dispel the idea of a uniform imperial perspective leading toward insular empire, this contemporary reaction demonstrates that substantial portions of the nation favored the more aggressive, more outward-looking foreign policy that increasingly characterized the decade.

Cleveland's denunciation in 1895 of British claims in a border dispute between Venezuela and British Guiana conformed more closely to the temper of the time. With both the capacity to block European advances and unobstructed access to the Orinoco River and to potential South American markets at stake, Secretary of State Richard Olney declared U.S. "fiat" equivalent to "law" in the Western Hemisphere and demanded (successfully) that Britain arbitrate the dispute.[40] Commercial considerations also heightened American attention to developments in China in the mid-1890s. Following Japan's victory in the Sino-Japanese War, the major European countries appeared poised to dissect the Celestial Empire and thereby endanger future U.S. sales and investments. Although the most energetic of Washington's interventions in China had assisted missionaries in the 1880s and 1890s, officials also searched for ways to safeguard the fabled "China Market" even as developments closer to home diverted their attention.

These developments, which constituted the decade's critical international events, centered on the Cuban revolt against Spanish colonial rule. The nation had adopted a more aggressive foreign policy against the backdrop of the social malaise and depression of the 1890s. Nevertheless, the occasion and the opportunity for the century's final phase of empire came with the Spanish-Cuban-American War. This latest Cuban campaign for independence had begun in 1895 and impinged upon a variety of U.S. interests. The revolutionaries' scorched-earth policy threatened some $50 million in American investments, and the war devastated trade with the island. U.S. efforts to enforce neutrality legislation and to protect its own citizens also proved costly, and the ongoing hostilities constituted an objectionable source of disorder and instability.

From the foreign policy perspective, officials worried that some stronger European power might displace the Spanish and thereby jeopardize potential U.S. canal routes and Caribbean domination and that preoccupation with Cuba precluded proper attention to trade prospects in China. Domestically, many worried that the resultant uncertainties endangered full economic recovery from the depression and intensified political partisanship and rancor. Much of the latter resulted from wrangling over which party was more concerned with and more prepared to alleviate the suffering of the Cuban people. Spanish efforts to segregate the general populace into reconcentration camps and thereby isolate the rebels had proved disastrous. Tens of thousands died of starvation and disease in these camps without weakening the revolutionary cause, and sensational American newspaper coverage fanned U.S. indignation and prompted demands for intervention to curb alleged Spanish cruelties.

With his inauguration as president in March 1897, William McKinley was cast into the vortex of this diplomatic and political maelstrom. Described by his successor, Theodore Roosevelt, as possessing "no more backbone than a chocolate eclair," McKinley once was dismissed as a cowardly, bumbling political opportunist who was driven into an unnecessary war by the yellow press and an aroused public opinion. Unable to provide clear conceptual or personal leadership, he had subsequently captained a relatively rudderless ship of state to end-of-the century empire almost "by accident." More recent scholarship effectively challenges this portrayal. In fact, McKinley was an expert and subtle manager of men who maintained clear control over his administration and its foreign policy and was quite "modern" in his management of public opinion and the Congress, both of which he more often led than followed. Moreover, when viewed in light of the nation's long-standing imperial ideology and practice, assertive U.S. policy in the 1890s, the 1896 Republican platform, and the internal logic of the president's actions, neither American intervention in Cuba nor this latest phase of empire can be termed accidental.[41]

Although McKinley's successful campaign in 1896 had not featured foreign policy, the Republican platform embodied much of the imperial perspective. It called for annexation of Hawaii, purchase of the Virgin Islands, construction of an American-owned Nicaragua canal, European withdrawal from the Western Hemisphere, and Cuban independence. McKinley's response to the Cuban crisis reflected these concerns and a determination to restore the order deemed essential to solid domestic economic recovery, to continued Republican political success, and to viable commercial and strategic foreign policy positions. From June 1897, McKinley pointedly threatened U.S. intervention if the Spanish failed to end the fighting and Cuban suffering. By refusing to support Spanish overtures unacceptable to the Cuban revolutionaries, he essentially demanded Cuban independence and rendered war highly likely, given that the Spanish rejected separation and the Cubans would accept nothing less.

Three events that took place early in 1898 revealed Spanish inability and unwillingness to meet McKinley's conditions. In January, Spanish loyalists in Havana rioted in opposition to a plan for partial Cuban independence; this demonstrated that neither the Cubans nor Spanish supporters were amenable to Madrid's reform proposals. On February 9 the New York *Journal* published a private letter from Enrique Dupuy de Lôme, the Spanish minister in Washington, in which the ill-fated diplomat incited public outrage by deriding McKinley as "weak and a bidder for the admiration of the crowd."[42] Even more significantly, de Lôme suggested that Spanish reforms in Cuba and negotiations with the United States were insincere delaying tactics. Six days later, the explosion of the battleship *Maine* in Havana Harbor and the resulting death of more than 250 U.S. sailors further revealed Spanish powerlessness to restore order and suggested possible treachery as well. When Spain refused McKinley's demands for an armistice and eventual Cuban independence, the president opted for war in early April.

In so doing, McKinley recognized the broad popular sympathy for the Cubans and understood Republican fears of losing the November congressional elections if the Cuban problem were not resolved. However, neither popular nor political pressure had driven the chief executive to war. The potential use of force had been central to his policy over the previous year, and war followed logically from this approach and the events of January and February. The president personified the current of genuine American sympathy for Cuban suffering, but he supplemented humanitarian motives with clear concern for U.S. dominance in the Western Hemisphere and for investments and trade in Cuba, and he agreed with key American businessmen in late March that ongoing uncertainty was intolerable. The president also monitored events in the Far East where, in the words of an editor close to the administration, "as soon as Cuba is out of the way the present Chinese complications are likely to develope [*sic*] a great deal of interest for us."[43] In short, McKinley and the nation acted from multiple motives. The "president did not want war, but he did want results that only war could bring"[44]—an end to the fighting in Cuba and the uncertainties it created for the American economy and politics, the imposition of order and stability and the reassertion of U.S. dominance in the Caribbean, and the freedom to pay greater attention to events in China. The intervention continued the assertiveness already established in the 1890s. Given this pattern, the long-held beliefs undergirding an expansionist foreign policy, and the prior implementation of this policy, forceful intervention was more predictable than haphazard.

Described by Secretary of State John Hay as "a splendid little war," the conflict lasted little more than three months and ended in a complete U.S. victory and the military occupation of Puerto Rico, Guam, and the Philippines as well as the annexation of Hawaii. Both Puerto Rico and Guam were perceived as the kind of strategic island bases that Mahan and others had advocated, and their subsequent annexation occasioned relatively little debate. Anti-imperialists objected much more strenuously to the formal acquisition of Hawaii in July 1898, but even opponents of expansion recognized the long-standing validity of Blaine's inclusion of the islands as a part of the "American system." Moreover, in 1898 two decisive considerations augmented the well-established arguments for annexation. First, the dispatching of U.S. troops to fight the Spanish in the Philippines rendered Hawaii an even more important strategic base en route to military operations, and the prospect of a naval station in the Philippines further enhanced Pearl Harbor's value as a stepping stone en route to Asian markets. Second, massive Japanese immigration after 1885 and angry protests by the Japanese government over the mistreatment of its citizens seemed to endanger ongoing white, American domination of the islands.[45]

The United States' domination of Cuba and the Philippines was more instructive concerning the nature of turn-of-the-century imperialism. Many Americans had long coveted Cuba, and as Spanish power declined in the late nineteenth century, Cuba, like Hawaii, was steadily integrated into the North American system. By the 1880s nearly 94 percent of Cuba's sugar production was exported to the United States and, in the following decade, American investors increasingly acquired the island's important sugar companies and plantations. American capital and technology was also responsible for Havana's gas lighting, for the island's railroads, bridges, and elevators, and for Cuba's only international cable communications—to New York and New Orleans rather than to Madrid. Even the growing Cuban attraction to baseball over bullfighting testified to the increasing American influence at Spanish expense.[46]

Just as this "Americanizing" process paralleled aspects of the U.S. presence in Hawaii, Americans held Cubans and their culture in the same low regard as they did Hawaiians or Native Americans. General Samuel B. M. Young observed that the "insurgents are a lot of degenerates, absolutely devoid of honor and gratitude. They are no more capable of self-government than the savages of Africa." If the Cubans were left to their own devices, an American reporter concluded characteristically, the island would be given "over to a reign of terror—to the machete and the torch, to insurrection and assassination." If the United States was "to save Cuba, we must hold it."[47]

Ironically, Congress seemed to have precluded this option as the nation moved toward war in April 1898. While approving McKinley's request for the use of force, the legislators had added the Teller Amendment, which pledged that the United States would not annex Cuba. Backers of the measure were less concerned with protecting Cuban liberties than with avoiding responsibility for $500 million in Spanish bonds tied to the island and with shielding the domestic sugar beet industry from competition; still, the amendment complicated U.S. policy. As newspaper editor Whitelaw Reid wrote McKinley, there was a critical inconsistency in going to war to restore order in Cuba and simultaneously disclaiming any right of "sovereignty, jurisdiction, and control." To expel Spain and not establish U.S. control, Reid warned, would yield another "Hayti [*sic*] nearer our own coast."[48]

McKinley and his advisers resolved this dilemma by ignoring Cuban aspirations for independence and by imposing a protectorate over the island. At the time of U.S. entry into the war, McKinley refused to recognize diplomatically the Cuban revolutionary government. During the fighting the American military ignored the Cuban commanders, and the Cubans were excluded from the negotiation of both the Spanish surrender and the postwar peace settlement. What had begun as a Cuban-Spanish conflict ended as the Spanish-American War. This process culminated in 1901 with the Platt Amendment to the U.S. Army Appropriations bill, which made the ending of military occupation conditional upon Cuba's agreement to make no other financial or political agreements compromising its independence, to sell or lease naval bases to the United States, and to accept future U.S. interventions to maintain order. Under intense pressure, Cuba wrote these conditions into its 1901 constitution, and General Leonard Wood, the U.S. commander in Cuba from 1899 to 1902, succinctly noted that Cuba retained "little or no independence."[49] According to historian Louis A. Pérez, Jr., American "intervention transformed a Cuban war of liberation into a U.S. war of conquest."[50]

The economic and cultural aftermath of the war was similarly imperial. A 1903 reciprocity treaty provided U.S. goods with tariff preferences in Cuba and funneled Cuban sugar to the mainland. Over the ensuing twenty years, investments in Cuban sugar multiplied to $600 million and American companies tightened their hold on the island's public utilities, port facilities, and industries. During the U.S. occupation, a new school system was instituted with an emphasis on the teaching of English and on personnel and institutional interchange with the mainland. Several hundred Protestant ministers and their aides also descended on the island, and with the U.S. presence came a new legal code and new standards of sanitation. Clearly, formal annexation was not required for military, economic, or cultural domination.

Unrestrained by pledges such as the Teller Amendment, the United States extended formal colonial rule over the Philippine Islands. Of the war's various outcomes, this action most often has been cited as a "departure from American traditions. . . . Never before had land thousands of miles away and inhabited by millions of people been acquired."[51] Certainly adding seven million Filipinos and seven thousand islands, which never had been envisioned (as had Cuba or Hawaii) as part of an American system and were located more than eight thousand miles from Washington, was a departure; without the opportunity afforded by the war, it is difficult to imagine the United States conquering and annexing the Philippines. But this departure is best viewed as a difference in degree rather than kind—especially when considered against the United States' established imperial ideology and practice and against the domination of Native Americans, Hawaiians, and Cubans. When assessed from these perspectives, making the Philippines a colony conformed rather closely to "American traditions."

Once again the rationale for U.S. actions embodied familiar, self-interested economic and strategic arguments. Together with Hawaii and Guam, the islands were declared essential to acquiring "the wealth of the Orient"; with the "advantages abroad which the Philippines would give us," the Chicago *Inter-Ocean* was confident that the United States would "become the greatest commercial power on earth."[52] Maintaining the security of a naval and commercial entrepôt at Manila required possession of all the islands, and granting the Filipinos independence would have created, according to McKinley, a "golden apple of [international] discord" and initiated competition and possible war among Germany, Japan, and Britain.[53]

Once again the United States possessed the power first to defeat the Spanish at Manila Bay in May 1898 and subsequently to suppress the Filipino insurgents who had been fighting the Spanish prior to U.S. intervention and who continued to struggle for national independence until 1902. As in the past, Americans considered the nonwhite Filipinos as racially and culturally inferior and as incapable of establishing and maintaining a viable state. President McKinley proclaimed a responsibility to "educate the Filipinos, and uplift and civilize and Christianize them,"[54] and General William Shafter concluded that it was necessary to kill the guerrillas so that the "remaining half of the population could be advanced to a higher plane of life."[55] Adopting this tactic, more than 126,000 U.S. soldiers served in the war to defeat these "niggers" and "brown men."[56] The cost of the campaign was appalling: 4,200 American lives lost and an expenditure of $400 million, approximately 18,000 Filipino battle deaths, and more than 100,000 dead from disease and starvation.

Yet again the American occupation took the form of an "experiment in self duplication" through the attempted transfer of American values and institutions.[57] For example, English became the language of instruction for a public school curriculum that combined the lessons of a Massachusetts elementary school and

"DECLINED WITH THANKS." Uncle Sam declines "anti-fat" medicine offered by antiexpansionists, while tailor McKinley prepares to accommodate his wider girth with rational expansion and enlightened foreign policy. *Puck*, September 5, 1900. *Courtesy Library of Congress*

contemporary industrial training for African Americans. U.S. officials attempted to reform municipal government in accordance with the American practices and to facilitate American investments, and Protestant missionaries were again prominent. The Reverend Wallace Radcliffe representatively endorsed "imperialism, not for domination but for civilization; not for absolutism but for self government." "I believe in imperialism because I believe in foreign missions," he continued. "The Church must go where America goes."[58]

These parallels between U.S. policy in the Philippines and interactions with Native Americans, Hawaiians, and Cubans were hardly coincidental. When viewed through the analytical lens of empire, late nineteenth-century foreign relations evidenced much deliberateness and continuity, and the acquisition and domination of the insular empire may not be dismissed as accidental. While there was neither a unanimously accepted "master plan"[59] nor a completely consistent series of actions, U.S. policy throughout the century exhibited an imperial ideology that portrayed nonwhites as inferior, propounded the existence of an American mission and destiny for national greatness, invariably categorized U.S. territorial acquisitions as necessary to national security or strategic stability, and persistently linked commercial expansion and economic prosperity. Acting on this belief system, Americans had employed superior power to acquire territory from weaker neighbors on the continent, whether they had been French or Spanish colonials or Mexicans and Native Americans. Therefore, treating Hawaiians, Puerto Ricans, or Filipinos in like fashion was not exceptional. The same may be said for imposing a colonial status on these new American subjects. Here again, depriving Hawaiians, Puerto Ricans, or Filipinos of the liberties and constitutional rights accorded to American citizens or seeking to transform them culturally assumed forms virtually identical to previous treatment of Native Americans. Moreover, extending this analysis to include nonstate actors, such as businessmen and missionaries, reinforces the patterns.

Historians adopting this general analytical approach have reached differing conclusions. Walter L. Williams has suggested that "Philippine annexation" be viewed "as the last episode of a nineteenth-century pattern of territorial acquisition and direct political rule of subject peoples." Placing greater emphasis on economics than on territory or colonialism, Walter LaFeber contended that McKinley's "objective was not a colonial empire but the minimum territory needed to obtain his conquest of world markets, along with the taking of strategic points necessary to protect that conquest." Edward P. Crapol has offered a synthesis treating the Gilded Age as a "period in which the first empire, a landed continental empire, reached fruition, then quickly faded, to be superseded by a second, insular empire that . . . briefly became the dominant paradigm of American imperial history." Connecting the two forms of empire were the "dual traditions of colonialism" as applied to Native Americans and "oceanic commercialism."[60] Regardless of individual emphasis, each of these historians has isolated the key to understanding the course of late nineteenth-century U.S. foreign relations. The essential theme running through the concepts of "transformation," "old" versus "new," and "emergence as a great power" was the ongoing evolution of different phases of empire.

Notes

1. Charles S. Campbell, *The Transformation of American Foreign Relations, 1865–1900* (New York, 1976); Robert L. Beisner, *From the Old Diplomacy to the New, 1865–1900* (Arlington Heights, IL, 1986); Ernest R. May, *Imperial*

Democracy: The Emergence of America as a Great Power (1961; reprint ed., New York, 1973); Walter LaFeber, *The New Empire: An Interpretation of American Expansion, 1860–1898* (Ithaca, NY, 1963).

2. For the most recent historiographical assessments of this period see Hugh DeSantis, "The Imperialist Impulse and American Innocence, 1865–1900," in *American Foreign Relations: A Historiographical Review*, ed. Gerald K. Haines and J. Samuel Walker (Westport, CT, 1981), 63–90; Edward P. Crapol, "Coming to Terms with Empire: The Historiography of Late Nineteenth-Century American Foreign Relations," *Diplomatic History* 16 (Fall 1992): 573–97; and Joseph A. Fry, "Imperialism, American Style, 1890–1916," in *American Foreign Relations Reconsidered, 1890–1993*, ed. Gordon Martel (London, 1994), 52–70.

3. For discussion of the definition of imperialism see Fry, "Imperialism, American Style," 52–54, 63–64.

4. Paul Kennedy, *The Rise and Fall of the Great Powers: Economic Change and Military Conflict from 1500 to 2000* (New York, 1987), 192. For the most sustained attempt to apply world systems analysis to U.S. foreign policy in this period see Thomas D. Schoonover, *The United States in Central America, 1860–1911: Episodes of Social Imperialism and Imperial Rivalry in the World System* (Durham, NC, 1991).

5. Daniel R. Headrick, *The Tools of Empire: Technology and European Imperialism in the Nineteenth Century* (New York, 1981).

6. Kenneth J. Hagan, *This People's Navy: The Making of American Sea Power* (New York, 1991), 182–232; David M. Pletcher, *The Awkward Years: American Foreign Relations under Garfield and Arthur* (Columbia, MO, 1973), 122–25.

7. David M. Pletcher, "1861–1898: Economic Growth and Diplomatic Adjustment," in *Economics and World Power: An Assessment of American Diplomacy since 1789*, ed. William H. Becker and Samuel F. Wells, Jr. (New York, 1984), 122–23; Walter LaFeber, *The American Search for Opportunity, 1865–1913* (New York, 1993), 21–31.

8. William Appleman Williams, *The Roots of the Modern American Empire: A Study of the Growth and Shaping of Social Consciousness in a Marketplace Society* (New York, 1969), 301.

9. LaFeber, *New Empire*, 106.

10. Robert Bruce Davies, *Peacefully Working to Conquer the World: Singer Sewing Machines in Foreign Markets, 1854–1920* (New York, 1976); Chu-yuan Cheng, "The United States Petroleum Trade with China, 1876–1949," in *America's China Trade in Historical Perspective: The Chinese and American Performance*, ed. Ernest R. May and John K. Fairbank (Cambridge, MA, 1986), 205–33; Pletcher, "Economic Growth and Diplomatic Adjustment," 117–71; Robert Zevin, "An Interpretation of American Imperialism," *Journal of Economic History* 32 (March 1972): 343–44.

11. David Healy, *U.S. Expansionism: The Imperialist Urge in the 1890s* (Madison, WI, 1970), 246; Walter LaFeber, *The American Age: U.S. Foreign Policy at Home and Abroad, 1750 to the Present* (New York, 1994), 161.

12. Michael H. Hunt, *Ideology and U.S. Foreign Policy* (New Haven, CT, 1987), 192.

13. For Beveridge see Hunt, *Ideology and U.S. Foreign Policy*, 38, and Emily S. Rosenberg, *Spreading the American Dream: American Economic and Cultural Expansion, 1890–1945* (New York, 1982), 41. For U.S. imperial ideology before, during, and after the Gilded Age see Hunt, *Ideology and U.S. Foreign Policy*; William Appleman Williams, *Empire as a Way of Life* (New York,

1980); Reginald Horsman, *Race and Manifest Destiny: The Origins of American Racial Anglo-Saxonism* (Cambridge, MA, 1981); and Albert K. Weinberg, *Manifest Destiny: A Study of Nationalist Expansionism in American History* (1935; reprint ed., Chicago, 1963).

14. For the quotes see Healy, *U.S. Expansionism*, 10, 26. For the broader apprehensions see Edward P. Crapol, *America for Americans: Economic Nationalism and Anglophobia in the Late Nineteenth Century* (Westport, CT, 1973); and Schoonover, *United States in Central America*.

15. Ernest R. May, *American Imperialism: A Speculative Essay* (1968; reprint ed., Chicago, 1991); Healy, *U.S. Expansionism*, 9–33.

16. Hunt, *Ideology and U.S. Foreign Policy*, 40.

17. Robert L. Beisner, "Thirty Years Before Manila: E. L. Godkin, Carl Schurz, and Anti-Imperialism in the Gilded Age," *Historian* 30 (August 1968): 572.

18. Healy, *U.S. Expansionism*, 216; Robert L. Beisner, *Twelve Against Empire: The Anti-Imperialists, 1898–1900* (New York, 1968), 97.

19. For Schurz see Healy, *U.S. Expansionism,* 217; for Atkinson see Beisner, *Twelve Against Empire*, 102–6.

20. Tennant S. McWilliams, *The New South Faces the World: Foreign Affairs and the Southern Sense of Self, 1877–1950* (Baton Rouge, LA, 1988), 3–67. Most southerners endorsed commercial expansion. See ibid.; McWilliams, "The Lure of Empire: Southern Interest in the Caribbean, 1877–1900," *Mississippi Quarterly* 29 (Winter 1975–76): 43–63; Joseph A. Fry, *John Tyler Morgan and the Search for Southern Autonomy* (Knoxville, TN, 1992); and Patrick J. Hearden, *Independence and Empire: The New South's Cotton Mill Campaign, 1865–1901* (DeKalb, IL, 1982).

21. This is Crapol's term. See "Coming to Terms with Empire," 594.

22. Hunt, *Ideology and U.S. Foreign Policy*, 53.

23. Brian W. Dippie, *The Vanishing American: White Attitudes and U.S. Indian Policy* (1982; reprint ed., Lawrence, KS, 1991), 135.

24. Hunt, *Ideology and U.S. Foreign Policy*, 55. See also Horsman, *Race and Manifest Destiny*, 103–4, 107, 191–93; and James O. Gump, *The Dust Rose Like Smoke: The Subjugation of the Zulu and the Sioux* (Lincoln, NE, 1994).

25. Robert W. Rydell, *All the World's a Fair: Visions of Empire at American International Expositions, 1876–1916* (Chicago, 1984), 112, 149. See also Frederick E. Hoxie, *A Final Promise: The Campaign to Assimilate the Indians, 1880–1920* (Lincoln, NE, 1984), 83–94.

26. Walter L. Williams, "United States Indian Policy and the Debate over Philippine Annexation: Implications for the Origins of American Imperialism," *Journal of American History* 66 (March 1980): 827–28.

27. John R. Wunder, *"Retained by the People": A History of American Indians and the Bill of Rights* (New York, 1994), 17, 35.

28. Williams, "United States Indian Policy," 827, 830–31; David H. Burton, *Theodore Roosevelt: Confident Imperialist* (Philadelphia, 1968), 70; Fry, *John Tyler Morgan*, 196.

29. Ralph S. Kuykendall, *The Hawaiian Kingdom, 1778–1854: Foundations and Transformation* (Honolulu, 1938), 101.

30. James C. Thompson, Jr., Peter W. Stanley, and John Curtis Perry, *Sentimental Imperialists: The American Experience in East Asia* (New York, 1981), 45. See also Paul W. Harris, "Cultural Imperialism and American Protestant Missionaries: Collaboration and Dependency in Midnineteenth-Century China," *Pacific Historical Review* 60 (August 1991): 309–38.

31. Ruth Tabrah, *Hawaii: A Bicentennial History* (New York, 1980), 37–93; Roger J. Bell, *Last among Equals: Hawaiian Statehood and American Politics* (Honolulu, 1984), 9; Kuykendall, *Hawaiian Kingdom*, 116, 167–68, 336, 353–62. In 1891 native Hawaiians made up 34,436 of a total population of 89,990. The great majority of the remaining 55,554 were Chinese, Japanese, and mixed races. See William Adam Russ, Jr., *The Hawaiian Revolution, 1893–1894* (Selinsgrove, PA, 1959), 32.

32. Russ, *The Hawaiian Revolution, 1893–1894*, 10–34.

33. Bell, *Last among Equals*, 18.

34. Ray Ginger, *Age of Excess: The United States from 1877 to 1914* (New York, 1975), 164.

35. Beisner, *From the Old Diplomacy to the New*, 74–76. See also Richard Hofstadter, "Manifest Destiny and the Philippines," in *America in Crisis*, ed. Daniel Aaron (New York, 1952), 173–200.

36. Turner and Strong quoted in LaFeber, *New Empire*, 70, 78.

37. Healy, *U.S. Expansionism*, 160.

38. For Cleveland and Gresham see LaFeber, *New Empire*, 197–229, and Charles W. Calhoun, *Gilded Age Cato: The Life of Walter Q. Gresham* (Lexington, KY, 1988), 121–222.

39. Calhoun, *Gilded Age Cato*, 221–22.

40. Campbell, *Transformation of American Foreign Relations*, 200.

41. Roosevelt quoted in Joseph A. Fry, "William McKinley and the Coming of the Spanish-American War: A Study of the Besmirching and Redemption of an Historical Image," *Diplomatic History* 3 (Winter 1979): 77. For the more positive assessment of McKinley see Lewis L. Gould, *The Spanish-American War and President McKinley* (Lawrence, KS, 1982); Robert C. Hilderbrand, *Power and the People: Executive Management of Public Opinion in Foreign Affairs, 1897–1921* (Chapel Hill, NC, 1981), especially pp. 4, 9, 27–28. See also the most recent study, John L. Offner, *An Unwanted War: The Diplomacy of the United States and Spain over Cuba, 1895–1898* (Chapel Hill, NC, 1992), which is meticulous and thoughtful, though somewhat less positive in its portrayal of McKinley.

42. Offner, *Unwanted War*, 116.

43. Beisner, *From the Old Diplomacy to the New*, 129; Thomas J. McCormick, *China Market: America's Quest for Informal Empire, 1893–1901* (Chicago, 1967).

44. LaFeber, *American Age*, 202 (quote). For a parallel assessment see Beisner, *From the Old Diplomacy to the New*, 129.

45. William Michael Morgan, "The Anti-Japanese Origins of the Hawaiian Annexation Treaty of 1897," *Diplomatic History* 6 (Winter 1982): 23–44.

46. Louis A. Pérez, Jr., *Cuba and the United States: Ties of Singular Intimacy* (Athens, GA, 1990), 59–73. See also Pérez, *Cuba between Empires, 1878–1902* (Pittsburgh, 1983); idem, *Cuba under the Platt Amendment, 1902–1934* (Pittsburgh, 1986).

47. Pérez, *Cuba and the United States*, 99–100.

48. David F. Healy, *The United States in Cuba, 1898–1902: Generals, Politicians, and the Search for Policy* (Madison, WI, 1963), 28.

49. Ibid., 178.

50. Pérez, *Cuba and the United States*, 97.

51. Campbell, *Transformation of American Foreign Relations*, 296.

52. Healy, *U.S. Expansionism*, 66–67.

53. Joseph A. Fry, "In Search of an Orderly World: U.S. Imperialism, 1898–1912," in *Modern American Diplomacy*, ed. John M. Carroll and George C. Herring (Wilmington, DE, 1986), 7.

54. Gould, *Spanish-American War and President McKinley*, 109.

55. Richard E. Welch, Jr., *Response to Imperialism: The United States and the Philippine-American War, 1899–1902* (Chapel Hill, NC, 1979), 34.

56. Ibid., 101–3.

57. Glenn Anthony May, *Social Engineering in the Philippines: The Aims, Execution, and Impact of American Colonial Policy, 1900–1913* (Westport, CT, 1980), 17; Peter W. Stanley, *A Nation in the Making: The Philippines and the United States, 1899–1921* (Cambridge, MA, 1974).

58. Stuart Creighton Miller, *"Benevolent Assimilation": The American Conquest of the Philippines, 1899–1903* (New Haven, CT, 1982), 18; Kenton J. Clymer, *Protestant Missionaries in the Philippines, 1898–1916: An Inquiry into the American Colonial Mentality* (Urbana, IL, 1986).

59. This is Hunt's term. See *Ideology and U.S. Foreign Policy*, 38.

60. Williams, "United States Indian Policy," 831; LaFeber, *American Search for Opportunity*, 156; Crapol, "Coming to Terms with Empire," 593. See also Charles Vevier, "American Continentalism: An Idea of Expansion, 1845–1910," *American Historical Review* 65 (January 1960): 323–35.

Suggestions for Further Reading

Beisner, Robert L. *From the Old Diplomacy to the New, 1865–1900*. Arlington Heights, IL, 1986.

Campbell, Charles S. *The Transformation of American Foreign Relations, 1865–1900*. New York, 1976.

Crapol, Edward P. "Coming to Terms with Empire: The Historiography of Late Nineteenth-Century American Foreign Relations." *Diplomatic History* 16 (Fall 1992): 573–97.

Field, James A., Jr. "American Imperialism: The Worst Chapter in Almost Any Book." *American Historical Review* 83 (June 1978): 644–68.

Fry, Joseph A. "Imperialism, American Style, 1890–1916." In *American Foreign Relations Reconsidered, 1890–1993*, ed. Gordon Martel, 52–70. London, 1994.

Gould, Lewis L. *The Spanish-American War and President McKinley*. Lawrence, KS, 1982.

Gump, James O. *The Dust Rose Like Smoke: The Subjugation of the Zulu and the Sioux*. Lincoln, NE, 1994.

Healy, David. *U.S. Expansionism: The Imperialist Urge in the 1890s*. Madison, WI, 1970.

Holbo, Paul S. "Economics, Emotion, and Expansion: An Emerging Foreign Policy." In *The Gilded Age*, ed. H. Wayne Morgan, 199–221. Syracuse, NY, 1970.

Hunt, Michael H. *Ideology and U.S. Foreign Policy*. New Haven, CT, 1987.

LaFeber, Walter. *The New Empire: An Interpretation of American Expansion, 1860–1898*. Ithaca, NY, 1963.

————. *The American Search for Opportunity, 1865–1913*. New York, 1993.

May, Ernest R. *Imperial Democracy: The Emergence of America as a Great Power*. 1961. Reprint edition, New York, 1973.

McCormick, Thomas J. *China Market: America's Quest for Informal Empire, 1893–1901*. Chicago, 1967.

Offner, John L. *An Unwanted War: The Diplomacy of the United States and Spain over Cuba, 1895–1898*. Chapel Hill, NC, 1992.

Plesur, Milton. *America's Outward Thrust: Approaches to Foreign Affairs, 1865–1890*. DeKalb, IL, 1971.

Pletcher, David M. "1861–1898: Economic Growth and Diplomatic Adjustment." In *Economics and World Power: An Assessment of American Diplomacy since 1789*, ed. William H. Becker and Samuel F. Wells, Jr., 119–71. New York, 1984.

Rydell, Robert W. *All the World's a Fair: Visions of Empire at American International Expositions, 1876–1916*. Chicago, 1984.

Williams, Walter L. "United States Indian Policy and the Debate over Philippine Annexation: Implications for the Origins of American Imperialism." *Journal of American History* 66 (March 1980): 810–31.

Williams, William Appleman. *The Roots of the Modern American Empire: A Study of the Growth and Shaping of Social Consciousness in a Marketplace Society*. New York, 1969.

13

Law and the Constitution in the Gilded Age

Michael Les Benedict

In the Gilded Age, legal institutions were required to cope with the immense social and economic changes that attended the development of the modern industrial state. Those changes led to calls for government action that challenged the traditional understanding of the government's role in a state dedicated to liberty. To preserve freedom, many Americans countered calls for increased regulation with the philosophy called "laissez-faire"—the idea that the economy works most efficiently when the government maintains a hands-off policy. During the final decades of the nineteenth century the courts reinforced this understanding by interpreting the U.S. Constitution to limit the ways in which government could regulate property. At the same time, they interpreted both the Constitution and ordinary legal principles in a manner that encouraged economic enterprise. Finally, the federal courts interpreted the Constitution to restrict the power of the federal government to regulate industrial production, as distinct from interstate commerce.

In essence, the courts created a body of doctrine that historians call laissez-faire constitutionalism. Their activities had a profoundly conservative effect on public policy, leading those who favored social and economic reform to denounce them as the conscious tools of powerful business interests. Because the Supreme Court is the highest and most visible court in the United States, reformers were especially bitter about the support it gave to laissez-faire constitutionalism.

Until recently most historians have shared this view, interpreting laissez-faire constitutionalism as growing out of the probusiness biases of Gilded Age judges and lawyers, who consciously favored property rights over human rights. Beneath the legal rhetoric, they charged, "the major value of the [Supreme] Court . . . was the protection of the business community against government."[1] The courts were "an arm of the capital-owning class."[2] The rules that governed such nonconstitutional areas of the law as employer-employee relations, the interpretation of contracts, and responsibility for accidents and personal injuries all served to promote economic development at the expense of basic fairness.

As early as the 1960s some legal and constitutional historians began to offer more nuanced analyses. In the past ten years they have significantly revised the older view of Gilded Age law and constitutionalism. Recent interpretations stress the connection between law, public policy, beliefs about civil liberty, and the deeply held moral convictions that characterized the age—what cultural historians sometimes call Victorian moralism. These interpretations are based on a new appreciation of the way law and public policy were shaped by these broader values.

The Transformation of Legal Institutions in the Gilded Age

Law plays a crucial role in American social and economic life. Because most U.S. citizens have moved freely and often from place to place, have diverse religions and ethnic origins, and reject the idea of fixed social status and hierarchy, and because the commercial system early encouraged arm's-length dealing between strangers, Americans have generally lacked the informal institutions for resolving disputes that characterize many other cultures. As a result, they long have been known for their litigiousness. They came to regard the courts as the primary forum for the resolution of ordinary disputes. Minor conflicts, both civil and criminal, were brought to informal courts administered by justices of the peace, city aldermen, mayors, and other minor officials, who were rarely lawyers. If the issue was substantial, it might be referred to a more formal court of record, which maintained an account of the proceedings so that a decision could be appealed to a yet higher court.

As the American economy developed, more and more business disputes were brought before the courts of record.

Acting in accordance with precedents, courts of record developed rules to prescribe behavior in various situations, and Americans accepted these rules—known as "the common law" in America and England—as the basic legal regulations governing human relations. Under this system, changes in American society led to disputes that had to be settled in courts well before they came to the attention of legislatures. Therefore, courts often were the first institution of government to articulate public policy. Adhering to precedent, judges were reluctant to change common-law rules once they had been firmly established. That was the job of the legislatures who thus built on the common-law foundations created by the judges, harmonizing inconsistent decisions and modifying rules that seemed inappropriate.

This approach worked well for Americans, and, during the late nineteenth century, they still preferred to develop public policy through this loosely organized system of dispute resolution followed, if necessary, by legislation. This was in stark contrast to the alternative that developed in most of Europe, where legislatures and government bureaucracies established detailed codes of conduct and judges merely applied them. The United States was slow to develop administrative agencies to help regulate the economy and other aspects of life. The largest federal bureaucracies were the postal service and the pension bureau, which served veterans and their families. Not until 1887 did Congress create the first national regulatory agency, the Interstate Commerce Commission.

In the absence of regulatory bureaucracies, the courts were central to the American economic system. They provided the prime forum for resolving business disputes, which sometimes involved basic questions about economic relations. Thus, as the American economic system was transformed in the second half of the nineteenth century, the courts were the first and principal institution to adjust law to the changes. When Congress, the state legislatures, and newly invented regulatory agencies acted, they often did so in response to complaints about prior judicial decisions. Statutes generally changed the law rather than established it; the courts set the status quo, and proponents of change had the handicap of having to disturb it.

Fulfilling such crucial economic responsibilities, lawyers grew in number and prestige. Firms grew larger and practitioners began to specialize. Corporate law became the dominant and most prestigious field. Leading lawyers worked to improve professional standards and legal education, founding the American Bar Association in 1878, while state bar associations took leading roles in licensing practitioners. The law was too important to be left to nonlawyers. Even before the Civil War the old practice of naming them to serve on courts had been dying out; by the late nineteenth century it was unheard of. Laymen still served as justices of the peace, but they were stripped of most of their legal responsibilities. There were constant calls to replace the informal legal jurisdiction of local officials with that of formal courts, staffed with trained lawyers.

Demands for such changes became a staple part of the larger movement to reform city governments, and by the 1870s they began to succeed. Therefore, as courts played an ever more important role in the economy, their role in resolving differences among ordinary individuals shrank. Disputes over business-related matters displaced minor disagreements among neighbors as the main items on a court's agenda. With professionalized courts demanding adherence to formal legal procedures and precedents, it became more difficult for average citizens to take their own complaints to court. Law enforcement was systematized, making it difficult for ordinary people to prosecute neighbors for minor offenses; doing so became the prerogative of the police and the government prosecutor. In effect, the primary function of courts came to be to serve the economy. The Gilded Age witnessed the beginning of the alienation of ordinary Americans from legal institutions.

The pressure to professionalize the bar led to reforms in legal education. Before the Civil War most lawyers had entered the profession by apprenticing with practitioners. Now many states began to demand tougher tests and standards. Law school replaced apprenticeship as the normal mode of legal education. Coinciding with the growing importance of law schools came a revolution in their approach to training. Identified with Christopher C. Langdell, dean of the prestigious Harvard Law School, the new system replaced rote learning of rules and precedents from lectures with the analysis of key cases. Guided by a skilled teacher, students distilled from the cases the principles that seemed to underlie the decisions and applied them in the classroom to new fact situations. Such training elevated the law from a trade to a profession.

Langdell's revolution in legal training, which spread to all the leading law schools, reflected a new understanding of law in general. Rather than a body of specific precedents and rules that governed each case, it was a body of general principles that could be scientifically determined and applied to varieties of factual situations. It was not the precedent that made the law; it was the underlying principle. This growing conviction that law was a science increased the tendency toward what legal historians have called "legal formalism." Lawyers believed that courts could find the correct answer to any legal question by identifying and applying the principle established by the precedents in similar cases. Correct legal reasoning led to correct results independently of the particular context. Evidence of the actual effect a decision might have on the parties or on society was irrelevant.

Another important change in the legal system that took place during the Gilded Age was the increased importance of the federal courts. The Constitution created a federal court system parallel to the state system and sketched its jurisdiction, but with a few exceptions it empowered Congress to define the details. The Constitution gave the federal courts no jurisdiction over questions between citizens of a single state arising under that state's law. Cases among citizens of several states could be brought into the federal courts, but Congress made it difficult for defendants to move them there once proceedings had begun. It gave state and federal courts concurrent jurisdiction over many cases that arose under federal laws. Even more significant, when defendants in state courts claimed rights under federal law or the Constitution, in most cases Congress provided no mechanism to remove the case to the federal courts. If the state court refused to recognize the claim, the only recourse was a final appeal to the U.S. Supreme Court.

As the transportation and communications revolution created a national economy that crossed state lines, businessmen complained that the system subjected them to a welter of conflicting laws and court interpretations. Out-of-state businesses charged that they were subjected not only to the biases of home-state juries but also of home-state judges, who were often elected and subject to political pressures. During the Civil War and Reconstruction, Congress began to expand the circumstances in which cases could be removed to the federal courts, whose judges were appointed for life and thus insulated from popular opinion. Finally, Congress passed the Judiciary Act of 1875, which gave federal courts jurisdiction whenever a party asserted a right secured by a federal law or the Constitution and made it possible to remove all such cases from the state courts to the federal courts. The result was a rapid increase in the business of the federal courts, buttressing free trade among the states, speeding the development of the modern national market, and establishing commercial rules that often served business rather than consumer interests.

Laissez-faire Economics

By its nature, the American legal system tends to reinforce conservatism in matters of public policy. The rules established by judges—the common law—define the status quo. Legislation does not inaugurate public policy; it changes it. In the late nineteenth century, a time of immense and rapid change, the natural conservatism of the law was reinforced by a more general conservatism that dominated American thought. Most American intellectuals viewed government regulation of business and other economic institutions with deep suspicion. In part, this attitude reflected a deep skepticism, fostered by the failure of Reconstruction, about the ability of government to effect any positive changes in society.[3] In the wake of that failure, most American intellectual leaders who called for "reform" advocated less, rather than more, government action to deal with problems. Gilded Age reformers believed that the wise legislator recognized the limits of government's power to effect change in any area of life.

Such convictions were reinforced by "classical" or "laissez-faire" economic thought. Classical economic thought had become more and more dominant among economists in the one hundred years since the great economic philosopher Adam Smith had first combined its strands and articulated it in *The Wealth of Nations* in 1776. By the 1870s it was almost universally accepted by American intellectuals. Economists might disagree on how to apply its tenets, but not on its basics. Those who articulated different views were scorned as crackpots.

Classical economists believed that economic relations were governed by laws that grew out of human nature—especially the rule that people try to secure the greatest possible economic benefit with the least possible effort. This inevitably led people to trade their goods and skills for things of value to them, making the best possible deals. No good, service, or labor had intrinsic value; it was worth what people agreed to pay for it in a free bargain. The results of such bargains varied according to the law of supply and demand: the greater the demand for some good, service, or skill, and the scarcer its supply, the higher its price.

Laissez-faire theory held that resources would be used most efficiently if people were free to provide any goods, service, or labor they wished and to trade freely for them—that is, if there were a free market, and particularly if that free market extended over a broad polity such as the United States. If goods, skills, or services were scarce and in demand, the high price they brought would lead people to provide more of them, bringing the price down. Ultimately supply and demand, and hence prices, would come close to a perfect balance, with society producing goods, services, and skills to match the demand for them. Such an efficient use of resources secured the greatest possible prosperity. Government interference in the economy disrupted this efficiency and reduced prosperity. The best rule for government, therefore, was laissez-faire, the "let-alone" principle.

Although these ideas were widely accepted among academics and intellectuals, the American government never adhered to laissez-faire economics. Both before and after the Civil War local and state governments subsidized canal and railroad building and promoted their economies with public works. The national government administered a protective tariff, a customs duty designed to help domestic production by increasing the price of imported goods. It subsidized the building and operation of canals, railroads, steamship lines, roads, and telegraphs, and it promoted mining and agriculture by giving land to settlers who agreed to develop it.

It was not so much laissez-faire economics that appealed to Americans as an understanding of liberty that it reinforced. Laissez-faire taught that government interference in the free market was not only economically inefficient but also unfair. The free market determined value and distributed resources fairly according to supply and demand. Government interference was designed to alter that distribution, giving to some individual or group an economic benefit they would not otherwise have. To advocates of laissez-faire, this was "class legislation" in that it benefited one part of society at the expense of the rest. Class legislation was the great evil that was potential in all government. To permit it would make control of the government the object of a great struggle among contending interests, encouraging bribery, electoral fraud, and ultimately threatening democracy itself.

Laissez-faire's concern with class legislation resonated with traditional American opposition to the use of government to secure special privileges. In the context of the earlier nineteenth century, this meant opposition to special privileges for the rich and powerful and support for equal rights and equal opportunity. In nations that lacked democratic government, small, powerful elites perverted public policy, robbing the many to benefit the few. But the danger was no less in democracies. "Now that the governmental machine is brought within everyone's reach, the seduction of power is just as masterful over a democratic faction as ever it was over king or barons," William Graham Sumner, the most popular exponent of American laissez-faire, observed acidly.[4] The only difference was that the threat now lay in the opposite direction—that the many would plunder the few. This was the heart of "socialism" and "communism"—the explicit promise to use government to redistribute wealth; therefore, laissez-faireists saw any legislation designed to interfere with the free market's determination of the value of goods, services, and labor as "socialistic" or "communistic." Nonetheless, laissez-faire moralism was not aimed only at "socialistic" legislation. Its advocates denounced subsidies for business, including the protective tariff, as well.

Laissez-faire also comported with Victorian moral convictions. It linked economic success with hard work, perseverence, ambition, and good morals. The labor of those who cultivated such characteristics would be in greater demand than that of the slothful and dissolute. The energy of businessmen who provided needed goods, the creativity and perseverence of those who developed new products, the ambition of those who secured good educations all would be rewarded. Those who surrendered to their baser instincts and passions would sink into the poverty and degradation they deserved. Thus, those who believed in laissez-faire saw the economic system as a great engine for the promotion of a moral society. By rewarding the undeserving poor, class legislation undermined the moral underpinnings of the American economic system.

Laissez-faire Constitutionalism

Given these understandings, it should not be surprising that legislators, lawyers, and judges developed rules that promoted a free market. "Restraint of trade" and "monopoly" (the effort to prevent people from freely buying and selling goods or providing services) were against the law throughout the United States. State authorities prosecuted monopolies vigorously and with a good deal of success. In 1890, Congress reinforced state antimonopoly policies with the Sherman Antitrust Act. Conspiracies to restrain trade could be enjoined—that is, forbidden—by judges, and those who persisted in the offense could be punished, even in the absence of statutes.

To ensure economic freedom and promote individual responsibility, legislatures and judges promoted maximum freedom of contract. They eliminated old laws that denied married women control over their property and earnings. Similarly, congressional legislation and the Fourteenth Amendment secured the equal rights of African Americans to make contracts. Judges set aside old legal rules that restricted who could make contracts, allowed judges to set aside contracts that seemed unfair to one of the parties, or limited the sorts of terms people could agree to. Each person was free to make his or her own agreements, and each person was obligated to live up to them.

When people were harmed by the actions of others, nineteenth-century law stressed the centrality of "fault"—that is, a person was liable for harm done to another only when he or she was at fault. Such a rule eliminated old standards of "strict liability" that held people responsible for harm they or their employees did regardless of fault. The old law discouraged people from developing new businesses, such as railroads, that in their nature caused some injury to others. Americans wanted no such obstacle to economic development.

The stress on fault also corresponded to the Victorian moral order, in which people who acted responsibly were rewarded and those who did not were punished. It seemed not only economically unwise but also basically unfair to hold people liable for injuries resulting from their activities no matter how careful they had been. For the same reasons judges developed the notion of "contributory negligence"—that is, the rule that injured parties could not secure compensation for injuries for which they were partially responsible. They rejected old rules that had held employers strictly liable for injuries employees suffered on the job. Instead they applied the "fellow-servant rule," first developed in the 1840s, holding that employers were not liable for injuries caused by the negligence of other employees. As a result, employees were encouraged to exercise due care, and liability was imposed upon those who were at fault, judges said. It was wrong to hold an employer responsible for events over which he had no control.

The courts also buttressed the influence of laissez-faire ideas in public life, developing a body of doctrines that legal scholars call laissez-faire constitutionalism. Laissez-faire suspicion of class legislation reinforced similar concerns that were deeply embedded in American constitutional law. Since the early days of the Republic, judges had been accustomed to distinguishing regulations that appropriately served the general welfare from those that conferred special benefits on privileged people or interests. Legitimate regulation was part of the "police power" that governments used to control behavior and regulate the use of property for the general welfare. Governments could exercise this power to suppress activities that affected public morality, such as gambling and prostitution; they could ban saloons and outlaw the sale of liquor; they could regulate dangerous occupations or the use of dangerous materials; they could impose quarantines to prevent the spread of disease. But it was not a valid exercise of the police power simply to give a favored person or group a special privilege—for example, a monopoly, a tax break, or a subsidy. Such class legislation, by giving benefits to some at the expense of others, violated the principle, incorporated in most state constitutions and the Fifth Amendment to the Constitution, that no person could be deprived of property without "due process of law."

Courts had precedents and rules to guide them in determining when laws were within the police power. The clearest cases involved laws that reinforced traditional common-law rules that restrained behavior and the use of property—for example, laws that suppressed nuisances, prevented trespasses, or set standards of careful behavior. Less clear were laws that required people to give up their businesses, such as prohibition laws; that controlled access to occupations, such as licensing laws; that severely limited the use of property, such as laws restricting the length of wharfs; or that subsidized private corporations with tax money. Before the Civil War, judges usually found that laws coming under challenge met the general-welfare requirement, but in several instances state courts found that such legislation unconstitutionally deprived people of liberty or property without due process. In 1868, Michigan supreme court judge Thomas McIntyre Cooley published *A Treatise on the Constitutional Limitations Which Rest upon the Legislative Power of the States of the American Union*, bringing the precedents for holding class legislation unconstitutional to the attention of lawyers and judges.[5] The same year the American people ratified the Fourteenth Amendment, which forbade any state from depriving persons of life, liberty, or property without due process of law. After that, the federal courts could apply Cooley's precedents to overturn class legislation in the states.

Troubled by demands that the state and federal governments take action to help those losing ground because of economic changes, advocates of laissez-faire immediately began to call upon both the state and federal courts to enforce the constitutional limitations. Although they objected to special subsidies to businesses, they were especially worried about federal financial policy, which used paper money to inflate the currency in the interest of debtors and entrepreneurs. They denounced the so-called Granger laws, passed in some of the midwestern states at the behest of farmers and shippers, creating commissions to regulate the rates charged by railroads and grain warehouses as well as their business practices. Advocates of laissez-faire also objected to laws limiting the work day to eight or ten hours, laws preventing employers from refusing to contract with union members, and laws imposing stricter employer liability for workplace accidents.

In the 1870s lawyers in state after state began to challenge laws that their clients claimed infringed upon their liberty or took their property without due process of law. At first judges tended to sustain the laws as valid exercises of the police power, finding that they did in some way serve the general welfare. But those urging courts to apply the requirement more strictly began slowly to win victories. Judge Cooley provided one in Michigan, where he convinced fellow judges of the state supreme court to rule railroad subsidies unconstitutional in 1870. Iowa's supreme court did likewise, and Maine's justices applied the same principle to rule other business subsidies unconstitutional. It should be noted that these first victories for laissez-faire constitutionalism overturned laws benefiting businesses rather than harming them.

Laissez-faire principles informed legal arguments against paper money, which were at first accepted and then rejected by the Supreme Court in *The Legal Tender Cases* in 1869 and 1870.[6] Opponents of paper money had to fight it in Congress and finally succeeded in returning the United States to the gold standard in 1879. Believers in laissez-faire fought the protective tariff as well, but with less success.

The quest for tighter judicial control of class legislation came to the Supreme Court in *The Slaughterhouse Cases* of 1873.[7] To combat recurring outbreaks of yellow fever and other diseases in New Orleans, the Louisiana state legislature had passed a law that required butchers to kill their animals in a single slaughterhouse outside the city. In exchange for building it, the law gave a single company a monopoly over it, putting hundreds of butchers out of work. They sued, arguing that the law deprived them of the privileges and immunities of citizens of the United States in violation of the new Fourteenth Amendment. The Court upheld the law, following the tradition that laws to protect the public health were well within the police power. But four of the nine justices, led by Justices Stephen J. Field and Joseph P. Bradley, agreed with the butchers. They would have ruled the law unconstitutional, both as a deprivation of the privileges of citizenship and as a deprivation of liberty without due process of law.

The legal resistance to the state laws authorizing railroad commissions to set rates was even more bitter. Lawyers for the affected railroads and warehouses brought suits in several federal district courts to prevent enforcement of the laws, which they argued violated the Fourteenth Amendment by depriving the owners and stockholders of the benefit of their property without due process of law. Over Field's dissent the Supreme Court again rejected the argument in *Munn v. Illinois*, and other Granger cases, decided in 1877.[8] Railroads, grain warehouses, and some other types of businesses always had been considered specially "affected with a public interest" and therefore subject to more stringest regulation than other businesses, the majority of the justices said. Nonetheless, the majority did not repudiate the fundamental principle that a law that arbitrarily deprived a person of property, without serving a public purpose, would be unconstitutional class legislation. Field continued to agitate for stricter judicial scrutiny of possible class legislation, securing decisions sustaining his views in the Ninth Circuit federal courts over which he presided.

By the 1880s those who feared class legislation were gaining ground in the state and federal courts. Like middle-class Americans in general, judges were alarmed by the rising conflict among farmers, workers, and the huge businesses spawned by the transformation of the American economy.

The courts played a significant role in making the situation worse. They conceded the right of workers to organize unions and

Judicial Architect of Laissez-faire Constitutionalism. Stephen J. Field, associate justice of the U.S. Supreme Court, 1863–1897. *Courtesy Library of Congress*

to go out on strikes, but they destroyed their effectiveness by denying that striking workers could prevent other workers from taking their places. Moreover, they could not encourage sympathy strikes or organize boycotts. All of these activities were illegal restraints of trade. When strikers nonetheless tried to obstruct the hiring of replacements or organized boycotts, employers sought court injunctions ordering them to stop. If they persisted, employers could call on local police or the state militia to enforce the orders. If judges and local law enforcement officials cooperated, employers could deputize their own private army of injunction enforcers/strikebreakers.

As a result of such applications of the law, strikes often degenerated into violence. Many workers were radicalized, denouncing the government and the courts as the tools of business. Many accepted the Marxist socialist argument that government always acted in the interests of the class that controlled it. Many others were swayed by the anarchist position that the answer was to eliminate government itself. Given the antilabor bias of the common law, even moderate labor leaders were perceived as dangerous radicals.

Many state and local courts and government officials were reluctant to intervene in labor disputes, but the unelected judges of the federal courts proved especially hostile to strikes and boycotts. They first issued injunctions in strikes against bankrupt railroads, which by law were placed under federal court supervision, and often imposed wage reductions. After Congress passed the Sherman Antitrust Act in 1890, federal judges interpreted it to authorize injunctions against any labor-organized boycott that would affect interstate commerce. Employers went to the federal courts to seek injunctions instead of to the less sympathetic local courts. The Supreme Court soon recognized a general power in the federal government to take vigorous measures to suppress strikes that interfered with interstate commerce. In 1895 it sustained the imprisonment of the president of the American Railway Union, Eugene V. Debs, one of the most important labor leaders in the nation, for defying such an injunction.[9]

Under these circumstances farm and labor leaders redoubled their calls for state and federal legislation to protect the interests of workers. Both radical and more moderate labor leaders organized immense demonstrations of workers calling for changes in the American economic system. Many farmers sympathized. By the 1880s coalitions of radicals and reformers were organizing political parties to challenge the system. By the 1890s the Populist party had emerged as a real threat to the Democrats and Republicans, and elements of the Democratic party itself were flirting with some of the measures the Populists favored, such as an income tax levied on the wealthy, national ownership of transportation and communication facilities, a government-mandated eight-hour workday, changes in labor law and limitations on labor injunctions, and inflation of the money supply by freely coining silver as well as gold. Many state legislatures began to pass such laws, and, in 1894, Congress passed a tax on yearly incomes greater than $4,000, a substantial sum that separated the wealthy from the middle classes. Populism seemed to promise class legislation on a grand scale.

The result was a significant hardening of conservative lines in the 1890s. As more and more Americans worried about the rise of radicalism, judges became more suspicious of legislation that interfered with the free market. They took a sterner look at laws that regulated business practices to protect consumers, small businesses, and farmers. They were particularly skeptical of claims that laws regulating the hours of labor and working conditions were designed to promote health or other aspects of the general welfare. More and more courts began to rule such laws unconstitutional in the 1880s and 1890s. It was particularly crucial to uphold the right of individuals to contract freely, judges insisted. Except in extraordinary circumstances, restrictions on the hours people could work, on the type of payment they could agree to, and on other conditions of employment unconstitutionally deprived employers and employees of the liberty of contract without due process of law. Due process required more than proper court proceedings, the judges ruled. The *substance* of such laws deprived people of their rights. The due-process clauses of the state constitutions and the Fifth and Fourteenth Amendments to the Constitution required not only appropriate legal procedures but also *"substantive* due process of law," as this doctrine came to be called. This meant that courts had the responsibility to evaluate the substance of laws to see that they were reasonably connected to the general welfare. This was not a new idea, but the vigor with which many courts now carried it out was new. Judges seemed to be second-guessing legislators about whether or not laws were necessary.

Many state courts, as well as the Supreme Court, wavered in their application of substantive due process. Extreme laissez-faireists, such as Justices Rufus W. Peckham and David J. Brewer, who inherited Field's mantle, urged strict scrutiny of any legislation that seemed to interfere with the free market. Justice John Marshall Harlan led the justices who called for greater judicial restraint. With Brewer and Peckham dissenting, the Court sustained laws restricting the working hours of miners in the key case of *Holden v. Hardy* in 1898.[10] Mining was traditionally considered a dangerous occupation subject to special restrictions, the Court observed. But

the Supreme Court was affected by the growing fear of radicalism
and class legislation. Its decision in Debs's case in 1895 reflected
the general panicky reaction of conservatives to the nationwide railway strike and boycott of the previous year. Also in 1895 the Court
ruled that the income tax law passed the previous year was unconstitutional, despite the fact that it had sustained the constitutionality of a similar tax twenty-four years earlier.[11]

The Court also began to restrict the power of the state railroad
commissions. In 1890 it ruled that due process required that the
reasonableness of any rate set by a railroad commission be review-
able by the judiciary, in effect inviting railroads to appeal commission decisions.[12] In 1897 the Court imposed its own rule for
determining fair rates and required state decisions to conform to
it.[13] It declared that the Interstate Commerce Commission, created
by Congress in 1887, did not have the power to set rates at all.[14]

The Supreme Court's drift toward laissez-faire constitutionalism culminated in 1905 with the great case of *Lochner v. New York*,
in which the majority of the justices overturned a New York law
limiting the workday of bakers to ten hours.[15] Four of the justices,
three of them joining Harlan's dissent, would have sustained the
legislation as a reasonable use of the police power to protect the
health of the workers and the community. They believed it would
be wrong to assume that the state had acted in bad faith. But by
now the majority of the justices were supersensitive to the danger
of class legislation, and they assumed the worst. The legislature's
claim that it was protecting the health of the bakers and consumers
of bread was merely a subterfuge, they charged. Baking had never
been considered a dangerous occupation. The real purpose of the
bill was to regulate the hours of labor. If the Court sustained it,
states could pass similar regulations of any industry. In effect, the
Court was saying that the states could apply their police power only
in traditional ways for which there were clear legal precedents.
They could not use it to deal with new problems arising out of industrial development, such as the imbalance in power that led to
one-sided contracts between farmers and railroads and between
workers and employers.

As the Supreme Court used the doctrine of substantive due process of law to restrict state and federal power to regulate business,
it also set limits as to what industries the federal government could
regulate at all. Conservatives worried that Congress might invoke
its authority to regulate interstate commerce to control the produc-

tion of all goods intended for shipment out of state. To preclude such legislation the Court drew a strict line between commerce and production. The Constitution authorized Congress to regulate how goods were traded beyond state lines; it could not regulate manufacturing, mining, or agriculture itself, no matter how much their practices affected the national economy.[16]

This doctrine compounded the difficulty states faced in regulating their industries. Even where the courts permitted the exercise of police powers over business, to do so would give advantages to unregulated competitors in other states. Only uniform national regulations could overcome this problem, and the Supreme Court's distinction between commerce and production made that alternative unconstitutional.

By adopting laissez-faire constitutionalism, the courts exercised even greater influence on public policy than they had before—a bulwark of conservativism against demands for legislation to deal with the massive social and economic changes that attended late nineteenth-century development. Yet, convinced that formal legal reasoning compelled their conclusions, most lawyers and judges denied charges that they were taking sides on deeply divisive political issues. They insisted that the social consequences of their decisions were irrelevant to the process by which they made them.

Opposition to Laissez-faire Constitutionalism

By the 1890s the courts' commitment to laissez-faire constitutionalism raised vocal objections from farmers, organized labor, progressive lawyers and judges, and others who urged government action to deal with the problems raised by modern commercial and industrial development. Populist congressmen submitted bills to curb judicial power and make the federal judiciary elective. Both the Populist and Democratic party platforms of 1896 called for the reversal of laissez-faire decisions.

Nearly all the critics of laissez-faire constitutionalism accepted the traditional view that courts should distinguish between legitimate exercises of the police power and unconstitutional class legislation. They criticized the rigor of the scrutiny that the courts were now imposing on government regulations. Courts used to take pains to defer to legislative determinations about what regulations served the general welfare. Only arbitrary regulations, demonstrably serving special rather than general interests, were to be overturned as denials of due process. Now, they argued, conservative judges were imposing their own views of what was reasonable. If they disliked a law, meaning they would have voted against it as legislators, they ruled it unconstitutional. In so doing, they were usurping the legislative function and threatening democracy.

Moreover, conservative judges' understanding of the relationship among working conditions, poverty, health, crime, and other social problems was too narrow, the critics charged. Surely it was reasonable for a legislature to conclude that contracts that required overly long workdays, or that imposed other onerous burdens on employees, affected their health and morals. Indeed, was it not reasonable to conclude that the public interest in easing class conflict was served through legislation designed to ameliorate the conditions under which the weakest and poorest groups in society lived, even if that meant transferring wealth from one group to another? Deciding what laws might reasonably promote the general welfare required an analysis of actual social conditions, the critics argued. The formalist notion that one could apply the law without attention to the specific context was dead wrong. Appropriate legal judgments required what would soon be called "sociological jurisprudence," not formalism.

Finally, a few critics, most notably Massachusetts supreme court justice Oliver Wendell Holmes, who would be appointed to the Supreme Court in 1903, attacked the basic idea that judges could distinguish between reasonable exercises of the police power and arbitrary class legislation. Holmes presented his arguments in articles, books, and dissenting judicial opinions; his dissent in the *Lochner* case, which trenchantly presented his skepticism, became more famous than Harlan's more traditional one. As long as legislatures and courts followed the appropriate procedures in making and enforcing laws, Holmes insisted, the standard of due process had been met. The whole concept of substantive due process was too vague. Inevitably, it led courts simply to substitute their will for that of the majority. Courts should defer to legislatures, overturning laws only when they violated the clearest commands of the state and federal constitutions, he concluded.

By the turn of the twentieth century, the judiciary's adoption of laissez-faire constitutionalism was leading to a crisis. The Progressive Era (approximately 1900–1917) would witness a broad attack on legal formalism and on the judiciary itself, but not until the New

Deal of the 1930s would laissez-faire constitutionalism finally be laid to rest.

Notes

1. Robert G. McCloskey, *The American Supreme Court* (Chicago, 1960), 105.
2. Arthur S. Miller, "Toward a Definition of 'the' Constitution," *University of Dayton Law Review* 8 (Summer 1983): 647. For other statements of the older interpretation of laissez-faire constitutionalism see Robert G. McCloskey, *American Conservatism in the Age of Enterprise* (Cambridge, MA, 1951); Max Lerner, "The Supreme Court and American Capitalism," *Yale Law Journal* 42 (March 1933): 668–701; and John P. Roche, "Entrepreneurial Liberty and the Fourteenth Amendment," *Labor History* 5 (Winter 1963): 3–31.
3. During the period of Reconstruction that followed the Civil War, northerners optimistically believed that they could remodel the South along progressive northern lines by enfranchising the former slaves, encouraging economic development, and developing educational facilities. Instead, the South appeared to sink into violence and corruption. (Opponents of change in the South exaggerated the degree of corruption, but most northerners believed their charges.) To learn more about Reconstruction consult Eric Foner, *Reconstruction, 1863–1877: America's Unfinished Revolution* (New York, 1988). For a brief overview see Michael Les Benedict, *The Fruits of Victory: Alternatives in Restoring the Union, 1865–1877*, rev. ed. (Lanham, MD, 1986); or Michael Perman, *Emancipation and Reconstruction, 1862–1879* (Arlington Heights, IL, 1987).
4. William Graham Sumner, "State Interference," in *Essays of William Graham Sumner*, 2 vols., ed. Albert G. Keller and Maurice R. Davie (New Haven, CT, 1934), 2:149. Sumner originally published the essay in 1887.
5. Thomas M. Cooley, *A Treatise on the Constitutional Limitations Which Rest upon the Legislative Power of the States of the American Union* (Boston, 1868).
6. *Hepburn v. Griswold*, 75 U.S. 603 (1869); *Knox v. Lee*, 79 U.S. 457 (1870).
7. *The Slaughterhouse Cases*, 83 U.S., 36 (1873).
8. *Munn v. Illinois*, 94 U.S. 113 (1877).
9. In re Debs, 158 U.S. 564 (1895).
10. *Holden v. Hardy*, 169 U.S. 366 (1898).
11. *Pollack v. Farmer's Loan and Trust Company* (I), 157 U.S. 429 (1895); *Pollack v. Farmer's Loan and Trust Company* (II), 158 U.S. 601 (1895).
12. *Chicago, Milwaukee and St. Paul Railway Company v. Minnesota*, 134 U.S. 418 (1890).
13. *Smyth v. Ames*, 169 U.S. 466 (1897).
14. *Cincinnati, New Orleans, and Texas Pacific Railway Company v. I.C.C.*, 162 U.S. 184 (1896); *I.C.C. v. Cincinnati, New Orleans and Texas Pacific Railway Company*, 167 U.S. 479 (1897).
15. *Lochner v. New York*, 198 U.S. 45 (1905).
16. *U.S. v. E. C. Knight Company*, 156 U.S. 1 (1895).

Suggestions for Further Reading

Benedict, Michael Les. "Laissez-faire and Liberty: A Re-Evaluation of the Meaning and Origins of Laissez-faire Constitutionalism." *Law and History Review* 3 (Fall 1985): 294–331.

————. "Victorian Moralism and Civil Liberty in the Nineteenth-Century United States." In *The Constitution, Law, and American Life: Critical Aspects of the Nineteenth-Century Experience*, ed. Donald G. Nieman, 91–122. Athens, GA, 1992.

Fine, Sidney. *Laissez-faire and the General-Welfare State: A Study of Conflict in American Thought, 1865–1901*. Ann Arbor, MI, 1956.

Gillman, Howard. *The Constitution Besieged: The Rise and Demise of Lochner-Era Police Powers Jurisprudence*. Durham, NC, 1993.

Gold, David M. *The Shaping of Nineteenth-Century Law: John Appleton and Responsible Individualism*. Westport, CT, 1990.

Hamilton, Walton H. "The Path of Due Process of Law." *Ethics* 48 (April 1938): 269–96.

Horwitz, Morton J. *The Transformation of American Law, 1870–1960: The Crisis of Legal Orthodoxy*. New York, 1992.

Jacobs, Clyde D. *Law Writers and the Courts: The Influence of Thomas M. Cooley, Christopher G. Tiedeman, and John F. Dillon upon American Constitutional Law*. Berkeley, 1954.

Jones, Alan. "Thomas M. Cooley and 'Laissez-faire Constitutionalism': A Reconsideration." *Journal of American History* 53 (March 1967): 602–27.

Kens, Paul. *Judicial Power and Reform Politics: The Anatomy of Lochner v. New York*. Lawrence, KS, 1990.

McCurdy, Charles W. "Justice Field and the Jurisprudence of Government-Business Relations: Some Parameters of Laissez-faire Constitutionalism." *Journal of American History* 61 (March 1975): 970–1005.

————. "The Roots of Liberty of Contract Reconsidered: Major Premises of the Law of Employment, 1867–1937." *Supreme Court Historical Society Yearbook* (1984): 20–33.

Paul, Arnold M. *Conservative Crisis and the Rule of Law: Attitudes of Bar and Bench, 1887–1895*. Ithaca, NY, 1960.

Pisani, Donald J. "Promotion and Regulation: Constitutionalism and the American Economy." *Journal of American History* 74 (December 1987): 740–68.

Porter, Mary Cornelia. "That Commerce May Be Free: A New Look at the Old Laissez-faire Court." *Supreme Court Review* (1979): 135–59.

Ross, William G. *A Muted Fury: Populists, Progressives, and Labor Unions Confront the Courts, 1890–1937*. Princeton, NJ, 1994.

Schwartz, Bernard. *Main Currents in American Legal Thought*. Durham, NC, 1993.

Steinberg, Allen. *The Transformation of Criminal Justice: Philadelphia, 1800–1880*. Chapel Hill, NC, 1989.

Tomlins, Christopher L. *The State and the Unions: Labor Relations, Law, and the Organized Labor Movement in America, 1880–1960*. New York, 1985.

Twiss, Benjamin R. *Lawyers and the Constitution: How Laissez-faire Came to the Supreme Court*. Princeton, NJ, 1942.

14

Public Policy and State Government

Ballard C. Campbell

Americans have had a long love-hate relationship with their state governments. The most glorious moment in the history of these institutions occurred during the Revolution, when Americans transformed British colonies into sovereign states, which played an indispensable role in winning independence. In 1787 delegates from the states journeyed to Philadelphia, where they drafted a constitution that integrated the original thirteen states into a stronger national union. Thereafter the number of states increased, reaching thirty-four at the outbreak of the Civil War, when eleven seceded and formed the Confederate States of America. The South's defeat on the battlefield ended the possibility that a state could unilaterally withdraw from the Union and confirmed the idea that state-making and national expansion evolved in tandem. Two states were admitted during the war, and nine more, created out of territories in the Plains and western regions of the country, entered the Union between 1865 and 1900.

By the Gilded Age the reputation of state government had slipped considerably. Originating from numerous quarters and sometimes expressed as outraged condemnation, criticism of their flaws and failures was the most conspicuous theme in the popular writing about state government in the Gilded Age. Often taking these opinions at face value, historians have made the indictment thesis the dominant interpretation of state politics in the late nineteenth century.[1] This critique of governance actually blends two distinct points of view that circulated during the era. One strand of contemporary criticism held that state legislatures were hyperactive bodies that enacted too many laws. Articulated by conservatives such as William Graham Sumner, a sociologist, and Edwin L. Godkin, a journalist, as well as lawyers, jurists, academicians, and others, these commentaries faulted the states for using their powers irresponsibly. Critical of the propensity of the states to restrict personal freedoms and uses of private property, many of these observers believed that the failure to impose limits on state lawmaking jeopardized individual liberties and imperiled the foundation of the Republic.

The second line of indictment came to the opposite conclusion. The states, according to these critics, did too little or, at least, too little of the right thing. Purportedly caught in the grip of big business, party bosses, and laissez-faire ideology, state legislators were charged with failure to respond effectively to the challenges of the times. Expressions of this sentiment poured forth from protest political parties, such as the Greenbackers, Antimonopolists, Populists, and Socialists, as well as from individual reformers, clergy, and journalists. Although advocacy of sweeping changes in governance represented a minority view in the Gilded Age, the suggestions aired during these years laid the intellectual foundation for reform in the early twentieth century.

Whether associated with the Left or the Right, critics agreed that the state legislatures were a primary source of the era's political problems. They denounced these forums as hopelessly inept and infinitely corruptible, partly because they attracted political opportunists who allegedly sold their services to the highest bidder, and partly because many of their members were puppets of party bosses who dictated voting instructions to their minions. New York's assembly had a reputation as one of the most dishonest bodies. "The Legislature at Albany," snorted Godkin, "is a school of vice, a fountain of political debauchery" whose members could not resist the temptation of extorting rich men and successful corporations.[2] James Bryce, the British author of *The American Commonwealth*, a standard survey of government in the United States for years after its appearance in 1889, added that "the state legislatures are not high-toned bodies." Offering opportunities for political amateurs to rush new statutes into law during brief and sometimes frenetically paced sessions, meetings of the legislatures were, according to Bryce, widely regarded as "dangerous." Citizens looked forward to these convocations "with anxiety" and saw their "departure as a deliverance."[3] Bryce's unflattering portrait of the state legislatures became the dominant interpretation among historians, who routinely wrote off these bodies as woefully corrupt and unable to cope with the challenges of their age.[4]

The allegation of legislative corruption must be understood in the context of Gilded Age politics. Despite his understated cynicism, Bryce believed that most state legislators were honest, an opinion seconded by other knowledgeable observers of his day.[5] Contending that a few bad apples spoiled the barrel, he fingered big-city lawmakers who represented political party machines and foreign-born voters, and white southerners who abetted racial injustice, as the culprits who sullied the reputation of state lawmakers in general. In addition to genteel upper-class biases, which colored the views of people such as Bryce, another source gave rise to charges of legislative corruption. Lobbying on a widespread scale at state capitols by paid agents of private businesses was a new phenomenon in the post-Civil War decades. The image of special interests using their financial power to extract favors from legislators, even when bribery was not involved, violated Jacksonian strictures against "class legislation."[6] Paid lobbying, especially by commercial groups, in other words, was widely regarded as unethical. Even conservatives such as Godkin, who faulted lawmakers for "doing too much," agreed, although his main complaint was legislative overactivity. Nine-tenths of these laws "will do no good," he wrote, and the other tenth "will do positive harm."[7] Godkin, like many other defamers of the political system, made the state legislature (and city councils) the whipping boys for policy outcomes they did not like. He and other critics often resorted to inflated rhetoric and exaggerations to dramatize their case. Reality, however, usually was a much tamer affair.

If state legislatures suffered any fault, it was an excess of democracy. Convening in regularly scheduled sessions for only a few months every other year (only six legislatures met annually), with a membership composed largely of part-time politicians who seldom served more than two terms and were paid a pittance, and lacking the aid of a professional staff, permanent support services, or lavish expense accounts, the state legislatures were citizen forums that tended to reflect the dominant outlooks in their communities. Most state lawmakers were members of the middle class. Political parties played an important role in the selection of leaders in northern legislatures and influenced voting decisions on some but not most policy questions. Equally instrumental in the lawmakers'

approach to policymaking was their sense of constituent preferences, the weight of policy precedent, and political philosophy.[8]
Moreover, one of the most influential political tenets of the era was
an admonition against unnecessary uses of public authority.

Despite the persistence of this traditional political maxim, state
legislatures enacted an enormous body of law in the last third of
the nineteenth century. No less an authority than Bryce noted the
contradiction between the lip service accorded the theory of laissez-
faire and the reality of the "new democracies of America," which
were "just as eager for state interference as the democracy of England."[9] This outpouring of statutes has offered fertile ground for
historical research, much of which rebuts the indictment thesis of
Gilded Age politics. Many of these studies have examined politics
and policy in a single state or a regional cluster of states, or in a
particular city. A few bold scholars have surveyed the policy actions of the states and large cities nationwide.[10] Other researchers
have focused on specific policies such as railroad and insurance
company regulations, protection for workers, school reform, public health, agriculture research, criminal law and police protection,
and moral restrictions on drinking, gambling, and prostitution.[11]
Economic and legal historians have examined various aspects of
economic policy, the courts, and changes in legal doctrines.[12] The
"new political history," which relies on social scientific research
methods, has opened up new perspectives on voters and elections.
The high voter turnout at the polls, widespread and sometimes fervent popular interest in politics, and close competition between
political parties and candidates in many elections documented in
this literature all contradict the claim that Gilded Age politics was
irrelevant, issueless, and insignificant.[13] Collectively, these various bodies of literature attest that the states were beehives of political activity throughout the Gilded Age.

Three legal principles anchored and sustained state governmental policymaking. The first of these tenets derived from the federal
system of government, which the U.S. Constitution had established.
In creating a national government of explicitly enumerated powers
(most of which are outlined in Article I, section 8), the Constitution in effect left to the states the prerogative to make policy in
numerous areas. Political pressures on Congress to confine its activity to a literal interpretation of its "enumerated powers" and hostility to the centralization of political power reinforced legal and

philosophical opinion that many subjects were properly the business of the states. In practice, throughout the nineteenth century the states and the central government attended to separate policy concerns. Scholars have labeled this division of labor "dual federalism." Bryce likened its operation to "a great factory wherein two sets of machinery are at work . . . each set doing its own work without touching or hampering the other."[14]

Within their broad range of authority the states were free to legislate on any subject not prohibited by their own constitutions nor disallowed by the U.S. Constitution. State and federal courts, which defined the legal boundaries of governmental powers, reiterated time and again that the states had wide authority over the health, safety, and morals of their citizens. It was not only their "right" but also their "solemn duty," the Supreme Court had said, to use their "police" powers to promote the public good. The police powers, the second legal foundation of state action, received a famous reaffirmation in *Munn v. Illinois* (1877), when the Supreme Court upheld the power of states to regulate private businesses that were "clothed with a public interest," such as grain storage elevators and railroads.[15]

The third legal platform that sustained lawmaking among the states was their authority to supervise local governments. State legislatures empowered city governments by issuing municipal charters, which lawmakers routinely amended by adding new powers or new restrictions. Local governments were, in essence, "instrumentalities of the State," which enumerated the prerogatives and obligations of the towns, cities, and counties, as well as special districts (such as for schools, sewers, water, and parks). This principle had fundamental relevance for Gilded Age legislators, who assigned the largest amount of civic administration such as public education, policing, road maintenance, and public health, as well as their funding, to local governments. State lawmakers placed an increasing number of mandates and policy options on local officials in the last decades of the century.[16] When state legal superiority over the counties and cities is viewed in conjunction with the effects of dual federalism and the police powers, one can see how Americans placed the heaviest civic burden on the shoulders of state and local government in the Gilded Age.

These constitutional principles and the ideological tenets that inspired them produced a highly differentiated and noncentralized political system. When attention shifts from the nation's capital to the wider canvas of state and local government across the United States, one sees not a single civic pattern but a diverse political landscape. One foundation of this diversity rested on the economic specialization of the states and regions, which ranged from lobster fishing in Maine, shoe manufacturing in Massachusetts, corn and hog farming in Iowa, and meat packing in Illinois to cotton planting in Mississippi, cattle ranching in Texas, copper mining in Arizona, and lumbering in Oregon. Illinois boasted the burgeoning metropolis of Chicago, while neighboring Iowa's largest city was but a fraction of the Windy City's size. New England was bedrock Republican country in most years, in comparison with the Democratic monopoly that arose in the South following the Populist uprising of the early 1890s. Interwoven among these political tendencies were profound social contrasts such as between New England Yankees and southern whites, whose speech and mannerisms differed from those of westerners and immigrant groups in the nation's polyglot cities. The public policies of the states also formed a matrix of contrasts. Within their realm of legal competency the states were free to adopt or reject legislation as they saw fit, and routinely they exercised this autonomy. The result produced varied blends of statutes, administrative arrangements, and court precedents across America. But there were some common patterns too, as policymakers adopted similar solutions to the economic, technological, and social problems of their era.

Massachusetts was a leader in experimenting with new public policies. Highly industrialized and urbanized compared with other states, the Bay State blazed a political trail by adopting a variety of statutory innovations during the latter decades of the nineteenth century. Table 14.1 lists the most important pieces of this legislation, which are arranged into seven general categories of policy. The table indicates that Massachusetts lawmakers developed a body of law in four broad policy areas: community standards of work and social behavior including education (see Social Policy, Workers), the economy (see Commercial Assistance, Commercial Regulation), public institutions (see Public Finance, Government), and public health and safety (see Health and Public Safety). The three dozen laws listed in the table merely skim the surface of statutory development in the Bay State.[17] Once begun, most programs were refined and expanded by amendments over the years.

Table 14.1 Massachusetts Policy Innovations in the Gilded Age

Social Policy
Compulsory education 1852
    tightened 1867, 1876
Board of Charities 1863
State college 1863 (became University of Massachusetts)
Veterans' disability assistance 1866
Women gain marital property rights 1874
Liquor: local option replaced statewide prohibition 1875

Workers
Bureau of Labor Statistics 1869
Ten-hour limit for children and women 1874
    strengthened 1892, 1900
Board of Labor Arbitration 1886
Compulsory payment of wages in money 1886

Commercial Assistance
Agricultural experiment station 1882
License pharmacists 1885
    dentists 1887
State aid for highways 1892
    Highway Commission 1893
Dairy Bureau 1892

Commercial Regulation
Banking 1851
Insurance 1866
Railroads 1869
Gas 1885
Electricity 1887
Small loans 1888

Health and Public Safety
State constabulary (forerunner of state police) 1865
Sanitary code for Boston 1868
Board of Health 1869
    water-standard regulations 1878
Prevent sale of adulterated food and drugs 1882
Metropolitan Sewer Commission 1889

Government
Civil service 1884 (state government and cities)
Secret ballot 1888
Registration of lobbyists 1890
Regulation of campaign finances 1892

Public Finance
Tax commission 1864
State supervision of county finances 1879
Tax railroads and telegraphs 1882
Inheritance tax 1891

Massachusetts can serve as a reference for reviewing activities of all the states during the Gilded Age. Because Bay State lawmakers were pioneers in many areas of policy, they established the outer boundaries of state action during the era. No state surpassed Massachusetts in the breadth of its statutory enactments, and many areas, especially the South, lagged considerably behind it. An innovator in matters such as health, labor law, and political reform, Massachusetts enacted laws that served as models for lawmakers elsewhere. Emulation of statutes and constitutional provisions among the states was a common practice in the Gilded Age, as it has been since the creation of the federal system. The increased proclivity of the states to "experiment" with innovative policies by the end of the nineteenth century led observers to call them "laboratories of democracy." The label has stuck to this day.

Social policy was a focal point of state action. Policymaking in this area tended to cluster around four topics: education, care of the indigent and unfortunate (orphans, the insane, the poor), morals, and women's rights. Although the state governments did not operate common schools, they did enact laws that mandated free public education supported by taxation. In 1867, New York and Indiana, for example, both eliminated tuition requirements for their common schools. New constitutions written during Reconstruction advanced education in the South, although the region continued to spend less on its schools than did northern communities and also erected a separate and inferior school system for black children. The South also lagged behind other states in adopting compulsory education requirements, which began in Massachusetts and spread to one-half of the states by 1890. The states also provided financial assistance to local communities for their grammar and high schools, founded normal schools for the preparation of teachers, and substantially increased their investment in the state universities. Massachusetts established a state college (the future university) in 1863 and admitted women to the Amherst campus in 1892.

As public education expanded, lawmakers subjected local authorities to greater centralized control, first through county school superintendents and later by state commissioners of education. Although usually administered by local officials, certification of schoolteachers increasingly was subjected to statewide standards, as were the curriculum, school building design, and textbooks, which states began to require to be issued without charge to students. As public education grew, teaching evolved into a full-time career in urban areas by the end of the century. New York and Illinois enacted pension laws in the 1890s for teachers in Brooklyn and Chicago, a sure sign of education's bureaucratization.

Because it intruded so directly on cultural values, education policy generated some impassioned controversies. Laws in Illinois and Wisconsin that required basic subjects to be taught in English, for example, provoked sharp denunciations from non-English-speaking groups in the early 1890s. Democrats led the effort to repeal the offensive provisions. The Gilded Age was awash in disputes over standards of moral conduct, with the effort to curtail the liquor traffic topping the list of divisive cultural issues. The anti-liquor movement evolved from the pre-Civil War temperance campaign that urged voluntary abstinence to a drive to make the manufacture and sale of alcoholic beverages a punishable crime. This goal pinched the sensitivities of various groups, pitting rural residents against urbanites, the middle class against workers, evangelical Protestants against Catholics and other liturgically oriented religious groups, and Republicans against Democrats. With so many overlapping blocs influencing policy outcomes, it is not surprising that lawmakers enacted a variety of solutions to the liquor problem, but county local option was the most common response. Under these laws saloons were licensed in localities whose residents voted to permit liquor sales.

Massachusetts settled on this choice in 1875 after experimenting with statewide prohibition. Iowans' attempt to ban all saloons in the 1880s foundered on wholesale evasion of the law and sizable defections from the Republican party, which had supported the experiment. Political pressures persuaded Republicans in the Hawkeye State to substitute a less stringent policy in 1894.[18]

Prohibition dogged the GOP in most northern states, as Democrats seized opportunities to accuse Republicans of usurping "personal liberty." The repeated divisions along party lines that occurred over liquor issues in most of the northern legislatures were often replicated on other social issues such as restrictions on activities on Sundays, prostitution, gambling and racing, the use of tobacco by minors, and obscenity. Less partisan debates erupted over laws affecting women such as restrictions on abortion, which swept through the states after the Civil War, as well as over legislation concerning divorce, rape, and control of marital assets.

Policies that affected workers often rested on social as much as economic rationales. Restrictions on child labor, which Massachusetts began in 1866 and subsequently strengthened, were linked to compulsory education laws and assumptions about appropriate activities for youngsters. Limitations on hours of female labor sprang from Victorians' notions about womanhood. Thirteen states restricted the hours per day for female workers by 1896, and twenty-eight states restricted child labor by 1900. Enforcement of these laws was lax, however, because legislators did not authorize enough factory inspectors. In some states, bureaus of labor statistics were responsible for the administration of labor laws. Appearing first in Massachusetts, bureaus of labor statistics had spread to half the states by 1889. Besides collecting data, interviewing workers, and reviewing labor laws, bureau commissioners suggested legislation to lawmakers on a wide assortment of issues. Some commissioners arbitrated strikes, although lawmakers tended to assign this function to separate agencies as the century progressed.

It is doubtful that the boards of labor arbitration helped workers very much, but the reform of liability laws that covered the collection of damages for injuries did have a positive effect. Under prevailing legal practice, workers who had been injured on the job, a common occurrence in occupations such as mining and railroading, had to demonstrate in court that they had not contributed to the accident. Some states, such as Wisconsin in 1893, removed "contributory negligence" and similar legal provisions as employer defenses against liability suits. States also set standards that sought to make industrial work safer and healthier; Massachusetts required fire escapes, toilets, and proper ventilation in factories in 1887 and placed restrictions on sweatshops soon afterward. The Commonwealth required that employers pay factory workers weekly money wages, a measure adopted in other states. Midwestern states regulated the weighing of coal, the basis on which miners were paid.

Policymakers seldom ventured beyond consideration of moral and safety standards for workers, but they exhibited considerable receptivity toward assistance for farmers and business proprietors. By the 1880s the states had created numerous boards and bureaus that promoted agricultural interests and often appropriated modest subsidies for them. Lawmakers established agricultural experiment stations, usually under the auspices of the state agricultural college, to conduct scientific research and advance practical concerns of farmers. When Congress began to subsidize the stations in 1887 through federal grants, one-half of the states had already set up research facilities and the remainder quickly followed suit. Dairy farmers were especially aggressive in seeking governmental help for their industry. Their influence was manifested in restrictions placed on the sale of oleomargarine and imitation cheese and in the enactment of pure milk laws. Western states created special water districts that enabled farmers to construct irrigation facilities financed by general taxation.

Irrigation projects represent a type of public improvement known as infrastructure, which aided trade and commerce as well as the general well-being of communities. State governments tended not to appropriate money directly for these projects, but rather to authorize the formation of local districts endowed with powers to construct facilities and to collect taxes and fees to pay for them. The responsibility for roads and bridges traditionally had been delegated to local authorities. The poor condition of rural roads received increased attention in the last two decades of the century. The first goal of the good roads movement was to require local residents to pay road taxes in money rather than in labor, as was the custom, and to place road work under the supervision of a trained expert rather than a locally elected overseer. These objectives had made only modest gains by 1900, by which time several eastern states, Massachusetts included, had authorized financial assistance to local governments for road construction and created state road agencies.[19]

Urban and commercial groups, the most active advocates of state involvement in roads, also sought changes in other policies affecting commercial activities such as the incorporation of businesses. Early in the nineteenth century, states had incorporated businesses on a firm-by-firm basis but later turned to general laws that transformed incorporation into an administrative process. Incorporation laws usually placed restrictions and obligations on business firms, but some states, New Jersey in particular, enacted provisions after 1889 that permitted greater latitude for entrepreneurs, especially by allowing multistate holding companies. New York and other states followed suit, thereby abetting the merger and acquisition movement of the 1890s. These consolidations fanned the flames of popular criticism of big business.

No business generated more impassioned debate or, probably, a greater volume of commercial law than the railroads, America's first big industrial business. Acting on the recommendation of Charles Francis Adams, Jr., the Massachusetts legislature created the Board of Railroad Commissioners in 1869 to monitor railroad activities. The Bay State law provided for a "weak" commission that lacked power to set rates and relied on investigation and publicity to uphold the public interest. Illinois, by contrast, adopted a "strong" commission (1873) that possessed rate-setting authority and was one of several midwestern states where railroad rate discrimination between places was an acutely vexatious issue in the early 1870s, especially for shippers who paid higher charges than competitors in nearby locations. Iowa and Wisconsin's so-called Granger laws responded to these complaints by fixing maximum rates by statute. The statutes' inflexibility, coupled with rate reductions by the railroad companies in the wake of the depression of the middle 1870s, led to the repeal of both laws. The direction in railroad regulation lay in the commission approach, which twenty-five states had adopted by 1887; ten states gave their agencies rate-setting powers. Iowa joined the trend in 1888 with a law that required that "all charges be reasonable and just" (the customary language), prohibited rebates (by which railroads pampered their favored customers), and outlawed short-haul, long-haul rate discrimination (the era's most troublesome railroad issue).

Iowa's action took place a year after Congress entered the field by the enactment of the Interstate Commerce Act, which placed interstate railroads under national supervision. The Supreme Court's *Wabash* decision (1886), which declared Illinois's rate control for lines that passed through the Prairie State unconstitutional, had created a regulatory void that invited federal intervention. Expansion of national supervision of the railroads eventually eclipsed the states' role in rate regulation, although for the remainder of the nineteenth century the states continued to set rates on intrastate traffic, as well as monitor other aspects of railroading such as adherence to safety standards and requirements for financial reports. But the understaffing of the commissions hampered their effectiveness, a story that was repeated in other state regulatory activities.

Legislative Activism in the States. The Chamber of the Massachusetts House of Representatives, which witnessed the enactment of many important laws in the late nineteenth century. *Courtesy Library of Congress*

Moreover, lawmakers were reluctant to tame certain railroad abuses such as the distribution of free passes to public officials.[20]

Economic policymaking often placed legislators in political cross-pressures between demands for laws to promote commercial enterprise and laws to ensure that constituents received uniform services at reasonable costs. Frequently faced with competing economic objectives but lacking foolproof solutions for balancing private and public interests, legislators customarily resorted to compromise. Thus, they enacted a battery of regulatory measures, whose impact usually was more a symbolic gesture to community sentiment than harmful to commercial enterprise.

As with other matters, the administrative design and effectiveness of economic policy varied among the states. State banks, insurance companies, and small loan operations (businesses that grew rapidly after the Civil War) came under greater public control in the latter decades of the century, as did natural gas and electric utilities. The licensing of trades and professions imposed entrance requirements and standards of conduct on practitioners, although these regulations customarily benefited the affected occupation. Massachusetts adopted licensing requirements for pharmacists, dentists, engineers, physicians, and lawyers in the last fifteen years of the century. Most regulatory controls were shaped to fit the contours of particular occupations and industries, but states also enacted antimonopoly laws between the late 1880s and 1900 that applied to business generally. While these statutes did not stop the growth of big business, they did provide the legal basis for vigorous antitrust campaigns in several states at the turn of the century.[21]

The effort to improve public health led lawmakers to prohibit certain commercial activities such as the adulteration of food and drugs and the slaughtering of diseased cattle. An equally important goal of the public health campaign, which centered in state boards of health (thirty-nine by 1900), sought to ensure safe water. Led by physicians and biologists, the Massachusetts Board of Health, the first state agency of its kind, was in the forefront of the clean water movement. Soon after the board's scientists demonstrated a causal link between organic pollution of water supplies and fatal disease, the legislature required that all municipalities submit plans for new water and sewer systems to the state board for approval. The quest to improve quality, as well as to ensure the adequacy of supply, prompted the creation in 1895 of the Metropolitan Water District, which constructed reservoirs to serve the Boston region. Members of health boards were a fertile source of policy recommendations on numerous matters, such as the pasteurization of milk and the regulation of slaughterhouses, whose waste materials were a widespread problem.

Although the general public probably had little comprehension of the scientific basis for public health controls, they could readily see reasons to maintain an orderly society. Each major disturbance of community harmony, such as a labor strike or urban riot, provoked demands on the states to provide for greater public safety. Gilded Age statute books swelled with new criminal laws, administrative arrangements to keep order (such as municipal police forces, sometimes placed under state control), and laws authorizing the construction of new prisons and reformatories. Requests for social controls rose during the hard times of the 1870s, when five years of depression turned thousands of unemployed men into tramps who wandered from community to community in search of work. Because local governments provided food and shelter to the indigent, municipal officials sought to prevent outsiders from flooding their communities and their limited tax resources. Vagrancy laws, which made begging and "wandering about" without visible means of support illegal, provided officials with the authority to keep the unemployed at bay. The Massachusetts state detective force, initially formed in 1865 to suppress violations of the liquor laws, helped to apprehend tramps in the Commonwealth. In the South, police used vagrancy laws to round up blacks who were leased to local businesses at a profit to the county sheriff and his deputies. If disorder overwhelmed the capacity of local police, governors could call out the militia, many of which were reorganized in the 1880s and received increased federal subsidies. State militias were mustered over three hundred times between 1877 and 1903 to keep the peace during labor strife.[22]

The authority to call out the militia, like the power to impose capital punishment, symbolized the enormous authority that state officials possessed. An increasing number of citizens during the Gilded Age thought that political parties abused these prerogatives and advocated curbs on partisan influence.[23] The major reforms of the political process during the period were the adoption of the secret, or Australian, ballot, which substituted state for partisan control of the printing and distribution of election ballots and allowed voting in private, and the institution of civil service rules, which substituted fixed procedures for patronage (wherein loyal party workers were rewarded with government jobs) for public hiring and appointments. Following the lead of Congress and New York in 1883, Massachusetts inaugurated civil service regulations for state employees in 1884 and gradually phased in the system for cities. Bay State lawmakers adopted the secret ballot in 1888, began the registration of lobbyists at the statehouse in 1890, and required candidates for elective office to report their campaign expenditures in 1892. Most states adopted secret ballot laws and, in the process, some added provisions that kept minor parties and fusion candidates off the ballot.[24] The southern version of election "reform" swept most blacks and many whites out of the enfranchised electorate. The implementation of civil service, like most administrative reforms, made only modest headway before the Progressive Era.

Public finance was a policy area closely connected to the political process, both in the volume of criticism the subject engendered and in the snail-like progress of reform. Three issues attracted the attention of fiscal reformers: the rising costs of state and local government; the apparent self-interest of partisan activists in increasing spending, taxation, and debt; and the ability of corporations to avoid taxation. During the last decades of the century, policymakers adopted several new state taxes such as levies on banks, railroads, corporations, mortgages, and inheritances and initiated a trend toward severing state government's dependence on property taxes, which were the bread and butter of local revenue. Progress toward administrative centralization, of which fiscal reform was a part, was also visible in state oversight of local finances.

A review of the statute books and court reports shows that state governments adopted laws on a broad array of issues during the Gilded Age. What accounted for this widening scope of state action? There is no simple answer to this question, which requires separate explanations for each area of policy and, frequently, for particular states. Broadly speaking, however, three general causes supplied the dynamics for state policy innovation. The first and most pervasive of these factors was the social and economic changes that were reshaping the society. The most momentous transformation was industrialization, a process that included the evolution of a commercialized economy, manufacturing and other business firms of unprecedented size and power, a work force increasingly dependent on wage labor, and rapidly growing cities with mushrooming needs for housing, water, transportation, and security. Industrialization also embodied new outlooks on the use of time, forms of human organization, and scientific knowledge. These overlapping strands of industrial change created a variety of new problems, many of which led Gilded Age Americans to call for government action. The impact of economic depressions increased their concerns. The downturn of the middle 1870s, for example, stimulated stricter vagrancy laws, closer supervision of banking, and new constitutional limits on indebtedness and taxation. The depression of the 1890s heightened criticism of big business and political parties.

Industrialization and associated social changes, such as immigration, laid the basis for a society increasingly characterized by distinct groups and specializations. Many of them formed organizations around their common interests, and some merged into state and national associations, which ran the gamut from church organizations to business associations and civic federations. Such interest groups, which recommended legislation to state lawmakers and lobbied for its enactment, constituted the second dynamic behind state policy innovation. The activities of public officials comprised the third factor. Some of these individuals were elected officers, such as state legislators and governors, and, in some states, administrative heads and judges. Appointed officials staffed state and local agencies, including the state colleges, while still other policy activists occupied quasi-official roles such as political party leaders who did not hold public office. Collectively, these officials put forward ideas about governing, cajoled colleagues for their support, and formally approved changes in policy. In the state legislatures outside the South, differences of opinion between Democrats and Republicans had some impact on policymaking, particularly concerning issues that touched on cultural values and the procedures of government. Parties had a smaller impact on economic legislation and public health issues.

Despite their policy experiments, the states manifested clear limits in their responses to social change. Problems such as unemployment, poverty, party patronage in government, and unequal treatment of nonwhites and women did not receive much effective attention at the statehouse. Four factors combined to restrain the scope of state reform. First, traditional political ideology, which warned of the dangers of government power, retained vitality in the late nineteenth century. Tenets of this way of thinking supported "economical" (low-cost) government, denounced bureaucracy and centralized control, and condemned policy favoritism for special interests. Reinforcing this classical republican ideology was the notion that natural forces governed the economy and worked best without government intervention, an outlook that gained wide assent in commercial and legal circles. Together, classical economics and traditional political ideology combined to sustain a laissez-faire philosophy that narrowed the range of policy options.

The insertion of many of these ideas into state constitutions was the second factor. This practice was as old as the Republic, but Americans continued to add restrictions to these charters throughout the nineteenth century. The depression of the 1870s stimulated a battery of new constitutional limitations on public finance such as the setting of lower maximum rates for property taxation and indebtedness, especially for municipalities. Legislatures imposed further restrictions in statutes and city charters. However composed, these legal provisions represented impediments to policymaking. Laws that appeared to violate these restrictions could be challenged in both state and federal courts. Federalism, the third constraint on policy innovation, offered Americans two legal forums through which to take state government to court. The vast majority of legal complaints about state action were rejected, but the occasional statute overturned by judicial review often received wide notice.[25] Finally, another artifact of the federal structure of government was competition among states to attract and retain business. Fears of alienating local enterprise probably deterred lawmakers from aggressive policy actions in some areas, especially concerning labor unions, wages, business regulation, and taxation.

Business leaders and lawyers watched state lawmakers closely on these issues and turned to laissez-faire and other arguments to dissuade legislatures from promiscuous action on them. The economically powerful, the successful members of the professional, social, and commercial establishments, and the middle class generally had disproportionate political power in the Gilded Age and thus held a firm grip on the rudder that steered the ship of state. Fearful of rapid and radical change and desirous of social stability and harmony, they accepted only incremental policy innovations. Political change customarily followed this gradual process. Even so, notable advances occurred in Massachusetts and elsewhere, laying the foundations for transformations that followed in the twentieth century.

Notes

1. For example, see Robert H. Wiebe, *The Search for Order, 1877–1920* (New York, 1967); John A. Garraty, *The New Commonwealth, 1877–1890* (New York, 1968); Morton Keller, *Affairs of State: Public Life in Late Nineteenth-Century America* (Cambridge, MA, 1977); Nell Irvin Painter, *Standing at Armageddon: The United States, 1877–1919* (New York, 1987); and Alan Dawley, *Struggles for Justice: Social Responsibility and the Liberal State* (Cambridge, MA, 1991).

2. Edwin L. Godkin, "The Decline of Legislatures," *Atlantic Magazine* 80 (1897): 52.

3. James Bryce, *The American Commonwealth*, 2 vols. (New York, 1889), 1:515, 521.

4. For example, see Richard Hofstadter, *The American Political Tradition and the Men Who Made It* (New York, 1948), chap. 7; Samuel P. Hays, *The Response to Industrialism, 1885–1914* (Chicago, 1957), 105; Wiebe, *Search for Order*, 28; and Keller, *Affairs of State*, 244, 542–43.

5. Bryce, *American Commonwealth*, 1:515–17. See, for example, Albert Shaw, "The American States Legislatures," *The Contemporary Review* 56 (October 1889): 555–73; Raymond L. Bridgman, "Biennial Elections and Legislative Sessions," *New England Magazine* 8 (April 1893): 206–21; and Robert Luce, *Legislative Assemblies* (Boston, 1924), 422ff.

6. Margaret S. Thompson, *The "Spider Web": Congress and Lobbying in the Age of Grant* (Ithaca, NY, 1985), 54–69, 181–88; Herbert Hovenkamp, *Enterprise and American Law, 1836–1937* (Cambridge, MA, 1991), 123; Michael Les Benedict, "Laissez-faire and Liberty: A Reevaluation of the Meaning and Origins of Laissez-faire Constitutionalism," *Law and History Review* 3 (1985): 293–331.

7. Godkin, "The Decline of Legislatures," 52.

8. Ballard C. Campbell, *Representative Democracy: Public Policy and Midwestern Legislatures in the Late Nineteenth Century* (Cambridge, MA, 1980); William G. Shade, "State Legislatures in the Nineteenth Century," *Encyclopedia of the American Legislative System*, ed. Joel H. Silbey, 3 vols. (New York, 1994), 1:195–214.

9. Bryce, *American Commonwealth*, 2:422. In his chapter on "Laissez-faire," Bryce appended a table that listed policy areas of state action.

10. The Suggestions for Further Reading for this chapter provide some exemplary illustrations. Additional titles are listed in Ballard C. Campbell, *The Growth of American Government: Governance from the Cleveland Era to the Present* (Bloomington, IN, 1995), esp. chaps. 1, 3.

11. For examples, see the titles cited in Suggestions for Further Reading.

12. Donald J. Pisani, "Promotion and Regulation: Constitutionalism and the American Economy," *Journal of American History* 74 (1987): 740–68; Harry N. Scheiber, "Legislatures and American Economic Development," in *Encyclopedia of the American Legislative System* 3:1195–1215.

13. Paul Kleppner, *The Third Electoral System, 1853–1892: Parties, Voters, and Political Cultures* (Chapel Hill, NC, 1979); Samuel T. McSeveney, *The Politics of Depression: Political Behavior in the Northeast, 1893–1896* (New York, 1972); Dale Baum, "The Massachusetts Voter: Party Loyalty in the Gilded Age, 1872–1896," in *Massachusetts in the Gilded Age: Selected Essays*, ed. Jack Tager and John W. Ifkovic (Amherst, MA, 1985), 37–66. See also Joel H. Silbey's able overview in *American Political Nation, 1838–1893* (Stanford, CA, 1991).

14. Bryce, *American Commonwealth*, 1:318. On federalism see Harry N. Scheiber, "American Federalism and the Diffusion of Power: Historical and Contemporary Perspectives," *University of Toledo Law Review* 9 (1978): 619–80; and Campbell, *Growth of American Government*, chaps. 1, 3.

15. William R. Brock, *Investigation and Responsibility: Public Responsibility in the United States, 1865–1900* (Cambridge, England, 1984), chap. 3; and Stanley K. Schultz, *Constructing Urban Culture: American Cities and City Planning, 1800–1920* (Philadelphia, 1989), chaps. 3, 4, offer splendid reviews of the doctrine.

16. Jon C. Teaford, *The Unheralded Triumph: City Government in America, 1870–1900* (Baltimore, 1984), chap. 5.

17. Most of the entries in Table 14.1 are taken from historical writings about Massachusetts, including Richard H. Abbott, "Massachusetts: Maintaining Hegemony," in *Radical Republicans in the North: State Politics during Reconstruction*, ed. James C. Mohr (Baltimore, 1976), 1–25; Richard Abrams, *Conservatism in a Progressive Era: Massachusetts Politics, 1900–1912* (Cambridge, MA, 1964); Geoffrey Blodgett, *The Gentle Reformers: Massachusetts Democrats in the Cleveland Era* (Cambridge, MA, 1966); Alexander Keyssar, *Out of Work: The First Century of Unemployment in Massachusetts* (New York, 1986); Marvin Lazerson, *Origins of the Urban School: Public Education in Massachusetts, 1870–1915* (Cambridge, MA, 1971); James Leiby, *Carroll Wright and Labor Reform: The*

Origins of Labor Statistics (Cambridge, MA, 1960); Thomas K. McCraw, *Prophets of Regulation* (Cambridge, MA, 1984), on the Massachusetts Railroad Commission; Barbara G. Rosenkrantz, *Public Health and the State: Changing Views in Massachusetts, 1842–1936* (Cambridge, MA, 1972); and Robert H. Whitten, *Public Administration in Massachusetts: The Relation of Central to Local Authority* (1898; reprint ed., New York, 1969).

18. The Iowa story is told in Ballard C. Campbell, "Did Democracy Work? Prohibition in Late Nineteenth-Century Iowa: A Test Case," *Journal of Interdisciplinary History* 8 (1977): 87–116.

19. Ballard C. Campbell, "The Good Roads Movement in Wisconsin, 1890–1911," *Wisconsin Magazine of History* 49 (1966): 273–93; Charles L. Dearing, *American Highway Policy* (Washington, DC, 1941).

20. Brock, *Investigation and Responsibility*; Gerald D. Nash, *State Government and Economic Development: Administrative Policies in California, 1849–1933* (Berkeley, 1964).

21. James May, "Antitrust in the Formative Era: Political and Economic Theory in Constitutional and Antitrust Analysis, 1880–1918," *Ohio State Law Journal* 50 (1989): 257–395.

22. Allan R. Millett and Peter Maslowski, *For the Common Defense: The Military History of the United States of America* (New York, 1984), 249; Jerry M. Cooper, "The Wisconsin National Guard in the Milwaukee Riots of 1886," *Wisconsin Magazine of History* 55 (1971): 31–48.

23. Geoffrey Blodgett, "The Mugwump Reputation, 1870 to the Present," *Journal of American History* 66 (1980): 867–87; Richard L. McCormick, *The Party Period and Public Policy* (New York, 1986), chap. 6.

24. Peter H. Argersinger, " 'A Place on the Ballot': Fusion Politics and Antifusion Laws," *American Historical Review* 85 (1980): 287–306; John F. Reynolds and Richard L. McCormick, "Outlawing 'Treachery': Split Tickets and Ballot Laws in New York and New Jersey, 1880–1910," *Journal of American History* 72 (1986): 835–58.

25. Brock, *Investigation and Responsibility*, chap. 3; Keller, *Affairs of State*, 326, 355–66, 401–8; Melvin I. Urofsky, "State Courts and Protective Legislation during the Progressive Era: A Reevaluation," *Journal of American History* 72 (1985): 63–91.

Suggestions for Further Reading

Brock, William R. *Investigation and Responsibility: Public Responsibility in the United States, 1865–1900*. Cambridge, England, 1984.

Bryce, James. *The American Commonwealth*. 2 vols. New York, 1889.

Campbell, Ballard C. *Representative Democracy: Public Policy and Midwestern Legislatures in the Late Nineteenth Century*. Cambridge, MA, 1980.

Friedman, Lawrence M. *A History of American Law*. New York, 1985.

———. *Crime and Punishment in American History*. New York, 1993.

Grant, H. Roger. *Insurance Reform: Consumer Action in the Progressive Era*. Ames, IA, 1979.

Harris, Carl V. *Political Power in Birmingham, 1871–1921*. Knoxville, TN, 1977.

Keller, Morton. *Affairs of State: Public Life in Late Nineteenth-Century America*. Cambridge, MA, 1977.

Kousser, J. Morgan. *The Shaping of Southern Politics: Suffrage Restriction and the Establishment of the One-Party South, 1880–1910*. New Haven, CT, 1974.

Link, William A. *The Paradox of Southern Progressivism, 1880–1930*. Chapel Hill, NC, 1992.

McCormick, Richard L. *From Realignment to Reform: Political Change in New York State, 1893–1910*. Ithaca, NY, 1981.

Miller, George H. *Railroads and the Granger Laws*. Madison, WI, 1971.

Mohr, James C., ed. *Radical Republicans in the North: State Politics during Reconstruction*. Baltimore, 1976.

———. *Abortion in America: The Origins and Evolution of National Policy, 1800–1900*. New York, 1978.

Nash, Gerald D. *State Government and Economic Development: Administrative Policies in California, 1849–1933*. Berkeley, 1964.

Pisani, Donald J. *To Reclaim a Divided West: Water, Law, and Public Policy, 1848–1902*. Albuquerque, NM, 1992.

Thelen, David P. *The New Citizenship: Origins of Progressivism in Wisconsin, 1885–1900*. Columbia, MO, 1972.

Tyack, David, Thomas James, and Aaron Benavot. *Law and the Shaping of Public Education, 1785–1954*. Madison, WI, 1987.

Woodward, C. Vann. *Origins of the New South, 1877–1913*. Baton Rouge, LA, 1951.

Wright, James E. *The Politics of Populism: Dissent in Colorado*. New Haven, CT, 1974.

Index

About the Contributors

ERIC ARNESON received his doctorate from Yale University. He teaches at the University of Illinois at Chicago and is the author of *Waterfront Workers of New Orleans: Race, Class, and Politics, 1863–1923* (1991).

ROBERT G. BARROWS received his Ph.D. from Indiana University and is an associate professor of history at Indiana University-Purdue University at Indianapolis. His publications in urban history include *The Encyclopedia of Indianapolis* (1994), which he coedited.

MICHAEL LES BENEDICT holds a doctorate from Rice University and is a professor of history at Ohio State University. His books include *The Impeachment and Trial of Andrew Johnson* (1973) and *A Compromise of Principle: Congressional Republicans and Reconstruction, 1863–1869* (1974).

CHARLES W. CALHOUN received his doctorate in history from Columbia University. He is a professor of history at East Carolina University, and his publications on late nineteenth-century American politics include *Gilded Age Cato: The Life of Walter Q. Gresham* (1988).

BALLARD C. CAMPBELL received his Ph.D. from the University of Wisconsin, Madison, and teaches in the Department of History at Northeastern University. He is the author of *The Growth of American Government: Governance from the Age of Cleveland to the Present* (1995) and *Representative Democracy: Public Policy and Midwestern Legislatures in the Late Nineteenth Century* (1980).

STACY A. CORDERY holds a doctorate in history from the University of Texas at Austin. She is an assistant professor of history at Monmouth College in Monmouth, Illinois. Her articles on the family of Theodore Roosevelt have appeared in several journals, and she is currently completing a biography of Alice Roosevelt Longworth.

ROGER DANIELS received his doctorate from the University of California at Los Angeles and holds the Charles Phelps Taft Chair in history at the University of Cincinnati. He has published numerous works on the history of immigration, including *Coming to America: A History of Immigration and Ethnicity in American Life* (1990).

EDMUND J. DANZIGER, JR., received his Ph.D. from the University of Illinois. He teaches history at Bowling Green State University, and his publications include *Indians and Bureaucrats: Administering the Reservation Policy during the Civil War* (1974), *The Chippewas of Lake Superior* (1978), and *Survival and Regeneration: Detroit's American Indian Community* (1991).

LESLIE H. FISHEL, JR., was awarded his doctorate in history by Harvard University. Throughout his career he has served in a number of administrative posts, including director of the Rutherford B. Hayes Presidential Center in Fremont, Ohio. His publications include *The Negro in American Life: A Documentary History* (1967), which he edited with Benjamin Quarles.

JAMES RODGER FLEMING earned a Ph.D. in history from Princeton University and is an associate professor and director of the Science and Technology Studies Program at Colby College in Maine. His publications include *Meteorology in America, 1800– 1870* (1990) and *Science, Technology, and the Environment: Multidisciplinary Perspectives* (1994).

JOSEPH A. FRY did his doctoral work at the University of Virginia, from which he received his Ph.D. He is a professor of history at the University of Nevada, Las Vegas, and has written *Henry S. Sanford: Diplomacy and Business in Nineteenth-Century America* (1982) and *John Tyler Morgan and the Search for Southern Autonomy* (1992).

LEWIS L. GOULD, who received his Ph.D. from Yale University, is Eugene C. Barker Centennial Professor in American History at the University of Texas at Austin. He is the author of *The Presidency of William McKinley* (1980) and the editor of *American First Ladies: Their Lives and Their Legacy* (1995).

WORTH ROBERT MILLER received his Ph.D. from the University of Oklahoma and is an associate professor of history at Southwest Missouri State University. He is the author of *Oklahoma Populism: A History of the People's Party in the Oklahoma Territory, 1860–1920* (1987).

GLENN PORTER received his doctorate from Johns Hopkins University. Currently serving as director of the Hagley Museum and Library in Wilmington, Delaware, he is the author of *The Rise of Big Business* (1992) and general editor of the *Encyclopedia of American Economic History* (1980).